LOGICAL SELF-DEFENSE

LOGICAL SELF-DEFENSE

◆

UNITED STATES EDITION

Ralph H. Johnson
University of Windsor

J. Anthony Blair
University of Windsor

McGRAW-HILL, INC.

New York   St. Louis   San Francisco   Auckland   Bogotá   Caracas
Lisbon   London   Madrid   Mexico City   Milan   Montreal   New Delhi
San Juan   Singapore   Sydney   Tokyo   Toronto

LOGICAL SELF-DEFENSE

Copyright © 1994 by McGraw-Hill, Inc. All rights reserved.
Printed in the United States of America. Except as permitted under the
United States Copyright Act of 1976, no part of this publication may be
reproduced or distributed in any form or by any means, or stored in a data
base or retrieval system, without the prior written permission of the
publisher.

This book is printed on acid-free paper.

2 3 4 5 6 7 8 9 0 AGM AGM 9 0 9 8 7 6 5 4

ISBN 0-07-032666-5

This book was set in Garamond Light by Better Graphics, Inc.
The editors were Cynthia Ward, Judith R. Cornwell, and David Dunham;
the designer was Joan Greenfield;
the cover was designed by Carol A. Couch;
the cover illustrator was Cathy Hull;
the production supervisor was Paula Keller.
Arcata Graphics/Martinsburg was printer and binder.

Library of Congress Cataloging-in-Publication Data

Johnson, Ralph Henry.
    Logical self-defense / Ralph H. Johnson, J. Anthony Blair.—U.S.
  ed.
       p.   cm.
    Includes bibliographical references and index.
    ISBN 0-07-032666-5
     1. Fallacies (Logic)   2. Reasoning.   3. Critical thinking.
  I. Blair, J. Anthony, (date).   II. Title.
BC175.J63   1994
168—dc20
                                     93-36989

◆

About the Authors

RALPH H. JOHNSON, a native of Detroit, Michigan, was educated at Xavier University and received his doctorate in philosophy from the University of Notre Dame. He is Professor of Philosophy at the University of Windsor where he has taught since 1966. He is co-editor of the journal *Informal Logic* and co-chair of international symposia on informal logic held at the University of Windsor in 1978, 1983, and 1989. He has lectured and published widely on informal logic, fallacy theory, argumentation, and critical thinking. He is a founding member and currently a member of the Executive Committee of the Association for Informal Logic and Critical Thinking (AILACT), of the National Council for Excellence in Critical Thinking (NCECT), and of the Canadian Research Group on Argumentation (CARGA). He has given workshop presentations and has been a consultant on informal logic and critical thinking across the United States and Canada. His current research is on the theory of argument and the theory of reasoning.

J. ANTHONY BLAIR, a native of Ottawa, Canada, was educated at McGill University and the University of Michigan. He is Professor and chair of the Philosophy Department at the University of Windsor, in Ontario, Canada. He is co-editor of the journal *Informal Logic,* co-author of *Reasoning, A Practical Guide,* co-chair of the international symposia on informal logic at the University of Windsor in 1978, 1983, and 1989, and of the conferences on argumentation at the University of Amsterdam in 1986 and 1990, and co-editor of the proceedings of these conferences. He has lectured and published widely on informal logic, fallacies and fallacy theory, argumentation and critical thinking. He is a founding member and a board member of the International Society for the Study of Argumentation (ISSA) based in Amsterdam, a founding member of the Association for Informal Logic and Critical Thinking (AILACT), and a member of the Canadian Research Group on Argumentation (CARGA). He has given workshops on and consulted on informal logic and critical thinking in Canada and the United States. His current research is focused on fallacy theory, on the relations between informal logic and argumentation and on the criteria of argument assessment.

Contents

Preface

This United States edition of *Logical Self-Defense* is adapted from the current revision of the popular Canadian text of the same name. It is intended for a logic, reasoning, or critical thinking course that focuses on the interpretation and assessment of "real life" arguments. These are the arguments that people formulate and use for practical purposes in their everyday lives.

The text offers step-by-step guidelines for identifying and analyzing arguments. It outlines a theory of good argument to use for purposes of evaluating and constructing arguments. It presents a positive approach to argument assessment, viewing "bad" arguments as deviations from the patterns of good ones, usually open to improvement or repair. It contains guidelines for constructing arguments and for preparing and writing essays or briefs with an argued case for their thesis. Students are introduced to fallacies as practical and effective tools for evaluating arguments. Special methods for interpreting and assessing longer arguments are provided. Students are given guidelines to help them filter out the more reliable information from newspapers and television news—the sources of most of the "facts" about society and the world we use in our reasoning and arguments. The text also offers an array of devices to deal with the tricks and deceits of so much of today's advertising.

In this text the informal fallacies figure prominently as a multipurpose learning device in the following ways

- ◆ Working with fallacies using this text's approach helps students improve their ability to recognize, interpret, and evaluate arguments and to formulate clear, well-organized arguments themselves.
- ◆ Our fallacies are a manageable set of memorable labels for common mistakes in reasoning and argument, and of recurrent argument patterns.
- ◆ As introduced in this book, the fallacies give students the bite-sized quantities of material best suited for learning and mastery: big enough for ready identification and retrieval; small enough to be digested in a lesson or two.

- ◆ Students can experience success in manageable learning chunks, which is important in encouraging perseverance in what is, after all, hard intellectual work.
- ◆ Learning new fallacies requires analyzing ever new and different arguments, giving the practice in the skills that's needed for their mastery; and so as students' repertoires of fallacies accumulate, they progressively enrich their critical abilities.
- ◆ Fallacies learned earlier recur, so ongoing review of the fallacies occurs naturally.
- ◆ As more fallacies and corresponding patterns of argument are added, the subject gets increasingly complex, but at a gradual rate that students can handle.
- ◆ Most of the fallacy names are widely used, so students learn that critical discussion is a public activity of discourse communities, not solitary and private.
- ◆ Seeing that the occurrence of fallacies is widespread, students appreciate that their critical skills have immediate, practical applicability.
- ◆ Students become aware that they themselves have tended to commit various fallacies, and thus that these critical tools are applicable to their own thinking.

Instructors will be pleased, we hope, by the precision, rigor, and theoretical currency of the identifying conditions provided for each fallacy, along with ample illustrations about how to apply them using actual arguments, not invented and unrealistic fictions. These fallacy conditions, boxed for easy reference, play two roles. Like a field guide, they show students what to look for to identify fallacies in the exercises or other examples. And, like a statute, they specify the elements of the case students have to make when they construct arguments to show convincingly that a given fallacy has been committed.

A special virtue of this text, we think, is its roster of actual examples, both in the body of the text and in the exercises, culled from the live issues in contemporary United States, Canadian, and British society. Our experience suggests that students' practical ability to handle arguments is best honed on the arguments they might actually encounter. We have provided our analyses of the examples we've used to illustrate each fallacy. Readers may well disagree with our interpretations, and we welcome well-supported corrections or improvements. Students as well as instructors are welcome to write to us at Department of Philosophy, University of Windsor, Windsor, Ontario, Canada N9B 3P4.

Acknowledgments

We are grateful for the influence of the comments, the discussions, and the scholarly work of many friends and colleagues, including Derek Allen, Mark Battersby, Lorraine Code, Frans van Eemeren, Alec Fisher, James Freeman, Trudy Govier, Rob Grootendorst, Moira Gutteridge, Hans Hansen, David Hitchcock, Sally Jackson, Scott Jacobs, Howard Kahane, Erik Krabbe, Tjark Kruiger, Donald McCloskey, James McCurry, John McMurtry, John McPeck, Stephen Norris, Daniel O'Keefe, Kate Parr, Richard Paul, Robert Pinto, Christian Plantin, Nicholas Rescher, Michael Scriven, Francisca Snoeck Henkemans, Stephen Toulmin, Christopher Tindale, Perry Weddle, Douglas Walton, Mark Weinstein, and John Woods. As the editors of the journal *Informal Logic* for the past ten years we have had the benefit of monitoring the leading research in our field, for which we are immensely grateful. Four anonymous McGraw-Hill reviewers gave the penultimate revision the generosity of careful, constructive critiques and suggestions that led to significant improvements in this version of the book. To all, our thanks.

In addition, we thank the input of numerous classes of students over the past (good lord!) twenty years, and we thank for specific suggestions used in this edition: Brad Bowen, Hank van der Breggen, Debra Boussey, Pamela Courtenay Hall, Tony Couture, Charles Jones, Sandra Orsini, and Ken Saunders.

We would also like to acknowledge the role of Catherine O'Toole, one of our editors at McGraw-Hill Ryerson, Toronto. Through her determination, this book has finally been able to cross the border into the United States. We also gratefully acknowledge the support and help of the McGraw-Hill, Inc. staff in New York—Cynthia Ward, our editor, Judith Cornwell, senior associate editor, and David Dunham, senior editing supervisor—for numerous helpful suggestions and for catching many of our errors and infelicities.

Last, and most important, we thank our families for their patience and support: Maggie, Mary, Sean, and Matthew Johnson; June and Jay Blair.

Ralph H. Johnson
J. Anthony Blair

LOGICAL SELF-DEFENSE

INTRODUCTION

Much has been written about the consumer in our society, but little has been done to extend that viewpoint to the area of argumentation about social, political, and other topics of everyday concern. As citizens, we are showered with persuasive appeals. Pick up any newspaper or magazine, turn on the radio or TV, or check the mail that comes to the door. The teachers' union, the school board, the city council, irate taxpayers—they're all trying to gain our support: for higher salaries, or for lower salaries; for a strike, or for an injunction to block a strike; for city core redevelopment or for rezoning for a suburban shopping mall. Walkathons want us to walk, bikeathons want us to bike, telethons want us to phone in a pledge to support this or that cause. Your political party wants you to canvass for a local candidate; your senator wants you to fill out a questionnaire; a pollster wants your opinion about issues in the upcoming election. Last night's editorial suggested that pornography is demeaning to women and dehumanizes men. Is it true? Some mothers write letters to the editor favoring abortion on demand; other mothers write urging that abortion be outlawed. Who is right? We are urged to get out and jog; we're implored to quit smoking. Is a home of your own an unachievable dream? What are we to think and do about all these pleas and appeals?

Groups and individuals are incessantly vying for our support for their way of seeing things, for our acceptance of their views of what is true, important, or worth doing. The list of topics varies; the point is that we are consumers of beliefs and values as well as products. An important question thus emerges: How good are our buying habits? Some arguments are damaged goods. Buying a bad argument can, depending on the situation, do a person more harm than buying a defective CD player.

Assuming that your buying habits are in need of improvement and that you are willing to work to develop better ones; assuming, too, that you are not so naive as to think that you can listen to this symphony of persuasive appeals without being influenced by them, what are your options? What resources exist to help you sort out the good from the less worthy? How can you equip yourself to distinguish between good and bad persuasive appeals?

1

We think you need to become familiar with and able to take part in the practice of argumentation. This activity has its origins in ancient Greek society of the fifth century B.C.; since then, it has been a mainstay of intellectual culture, aiding generations of inquirers in pursuit of truth. Although our society has become image-oriented, argumentation is no cultural dinosaur. On the contrary, the practice of insisting on good reasons for believing and doing remains essential to the expansion of knowledge and to a free and democratic society.

We are convinced that argumentation is a powerful tool for assessing the value of the multitude of messages beamed at us and that with its aid, we will be better able to distinguish the good reasons for believing and acting from the bad ones. We hope that by working through this book you will acquire, to a significant extent, the knowledge, skills, and habits of mind you need to analyze arguments and so to believe and act on ever more solid grounds.

SECTION I
The Basic Tools

CHAPTER ONE

◆

Identifying Arguments

In this chapter we introduce the concept of argument that will be used in this book by distinguishing it from opinion. We then suggest ways of identifying arguments that are made in the prose of everyday settings.

Opinion versus Argument

There are few sure things in life anymore, but one of them is that people will always have opinions on almost every conceivable topic—from how to save the environment to how to save your soul, from what City Hall should do about waste disposal to what Israel and the Arab states should do to secure an enduring peace in the Mideast, from whether it will rain tomorrow to what makes a song a "classic." In fact, there are opinions about opinions; for example, "Everyone is entitled to their opinion."

By *opinion,* we mean simply belief or attitude. For example, suppose that you and a friend have just seen the classic movie *Casablanca* for the first time. You turn to your friend and ask, "Well what do you think? Did you like it?" What you are asking for is your friend's reaction to the movie, her first thoughts about it. Perhaps your friend says, "I thought it was terrific; I loved it." That is her opinion; in this case, a value judgment. But opinions can also be judgments of fact ("In my opinion, that big bird is an eagle"), predictions ("If you ask my opinion, the consensus will be that Navratilova had the greatest tennis career of the twentieth century"), or statements of faith ("In my opinion, God looks after those who are pure of heart").

OPINION

Any belief or attitude held or expressed by anyone.

People express their opinions in all sorts of contexts. They may do so simply to be sociable ("Rotten weather, isn't it?") or because they think others want to (or should) know their opinion ("Oh dear, that jacket does not go with those slacks"). Others, like TV commentators or newspaper columnists, get paid for their opinions. Some opinions are instant reactions, expressed in the heat of the moment or without deliberation. These opinions reveal more about their owner's state of mind at the time than they do about the subject. Others have been considered or thought through and convey reliable information about the subject. Physicians' medical opinions about their patients' health and attorneys' legal opinions about their clients' legal positions are supposed to have this latter feature.

The following is a clear example of an opinion, stated in a letter to a newspaper:

1   Thank you for your movie critic, Judy Gerstel. We can depend on her for a good appraisal of movies. Her critiques are usually right on.
        We prefer, however, the 10-point movie-rating system you used to use to the current 4-point system.

Marge and Mike Miller [fictitious names]

The Millers say they tend to agree with Judy Gerstel's movie reviews and express gratitude to the paper for using her as a movie reviewer. They also express their disagreement with the paper's new 4-point movie-rating system. These are their opinions. Period. Is Judy Gerstel really a good movie reviewer? Is the 10-point rating system better than the 4-point system? The Millers present no grounds for agreeing with their opinions.

Can one assess opinions? Sure. Opinions can be thoroughly thought-out judgments or vague impressions; they can be wise or foolish; they can be well-grounded or utterly baseless. (In a TV commercial for Gallo wines, a character says, "Isn't 'I just like it' good enough?" Maybe it is with wine, but when you get your doctor's opinion about whether your arm is broken or you're pregnant, "I just have a feeling . . ." is emphatically *not* good enough.)

What is an opinion worth? That's partly a matter of its function and partly a matter of whose opinion it is. If a local columnist is successful in getting people to think about a particular topic by expressing an opinion (even stridently), then the purpose may be achieved. A doctor's diagnosis ("medical opinion") of an athlete's injury will normally be more valuable than will that of a teammate.

Logicians are interested in arguments that are launched by expressions of opinion; that is, they are interested in the opinions *plus* the reasons or evidence advanced to support those opinions. The simple statement of an opinion can be the first step toward the construction of an argument. Unfortunately, for many people it's also the last. A further step is taken when, in addition to offering an opinion, the person goes on to offer reasons for it. What makes the citing of reasons or grounds for an opinion preferable to just stating it is that the reasons offer us a possible basis for agreeing with the stated opinion. By looking at how well the reasons support it, we can see whether we, too, should share the opinion.

Opinions lead to argument in a couple of ways. When an opinion is questioned or challenged, a natural response is to look for the grounds or evidence that support it (that constitute reasons to believe it). Such grounds constitute an argument for the opinion. Alternatively, when two opinions clash, the question naturally arises as to which is true or more plausible. Producing the reasons for preferring one of two conflicting opinions constitutes producing an argument in support of that opinion.

When people engage in a dispute, contesting each other's opinions (sometimes heatedly), we say they are *having an argument*. The discussion may not go beyond just repeating the disagreement:

> PRO: I really like *Casablanca*.
> CON: I don't, particularly.
> PRO: What? It's a terrific movie. It's a classic.
> CON: Maybe, but I can't get excited about it.

Often the discussion will go beyond the mere expression of disagreement, and one side will ask for the other's reasons (Pro: "What don't you like about it?" or Con: "What is there to it?"), and both sides may then try to state their reasons. What they put into words may be what led them to their opinions or it may be an after-the-fact defense of it. The expression of opinions functions as a natural starting point for the construction of reasoned support for them. When people state the grounds or reasons for their opinions, they are giving arguments for them—and these reasons are arguments that they, or someone else, "makes" or produces.

Starting out by *having* an argument, the disputants thus might turn to *making* arguments. Clearly, then, the word "argument" has at least these two uses.

TWO SENSES OF 'ARGUMENT'

1. An interaction, usually verbal and usually between two or more people, that is normally occasioned by a difference of opinion
2. What someone makes or formulates (reasons or evidence) as grounds or support for an opinion (the basis for believing it)

To get the benefit of any arguments associated with opinions, you have to be able to identify the expressions of opinion that are accompanied to some extent by reasons and so can serve as starters for argument and to distinguish them from mere opinion, i.e., opinion unattended by any attempt at support. Let's look at a couple of examples to bring this contrast home.

A few years ago, the *Los Angeles Times* ran a story about a trial in which a United States district court judge was quoted as having used the word "faggots" to refer to homosexuals. This story prompted several readers to write letters to the editor. Here is what one wrote:

2   So Judge Hauk referred to gays as faggots.

It seems the crooks, weirdos and rapists are all looking for acceptance from those of us who follow the straight and narrow, and frankly I'm sick of it.

If someone is caught in the act of committing a crime, shoot him with a gun, not a Taser!

This writer surely expressed his opinion. His reaction was intense, but what was he trying to say? Was he claiming that gay men are crooks, weirdos, and rapists and that therefore it's all right to call them insulting names? Or was he just angry about some particular recent cases where he thought the accused had expected approval just because they were homosexual? His comments were not very well thought through. He seemed to want to defend the judge's use of the term "faggot" but we aren't given any clear reasons why it is defensible. The tone here is certainly strident, anticipating disagreement, but the contents leave little room for interplay or evaluation. As far as argumentation is concerned, this expression of opinion is a nonstarter.

Contrast the opinion in 2 with the next one, also about Judge Hauk's comment.

3   Judges should be fair and honest to handle all proceedings in a just and unbiased way. If Judge Hauk has such prejudices against homosexuals, how many of what other prejudices does he have? How could people of the United States expect Hauk and judges like him to be fair and give out sentences or unbiased opinions when obviously he has prejudices against certain people?

The second writer's opinion was that Hauk was biased (an opinion based on the judge's reference to homosexuals), but she went on from this opinion to express another view in the form of wondering whether this judge can be fair. This expression of opinion has both structure and motion; it is headed in a direction, toward a goal, and it is not hard to see roughly what that goal is: opposition to Judge Hauk or to any judge with prejudices. The support for this opinion—that judges should be fair and honest and that prejudiced judges cannot give out fair sentences or opinions—we can evaluate logically, unlike the first case, which had no clear structure or direction. And there is another important difference: Perhaps both writers sought to persuade us, but the second writer was more rational. She gave us organized reasons; the first writer gave us a jumbled, unformed reaction.

From the presentation of opinion in the second letter (though not from the first), it is possible to make a reasonable guess at the argument the second writer intended to make.

By *an argument that is made,* we mean reasons that someone has collected which that person thinks show that another claim is true, or at least deserves consideration. The reasons might consist of claims the person making the argument thinks up, borrows from other people, or gathers through research. The person thinks that anyone who accepts the reasons is thereby committed to accepting the claim alleged to follow from them. Thus, for example, if you accept that today is Tuesday, then you are led to accept that tomorrow is Wednesday. Suppose we make the argument that Yvan should be given the winner's prize because he won the race and the prize should go to the person who won the race. In making that argument, our thinking is that if you agree both that winning the race is the only basis needed for deserving the winner's prize and that Yvan won the race, then you are led to accept that Yvan deserves the winner's prize. So *an argument someone makes* is a collection of claims (or statements) that point the way from the acceptance of one group of claims to the acceptance of the remaining claim.

Because the second expression of opinion about Judge Hauk's ruling is much closer to fitting this definition than is the first one, we want to distinguish between the two. The first is pure opinion, while the second, which gives reasons but is not very clear about exactly what those reasons are supposed to show, is what we'll dub (for want of a better term) "proto-argument."

The expressions of opinion we call *proto-arguments* differ from arguments proper more in terms of their structure than in terms of their purpose. In an argument (as product), a certain structure is evident: (1) a clear opinion, or "claim"; (2) support for that opinion; and (3) the path by which the support is supposed to lead to the opinion. It is the absence of (2) or (3), or both, which identifies a proto-argument and the absence of (2) that marks mere opinion. Yet both proto-argument and fully explicit argument make an attempt to persuade rationally by dispensing reasons.

The citing of reasons is a distinguishing ideal of constructed arguments because there are other methods of persuasion, other tactics that people use to attempt to induce belief and action. There is the appeal to one's blind faith in authority: "This is your Leader speaking!" There's the appeal to force and fear: "I have a gun! Gimme the money." There is the appeal to one's vanity or insecurities: "Someone with your obvious intelligence can see that our policies are clearly right-minded." There's the appeal to personal loyalty: "We've been friends a long time. Believe me when I say I didn't do it" or to group loyalties: "All good environmentalists will oppose this bill."

Such methods of inducing belief or influencing actions may, in some situations, be legitimate. A 4-year-old child is generally not going to be persuaded rationally to keep from running into the street, so one may have to resort to some combination of force and fear to keep the child out of the roadway. However, as we become mature and able to reason things out for ourselves, we are quite capable both of persuading others rationally and being so persuaded ourselves. Arguments have a prominent role in this enterprise.

A *constructed argument,* then, is a piece of linguistic communication (whether written or spoken) with a certain structure (support and claim) and function (rational support or grounding). The requisite structure and function cannot be rigidly specified. So far as structure goes, people's arguments will tend to have tacit or unexpressed parts and will vary in how clearly ordered they are. Argumentative expression ranges from relatively sketchy forms to those elaborated with systematic thoroughness and in fine detail. Most of the arguments we will be dealing with fall somewhere between these extremes. The first thing to do in appraising arguments is to get clear about what the argument is:

just what is offered as support and how it is intended to support the claim concluded (more about that in the next chapter).

So far as function goes, probably the most frequent use of arguments is to try to persuade another or others to accept or agree with the arguer's opinion. But arguments can have other purposes. For example, they can be used to investigate a hypothesis (by seeing what reasons might be given to support a claim), or to understand what one is committed to in accepting some claim (by seeing what other claims it leads to or supports), or to reinforce people's opinions (by giving them further reasons for believing what they are already disposed to believe and answering objections or criticisms). We say more about some of these topics in Chapter 12.

THE SENSE OF 'ARGUMENT' USED IN THIS BOOK

By 'argument,' we mean a claim, together with one or more sets of reasons offered by someone to support that claim.

The *claim* will be an opinion or point of view that someone has asserted and is defending. Any sentence expressing an opinion in that role expresses what is called a *conclusion* of the argument. Sentences expressing reasons or evidence put forward to support any conclusion express what are called the *premises*[1] of the argument. Offering reasons to support a claim amounts to trying to show that it is true or believable. (Sometimes the word 'argument' is used to refer just to the premises, as in "He had a good point, but the arguments he used to support it were weak.")

In the early part of this book, we deal with arguments that are not elaborated very extensively. We concentrate on what we call *snippets*; that is, very short arguments or segments of longer passages. This focus makes it easier for you to develop your logical skills and sensibility initially.

We began this chapter by talking about expressions of opinion as, in some instances, the preliminary step toward argument. But making an argument with a single reason for accepting a claim will usually be merely a preliminary to formulating a fully worked-out argument, which we will call a *case*. Let us explain. Disagreements about controversial matters are usually what lead people to make arguments. Making a well-rounded argument in support of a contending point of view in a controversy requires us not only to give arguments for it but to deal with the known objections to those arguments and with the arguments that seem to show that the position itself is wrong. For example, an argument that consists of a few reasons in favor of capital punishment but fails to deal with the well-known objections to those reasons and does not take into consideration and respond to arguments for opposing capital punishment moves in just one of three dimensions. What is needed here is a multidimensional set of arguments that seeks to (1) give reasons or evidence for the

---

[1] Also spelled 'premisses.'

conclusion, (2) rebut objections to those reasons, and (3) rebut arguments for the opposite viewpoint. This multidimensional set of arguments is what we have in mind by the idea of a case. In Chapters 12 and 13, we have more to say about cases. In the meantime, we will mostly be considering arguments that move in only one or two of the three dimensions.

Identifying the Argument

We now turn to the essential preliminary stage leading to the logical appraisal of arguments: arriving at a clear understanding of what the argument is prior to evaluating it. A physician cannot treat a disease or injury properly without diagnosing it correctly. An attorney cannot advise a client properly without knowing the precise and full particulars of the client's situation. Nor can a reasoner evaluate an argument properly without a precise understanding of what the argument is.

When people talk or write, they don't always clearly signal when they intend to make their arguments. As we have noted, even when they are clearly *having an argument* (that is, disagreeing and disputing), they don't always *make* any arguments (that is, give any reasons to back up their opinions). So when interpreting what someone has said or written, we must, at the outset, make a judgment as to whether an argument has been made at all.

In practice, deciding whether someone has made an argument cannot be disassociated from deciding what the constituent parts and structure of the argument are. It's like deciding whether an ad has a subliminal message: You can't decide that there's a message there without identifying what the message is. To simplify our exposition, however, we have artificially separated these two intertwined tasks. In the remainder of this chapter, we will list some indicators of the presence of an argument, compare argument with a look-alike, and offer some advice. Then, in Chapter 2, we will focus on the problem of *reconstruction:* extracting the argument and displaying its structure.

We also restrict our discussion to arguments expressed in language and, for practical convenience, to examples from published, written sources. The first question to ask when trying to determine whether a passage of prose might contain an argument is, Why suspect there is an argument here? But there is an ambiguity in this question. On the one hand, the author might be intending to produce an argument. On the other hand, the passage might contain a set of statements that could be arranged so as to constitute an argument regardless of whether the author intended to be producing one. Either case can have two versions. In one, whether intended as an argument or not, the argument is a good one. In the second version, the argument is not a good one. And if not good as it stands, it either can be repaired or improved or is beyond help and should be abandoned. So which case do we have in mind in asking about a passage, Is there an argument here? For our purposes, we will be trying to discern what the author had in mind. If he or she intended to make an argument, then whether it is a good argument or a bad one and whether it can be fixed or not, we will say there is an argument in the segment of writing. In deciding whether an argument by the author is present, several different kinds of clues are available.

Evidence of the Author's Intention

Writing or talking aims at some end or goal. Talking and writing are actions and thus performed for a purpose. Ask yourself, What was the author's purpose here? Since one of the most common reasons for making arguments is to use them to persuade others to believe something or to do something, it's helpful to ask, Is the author trying to persuade some audience to accept some claim or to perform some action? Is the author trying to prove or establish some point of view? If so, what is the viewpoint or action, and what are the reasons given?

Sometimes a writer is helpful enough to make her intent clear. She might say: "Now here is what I believe, and here's why I believe it" or some equivalent. Then you know you have an argument, and the only remaining question is what exactly the contents and structure of the argument are. What are the premises and the conclusion, and how are the premises organized?

Unfortunately for readers, such explicit statements of intent are rare. In their absence, there are three principal sources of evidence to determine the authors' aim and to discern the details of any argument they have produced: (1) *verbal clues,* special argument-indicating expressions in the language; (2) *situational clues,* the context in which the passage was written or spoken; and (3) *internal logical clues,* the logical or evidentiary relations between the statements in the passage. We'll take up each in turn.

Argument Indicators

When someone writes, "Bat and pigeon droppings contain parasites that can be fatal to humans, so you should wear reliable respirators when you renovate buildings that might contain such droppings," the word 'so' is a signal that the author means to be arguing. 'So' also indicates that the claim following it is the conclusion and that the claim preceding it is a premise. When someone says, "You should see that movie because the mountain scenery in it is spectacular," the word 'because' tells you that they are arguing and, specifically, that the statement prior to 'because' is what they are trying to persuade you of (the conclusion), and the statement following it contains a reason they think will persuade you (the premise).

Perhaps the most reliable textual clues to the author's intention to argue are these expressions that signal premises and conclusions. We have seen that they do two things at once: (1) imply the presence of argument and (2) point out the argumentative roles of the sentences they are juxtaposed with. As a competent language user, you are familiar with words like 'so' and 'therefore,' 'because' and 'since,' and you know how to use them to indicate your own intentions to argue, but you might not have paid explicit attention to the *way* they work.

As we have just illustrated, argument indicators can be divided into two groups according to the argumentative function of the clause to which they are attached. The ones we call *conclusion indicators* introduce clauses stating one or more of the conclusions of an argument; the ones we call *premise indicators* introduce clauses stating one or more of the premises of an argument. (In case you happen to run across it somewhere, the grammatical label for these premise and conclusion indicators is *illatives.*)

CONCLUSION INDICATORS

therefore	thus	it follows that
so	accordingly	I conclude that
hence	and [so]	my conclusion is

These are words that almost invariably introduce the clause expressing an argument's conclusion. The clearest conclusion indicator of all is 'therefore,' which rarely fails to play this role (though there are exceptions, so you can't use it blindly). 'So' used as a conjunction is a synonym of 'therefore.' (Thus people who say "so therefore . . ." want to leave no doubt in your mind that "here comes my conclusion!") Other terms that signal the presence of a conclusion by preceding it are 'hence,' 'thus,' and 'accordingly' when they are used as conjunctions. 'It follows that' and 'I conclude that' are almost invariably conclusion-indicating phrases, but 'in conclusion' usually marks the end of a piece of prose—either the last point or a final summary—and not necessarily the conclusion of an argument (that is, the claim being argued for). 'Consequently' sometimes indicates an argument's conclusion, but sometimes it points to something being explained, not something being argued for. (We discuss the important distinction between argument and explanation later in this chapter.)

PREMISE INDICATORS

because	given that
since	granted that
for	for the reason that

These are words that are usually followed immediately by one or more of the premises of an argument. 'Since' (the conjunction, not the adverb) strongly suggests that the clause following it states an argument's premise. 'For' (the conjunction, not the preposition) sometimes indicates argument, sometimes explanation. Similarly, 'because' marks either an explanation or an upcoming set of premises. 'Given that' and 'granted that' sometimes indicate premises and sometimes just introduce the conditions of something. Some references to 'reasons' indicate the premises of arguments; others indicate explanations.

Keep an eye out for premise and conclusion indicators. Together with other evidence they can be decisive, but alone and out of any context they are like the rules of spelling: There are exceptions. Also, too often just when you need one to indicate that an argument is intended or to cue you to the role of a particular statement in an argument, your author lets you down by failing to provide any.

Context

Besides going by premise and conclusion indicators, look to *context* to help divine the author's intentions. There is context in the sense of the *habitat* of the communication; i.e., where you find it. In certain locations, arguments are the norm: courts of law, legislatures, articles in scholarly and scientific journals, to name but three. In other locations, arguments are rare; for example, in lyric poetry, pornography, comedians' routines, or prime-time TV commercials (as we'll contend in Chapter 11). In between are contexts that are hospitable to arguments, yet often enough have argument-free prose. Here we'd put letters to the editor, editorials, "opinion" columns, political speeches, college lectures.

Context can also mean the situation that is the *occasion* for the communication; i.e., when you find it. For example, if your local newspaper has been reporting a battle at City Hall over contracting out garbage collection to a nonunion company and laying off workers in the city's unionized sanitation department, then you can bet on finding arguments in the interchanges at city council meetings and in letters and opinion and editorial columns of the paper. In general, when there is a dispute with two or more sides in contention, expect the people involved to be intending to give reasons why their particular view should prevail. Include here all the "hot" issues of the day: environmental ethics, affirmative action, nuclear power, policies dealing with AIDS, biomedical ethics, business ethics, tax policies, trade and tariff policies, capital punishment, gun control, abortion, euthanasia, suicide, school board policies, foreign policy, and so on. The same holds when someone takes a public position that runs counter to the conventional wisdom, even if there isn't a public dispute about it yet.

The last paragraph deserves elaboration. It seems to be a convention of communication via speech that if someone asserts something to be the case and another person questions or doubts that claim, the person making the assertion owes an account of why he or she thinks it is true. This obligation, or *onus*, is

---

BURDEN OF PROOF

When someone asserts an opinion to which there are well-known objections, the asserter has an obligation, if it is so requested, to provide a reason for accepting the opinion.

what is known in legal argumentation and organized debate as *the burden of proof.*

The burden-of-proof rule is a convention of communication, so people adept at communicating usually try to discharge their obligation by supplying the requisite support for contentious claims. So, as interpreters of prose where controversial claims are advanced, we are justified in trying to interpret the writing as containing argumentation, at least if we can do so without distorting it. For example, when Oliver Stone's movie *J.F.K.* makes the implied claim that there was a conspiracy involving the FBI, the CIA, some Supreme Court justices, and other highly placed federal government officials to conceal the real facts of the assassination of President Kennedy, Mr. Stone incurs the burden of proof because his allegation is highly controversial. It's fair to interpret the movie as representing his argument in support of it.

Logical Structure

There is a fourth resource (besides the writer's avowed intention, premise and conclusion indicators, and contextual evidence) available for deciding whether a piece of writing is intended to be argumentative: its logical structure. Ask yourself, Can its statements readily be fitted together to form a sensible argument? Do some of them actually lend support to others? Is it easy to see how the author might have thought that some claims support others (even if they don't)?

The point is this: If you can reconstruct from the prose an argument that someone could put forward sensibly, then you have some evidence that the author intended to be making that argument in that passage. You have to be cautious. The "argument" so reconstructed might be a logically bad one (we go into the standards of a good argument in Chapter 3), and you don't want to attribute to someone a bad argument unless you have no choice. Why not? The reason is a general principle of interpretation called the *principle of charity*.

PRINCIPLE OF CHARITY

Provide the most favorable logical interpretation of what someone has written or said that is consistent with all the available evidence relevant to its interpretation.

Unless there are special reasons for not doing so, when we communicate competently it seems that we try to live up to certain norms. For example, we try to give accurate and relevant information in adequate amounts for the purposes at hand. Hence, when we make and offer arguments, we normally try to make them logical. This feature of communication is what lies behind the principle of charity. The idea is that since (normally) an author will be *trying* to make logical arguments, it follows that if, in interpreting a passage, we reconstruct the most logical argument we can make it out to contain, then that probably will be the argument the author intended to make. A corollary of the principle of charity is that if we can take a particular passage in two ways—either as a stupid argument or as, more sensibly, something else—and if either makes sense in the context, then we should assign the second interpretation.

Any piece of writing will approximate one of the following five models, and the principle of charity directs the associated verdict in each case.

1. The prose yields a logically good argument, and nothing in the context points against that interpretation. Verdict: Treat it as an argument.
2. The passage yields an argument that in the context, there is some reason to think the author intended, but it is not a logically good argument. In that case, you have to decide between two options: (*a*) the author did not intend to argue, in which case he cannot be made out to have argued badly, but the cost is that it is hard to make sense out of what he was intending to do, or (*b*) the author intended to argue, in which case there is a reasonable interpretation of the function of his communication, but the cost is that he has to be taken to have argued badly. Verdict: Sometimes (*a*) sometimes (*b*) depending on the specifics of the communication and the context; sometimes there is no way to decide.
3. The passage yields an argument, but only a logically bad one, and there is an alternative interpretation based on context. Verdict: Call it, not an argument, but, instead, whatever it seems to be (a joke, a piece of sarcasm or irony, simply an opinion, or whatever).
4. The piece of prose might be construed to yield a partial argument or moves in the direction of argument, and the context is favorable to reading it as argumentative, yet what is stated is so tentative or so unformed that to reconstruct an argument out of it would require, in effect, creating an argument oneself, based on the hints the author gives. Verdict: Call it proto-argument.
5. What has been said is nonargumentative. Verdict: No argument. The author is doing something besides making an argument.

A Word of Warning

This is a book about arguments. Because it deals almost exclusively with arguments, as you read it and work your way through the exercises you may find yourself inclined to see arguments under every rock and behind every tree. Perspective is important. Lots and lots of written and spoken communication— most of it, in fact—is *not* argumentative. People complain, crack jokes, express outrage, pontificate, praise, register observations, make snide comments, make requests, make small talk, ask questions, recommend, ridicule, stand on their dignity, pass the time of day, describe situations, tell stories. . . . The list could go on and on, and none of this is argument. Also, as already emphasized, we are following the policy of withholding the title "argument" from expressions of opinion and proto-arguments. Critical judgment means discrimination in using the honorific term 'argument' and in applying the critical apparatus that goes with it.

Examples

Here are two examples, together with as much background as we have available about them, to illustrate some of the above points.

All we know about this passage is that it was a letter written to a columnist for the Newark, New Jersey, *Star Ledger* and printed there.

4   Dear Emily:

I wish you'd write something about people who are unfeeling about pets. I've had visitors talk disparagingly about my cat and within her earshot. These same people would be highly indignant if I made a similar remark about one of their children. I can't understand such a lack of feeling.   —Irate

Next is a passage from Neil Postman's critique of television, *Amusing Ourselves to Death* (Penguin Books, 1985). Postman has written in an earlier chapter that his "book is an inquiry into and a lamentation about the . . . decline of the Age of Typography and the ascendancy of the Age of Television."

5   But there is still another reason why I should like not to be understood as making a total assault on television. Anyone who is even slightly familiar with the history of communications knows that every new technology for thinking involves a trade-off. It giveth and it taketh away. . . . We must be careful in praising or condemning because the future may hold surprises for us. (p. 29)

Before reading any further, decide for yourself whether these excerpts should be construed as containing arguments. Then put down your reasons for arriving at your judgment in each case. After you have done that, read our verdicts in the following paragraphs:

We think "Irate" is expressing his indignation at how people can be unfeeling about pets and making a request of the columnist to whom he is writing. We don't think there is any point in trying to tease an argument out of this letter. "Irate" finds an inconsistency between what people do and what they expect others to do (they'll criticize your cat and hurt your feelings but be upset if you criticize *their* children and thus hurt *their* feelings). He expresses puzzlement, or perhaps dismay, over this phenomenon. If you try to make "Irate" out to be arguing, you have to attribute to him an argument that employs a silly analogy, namely: "Cats, like children, have feelings; and so, just as you shouldn't insult a child, you shouldn't insult a cat." So here is a model-4 situation. You have a choice between (1) interpreting the letter to yield a bad argument and (2) interpreting it as not functioning to express an argument at all but doing something else. In the context, the latter is entirely reasonable. The letter is expressing feelings and making a request (the principle of charity indicates this option).

We think the excerpt from Postman's book does contain an argument. The clearest indication is the author's own words, "But there is still another reason why. . . ." These words indicate explicitly that the author intends to support his claim that he should not be understood to be making a total assault on television. A second factor is the context. As the quote in the background states, Postman's book is a lament about television. We would expect, therefore, to be given a reason for any qualification of that lament, which our passage clearly is. Finally, the excerpt itself readily yields up a logically sensible argument, one which goes roughly as follows:

6   Every new technology for thinking brings new benefits and causes the loss of benefits from the technology it replaces.
Therefore:
   The future may reveal some hitherto unappreciated benefits of television.
Therefore:
   It would be a mistake to claim television has no benefits.
Therefore:
   Do not understand Postman to be making a total assault on television.

The argument we attribute to Postman is, moreover, a very plausible one. So there are several reasons to interpret this segment as containing an argument, and no reason not to. Whether we have interpreted the argument accurately we leave to your judgment.

Argument and Explanation

One understandable source of confusion in identifying arguments is their similarity to explanations. An argument and an explanation are quite different nonetheless. They perform different functions. The job of an argument, as we've seen, is to present reasons for accepting a claim. An explanation, on the other hand, is used to make something intelligible or understandable. Often explanations do this by showing how the thing came about, how it came to be; thus we get explanations that do their work by showing the cause or origin of an event or at least the factor(s) that made the difference in its coming to be. At other times, explanations work by giving the meaning or significance or a phenomenon or event. Both of these functions of explanations are illustrated in a *New York Times* story about a farmer in Hills, Iowa, who killed three people and then committed suicide. The headline was "Deaths on the Iowa Prairie: Four New Victims of the Economy," and the report said the deaths "were the latest in a series of violent outbursts across the Middle West" caused by the depressed farm economy.

   The presence or absence of an attempt to support a claim is one way of distinguishing argument from explanation in practice. Ask, Does the writer say anything to try to establish the claim? to show that it is true? to persuade us to accept it? If the answer is "yes," you are looking at an argument; if "no," then it is not an argument. And you can ask, Is the writer taking the claim's truth for granted—treating it as given or as already established—and offering an account of why it is? If the answer here is "yes," then you have an explanation. Unfortunately, you cannot rely on premise and conclusion indicators or other terms alone to mark the argument/explanation distinction. For example, 'because' can introduce either, and what's called a "reason" can be either.

   Further complications:

1. An explanation can be used in an argument. For instance, an explanation of why the accused could have had no motive for committing the crime can contribute to an argument supporting the accused's innocence.
2. An argument can be used in an explanation. Postman's argument to show that television is probably not without benefits explains why he is not totally critical of TV.
3. There will be cases in which either interpretation—argument or explanation— seems equally plausible, or where, as in the following example, both explanation and argument occur simultaneously.

7   Wiring in new construction is seldom a problem since all studs and ceiling joists are exposed and accessible. (*Reader's Digest Complete Do-It-Yourself Manual,* 1973, p. 264.)

Here the subordinate clause explains why wiring in new construction is seldom a problem and, at the same time, gives a reason for believing that it's seldom a problem.

   We grant the complications and acknowledge the difficulty of marking the distinction in certain cases, but we still contend that the two functions of arguing and explaining are conceptually distinct. It is the interpreter's task to sort the two out and to identify only arguments as "arguments."

Explanation   Information that is supposed to indicate the origin, cause, meaning, or significance of an event or other phenomenon. (Example: "She's the best tennis player on the team because she has had better coaching, is in better shape, and practices a lot more than anyone else.")

Argument   Information that is supposed to establish that a proposition is true or otherwise worthy of belief or acceptance. (Example: "She consistently defeats all her teammates, so she's the best tennis player on the team.")

Reading Carefully

One of the payoffs of a study of argument and from practice identifying, reconstructing, and assessing arguments is that your reading will improve. You'll read more carefully, with greater attention to detail and more discrimination among different possible interpretations, than you did before, because such care is necessary to identify, reconstruct, and assess arguments. We have here what's called a *bootstrapping problem*. To learn how to do *x* well, you must start by trying to *x* well. In other words, you have to lift yourself up by your own bootstraps. Bootstrapping problems are common and far from insurmountable. We encounter them any time we learn a skilled activity, be it entirely mental (for example, chess) or mental and physical (for example, golf). To learn to play chess or golf well, you must try to play chess or golf well. Similarly, to learn to read prose with care in order to discern with discrimination whether it contains an argument and, if so, what argument, you must begin by trying to read carefully.

To be sure, the admonition "Read carefully!" is no more helpful to the budding argument analyst than "Play the piano beautifully!"[1] is to the budding pianist. So we offer a few pieces of advice based on experience with miscommunication.

Communication theorists have discovered that when one person (the sender) communicates to another (the receiver), the receiver is not like an empty cassette that simply records the sender's message. Instead, the message is mediated by a complex group of filters, an interacting network of cognitive and affective states, that are built into the receiver. Many of these help the communication, as when they supply needed context and background meanings. But sometimes they distort the message, and when they do, the message received is not the message sent. The result is misinterpretation.

A major cause of misinterpreting what others have said or written is the habit of "reading into" their actual words meanings that are not there, meanings based on the receiver's expectations or on his purely personal associations with the sender's words or expressions. Our main advice about reading carefully, then, is directed to breaking that habit. If you can train yourself in your reading to distinguish the following four things, you'll be on the way to avoiding such misinterpretation.

1. what someone asserts in writing or uttering a given sentence
2. what is consistent with what the person asserts
3. what that assertion strictly implies
4. what that assertion supports but does not strictly imply.

To explain these distinctions, we will apply them to examples.

1. What someone *asserts* is what she intends to be understood to mean. It can be paraphrased in a roughly equivalent sentence. Thus, when Professor Onora O'Neill begins her book *Constructions of Reason* (1989) about Kant's moral philosophy with the sentence (p. 3)

8   I start with two puzzles about Kant's account of reason.

[1] We are grateful to Moira Gutteridge for persuading us of the importance of this point and for this analogy.

she has asserted that there are at least "two puzzling or curious features of what Kant says about reason" and that she is, to paraphrase, beginning her book with a discussion of them.

2. Has Professor O'Neill asserted (*a*) Kant's account of reason contains only two puzzles, (*b*) Kant's account of reason is totally puzzling, (*c*) Kant's account of reason is totally mistaken, or (*d*) Kant's account of reason contains some mistakes, or (*e*) these two puzzles can be explained away? No, she has asserted none of these. It's true that each one is consistent with 8 (that is, if what she asserts in 8 is true, each of *a* to *e* could be true). Two statements are *consistent* if they can both be true at the same time.

3. One assertion *strictly implies* another when the second cannot be false if the first is true. For example:

9   Proper footnotes allow the reader to check sources and to verify information.

implies that

10   Proper footnotes contain enough accurate information to permit the reader to find the source of the footnoted passage.

Passage 9 implies passage 10 because if 9 is true, then 10 has to be true also. If proper footnotes are to allow a reader to check sources and verify information, then they must contain enough accurate information to enable the reader to locate the sources they refer to.

4. One statement can support another without implying it. A statement *supports* another if it constitutes a reason for believing it even if it does not strictly imply it. Consider the following two assertions that Edward Herman and Noam Chomsky make in their book *Manufacturing Consent* (Pantheon, 1988, pp. 18-19.)

11   [1] The mass media are drawn into a symbiotic relationship with powerful sources of information by economic necessity. . . . [2] Economics dictates that they concentrate their resources where significant news often occurs, where important rumors and leaks abound, and where regular press conferences are held. [Numbers added.]

Now, if indeed the costs of news gathering require the mass media to locate their resources as Herman and Chomsky assert, then since capitals such as Washington, Beijing, Tokyo, London, and Paris are such locales, and these are also the centers of government power and governments' distribution of information, then you can see how the mass media might be drawn into some sort of relationship with those sources. So [2] supports [1], but [2] doesn't strictly imply [1]. It could be true that economics dictates such a concentration of media resources, yet the media are able to maintain firm arm's-length relationships with powerful sources (such as governments and lobbies). The first sentence could be false even if the second were true. In fact, that is exactly what some critics of the Herman-Chomsky thesis maintain.

Our main advice about reading carefully, then, comes down to this: When you are reading, do your best to keep track of exactly what the author asserts. Do not add to it by reading in possible interpretations even if the interpretations are consistent with what the author asserts and even if the author might well believe them too. Keep separate also what the assertion strictly implies. Although the author may be committed to what his or her assertions imply, it is one thing to *say* something (that is, put it into words) and quite another to *imply* it. An author might not realize what his assertions imply, and once those implications are pointed out to him, he might take back what he said rather than commit to its implications. Finally, do not attribute to the author what you think his or her assertions might support. The author might disagree or have never thought about it.

Two final general suggestions about careful reading. First, keep an eye out for the premise and conclusion-indicating terms noted above. Second, attend to the semantic cues we refer to in Chapter 2 in our discussion of reconstructing arguments.

Summary

In this chapter we first introduced the concept of "argument" as reasons that one makes or gives in support of a claim, thus distinguishing an argument from opinion and proto-argument, on the one hand, and from a quarrel or a fight, on the other hand. Then we took on the problem of deciding when an argument has been given in a piece of writing. We noted that the author's intentions, premise and conclusion indicators, cues from the context, and the logical structure of the prose all can help you determine the presence of argument. We warned against seeing arguments everywhere, distinguished between arguments and explanations, and suggested how you might try to read with discrimination.

Chapter 2 is devoted to techniques of rewriting and displaying the structure of shorter arguments. In Chapter 13 we introduce a method for displaying the structure of longer arguments.

EXERCISES

These examples will give you practice in discriminating among occasions when someone is clearly giving an argument; when someone is simply offering an opinion; when someone's communication falls somewhere in between, in the gray area of proto-argument; and when someone is doing something else entirely. In each passage below, decide whether there is argument, proto-argument, opinion, or none of these. If it is one of the first three, write out the opinion being offered or the conclusion being argued for. In each case, briefly support your interpretation. Often it is impossible to make a judgment about a piece of writing without information about its context. When needed, such information is provided in the introduction to the example.

1. The word "basically" is a stall word, and any sentence starting out with it signals fuzzy thinking and a desire not to offend. [From the annual list of misused, overused, and useless words compiled at Lake Superior State College, Sault Sainte Marie, Michigan.]

2. If you are getting a refund, you should file your tax return early. That way, you'll have the money sooner to spend or to invest.

3. In their book *Trusting Ourselves: The Sourcebook on Psychology for Women* (Atlantic Monthly Press, 1990), Karen Johnson, M.D., and Tom Ferguson, M.D., list four stages or phases in the development of alcoholism; and in the footnote where they cite their source, they add (p. 359, note 40):

   These phases have been developed based primarily on the study of male alcoholics. Consequently they may not be fully applicable to women.

4. Landscape designer Linda Sheehy has several suggestions for people who hate grass or who have shaded yards where grass won't grow. She recommends several types of ground cover, including periwinkle, snow-on-the-mountain, Japanese birch, and bungleweed. They can be trimmed once or twice a year or not at all, Sheehy says, but the flowers should be cut off. [From a newspaper article.]

5. At college, it's a good idea to spend as much of your time outside class and labs as you can reading and writing and talking about what you're learning. So it is a mistake to take a part-time job while attending college if you can afford not to.

6. Lawrence Weschler wrote a "Reporter at Large" column about Poland in *The New Yorker* magazine (December 10, 1990, pp. 86ff.). Referring to the turbulent events in Polish politics in the first year of the Solidarity-dominated government, after four decades of Communist rule in that country, Weschler wrote:

   All of which [the turbulent political events] I found surprising, since at first blush, anyway, so much of Poland's material situation seemed to have improved so dramatically since my last visit, a year ago.

7. The means used to obtain pleasure may be bad, but it does not follow that the pleasure so obtained is itself bad. Therefore the immorality of some pleasurable activities does not refute the claim that pleasure is good in itself.

8. The press has no right to encourage criminal activity (i.e., illegal news gathering) in order to usurp the function of the police or FBI. Except in extreme circumstances which warrant breaking the law, this is not a case where the end justifies the means. [From a letter to the editor.]

9. Further to an item regarding services across the Irish Sea, I would like to correct a number of inaccuracies. The writer states that the service operates from Larne to Stranraer by hovercraft. In fact the service operates from Stranraer to Belfast and is served by a SeaCat, which is the world's largest car-carrying catamaran. [Letter to the editor.]

10. I am tired of being regarded as prejudiced because I do not approve of homosexuality. All my life I have been taught to believe that homosexuality is a sin. The vast majority of people once believed the same thing.

    Morality does not change; that is one of the defining attributes of God. Any intimate physical activity between two people who are unmarried is wrong. [Letter to the editor during the controversy over gays in the military at the outset of the Clinton administration in 1993.]

11. Why won't our military leaders wake up? Homosexual activity is here to stay, and no high-tech weaponry can take it away. [Letter to the editor during the controversy over gays in the military at the outset of the Clinton administration in 1993.]

12. Despite all the homosexual rhetoric foisted upon us, there is a holy God who condemns homosexuality.

    How strange quite "heterophobic" columnists are about the results of this aberrant lifestyle. Let's have some honesty in print instead of emotion. [Letter to the editor during the controversy over gays in the military at the outset of the Clinton administration in 1993.]

13. The furor over gays in the military is sickening. America has a long history of legally discriminating against its own, from African Americans to women.

    I spent more than five years in the Air Force. In 1960, I roomed with a young man who was gay, and almost everyone in my unit knew it. We lived in a three-person room in a dormitory. It never caused a problem. He never attempted a pass at anyone. He carried himself as a professional soldier, and we respected him for that.

    I doubt that any of the sailors involved in the Tailhook affair was gay. Yet their abusive behavior toward women was tacitly condoned by their superiors, until it became a full-blown scandal. [Letter to the editor during the controversy over gays in the military at the outset of the Clinton administration in 1993.]

14. The suggestion by Detroit Schools Superintendent Deborah McGriff that schools be closed if they do not improve is a shortsighted response to public school failure and will do nothing to remedy our city's educational woes.

    Detroit's educational crisis is the product of a myriad of social, economic, and environmental problems. Public school classrooms are overcrowded, and teachers are ill equipped to handle the social and environmental baggage many young people bring to school. The ineffectiveness of teachers is simply one of the broken spokes in a tattered wheel. The problems of education in our city are systemwide and require a systemwide solution.

    Until our top school administrators and government officials decide to address those problems directly, closing ineffective schools will be fruitless. [From a letter to the editor in a Detroit newspaper.]

15. The following letter to the editor was written in response to an item headlined, "Capon Crusader Wins Case."

    So, "The Ontario Chicken Producers Marketing Board has lost a bid to shut down the provinces' only known producer of capons"?

    The lack of research on the part of your reporter which this statement reveals is appalling. I myself, in my time have produced four Capons, and, although my wife now refuses to cooperate in any further production, I can claim membership in a small but expanding industry.

    Anthony C. Capon

16. When we're asleep, we have no control over our mental processes. When we're dreaming, we aren't attentive, focused, or logical; and we can't have clear ideas. Nor can we evaluate our impressions and feelings or cross-check with other people.

    That's why the seventeenth-century philosopher René Descartes regarded dreaming as incompatible with knowledge. . . . Entrancing and moving as many dreams are, I agree with Descartes's view that dream thought is unreliable. [From a newspaper article on dreams by Trudy Govier.]

17. It is difficult to understand your dreams; it is next to impossible to learn anything at all from them if you approach them with scorn and derision. However, when treated with respect, openness, and appreciation, they may reveal their secrets to you. Dreams offer a deep source of wisdom to those willing to listen. "Listening" means, among other things, letting go of logic and reason and letting in feelings and intuition. [From a newspaper article by Sarah Shadowitz responding to Govier's article excerpted in 16.]

18. I was paid little for my fortnightly reviews, but every other Monday I was able to stagger to the railway station with two big book-crammed suitcases and take the train to Charing Cross and then a taxi to L. Simmonds on Fleet Street, there to sell all my review copies (except the few I wished to keep) at half the retail price. The bank notes I received were new and crisp and undeclarable to the Inland Revenue. They paid for the groceries and the odd bottle of cognac. This was the real reward of reviewing. [From the introduction to *99 Novels, The Best in English since 1939,* by Anthony Burgess, Summit, New York, 1984.]

19. In *Trusting Ourselves*, the book by Johnson and Ferguson cited in 3, the authors write in their first chapter, titled "Historical Perspective," as follows (p. 20):

> By the mid-1920s, the behaviorist school of psychology began to challenge mainstream psychiatry and psychology. Behavioral theorists believe that most human behavior is learned rather than driven by instinct. By the 1950s, they had developed a comprehensive and systematic approach to clinical problems that has continued to grow exponentially. When people experience psychological distress, behaviorists are able to offer a selection of techniques that are designed to reduce the individual's anxiety and help them master uncomfortable situations. These strategies have been particularly useful in reducing severe panic disorders and agoraphobia.

20. The following passage is adapted from a fall 1990 issue of a Chicago promotional magazine's regular column about current events in that city.

> Experience what it was like to live and work here a century ago at the Chicago Historical Society's multimedia exhibition, "A City Comes of Age: Chicago in the 1890s." The story will be told through six characters who represent the diversity of the decade: an entrepreneur, a domestic worker, a laborer, a skilled craftsman, a meat packer, and a child laborer. This fin de siècle flashback opens on October 24 and continues through July 15, 1991. For more information, call 642-4600.

21. The following selection is from Mary Midgley's book *Animals and Why They Matter* (The University of Georgia Press, Athens, 1984, p. 108). It is from a section discussing the nonexclusivity to their own species of animals.

> . . . species loyalty in social animals, strong though it is, is not necessarily exclusive. . . . Thus Jane Goodall describes how, even in the wild, a somewhat juvenile chimp finds a playmate in a young baboon. . . . More remarkable still, an outsider may be cherished even when one's own species is present. A clear instance is the well-established tendency of race-horses to become attached to some apparently unimpressive stable-companion, such as a goat or even a cat, and to pine if they are separated from it.

22. Allan Bloom's book critical of university education in America, *The Closing of the American Mind* (Simon and Schuster, 1987), raised a storm of controversy. Below is our reconstruction of a point made by the American philosopher, John Searle.

The vigorous objections made by Allen Bloom's critics have tended not to touch on the theory of higher education. But Bloom's theory is as much open to challenge as is his practical advice. For example, he does not properly appreciate the importance of the study of history. And he fails to recognize the achievements of contemporary analytic philosophy.

23. Both the women's movement and the newly emerging "men's movement" have been much discussed recently. One commentator made the following observation about one such article.

> The December issue of *New Age* magazine contains an interview with Georgetown linguistics professor Deborah Tannen, who confirms what many of us have long suspected—that men and women talk to each other in very different ways. "For males," says Tannen, "conversation is the way you negotiate your status in the group and keep people from pushing you around. Females, on the other hand, use conversation to negotiate closeness and intimacy; talk is the essence of intimacy."

24. In an article in *The Wine Spectator,* a monthly magazine about wines, Steve Heimoff wrote an article about the best size of bottle to buy ("The Big Bottle Debate," December 15, 1990, p. 91). In his article, Heimoff includes the following quotation:

> "I'd say, buy according to your usage pattern," advises Abdallah Simon, chairman of Seagram Chateau & Estate Wines Co. in New York, a leading importer of Bordeaux [wines]. "If you're a small family unit, there's nothing more desirable than 750-milliliter bottles. If you're having (larger) dinner parties, certainly the magnum [1.5 litres] is more attractive and desirable."

25. The passage below comes from a booklet containing advice on how to be an environmentally sensitive consumer and citizen.

> *Compost Pits*
>
> Compost "pits" work every bit as well as compost bins. So if you are a lousy carpenter, or don't demand geometric perfection in your garden, follow the example and advice of Cynthia Grower, president of the Society of Organic Gardeners: "Just dig a hole and throw your wet garbage into it. Cover it with leaves or grass clippings and a bit of the soil you removed. Dig some out from underneath when you want to use it."

26. The passage below opens an article about Robin Williams, the actor and comedian, written by Joe Morgenstern and appearing in *The New York Times Magazine* (November 11, 1990), p. 33.

> On a movie set, Robin Williams wears two heads. When the camera rolls, he is an actor of great authority and accomplishment. Between takes, he is himself, or a stand-up version of himself, giving little performances for his fellow performers.

27. John F. Burns, Toronto bureau chief of *The New York Times,* was on assignment in the middle east in the autumn of 1990 following the Iraqi invasion of Kuwait. The following passage is from his article "Days and Nights in Baghdad," which appeared in *The New York Times Magazine* (November 11, 1990, p. 54). Baghdad is the capital of Iraq, Hussein was the President of Iraq, and the Iran-Iraq war was a ten-year war that ended in stalemate in 1989.

> *Sept. 28.* In the morning, things are looking up. Along with other reporters, I have been invited on a trip to Basra, Iraq's second-largest city, and to the battlefield at Fao, where Hussein's army lost 53,000 men in the fiercest fighting of the Iran-Iraq

war. We are eager for a chance, no matter how fleeting, to talk to ordinary Iraqis and find out how they feel about the prospect of a new war, over Kuwait. But once in Fao, in Basra's central bazaar, our guides discourage such contacts, pushing us along whenever conversations start.

28. The excerpt below is from a sixty-five-page brochure put out by Killington Limited, the company that runs the Vermont ski resort called Killington. The brochure describes the lodging, dining, and skiing facilities on and surrounding Killington mountain and contains detailed suggestions for putting together vacation packages that include transportation, room and board, ski rentals, lessons, and lift tickets. The passage, on page 13, has the headline "Choose your vacation from these exciting Ski Plans."

> For many of us, the fun of going on vacation begins with the planning. Especially if you save time and money in the process. Rather than arriving at Killington and spending precious skiing time assembling the components of your ski vacation, we'd like to suggest that you make your arrangements before you get here.

29. The following is an excerpt from Charles Dickens's *A Christmas Carol*. Scrooge had just been asked by some fellow businessmen to donate to a charitable fund to supply some food and presents to the destitute. Scrooge turned them down, claiming that the prisons and workhouses were already available. Pressed by the soliciting visitors, Scrooge responds as follows:

> "I wish to be left alone," said Scrooge. "Since you ask me what I wish, gentlemen, that is my answer. I don't make merry myself at Christmas, and I can't afford to make idle people merry. I help support the establishments I have mentioned [prisons and workhouses where the destitute could stay]: they cost enough; and those who are badly off must go there."

30. The following was inspired by a passage in a column by Tom Wicker in *The New York Times* that ran late in 1990.

> There are many Americans who regard driving a car as an inalienable right. But the nation needs to double, from $13-billion to $26-billion, its current annual spending just to maintain or repair to minimum standards the highways that now exist. In addition, $50-billion is needed to repair or replace 240,000 bridges. Others prefer to fly. But about $1-billion a year for the next 10 years is needed just to maintain existing flying conditions—which most travellers agree are poor—and only minimally to relieve airport congestion.

31. The passage that follows is by the English philosopher Thomas Hobbes from his book *Leviathan* (1651, Part I, Ch. 13). The language is nearly 350 years old so it's a little old-fashioned, but if you go over it a couple of times, you should be able to follow it.

> . . . it is manifest that, during the time men live without a common power to keep them all in awe, they are in that condition which is called war, and such a war as is of every man against every man. . . .
>
> Whatsoever . . . is consequent to a time of war where every man is enemy to every man, the same is consequent to a time wherein men live without other security than what their own strength and their own invention shall furnish them withal. In such condition there is no place for industry, because the fruit thereof is uncertain; and consequently no cultivation of the earth; no navigation nor use of the commodities that may be imported by sea; no commodious building; no instru-

ments of moving and removing such things as require much force; no knowledge of the face of the earth; no account of time; no arts; no letters; no society; and, which is worst of all, continual fear and danger of violent death; and the life of man solitary, poor, nasty, brutish, and short.

32. Below is one of the most famous passages in western philosophy, from Part IV of the *Discourse on Method* by René Descartes (1637, translated by John Cottingham, Robert Stoothoff, and Dugald Murdoch, *The Philosophical Writings of Descartes,* Cambridge, 1985, p. 127).

> I resolved to pretend that all the things that had ever entered my mind were no more true than the illusions of my dreams. But immediately I noticed that while I was trying thus to think everything false, it was necessary that I, who was thinking this, was something. And observing this truth *"I am thinking, therefore I exist"* was so firm and sure that all the most extravagant suppositions of the sceptics were incapable of shaking it, I decided that I could accept it without scruple as the first principle of the philosophy I was seeking.

◆

CHAPTER TWO

Interpreting Arguments

Introduction

Even when there can be no doubt that a person intended to be making an argument, it is often not clear what the contents and structure of that argument are. People don't always set out their opinions and their grounds for them clearly and explicitly. As evaluators, we usually have to interpret what they say so as to get as clear and accurate a picture as possible of the argument or arguments they are expressing. Doing so usually entails reconstructing the argument, an effort that resembles trying to infer the materials and structure of a house from a photograph of it: We have to infer details and what is under the surface from a partial view.

This chapter contains guidelines for extracting and setting out an argument in a piece of writing. At the end of the chapter, we give an example illustrating how the guidelines work.

Conclusions

If you have already established that there is an argument present in a given passage, that means you have identified some view or claim that the author is defending. This is the author's conclusion.

Sometimes the author's viewpoint is not explicitly stated. You have to draw inferences from what's written and from its context in order to attribute this claim to the author. We call this a *missing conclusion* since it is missing from what was explicitly stated. The principle of charity requires that in attributing a missing conclusion you formulate the most plausible claim consistent with the rest of the passage and its context.

For example, suppose you are camping and about to fill your drinking-water canteen from a stream when your companion says, "I think that water isn't safe, and we don't want to risk getting sick." Clearly, she intends some such conclusion as, "You shouldn't fill your canteen from that stream," and it would be appropriate for you to attribute that conclusion to her.

Remember, we are talking about a "conclusion" in the sense of the opinion or viewpoint the author supports in an argument and not about a conclusion in the sense of the ending of a piece of prose: the final sentence or the last part. A conclusion in the first sense can be located anywhere in the passage; it is just as likely to be the first statement as the last one, and it can be situated anywhere in between. When someone says, "In conclusion . . ." or "I conclude with . . ." they are introducing their final remarks; when they say, "I conclude that . . ." or "My conclusion is . . ." they are introducing the claim they are backing up in an argument.

Premises

For something to be an argument and not just a statement of opinion, there have to be *premises*, reasons put forward to support the opinion. Write these premises out, and try to organize them in relation to one another.

Do two or more of the premises work as a unit to support the conclusion? Example: "My dentist is a graduate of the University of Kentucky. He has a diploma from Kentucky on his office wall, and it's improbable that he would have a Kentucky diploma on his wall if he weren't a Kentucky alumnus." Here, (1) "My dentist graduated from Kentucky," and (2) "It's improbable that my dentist would have a Kentucky diploma on his wall if he weren't a Kentucky alumnus" combine to support the conclusion.

Do some premises function as reasons for the position quite independently of the others? Example: "It's a good idea to eat lunch. It gives you energy in the afternoon, and it keeps you from getting hungry and eating junk food, which is bad for you." In this case, energy gain and junk-food avoidance are two distinct and independent reasons for eating lunch.

Some reasons or evidence provide support not by backing up the conclusion, but by backing up the premises that do directly support the conclusion. "This course is too hard for me. I can't understand the readings. I spent the whole weekend trying to understand Heidegger's *Being and Time*, one of the texts, and I couldn't grasp it at all." Here the weekend spent in the futile attempt to understand *Being and Time* is offered as evidence that the speaker cannot understand the course readings, which in turn is offered as evidence that the course is too difficult for him.

Semantic Indicators of Argument Structure

Besides the premise and conclusion indicators that we noted in Chapter 1, languages supply other words, expressions, and conventions that serve typically to point out the argumentative roles of the assertions they accompany. Here are some examples to give you the idea:

Item 1.   It is common to place the conclusion of an argument either at the beginning or at the end of a paragraph. This is definitely not a hard-and-fast rule because, first, stylistic considerations sometimes warrant placing the conclusion in the middle and, second, writers do not always organize their paragraphs in the clearest way possible. Still, the opening and closing sentences of a paragraph that seems to contain an argument are good candidates for the conclusion.

Item 2.   When one of two or more clauses joined by 'and' is a premise, then almost certainly the others are premises, too, and they will all be part of the same set. If one of two or more clauses joined by 'and' is a conclusion, then the others are probably conclusions, too. 'But,' 'moreover,' 'furthermore,' and 'in addition' play the same role as 'and.' (Examples: "She is young, moreover she's fit, so she'll heal quickly"; "He's new to the job, so he's enthusiastic but inexperienced.") But a word of caution: sometimes 'and' is short for 'and therefore,' in which case it functions as a conclusion indicator, preceded by a premise and followed by a conclusion. (Example: "He's very tired, and he should get some rest.")

Item 3.   When a clause asserting a premise is connected to another clause by 'but,' then the first clause often contains an objection to the conclusion and the second clause often contains a reason for overriding that objection. 'However' and 'although' play the same role. That is, 'but,' 'however,' and 'although' will often juxtapose an objection to the conclusion with rebuttal of that objection. (Example: "She's running behind, but her next appointment has canceled, so she should be able to see you for a few minutes.")

Item 4.   'Nevertheless' or 'but' often introduces a conclusion maintained *in spite of* the antecedently expressed reasons or evidence to the contrary. In other words, the arguer believes the conclusion is justified on grounds that override, take precedence over, or are weightier than the contrary evidence preceding 'nevertheless.' (Example: "He has no experience in accounting, nevertheless we should hire him because he's a genius in sales.")

Item 5.   'On balance,' 'everything considered,' and 'all in all' introduce a conclusion that the arguer believes is supported by the net weight of the evidence, which is arrived at by subtracting the grounds against the conclusion from the grounds in favor of the conclusion. Hence these expressions hint that you should look for both sorts of consideration, negative as well as positive ones. (Example: "The puppy isn't a purebred and it's not the color we wanted, but it'll grow into a big dog good for protection and it's supposed to have a wonderful disposition; all things considered, I think we should buy it.")

Restating Premises and Conclusion

You will often find it necessary to paraphrase the author's prose in order to make the meaning clear, to distinguish different premises lumped together in a single sentence, to separate premises from conclusions similarly grammatically combined, and to portray the reconstructed argument, with its meaning and structure, lucidly.

Here is an example to illustrate the point. In a review in *The New York Times Book Review* of Madonna's picture book, *Sex* (Warner Books, 1992), Caryn James wrote:

1 To regard [*Sex*] as a book at all, to debate its merits as photography or erotica, is to play into the hands of Madonna's hype machine. Worse, it is to misunderstand the nature of her art. She is not a singer or an actress or a model but a performance artist, and every word she utters is part of the act. "Sex"—which comes spiral-bound between metal covers and sealed in Mylar wrapping, the better to keep small children and unpaying browsers away—is one part of this fall's performance piece, a package that also includes her new album, called "Erotica," a music video and appearances on the covers of Vanity Fair and Vogue. Music, books and sound bites are all part of the same thing for Madonna.

When you reconstruct an argument, we suggest you restate each point in a distinct sentence. The goal is to make the original clearer without adding to or subtracting from its meaning. Here are our attempts with 1:

2 1. To debate the merits of *Sex* as photography or erotica is to play into the hands of Madonna's hype machine.

2. To debate the merits of *Sex* as photography or erotica is to misunderstand the nature of Madonna's art.

3. Madonna is not a singer or an actress or a model.

4. Madonna is a performance artist.

5. Every word Madonna utters is part of her performing act.

6. *Sex* comes spiral-bound between metal covers and sealed in Mylar wrapping the better to keep small children and unpaying browsers away.

7. *Sex* is one part of this fall's performance piece, a package that also includes her new album, called *Erotica*, a music video, and appearances on the covers of *Vanity Fair* and *Vogue*.

8. Music, books, and sound bites are all part of the performing act for Madonna.

We have numbered the statements above to be able to keep track of them. You can see that each numbered sentence contains exactly one statement, even though these eight statements occur in only five sentences in the original excerpt. Our restatements replace pronouns and demonstratives with the terms or phrases they refer to and contain some repetition. At a couple of points (5 and

8), we made explicit what we take James's references to be. As long as we have not changed the meaning or force of the writer's argument, those features turn out to be beneficial when we begin reorganizing the statements in order to display the structure of the argument most revealingly, for there is then never any doubt about what each separate statement asserts.

Internal Arguments

Often the premises of an argument turn out themselves to fit together as internal arguments within the whole body of support offered for the main conclusion. That is, some of the statements that support the main conclusion are themselves supported by other premises. Those statements in the middle thus have a dual role: With respect to the main conclusion they are premises, and with respect to the premises supporting them they are conclusions.

INTERNAL ARGUMENT

An *internal argument* is an argument whose conclusion is also the premise of another argument that directly or indirectly supports the position being argued for.

Consider the argument in the following excerpt from a letter to the editor critical of media claims to have special privileges:

3   Although the media likes to portray itself as the guardian of the public interest, it has no business doing so. It is essentially just another business whose goal is to make a profit, and so its actions are largely governed by self-interest.

We see four propositions asserted in this passage.

4   1. The media likes to portray itself as the guardian of the public interest.

2. The media has no business portraying itself as the guardian of the public interest.

3. The media is essentially just another business whose goal is to make a profit.

4. The media's actions are largely governed by self-interest.

In this argument the main conclusion is 2, which is backed up directly by 4, which is, in turn, supported by 3. That is, the media's being just another business out for a profit is given as a reason why the media's actions are governed largely by self-interest (note the 'so'), and the self-interest of the media makes sense as a reason why it should not portray itself as the guardian of the public interest. Sorting out the premises of an argument, then, involves looking for internal arguments as well as for premises directly supporting the main conclusion.

Missing Premises

Just as the arguer's conclusion might not be explicitly stated, so, too, you might find that one or more of its premises have been left out of the explicit statement of the argument. We call these *missing premises*. For example, if we argue "This is a textbook, so don't expect any jokes in it," we have left unstated the obvious premise that "Textbooks don't (usually) contain jokes." Alternatively, suppose we argue that "textbooks don't contain jokes, so don't expect any when you read this book." We have then left unstated the premise, "This book is a textbook."

MISSING OR UNEXPRESSED PREMISES

A *missing premise* is a statement that (1) is not expressed in the written or spoken argument but that (2) must be added to the explicit premises to make the set relevant as support for the conclusion. When interpreting a particular person's argument, a missing premise will also (3) be a proposition likely to be accepted by the arguer and (4) be one the arguer would likely use in addressing that particular audience.

The principle of charity applies to the formulation of missing premises just as it does to the formulation of missing conclusions. In trying to reconstruct the arguer's argument, your objective is to add to the stated premises the most plausible statement (consistent with the rest of the passage and likely to be believed by the arguer and used in addressing that audience) needed to make the whole set of premises relevant to the conclusion.

In practice, missing premises often work to make the stated premises relevant in either of two ways. They can be members of a set with two members: a general claim plus a particular claim. In that case, one of the pair is asserted explicitly, and the other is left unexpressed but understood. Our examples about jokes in this book illustrated this kind of missing premise.

5   1. Textbooks don't usually contain jokes. (generalization)

2. This is a textbook. (particular statement)

so 3. Don't expect jokes in this book.

If you find just the generalization, (1) and the conclusion (3) in what is stated, you need to supply the particular link (2). If you find just the particular statement (2) and the conclusion (3) in what is stated, the link that is needed is the generalization (1).

A missing premise can figure in an argument by being a missing conclusion at the same time. In such a case, the missing premise is a statement that follows from a stated premise and, in its turn, supports the conclusion. We can best explain by using an example. Consider this argument:

6   Government-funded efforts to save the whooping crane from extinction are paying off. Therefore, government funding of programs to preserve endangered species should be continued.

You can sense the relevance of the premise, yet one might wonder how the success of the whooping-crane project—that single project—relates to the desirability of funding future projects in general. However, if you read the stated premise as working logically to support a claim which links that particular project to the general conclusion, then the connection is made explicit. Here is how we would set it up:

7   1. Government-funded efforts to save the whooping crane from extinction are paying off.

   so 2. Government funding can be effective in helping to preserve endangered species. (missing premise)

   so 3. Government funding should be continued for programs to preserve endangered species.

The missing premise in such cases is both a missing conclusion of an internal argument and a missing premise in the argument leading directly to the original conclusion.

     In example 1 about Madonna's book, *Sex*, there is a missing premise in Caryn James's argument. James concludes (in part) that to debate the merits of the book's photography or erotica is to misunderstand the nature of Madonna's art. She offers the premise that Madonna is not a singer or an actress or a model. Clearly, James's argument relies on the missing premise that to debate the merits of its photography or erotica is to treat Madonna as a singer or an actress or a model.

Tree Diagrams

It is convenient to have in hand a technique for sketching the logical structure of an argument so you can see it at a glance. *Tree diagramming* (so called because the diagram of a complex argument looks like the outline of the branches and trunk of a leafy tree) is the most efficient device we have encountered. Here is how it works:

     (A) Assign a number to each statement in the segment of prose you are analyzing (it helps to write out each statement, breaking up sentences when necessary). Replace pronouns and demonstratives with their referents. We have already done this for previous examples. Here is another one:

8   Life without freedom is intolerable, so it is worthwhile to risk one's life to obtain or protect freedom. Maybe that's what is behind the slogan: "Live free or die."

The three statements in this passage would then be written out as three distinct sentences.

9   1. Life without freedom is intolerable.

2. It is worthwhile to risk one's life to obtain or protect freedom.

3. Maybe the source of the slogan "Live free or die" is the belief that it is worthwhile to risk one's life to obtain or protect freedom.

(B) Make a diagram, using the numbers to represent the statements they refer to and drawing an arrow from the set of numbers representing each premise set of an argument to the number representing the argument's conclusion. Use arrowheads pointing to the conclusion so there will be no ambiguity about which way the premise/conclusion relationship goes. The numbers of statements in the passage that do not figure in the argument will not appear in your tree diagram.

In our example, the first statement is used to support the second one. The third sentence neither supports nor is supported by either of the first two statements, so it plays no role in the argument. We would thus diagram the argument in our example as follows:

10
$$1$$
$$\downarrow$$
$$2$$

Notice that the number of the extraneous statement (3) simply does not appear in the diagram of the argument. Conventions about where to put the conclusion vary; we will put the number for the conclusion below the number(s) for the premises.

Number 10 is the diagram of a single argument, since there is just one set of premises supporting one conclusion.

(C) Add missing premises and conclusions, writing out each statement and assigning to each a letter of the alphabet (to distinguish them from the numbers representing explicitly stated premises and conclusions). Where two or more premises are relevant in combination, indicate that. We do so by placing a plus sign between adjacent premises.

Let us illustrate these points with an example we used above to introduce the idea of missing premises.

11　　There will probably be no jokes in this book because textbooks don't usually contain jokes.

Our restating, numbering, and tree diagram look like this:

12　　1. There will probably be no jokes in this book.

　　　　2. Textbooks don't usually contain jokes.

$$2 \\ \downarrow \\ 1$$

Our argument assumes that this book is a textbook, so to make our reasoning fully explicit we need to add the missing premise.

13　　*a.* This book is a textbook.

And we then need to revise our diagram to show where this missing premise fits in the argument.

14

$$\frac{2 + a}{} \\ \downarrow \\ 1$$

　　Number 14 is another single argument: one premise set and one conclusion.
　　(D) Where there is an internal argument, there will be an arrow pointing to a number (or letter) and an arrow from that number (or letter) and the others in its set pointing to yet another number (or letter). This shows that the middle statement is both a conclusion (of the internal argument) and a premise. We will use the whooping-crane example, slightly modified, to illustrate this point.

15　　Government-funded efforts to save the whooping crane are paying off, and I, for one, am delighted. This is clear evidence that government funding can be effective in helping to preserve endangered species. There is no question, therefore, that government-funded programs to preserve endangered species should be continued.

The statements found in example 15 are

16   1. Government-funded efforts to save the whooping crane from extinction are paying off.

2. I, for one, am glad that government-funded efforts to save the whooping crane are paying off.

3. Government funding can be effective in helping to preserve endangered species.

4. Government-funded programs to preserve endangered species should be continued.

In this argument, 2 is not evidence for any of the other claims, nor does any of the other claims support it, hence 2 is extraneous. (It is not uncommon for prose to contain statements that are parts of arguments mixed together with statements that play no role in any argument.) The conclusion indicators—"this is clear evidence that" and "there is no question, therefore, that"—tell us that the author intends the first statement to support the third one and the third one to support the fourth one. Hence we get the following tree diagram:

17

$$1$$
$$\downarrow$$
$$3$$
$$\downarrow$$
$$4$$

Number 17 is the diagram of a chain of arguments. The conclusion of one argument (3) is also a premise in another argument, the one which has 4 as its conclusion. We will leave it to you to decide if there are any unexpressed premises that should be added to the above argument.

(E) When there are, in effect, two or more distinct, independent grounds for a conclusion, think of each ground as a separate argument. Show them by grouping the numbers for each premise set and giving each set its own arrow pointing to the number of the conclusion in question. Here is an example of such an argument:

18   Capital punishment, in many cases, deters people from committing murder, and reducing the murder rate is, in itself, worthwhile. Executions are also less costly to society than is the alternative, life imprisonment. Someone who has murdered another person does not have as strong a claim on taxpayers' money as do other causes. And in any case, a murderer has, by the act of murder, forfeited his life, which means he no longer has a right to life. So can there be any doubt that the penalty for murder should be execution?

Writing out each statement we get

19   1. Capital punishment deters people from committing murder in many cases.

2. Reducing the murder rate is, in itself, worthwhile.

3. Capital punishment is less costly to society than is the alternative, life imprisonment.

4. Someone who has murdered another person does not have as strong a claim on taxpayers' money as do other causes.

5. A murderer has, by the act of murder, forfeited his life.

6. A murderer no longer has a right to life.

7. The penalty for murder should be execution.

The tree diagram of the argument looks like this:

20

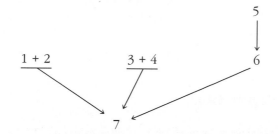

Number 20 diagrams a pattern of convergent arguments. There are three premise sets—(1 + 2), (3 + 4), and 6—which, independently of each other, are used to support one conclusion, 7. There is also a chain of arguments in 20: the argument from the premise (5) to the conclusion (6) and from the premise (6) to the conclusion (7).

A note of caution: Each arrowhead should point to one single, particular number or letter, never vaguely to a group of them and never to a plus sign. For any set of premises, there are one or more specific conclusions, and there should be a separate arrow pointing to each conclusion which that set of premises is intended to support.

If an argument is even a little bit complicated, its tree diagram will likely incorporate more than one of these patterns. In Chapter 13 we will introduce some modifications to these conventions for diagraming longer arguments.

For purposes of clarity and in order to save space in this book, we will adopt a combination of the tree diagram with typography, placing premises above their conclusions and indenting premises of internal arguments to the right. You may find this useful, too. For example, here is how we would print the whooping-crane example, 6 above, after analyzing its structure:

21   1. Government-funded efforts to save the whooping crane from extinction
             are paying off.

     3. Government funding can be effective in helping to preserve endangered spe-
        cies.

     4. Government funding should be continued for programs to preserve endan-
        gered species.

You will recognize elaborations of this basic scheme or standardization in later examples.

In order to identify premises and conclusions in an argument and to diagram their logical structure you must be able to distinguish between what belongs to the argument and what is extraneous to it. In making these judgments, you have to rely on your sense of logical flow, the support relationship that binds premise and conclusion together. The judicious use of tree diagrams can also help you reject various possibilities and detect missing premises and conclusions. Once the outline of an argument's structure is clear, it becomes easier to recognize peripheral material.

Surface and Depth Analysis

The job of the critical reader or listener would be much easier if people always presented their arguments in straightforward assertions. The rhetorical flourishes and turns of phrase that lace most pieces of writing are there for a purpose, but they present a challenge to the interpretation, to figuring out just what was meant. When someone is not expressing himself in straightforward literal terms, you need to decide what he means. Much of the time, it will be possible to get beneath the surface meaning (the metaphor, the literal meaning) to its deeper meaning.

Consider the following example. It is an excerpt from a newspaper column in which the writer defends police officers against public criticism.

22   Police officers are damned if they do and they are damned if they don't. How often
         do we hear comments from the public when they see traffic violations or hear of
         unsolved crimes to the effect that there is never a police officer around when one

needs one? But when the officer is doing his job these same people complain the loudest.

Numbering the statements and restating the rhetorical question, we get

23 1. Police officers are damned if they do and damned if they don't.

2. We often hear people complain, when they see traffic violations or hear of unsolved crimes, that the police are not there when they are needed.

3. The same people complain the loudest when the police are doing their jobs.

24 We get the following tree diagram:

$$\frac{2 + 3}{}$$
$$\downarrow$$
$$1$$

But this analysis misses the point. Look again at 22 and our formulation of its component statements in 23. Both 1 and 3 fall short of declaring their meaning, and so some interpretation is needed. When the writer says that "police officers are damned if they do and damned if they don't," what is the likely meaning? In this context, we would say that the writer means
1. (Restatement) Police officers are criticized when they succeed in enforcing the law, and they are also criticized when they fail to enforce the law.
The third statement is a bit trickier to handle. Although the writer says that people complain when the police are doing their job, we don't want to saddle her with the silly assertion that people who want the police to arrest speeders complain whenever they do that because that is manifestly not what she means. How then to put it? We hypothesize that she is probably thinking this: Some people squawk when they get a ticket even though they believe that *other* people should be ticketed. That is the sort of inconsistency that the writer appears to have in mind. So we would rephrase 3 as
3. (Restatement) The same people complain the loudest when the police ticket them for a violation of the law.
Our advice: Without distorting the passage and its context, and taking care to make your interpretation no less clear and plausible than the original, be prepared to look beneath the surface, literal meaning of a piece of writing to find the deeper meaning that is probably intended. Once again, the principle of charity is at work: Assume that the person you are interpreting is taking the most sensible position, making the most plausible assertions consistent with the rest of the passage and its context.

Postpone Evaluation

It is tempting when interpreting arguments to make the mistake of judging the argument before you have set it out clearly. You can't turn off that critical radar, and it keeps beeping once you sense a logical error in the argument you are interpreting. But the effect, too often, is that you are distracted from giving the argument a fair shake. You don't interpret it accurately or fairly because you are already intent on criticizing it.

INTERPRETATION RULE

Withhold judgment of the merits of the argument until you have set it out as fully, accurately, and fairly as you can.

A corollary of this rule is, When you think you have spotted an error, double-check. Ask yourself, Am I sure that I have understood this passage correctly? Is this really what the person is arguing?

This advice has a second side to it. Just as your hostility to a thesis can lead you to jump prematurely to condemn the arguments someone offers in support of it, so, too, can your identification with or loyalty toward an opinion lead you to gloss over possible problems in the grounds advanced on its behalf. If either attitude causes us to misidentify what exactly the argument is, then subsequent assessment will obviously be thrown off.

As is so often the case, there is a complicating factor. We have seen that in order to decide what an argument is, we must frequently make a judgment about what would be a plausible argument, given the surrounding discussion and its context. We have to evaluate in order to interpret. How, then, can the rule to postpone evaluation be right? The answer lies in a necessary and defensible distinction between evaluating for the purpose of interpretation and evaluating the resulting reconstructed argument. When interpreting, you must work within the limits of what the person said and what, given all the relevant factors, you have good reason to believe he or she intended to convey. You cannot change those things to make a logically better argument. Your interpretive goal is to give a fair reconstruction of the argument, and that means opting for more plausible over less plausible formulations, everything else being equal. When criticizing the resultant reconstructed argument, however, you are under no such constraints. Then all the standards of good logic, which we shall be introducing in Chapters 3 through 9, must be brought to bear. In sum, first figure out what the author's argument is, trying to be fair and accurate. Only then should you begin to assess the merits of the argument.

A More Complex Example

Now let us put all this advice to work on a complicated, real-life example. We begin by giving some relevant background information about the example, a letter to the editor of the *Detroit Free Press*.

In Michigan a few years ago, there was a (successful) campaign to make seat-belt use compulsory. As you can imagine, the issue was hotly debated. The *Detroit Free Press* gave its support to a seat-belt bill already in the state legislature with an editorial in late May 1982. In early June, it published several letters to the editor written in reaction to its editorial and to support for the seat-belt bill in general. Here is one of these letters:

25   They are starting about seat belts again, but if the law is passed, I will be the first to demand a cell in jail. I will not wear a seat belt.

Eleven years ago, I was thrown into the windshield when my van went into a 7-foot ditch filled with 5 feet of water. Quick thinking by a farmer, who dived into the water and got me out, saved my life. Had I been wearing a seat belt, there is no way he could have undone it and rescued me. I have suffered daily and spent more time in the hospital than out, but I'm still alive.

The seat-belt law is one of the reasons I miss the beautiful country drives through Canada.

L. R. J.
River Rouge, Michigan

Is L. R. J. offering an argument here? If so, what is it? If you think there is an argument here, we agree with you, but can we justify our judgment?

Here is how we would try. First, notice that the context is a natural one for argument. The letters-to-the-editor column of a daily newspaper is where people present and defend their opinions about controversial issues of the day. Second, the particular occasion for L. R. J.'s letter is the controversy over whether seat-belt use should be made mandatory in Michigan. Controversies are natural incubators for arguments; people are trying to convince others which side to take in the dispute. These two factors create a strong presumption in favor of interpreting L. R. J. as arguing.

Looking at the letter, there are no premise or conclusion indicators, so the next move is to see if L. R. J.'s letter can be reconstructed in a way that makes sense as an argument.

On the surface, it might seem that L. R. J. is simply announcing his own intentions and explaining them to *Free Press* readers. He is never going to wear a seat belt; he'd go to jail first because he was in an accident that would have killed him had he been wearing a seat belt. But this interpretation is implausible. Why should anyone write a letter to the paper to announce private intentions? We cannot see any sensible point to doing so. On the other hand, there is good reason to go on record with a position on a particular piece of legislation. Such public expression of our opinions is one means that we use to try to shape laws and policies.

If we go beneath the surface of the mere grammatical form of L. R. J.'s letter, it is easy enough to see that he is writing to oppose making seat-belt use compulsory in Michigan. His opinion might be stated thus:

a. Seat-belt use should not be made mandatory in Michigan;
or, possibly, *a*.1, The bill before the Michigan legislature that would make seat-belt use compulsory should be defeated.

It's true that L. R. J. makes no explicit reference to Michigan or the Michigan bill, but he refers to the debate: "They are starting about seat belts again," and he is writing in Michigan to a Michigan newspaper, so we presume he is taking a position on the issue there, although he clearly has a more general position, too, for he states categorically that he will not wear a seat belt, and presumably that means anywhere (he stays out of Canada, where seat-belt use is required).

We've said that L. R. J. is taking a position and not just announcing his private intentions, but that doesn't show that he is arguing for his position; he might be only expressing an opinion and letting it go at that, as people often do. In fact, though, we can construe his letter as containing an argument for his position as soon as we take into account the middle paragraph, where he recounts the accident he was in eleven years ago. Once again, we have to go beneath the surface of the personal anecdote to the underlying point. We take L. R. J. to be arguing that there can be accidents in which the wearing of a seat belt can contribute directly to the death of the occupant of the vehicle. L. R. J.'s personal experience has no bearing on the issue—it is irrelevant—unless it is taken as evidence for a general claim about one risk of wearing a seat belt. So we see L. R. J.'s argument shaping up (roughly) as follows:

26

          b. I was in an accident in which I would have died had I been wearing a seat belt.

    c. Wearing a seat belt can cause death in an accident.

  d. It can be life threatening to wear a seat belt.

a.1 The Michigan bill to make wearing a seat belt compulsory should be defeated.

What we are proposing is that L. R. J.'s personal story can be seen to make sense as part of an argument for his position if it is taken to be intended as evidence for a more general claim, one which can, in turn, be hooked up as a relevant reason for accepting his position. We don't know if L. R. J. would agree with exactly the way we filled in the connections. He might have reasoned as we reconstructed his argument above; or he might have gone from *b* straight to *d*; or he might have gone from *b* to *c* and then straight to *a*.1. The reason we added *d* is that we can see it warranted as support for *a*.1 by a further general assumption; namely, that the state should not make the use of potentially life-threatening devices compulsory. Whatever general premise or premises we take to connect L. R. J.'s personal experiences with his conclusion, some such further premise that warrants this connection has got to be taken for granted as part of the argument. If L. R. J. just says, "It can be life threatening to wear a seat belt," you can respond, "So what? What's that got to do with the Michigan bill?" and to your question, L. R. J.'s obvious reply will be, "Plenty! The state shouldn't legislate things that are life threatening." Or, if L. R. J. wants to argue directly from *b* ("Wearing a seat belt can cause death in an accident") to his opposition to the Michigan bill, you can again insist, "What has the fact that wearing a seat belt can be responsible for a person's death in an accident got to do with rejecting the Michigan bill?" In that case, he needs to provide some justification for the connection such as: "The state shouldn't legislate the use of devices that can contribute to a person's death."

What we are doing here is reconstructing how L. R. J. might have intended his argument to run. We can make sense of what L. R. J. has written in his letter to the *Detroit Free Press* as an argument although doing so requires filling in some missing premises. To anyone who complains that we are taking liberties with L. R. J.'s letter, our reply is that the alternative is worse. Either L. R. J. intended to be arguing (in which case we have to reconstruct his argument and fill in some missing premises so the argument will be plausible and its premises will connect up with the conclusion) or else we must surmise that he took the trouble to write a letter to the paper just to tell a personal anecdote and announce to the world his private plans. We think the former interpretation is the more credible, even though the argument we have to attribute to L. R. J. turns out not to be the strongest one in the world.

We have answered both of our initial questions about L. R. J.'s letter, Is he arguing and, if so, what's the argument? at the same time. That was unavoidable: The only way to make a solid case that an argument is intended (in the absence of explicit notice to that effect from the author) is to extract a candidate and show how it is plausible. So you end up with two answers at the same time: "Yes, there is an argument here" and "Here it is: . . . ." To finish the job, we should put down, in completed form, alternative interpretations of L. R. J.'s argument.

27

> *b.* I was in an accident in which I would have died had I been wearing a seat belt.
> *c.* Wearing a seat belt can cause death in an accident.
> *d.* It can be life threatening to wear a seat belt.
> *e.* The state should not legislate the use of possibly life-threatening devices.
> *a.*1 The Michigan bill to make it compulsory to wear a seat belt should be defeated.

28

> *b.* I was in an accident in which I would have died had I been wearing a seat belt.
> *c.* Wearing a seat belt can cause death in an accident.
> *e.* The state should not legislate the use of devices that can contribute to death in accidents.
> *a.*1 The Michigan bill to make it compulsory to wear a seat belt should be defeated.

Is L. R. J.'s argument a good one? The topics of what makes good arguments and what distinguishes bad arguments are introduced in the next chapter, and pursued in Chapters 3 through 9.

Summary

In this chapter we dealt with the practical problem of extracting arguments from the passages of prose in which they are located—indeed, sometimes "embedded" or "buried" might be a more appropriate word. We saw that once you have determined that an argument is truly present, the task is to reconstruct it by separating it out from its surroundings and making its logical structure explicit. We listed a set of guidelines for interpreting the argument (first, identify and write out the conclusion, making it explicit if it is unstated; then, list the premises and try to get a clear picture of the pattern of their supporting relationships). In the process of doing this, you will often need to identify the missing premises; and we included some advice for that task. We introduced the convention of making a tree diagram to display the argument's logical structure. In following these steps, it is necessary to distinguish extraneous material from what belongs genuinely to the argument; and you will often find yourself having to dig beneath the surface of the writer's prose to bring out its deeper intended meaning. Throughout, there is a temptation to mix up your critical evaluation of the argument with your interpretation of its intended meaning. This critique of the argument must be postponed until you have it fairly represented.

If you have mastered the material so far presented, you have already made a solid start in developing the skills for appraising arguments. More likely, however, you will find it useful to turn back to the material presented in Chapters 1 and 2 from time to time as you proceed with the rest of the book.

EXERCISES

The following exercise is designed to give you practice in reconstructing arguments. We include passages that we believe contain arguments. Background information is also supplied, since it can help identify the argument's conclusion.

In writing up your reconstructions, use the conventions your instructor assigns. The conventions we use are as follows:

a. Write out each separate statement in the passage, whether it is part of a longer sentence or a sentence by itself and whether or not you initially think it is part of the argument. Give each statement a separate number. When necessary to make its independent meaning clear, rewrite the statement in your own words.
or
Photocopy the passage. On the photocopy, place square brackets around each separate statement and write a separate number next to each one, indicating clearly the statement to which each number refers. Rewrite statements in your own words when it is necessary to make their independent meaning clear.

b. Construct and write out a tree diagram of the argument. Include in the tree diagram only the numbers of statements that are premises or conclusions in the argument. Leave out of the diagram the numbers of statements that don't play any premise or conclusion role.

c. Write out any missing premises or conclusions that are tacitly at work in the argument and give each a separate letter of the alphabet.

d. Construct and write out a revised tree diagram of the argument, one in which you include the letters of missing premises and conclusions as well as the numbers of explicit premises and conclusions.

A. Follow your instructor's directions for the assigned passages from the exercises for Chapter 1 which you have identified as containing arguments.

B. Follow your instructor's directions for the passages assigned from the following set:

1. *Background:* The following excerpt from Plato's dialogue *Apology* concerns the trial of Socrates. Socrates is speaking.

   . . . to fear death, my friends, is only to think ourselves wise without really being wise, for it is to think that we know what we do not know. For no one knows whether death may not be the greatest good that can happen to man.

2. *Background:* For a while, University of Calgary philosopher Thomas Hurka wrote a weekly column about philosophical questions raised by public issues of the day. We have taken the idea for the following passage from one of Hurka's columns occasioned by the question of whether a United States-led war should be waged against Iraq over its invasion and annexation of Kuwait—a question made especially timely by the then-recent United Nations resolution declaring that a war could be justified after January 15, 1991, if Iraq failed to withdraw from Kuwait.

   Some wars are right and some are wrong. Most colonial wars, such as the Soviet invasion of Afghanistan, are immoral. But the Allies' participation in the Second World War was not wrong. What are the general principles that explain these differences? And what are the implications of such principles for the war we may soon face, a U.S.-led war against Iraq?

3. *Background:* Later in the same column, Hurka wrote something that we restate and extend as follows:

   There is in political theory, a theory of a "just war." According to the classical theory of the "just war," there are several conditions for legitimate military action. The first requirement is that the *cause* of the war be just. One cause that is generally regarded as just is resisting aggression. The aggression can be against your country or against another country. In the present circumstances, Iraq has committed aggression against Kuwait. Therefore, according to the first condition of the "just-war" theory, a United States-led war against Iraq to force it to leave Kuwait would be justified.

4. *Background:* Warren Berger wrote an article for *The New York Times Magazine* (November 11, 1990) about the Portland, Oregon, advertising company Wieden & Kennedy. Berger quotes a firm partner, Dan Wieden, explaining why the agency operates in a distinctively un-Madison Avenue style, away from the major advertising centers of New York and Chicago. "We don't get distracted here," Wieden says. "We're focused on creating good advertising, and nothing else." Berger comments:

   That Wieden & Kennedy has succeeded in doing just that is undeniable. The 8-year-old agency has emerged as one of the country's most celebrated advertising companies, creating some of the most original commercials of recent years, notably the "Bo Knows" ads for Nike, as well as a series, also for Nike, pairing the film maker Spike Lee with the basketball star Michael Jordan. Over the last two years, the agency's campaigns have won almost every major trophy in the business, including top prize at the Clio, the One Show, the National Addy and the Stephen E. Kelly awards.

5. *Background:* The following is our reconstruction of a point made by Warren Berger in the article cited in 4:

> The words "Just Do It" that are shown at the end of many Nike commercials seem to be a call to action, but there is no indication of what action is supposed to be performed. The injunction is extremely vague.
>
> For whatever reason, the approach seems effective. Some have argued that it can be blamed for violent thefts of expensive sneakers. The phrase, "Just Do It" seems to mean different things to middle class people and to people stuck in the ghetto. To the former, it means, "Go out and get fit," whereas to the teenager in the ghetto it means, "Forget morality, just take whatever you want." In other words, critics charge, the ad carries an immoral message.

6. *Background:* The following passage is from Chapter 3 of the Jean-Jacques Rousseau's *The Social Contract*, originally published in 1762 (Hafner, New York, 1947, pp. 8-9). Rousseau was discussing the claim that "might makes right."

> Let us suppose for a moment the existence of this pretended right [the right of the strongest]. I see nothing that can arise from it but inexplicable nonsense. For, if we admit that force constitutes right, the effect changes with the cause: all force which overcomes the first succeeds to its right. As soon as men can disobey with impunity, they can do so justifiably; and because the strongest is always in the right, strength is the only thing men should seek to acquire. But what sort of right is that which perishes with the force that gave it existence? If it is necessary to obey by force, there can be no occasion to obey from duty; and when force is no more, all obligation ceases with it. We see, therefore, that this word "right" adds nothing to force, but is indeed an unmeaning term.

CHAPTER THREE

◆

Fundamentals of Argument Construction and Evaluation

Introduction

Now that you know what an argument is and how to distinguish it from other forms of reasoning and discourse, we are going to deal with the basics of argumentation. First we discuss the process of evaluating arguments, then the process of constructing them.

Fundamentals of Argument Evaluation

Once you have identified and extracted an argument, you are ready to evaluate it, to ask, What are the logical merits and demerits of this argument? To answer this question, you need to have two things: (1) a general grasp of the criteria that enter into the logical evaluation of arguments and (2) practice in evaluating arguments.

Let's go back to what we said about the process of argumentation. We claimed that an argument is an attempt to trace a rational route from a starting point (premise or premises) to a destination (conclusion). "If you begin here with these premises," the argument says, "then, if you want to be consistent, you must wind up here." An argument is good to the extent that the route it proposes to trace from premises to conclusion is a solid one—like a good map, with directions that get you where you want to go. On the other hand, an argument is bad to the extent that the route it lays out is filled with detours, dead ends, roadblocks, and other pitfalls.

Before we present the criteria for assessing the merits of an argument, we want to introduce the notion that arguments can be thought of as located somewhere along a spectrum. At one end of the spectrum are the really good arguments; at the other end are the really bad arguments. Most arguments, however, can be found in the broad middle range, with both strengths and weaknesses. Rarely is an argument so good that it cannot profit from criticism;

and seldom is an argument so bad that it cannot be improved by criticism (most arguments with defects are capable of being revised so as to strengthen the argument). If you think a particular argument is airtight, that might be because you have not thought deeply enough about the issues or don't know enough about the positions it competes with. Or you have not really examined the argument closely (always a danger when the argument favors a position you agree with). If, on the other hand, you think a particular argument is worthless, that might be because you've saddled yourself with blinders and won't let yourself consider the possibility that such a line of argument might have merit. Most arguments fall into the middle band of the spectrum. The purpose of argument analysis is to enable you to see both the pluses and the minuses in an argument and thereby reach an overall verdict on the argument while guarding against premature acceptance or rejection.

A *logically good argument*, as we shall use this term, is one whose premises supply strong grounds for any reasonable person to accept the conclusion. In other words, a reasonable person would accept its conclusion, based on its premises, and would be justified in so doing.

It should be clear that the logical merit of an argument can be independent of its other virtues (or defects). Among the latter we count the clarity and elegance of its expression; its persuasiveness in the sense of its capacity to move the audience to agreement; its economy in the sense of supplying exactly the grounds needed, no less and no more. These extra-logical merits are not, however, incompatible with good logic; indeed, an argument that is good overall will have most, if not all, of these merits.

Utopian expectations about what is required for a decent argument are perhaps natural but should be resisted. By their nature, arguments come into being against a background of controversy, of diverse opinion and differing points of view. Moreover, the issues they address are usually difficult to resolve: how to prevent the devastation of the environment while yet supporting economic development, how to deal with the federal deficit, what to do about the rise in crime, and so on. The heterogeneity of beliefs and values surrounding these issues, combined with their complexity, makes it unrealistic to expect any argument to establish its conclusions as the final word and shut down all alternatives. That just won't happen. To require of a good argument that it prove its conclusion beyond any possible doubt or criticism is unrealistic. Proof may be an appropriate standard to invoke in geometry and algebra, but in the realm of everyday arguing about contentious issues, it is inappropriate. An argument may be quite good even without *proving* its conclusion true.

At the other extreme lies another mistaken attitude about evaluating arguments. Many people evaluate arguments by one standard only: Does it support my view or not? This is not a viable standard. If this were the standard, then the consequence must be relativistic because what one person regards as a strong argument (because supportive of his position), another rejects as weak (because it goes against her position). Adoption of such a standard would put subjectivity in the saddle and would, moreover, contradict the very ethos of argumentation, which is that the process of argumentation is a potential tool for assessing the merits of any position. To engage in the practice is to admit in principle the possibility that your premises do not constitute good grounds for your conclusion (even though at the moment you think they do).

In our view, logical evaluation requires sensitivity to the different positions on the table and to points of evidence. It requires that you be able to put yourself into the position of an intelligent and thinking bystander and ask, Quite apart from whether I am predisposed to accept or reject the conclusion, does this argument display the features of a good argument or not? Or better still, How many of the features that make an argument strong does this one possess?

Judgment of the logical merits of an argument will also depend on the purposes for which the argument is being appraised and on the circumstances in which the appraisal is made. For instance, in any real-life setting, an argument must be of manageable length because of the finiteness of time, energy, and money. Thus newspapers restrict the length of letters to the editor; opinion columns have a specified length; the brief you write for your boss is limited to five typed pages; and so on. In such circumstances, a good argument must include the essential lines of support and omit unnecessary details.

When it doesn't matter as much that the conclusion is true as that other considerations are satisfied, a "rough-and-ready" argument will suffice. For example, when you are eating at a restaurant, it's more important to order the meal and enjoy the conversation than it is to work out all the arguments for and against each menu selection. The best argument in this situation would identify the major determinants of a good choice: what you hate or can't eat and what you don't want to miss. Sometimes what matters most is avoiding a disastrous mistake, while any of a range of good choices will satisfy. Think of a team of architects and engineers discussing a design problem. In that case, the good argument will be most precise, detailed, well-confirmed, and complete about how to be sure the building won't collapse during an earthquake, and the good argument will be more speculative and open-ended about choice of finishing materials and colors.

Enough of the preliminaries. It's time for you to put your instincts to work on some examples. For each of the four examples that follow, we ask you to read the argument carefully and make sure that you have grasped it correctly. Then decide how strong you think the argument is, and write out your own reasons for the verdict. Only after thinking about how you would argue for your judgment should you proceed to compare your views with others.

Example 1.   A letter to Ann Landers read:

1   Dear Ann Landers:
     My 16-year-old cousin sent for your booklet called "Teenage Sex and Ten Ways to Cool It." She sent her 50 cents and the self-addressed envelope like it said at the foot of your column. When the booklet arrived, she read it right away and phoned me to say that it was very good and gave her a lot to think about. Well, Ann Landers, three months later she was pregnant and got married very fast. Her mother almost had a heart attack. What I want to know is, Why do you recommend booklets if they don't do any good?

                                                              Highly Disappointed

Example 2.   This example deals with highway speed limits. In the seventies, the speed limit on interstate highways was reduced from 70 to 55 miles per hour. In an article in *En Route* magazine, Len Coates objected as follows:

2   Yes, it is true that the 55 mph saves lives. The National Highway Traffic Safety Administration estimates that 4,500 lives have been saved by the 55 mph limit. But surely there are more cost-efficient ways of saving lives . . . such as equipping every house with a smoke detector (that would cost $50,000 to $80,000 per life) or putting more dialysis machines in hospitals ($30,000 per life).

Example 3.   This is an excerpt from Josiah Thompson's book *Six Seconds in Dallas* (New York: Bernard Geis, 1967) about the assassination of President John F. Kennedy. Thompson is discussing the question, Where did the first bullet go? (p. 39).

3   The testimony of Secret Service Agent Roy Kellerman adds weight to the theory that the first bullet only lodged in the President's back. Seated in the right front seat of the presidential limousine, Kellerman heard Kennedy yell, "My God! I'm hit" just after the first shot. . . . Since the projectile that caused the throat wound ripped his windpipe in passing, it seems unlikely that the President could have spoken after receiving the throat wound.

Example 4.   *Harper's* (March 1982) published an article by David Owen titled "The Secret Lives of Dentists" in which Owen discussed in great detail the hazards of being a dentist and the pressures dentists face, both financial and psychological. He stated: "The divorce rate in the profession has risen 12 percent in the last decade, and drug abuse, alcoholism, and suicide have also been on the rise." Many dentists took exception. One, whose letter was quoted in the May 1982 issue of *Harper's* (p. 5), stated:

4   If someone had read David Owen's article, "The Secret Lives of Dentists," to me, I would have sworn it had been published in the *National Inquirer*. This childish bunch of half-truths and snide innuendo is a low blow to a hard-working and dedicated profession. . . . I do not know a single case of a dentist who took his own life. An alcoholic dentist doesn't stay in business very long.

Before reading further, make your own judgments about each of the four arguments. Then compare your judgments with ours.

Example 1.   This is a weak argument. Intuitively, you might have reasoned that Highly Disappointed is jumping to a conclusion. He reasons from one case in which the booklet apparently failed to prevent someone from becoming pregnant to the (implied) conclusion that the booklet is not effective in general. If Highly Disappointed were reasoning more carefully (less in the throes of his disappointment), he would have seen that more evidence is needed to reach that general conclusion, such as how others who have read the booklet have been affected. The booklet's failure to convince one person would not show that it does no good at all. (*Note:* One can also raise the question of whether this case presents any evidence at all for the general thesis. Highly Disappointed's cousin may have read and then rejected the advice in the booklet. Moreover, there is some difficulty in deciding upon the criteria by which one should judge the effectiveness of such a booklet.)

Example 2.   This is a poor argument. It may be true that we could save lives by equipping every house with a smoke detector, but that has nothing to do with saving lives on the highway—which is what the argument is about here. Lowering speed limits doesn't interfere with installing smoke detectors.

Example 3.   We think this is a fairly strong argument. If the first bullet pierced Kennedy's throat (as some allege), then Kellerman could not have heard what he said he heard. Hence his testimony "adds weight to the theory that the first bullet only lodged in the President's back." Thompson's conclusion is presented in a qualified way ("adds weight," "seems unlikely"), and he presents contrary evidence later in the book (no one else heard what Kellerman heard the President say). But if the facts are as recorded in Example 3, they provide fairly compelling evidence that the first bullet did not pierce Kennedy's throat but lodged in his back.

Example 4.   This is argument limps badly. The dentist means to argue that Owen has his facts wrong. The dentist adduces two premises: (1) he does not know of a single dentist who took his own life, and (2) an alcoholic dentist doesn't stay in business very long. First, though we can grant that the first premise is true, it doesn't follow that Owen's claim about the rate of suicide is wrong, for this dentist's colleagues may not be representative of the profession. Second, the second premise needs to be defended with some reasoning and evidence, for it is not obviously true. Some alcoholics, including doctors, lawyers, and business executives, manage to keep working for years. Owens hasn't shown that dentists are different in this respect. It may be that Owen got his facts wrong (indeed, the dentist would have a more effective line of objection here had he challenged Owen to produce some evidence for his claims), but the dentist's argument does not succeed in showing that.

Looking back now, you will see that our exercise contained three weak arguments and one fairly strong one. In this text, we will often be focusing on bad arguments, why they are bad and how they might be improved. Such an emphasis runs the risk of creating the impression that all arguments are flawed. Not so.

One common complaint about the fallacy approach to argumentation is that it produces jaundiced students, determined in advance to flog any weakness in an argument but blind to its strengths.[1] It would be inappropriate here to engage in a defense of fallacy theory against such criticisms.[2] The set of observa-

---

[1] See Richard Paul, "Teaching Critical Thinking in the 'Strong Sense,'" *Informal Logic Newsletter*, 1982, pp. 4-8.

[2] Anyone interested in such a defense might consult "The Blaze of Her Splendors," Ralph H. Johnson, *Argumentation* 1 (1987), 239-253.

tions that follow should help you to understand the focus and framework in this text.

First, a solid game of defense is often the best offense. It surely helps. All that can be objected to is overuse of the defensive tools fallacy theory provides. But this is a problem for the teaching and learning of almost any new skill. The beginner initially wants to apply them, and at first lacks the skill and judgment to do so with discrimination. The same danger applies to any approach to logical criticism.

Second, the ability to spot flawed reasoning or dubious evidence in others' arguments can profitably be turned inward. Indeed, there is small profit in picking out weaknesses in the reasoning of others if one is unable to spot those same shortcomings in one's own arguments. By using knowledge of fallacies to be self-critical as well as being critical of the logic of other reasoners, you can double your gain and avoid one-sidedness.

Third, in the exercises that accompany each chapter, we will include specimens that we think are good arguments along with the bad ones to keep you on your toes and guard against an overly negative mind-set.

Fourth, from the outset you will be expected to give good arguments for this or that fallacy. In the long run, you are going to be given the responsibility of showing good judgment and discrimination in your evaluations. Are the flaws really serious ones or not? You will have to decide and to defend that decision.

We turn now to the crucial question, What are the criteria for good arguments? We are going to elicit these by looking at the arguments we have already presented and the ways in which these arguments violated the criteria. The flaws we will be discussing are called *fallacies*.

FALLACY

By *fallacy*, we mean a pattern of argumentation that violates one of the criteria a good argument must satisfy and that occurs with some marked degree of frequency.

A fallacy, as we understand the concept, is necessarily located in an argument. There are other meanings of the term *fallacy*, such as "a mistaken belief." The "gambler's fallacy" for example, refers to the mistaken belief that since a penny has landed on heads six times in a row, it is now "due" to land on tails. Our definition (see box) also requires that the pattern occur with some frequency. If we were to label every violation of a good argument's criteria a *fallacy*, we would have an unmanageably long list. Consequently, we restrict the term to those cases where the violation is frequent enough to be worth labeling.

In our evaluation of the examples, we made implicit reference to the criteria for good argumentation. It is time to make them explicit.

When we said that Example 1 was a weak argument because Highly Disappointed did not provide enough evidence to support his conclusion, we were implicitly appealing to the *standard of sufficiency*; i.e., that the premises of an argument must provide sufficient support for its conclusion. To illustrate the flaw in Example 2, we appealed to a different criterion. By saying that equipping homes with smoke detectors had nothing to do with saving lives on the highway, we were charging that the reason offered was irrelevant to the conclusion. We were implicitly appealing to the *standard of relevance*; i.e., that the premises of an argument must be relevant to the conclusion. Finally, we found that Example 4 was weak because we could not accept the dentist's premises. Here, we were implicitly appealing to the *standard of acceptability*; i.e., that the premises must be acceptable.

If you look back over the italicized words, the key words in our assessments, you will see that there are three different criteria that an argument must satisfy in order to be a good argument. First, the premises must be relevant to the conclusion: They must pass the relevance test. Second, the premises must provide sufficient support for the conclusion: They must pass the sufficiency test. Third, the premises must be acceptable: They must pass the acceptability test. We shall have more to say about each of these criteria in the next section. In Figure 3-1, we offer a graphic representation of them in the RSA Triangle. This figure identifies the criteria that a good argument must satisfy. An argument that fails to satisfy any one (or more) of these criteria is, in that respect and to that degree, a flawed argument.

In our way of approaching the study of fallacy, then, there are three basic kinds of fallacy: fallacies of relevance, fallacies of sufficiency, and fallacies of acceptability. However, in presenting the fallacies in the following chapters, we have used a different organization. In Chapter 5, we study fallacies that are in some way diversionary. In Chapter 6, we study fallacies that impersonate good arguments. In Chapter 7, we study fallacies that have a linguistic basis. In Chapter 8, we study fallacies that seek to persuade by intimidation. And in Chapter 9, we study the attitudes that cause people to reason fallaciously.

Other logical traditions take a different approach to what is required for an argument to be logically adequate. Logicians have typically distinguished two types of argument (or two types of inference found in arguments): an *inductive argument* (or inference), whose characteristic feature is that the premises render the conclusion probable; and a *deductive argument* (or inference), whose characteristic feature is that the conclusion follows necessarily from the

Figure 3-1 *RSA Triangle: The criteria that a good argument must satisfy.*

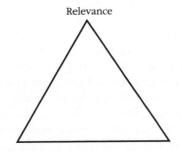

Relevance

Acceptability   Sufficiency

premises. Deductive arguments are characteristic of mathematics. Inductive arguments, on the other hand, are typically found in the empirical sciences. One kind of inductive reasoning that enjoys high profile in this society is the technique of sampling—featured in polling and opinion research. We discuss this briefly in Chapter 4.

If one accepts this dichotomy (which the authors of this text are not happy with), then one does not speak of across-the-board good arguments but, rather, of sound arguments (in the cause of deductive arguments) and strong arguments (in the case of inductive ones). The crucial question for evaluation then becomes, What constitutes soundness? or What constitutes inductive strength? Such matters are dealt with in most formal logic textbooks; we make no attempt to deal with these concepts in this text.

To conclude this section, we offer these additional observations about our approach to argument analysis. First, the fallacies we discuss are logical miscues that occur with some regularity in arguments in everyday discourse. You may find that our coverage of fallacies is narrower than that of some texts; i.e., we don't include as many fallacies as some do. We have listed only those that we believe show up with greatest frequency. A standard criticism of the fallacy approach to argument analysis is that there can be no complete inventory of fallacies because there is no complete list of the ways people go wrong in their reasoning. That may well be true, but it is of questionable relevance to our purposes. We believe there can be many lists that are useful without being complete; for example, lists of grammatical mistakes, lists of typically misspelled words, and lists of common reasons why a car's engine won't start.

Second, the fallacies we discuss all have names or labels selected with a view to indicating the flaw they embody. Some are vivid (*straw person*, *red herring*, *slippery slope*); others more pedestrian (*questionable cause*). What we want to impress on the reader at the outset is that the objective in learning the fallacy approach is *not* to enable you to throw these labels around in casual conversation to impress people with your logical savvy. It is never enough just to sprinkle your conversation with claims such as "that's a *red herring*." Most of the people you argue with will not have taken a logic or critical thinking course, so when you talk with them you have to make your points about arguments without resorting to the labels used in this text. The value of these labels is primarily *mnemonic*, to help you recall various sorts of mistakes in argumentation that people frequently make.

Third, our treatment of each fallacy centers around the identity conditions. These conditions serve a dual function. Not only do they define the fallacy but they guide you in your effort to show that the fallacy has been committed in a specific argument. Claiming that an argument is fallacious is not useful to you or the arguer unless you have good grounds for your opinion. You will need to make a reasonable argument to support your view.

Think of your role of a logical critic as like that of the prosecutor in a court of law. The prosecutor must show that there is enough evidence to convict a citizen of having violated a specific and named law or statute. The prosecutor would be laughed out of court were he to say, "He's guilty of something or other, but I can't say what." Nor can the prosecutor hope to get by with simple assertions (though he must assert). He cannot state, "The defendant shoplifted that Rollex," unless he can produce evidence of the crime (eyewitnesses, sworn statements, and so on). Similarly, you must be able to show that a given argument is guilty of a specified violation. To do this, you need to show that each of the fallacy conditions is satisfied in the case at hand. Mere assertions won't do the job. If you were to assert no more than some such unsubstantiated charge as "this premise is irrelevant to that conclusion" without arguing for your claim, your case would be thrown out of court for lack of evidence.

Fourth—and this harks back to a point made at the beginning of this chapter—the charge of fallacy is nothing more than an initial critical probe of the argument. It is an attempt to locate a possible weakness, not the bold (and sometimes arrogant) assertion that because of this flaw, the argument is worthless. Even if the charge of fallacy is justified in a given instance, that does not mean the argument cannot be repaired over the flaw. Nor does it follow that the conclusion of the argument is false. One may argue poorly or inadequately on behalf of a true statement (as conclusion) just as it is possible to argue well on behalf of a false (or unacceptable) belief. When you criticize an argument as fallacious, remember that all you have shown is that there is a potential obstacle on the route traced by the arguer from premises to conclusion. You have shown that the conclusion has not been adequately argued for. That leaves open the possibility that the arguer can revise the argument so that the conclusion is adequately supported.

With those observations behind us, we are ready to proceed with our discussion of argument construction.

Fundamentals of Argument Construction

It is a good idea to approach the construction of arguments in a methodical way, with a clear idea of your objectives. Otherwise, you risk using bad arguments, overlooking good ones, failing to cover your bases, and failing to be very persuasive.

What Is My Position?

First, ask yourself, What is my position? What, precisely, is it I want to argue for? Write out the answers to these questions.

Second, ask yourself, Have I stated one claim or more than one? It is quite common to bundle two or more different propositions together.

Suppose, for example, your claim is that abortion is wrong because it is murder. Notice that you have already made two claims: (1) abortion is wrong and (2) abortion is murder. It is best to separate distinct claims and argue for them separately. Is your claim made as clearly as it can be? Have you stated exactly what it is you want to argue for? Suppose you deal with your second claim—that abortion is murder—first. What, exactly, does that claim commit you to? When you call abortion *murder*, you are presupposing that it is wrong; and since you are probably interested in arguing for the second claim because you think it leads to the first, you are presupposing what you are arguing for when you call abortion *murder*. So it is best to revise your claim to avoid that flaw, claiming, instead, that "abortion is the taking of innocent life." Furthermore, since what you are talking about is abortion and not the taking of life in general (killing animals for food, for example), it would be better to restrict your second claim even further by saying "Abortion is the taking of innocent human life." Now your position is much clearer.

What Makes Me Think My Position Is True or Plausible?

It is a good idea at this point to try to formulate the reasons or evidence that have led you to believe the claim you want to argue for. Do you have one reason or several? Do your reasons fall into different groups? Here is where you write out a draft of your argument. This draft will almost certainly have to be revised later.

The same standards of relevance, acceptability, and sufficiency that you use to judge other people's arguments should be used to judge your own. We think a helpful way to do so is to think of the objectives of your argument.

What Is the Purpose of My Argument?

Having clarified your conclusion and set out the reasons or evidence that seem to you to support it, pause and consider what your aim is in formulating the argument. Several different purposes are possible, and each will lead to a different tailoring of the draft of your argument.

a. You want to persuade a particular person. In this case, ask yourself what beliefs or values you share with that person that you can appeal to. Also, since you think the person needs persuading, presumably he or she is opposed to your conclusion for some reason. So ask yourself what objections the person has, or is likely to have, to your conclusion. If you haven't done so already, you will need to find reasons that respond to those objections. There are three possible ways to get around objections. One is to show that the objections are mistaken. A second is to show that the objections, although true, do not really refute your position. The third is to change your position slightly, by qualifying it or weakening it in some other way, so that the objection no longer applies to it.

b. You want to prove or refute a point to a particular group. In this case, you need to consider more widely what beliefs or values you share with everyone in that reference group and what objections have been or might be raised against your position by any member of your intended audience.

c. You want to demonstrate your capacity to make a thorough case for your position. That is normally the aim you should have as a student writing an essay or fulfilling some other assignment. You need to show your instructor your capabilities. When you are assigned exercises from this book, for example, you are almost always asked to support your judgments. What is being requested, in effect, is that you give arguments to show that your answer is correct.

When you are demonstrating your competence, you may need to show that you are familiar with the issues and arguments related to your conclusion contained in some body of research literature. You could then borrow (with acknowledgment) arguments from that literature that you think are good ones and respond to criticisms of your position that were made in that literature.

If you are trying to defend your answer to one of the exercises in this book, the task is slightly different. In that case, you are usually trying to show that there is a flaw in someone else's argument. Your role is akin to that of a prosecuting attorney trying to establish that someone has committed a legal offense. The person whose argument you are critiquing presumably thought the argument was perfectly all right. So, were the person present, his or her role would be that of a defense attorney, trying to show that the prosecution's case is no good. It is not enough, therefore, just to state that the argument has some flaw. You must also give reasons that would persuade an impartial judge or jury. The argument is, as it were, "innocent until proven guilty" in the eyes of that impartial arbiter. The "judge" is the audience you have to persuade, and the presumption of the innocence of the argument from any flaw is what you will have to overcome in order to do so.

There are other possible objectives you may have in building an argument. For example, you may want to test the truth of a claim you are curious about. Is it true or false? You will try to find the strongest arguments that support it and the strongest ones against it so that you will be able to compare the merits of the two. But we will not go into this or any other possible goals here.

After you have made your arguments, it is always a good idea to review and revise them with a view to clarity as well as correctness. Is your reasoning easy to follow? You won't persuade a reader who can't see what you are driving at. Have you stated your premises and conclusions clearly? If either are vague or muddled, then your argument loses its force. Have you said anything in a way that could be interpreted differently from the way you mean it? Try to imagine yourself in the role of someone who holds a position contrary to yours and think about how this person is going to interpret what you have written. That exercise can lead to clarifying revisions.

We have listed a number of dos. Here are three don'ts. First, we recommend against using rhetorical questions (for example, "Who in his right mind would accept this claim?") when the purpose of your argument is to demonstrate your knowledge or understanding. In almost every case, you will end up with a claim that it is incumbent upon you to defend. It turns out, then, that rhetorical questions tend to be lazy ways of avoiding the onerous task of producing an argument to support the claim.

Second, be wary of using what you need to prove as part of your argument. For example, if you want to claim that an argument's premises are insufficient, it won't do to say, "The premises are insufficient because they don't provide enough evidence for the conclusion." What you need to prove is just that the premises don't give enough evidence. Or, if you want to argue that a premise is irrelevant, it won't do to say, "The premise is irrelevant because it gives no reason for that conclusion." Again, to prove irrelevance, what you have to show is that the premise supplies no reason.

Third, make sure that you are supplying the right kind of argument yourself. For example, don't argue that a premise is unacceptable by saying, "The premise hasn't been proved so it is unacceptable." Absence of proof does not show unacceptability. Instead, you must give some specific reason for doubting or questioning the premise.

Summary

In this chapter we have been concerned with the fundamentals of the process of argumentation. In the first part, we introduced you to the task of evaluating arguments by giving you some examples to work over. In our discussion, we introduced the concept of "fallacy," which will move center stage in the next section of the book—Chapters 4 through 9. In the second part of this chapter, we introduced you to the task of constructing arguments. Further discussion of this aspect of argumentation will be found in Section IV, "Advanced Argumentation."

EXERCISES

A. Exercises for Evaluating Arguments

Directions. For each extract assigned, decide if there are any arguments present, and, if so, whether they contain any of the fallacies you have studied so far. If you think there is no argument, explain what the function of the passage is. If you think any arguments are logically good ones, try to anticipate possible criticisms, and argue against such criticisms. If you think there are any fallacious arguments, write a critique supporting your judgment (see details below). If you think there is some fallacy not covered (yet), say so. While you may reasonably expect that these passages contain instances of the fallacies taken up in this chapter, understand that some passages may not contain arguments at all, some may contain argument with fallacies you have not encountered, and some of the arguments may be fallacy-free.

For *each* fallacy you identify, do the following in your critique: (1) identify: the argument's conclusion; the premise(s) in which the fallacy occurs; who commits the fallacy; and the name of the fallacy (if it is not one covered so far, describe it); (2) formulate an argument to convince a neutral observer that the fallacy you allege has indeed been committed; and (3) say whether any fallacy completely undercuts the argument or whether the argument can be repaired, and explain why you think so.

1. The February 15, 1993, issue of *Time* magazine, devoted to "The Chemistry of Love," occasioned this response from one reader:

   > Your story about love did readers a disservice by using the words *love* and *romance* interchangeably. Love comes from giving of oneself to another. Love is a commitment. It is a bond. It is a choice. Romance is nothing more than the icing on the cake.

2. An argument dealing with the abortion issue was cited in *Invitation to Critical Thinking.*[3]

---

[3] Barry and Rudinow, 2d ed., 1990, p. 234.

How can you deny that abortion is murder? The fetus is certainly alive, isn't it? And it certainly is human, isn't it? And it hasn't done anything wrong, has it? So you're talking about taking an innocent human life.

3. According to Barry and Rudinow,[4] the reasoning below was used by Lt. Col. Oliver North as his rationale for exchanging arms for hostages in Iran:

I'll tell you right now. I'd have offered the Iranians a free trip to Disneyland if we could have gotten Americans home for it.

4. After he took office in January 1993, President Clinton appointed Hillary Rodham Clinton to a task force on health care. One option the task force investigated was national health care, which prompted this response from a *Detroit News* reader:[5]

There isn't enough money in the country, much less the United States Treasury, to sustain a national health care program. Hundreds of billions of dollars would be spent annually just for "Band-Aid" treatments.

See also the examples of arguments from the exercises at the ends of Chapters 1 and 2.

B. Exercises for Constructing Arguments

5. Select an issue on which you have mixed feelings and thoughts. Construct an argument for and an argument against a position on that issue. The arguments should be fairly simple, consisting of several premises and a main conclusion each. What did you learn from this exercise? Discuss.

6. An important aspect of constructing arguments is being able to anticipate and defuse objections. Go back to the arguments you constructed for exercise 5. State an objection to each argument. Then answer the questions below.
   a. Is your objection an objection to a premise or an objection to the conclusion?
   b. As arguer, how would you respond to that objection?
   c. Rewrite the argument so that the objection and the response to the objection are incorporated into it.

[4] *Invitation to Critical Thinking*, 2d ed., 1990, p. 249.
[5] March 27, 1993.

SECTION 2
Fallacies

CHAPTER FOUR

◆

Three Basic Fallacies

Introduction

As we explained at the end of Chapter 3, the fallacies we take up in this chapter are basic because each stems from a violation of one of the three criteria. *Irrelevant reason* is the generic name for the fallacy that occurs when an irrelevant premise is introduced into an argument. *Hasty conclusion* is the generic name for the fallacy that occurs when the premises do not provide sufficient support for the conclusion. Finally, *problematic premise* is the generic name for the fallacy that occurs when a premise that is not acceptable is introduced into an argument. In our treatment of *problematic premise*, we also introduce two important instances of that fallacy: *begging the question* and *inconsistency*.

These three fallacies are generic in the sense that each of the fallacies we discuss in the following chapters is a more specific instance of one of them.

Irrelevant Reason

The first fallacy in our catalog is *irrelevant reason*. You may find it referred to by its Latin name, *non sequitur*, which translates to "it does not follow." Example 2 in Chapter 3 was an instance of this fallacy. The fact that lives can be saved by the use of dialysis machines is irrelevant to the issue of lives saved (or not) by the 55-mile-per-hour limit because the issue addressed in the argument is not how best to save lives but, rather, the effects of the reduction of the speed limit on highway safety. In this context, the question of how many lives might be saved by dialysis machines does not address that issue. On that basis, we judge it irrelevant.

We begin our treatment with a paradigm case of this fallacy. A Member of Parliament in Canada once charged, in the House of Commons, that the Federal Department of Health and Welfare had been cooperating with the Kellogg Company in permitting the sale of a cereal (Kellogg's Corn Flakes) that had "little or no nutritional value." Marc Lalonde, then the Minister of Health, seeking to rebut that charge, stated:

1   As for the nutritional value of Corn Flakes, the milk you have with your Corn Flakes has great nutritional value.

The implication of this claim in this context is that "Kellogg's Corn Flakes does have significant nutritional value." It is possible that Lalonde had a much stronger conclusion in mind. Maybe his view was that Kellogg's Corn Flakes has great nutritional value. But in setting forth his argument, we are required by the principle of charity (discussed in Chapter 1) to attribute to him the minimal statement that brings him into dialectical conflict with the opposing view. In interpreting an incomplete argument, we are obliged by the principle of fair play not to overcommit the arguer (as supplying the stronger implied conclusion would have done). We have thus reconstructed Lalonde's argument as follows:

2   1. The milk that one has with Kellogg's Corn Flakes has great nutritional value.
        a. Kellogg's Corn Flakes has significant nutritional value.

In our view, this is a bad argument because the premise furnishes no support for the conclusion. The nutrient properties of milk have no bearing on the nutrient properties of Corn Flakes, even if the two are usually consumed together. To determine the nutrient value of any food, one needs to measure the value of the food itself (its supply of protein, carbohydrate, fat, and so on), not the value of its companions.

One way to see the irrelevancy here is to construct a *counterexample*; i.e., an argument with a different subject matter, but one that uses the same type of reasoning, reasoning that is clearly bad. To illustrate the irrelevancy of Lalonde's reasoning, we construct these two counterexamples:

3   Salt has great nutritional value because the steak you sprinkle it on has great nutritional value.

4   Water has great nutritional value because the soup powder you mix it with to produce soup has great nutritional value.

In these examples, the premise clearly fails to support the conclusion because it is irrelevant to the conclusion. Lalonde's argument has the same pattern. In sum, Lalonde's premise is irrelevant to his conclusion, so the argument commits the fallacy of *irrelevant reason*.

The charge of *irrelevant reason*, as indeed any other charge of fallacy, constitutes an initial criticism of the argument and may well solicit a response. Lalonde (or someone who shares his view) could reject the criticism by showing how the premise, in conjunction with some as yet unmentioned assumption(s), would support the conclusion. Alternatively, Lalonde might persuade us that we had misunderstood his argument. Thus, when we make a charge of fallacy against an argument, we regard it as opening a critical discussion of some specific part of the argument—not as the definitive refutation of the argument.

Here is a second example. Asked to write an essay addressing the question of UFO sightings and whether such phenomena should be taken seriously, one undergraduate argued as follows:

5   I think UFO's should be taken seriously.
         I really enjoyed the movie *Close Encounters of the Third Kind*. It made me stop and think about UFO phenomena because the movie is about UFOs that landed here on earth and how people reacted to them.

The writer seems to be citing the movie *Close Encounters* in support of the implicit claim that UFO sightings should be taken seriously. Note, to begin, that this conclusion is itself vague; it could mean any number of things, from funding research on UFOs to educating people about them to not laughing at people who take UFOs seriously. We discuss vagueness in Chapter 7. The problem with this argument is in the relevance of the premise to the conclusion. What goes on in movies is no evidence of what goes on in the world at large. In movies, human beings can fly; there is life on other planets; and tomatoes become killers. None of these cinematic occurrences are any evidence that such things happen in real life. A movie does not provide relevant evidence about what takes place in the "real world." So the arguer's premise is irrelevant to the conclusion.

The two identity conditions of this fallacy may be formulated as below:

IRRELEVANT REASON

1. The arguer has put forth a premise as a reason for the conclusion.
2. The premise, considered in conjunction with the other premises, fails to satisfy the relevance requirement.

To suspect an argument of being guilty of *irrelevant reason* is one thing; to argue successfully for your charge of irrelevance is another. The boxed conditions are meant to guide you in the latter task. They tell you what you must do to show that an *irrelevant reason* fallacy has occurred in the argument under consideration.

A word about Condition 2. In the arguments we have considered thus far, there was only one premise. But Condition 2 is important because, although relevance is a property that individual premises of the argument must satisfy in and of themselves, the determination of relevance cannot occur in a vacuum. The other premises must be taken into account.

To illustrate how to use the boxed conditions, we will use the Corn Flakes example. Condition 1 is satisfied. Making the appropriate substitutions in that condition, we arrive at the following claim:

Condition 1.   Lalonde put forth "the milk you have with your Kellogg's Corn Flakes has great nutritional value" as a premise for his conclusion that Kellogg's Corn Flakes has significant nutritional value. It is obvious that Condition 1 is satisfied.

Condition 2.   The premise is irrelevant to the conclusion.

We must defend this claim, and we do so by replaying the line of reasoning set forth a few paragraphs back: "The nutrient properties of milk . . . companions." It is never enough merely to *assert* that the premise in question is irrelevant. To tip the scales of logic in your favor, you must justify your assertion. Otherwise the situation remains a standoff: Your undefended claim that the premise is irrelevant against the arguer's implicit (and likewise undefended) claim that the premise is relevant.

How can we satisfy condition 2? We turn to that difficult problem next.

First, as we said above, relevance (unlike truth) does not inhere in each individual premise but rather in an individual premise taken in conjunction with certain other items of evidence or information. (Sometimes these will be tacit or unexpressed.) Think of the sort of artificial case that makes for dramatic TV fare. The prosecutor asks: "Is the defendant left-handed?" The defense lawyer objects: "May the Court please, Your Honor, that question is surely irrelevant." Now the prosecutor jumps up and says, "But, Your Honor, we shall establish that the murderer has to have been left-handed, so if the defendent is left-handed, that is relevant to the question of whether he could have been the murderer." With the addition of that information, the light goes on, and the relevance of the premise becomes clear. Sometimes, then, a charge of irrelevance may be prompted by the arguer's failure to complete his or her reasoning. When that missing piece is provided, the logical focus changes from the question of the relevance of the original premise to the question of the acceptability of the newly added, relevance-supplying premise. But sometimes irrelevance occurs because the position has not been thought through carefully enough, and no additional premise with any plausibility at all can be found to supply relevance.

Second, one way to test for irrelevance is to assign truth values to the suspected premise and conclusion. (*Truth value* is a generic way of referring to the truth or falsity of a statement.) Assigning truth values requires logical imagination. You must say to yourself: "Let me suppose that O is true; does the truth of O suggest a truth value for T (the conclusion)?" That is, "If O is true (just supposing), does that give some basis for judging that T is true?" Or try it the other way: "If O is false, does that give some basis for supposing that T is false?" If, in both cases, the answer is "no," then you have some reason to assert that O is irrelevant to T. Let's try this strategy on the Corn Flakes example.

O = The milk you have with your Corn Flakes has great nutritional value.
T = Corn Flakes have significant nutritional value.

Suppose O is true; does that increase the likelihood of T's being true? No, for Corn Flakes and milk are two different and distinct food substances, each with its independent nutrient properties. Milk doesn't react chemically with Corn Flakes in such a way as to increase the nutritional properties of the Corn Flakes. Does

O's truth increase the likelihood of *T*'s falsehood? Not at all, for milk does not decrease the nutritional value of Corn Flakes any more than it increases it. Now suppose *O* were false; what difference would that make to *T*'s truth value? If milk were not very nutritional, that would neither increase the nutritional value of Corn Flakes (and so make *T* true) nor decrease it (and so make *T* false). The truth and falsehood of *O* and *T*, then, are totally independent; hence, *O* is irrelevant to *T*.

A second strategy for arguing irrelevance will emerge from consideration of the example we used in introducing the relevance requirement (Example 2 from Chapter 3). Recall that in that argument, which had to do with the new 55-mile-per-hour speed limit, the arguer stated:

6   There are more cost-efficient ways of saving lives . . . such as equipping every house with a smoke detector . . . or putting more dialysis machines in hospitals.

We argued that this premise has nothing to do with the conclusion (which is just another way of saying it's irrelevant). But how to argue for this? The conclusion has to do with saving lives on the highway; the premise has to do with a much broader and, at any rate, different category: saving lives in general. The strategy here is to categorize the issue addressed in the suspected premise and then show that it is different from the one being addressed in the conclusion.

We conclude our treatment of this fallacy with a classic case. In the early seventies, a doll being sold in toy stores all across North America was found to have the unsavory feature of allowing a small pointed spike to protrude if the head of the doll were removed, a feat that tests showed could be accomplished by infants. When parents discovered this danger, they complained to government agencies. Informed of these complaints, a spokesperson for the company that manufactured the doll stated:

7   All the legislation in the world isn't going to protect a child from the normal hazards of life.

To begin, we identify the implied conclusion, which we take to be "it would be inappropriate to draft legislation seeking to prevent the manufacture and sale of such dolls." The premise is relevant to the conclusion only if we assume that the dolls in question fall under the category of the "normal hazards of life." Admittedly, the category is rather broad and hard to define precisely; but one could classify as *normal hazards* things like busy urban streets, rusty nails left in planks, icy sidewalks, and roving dogs. Certainly the bounds of that category would have to be stretched to include within it a plaything such as a doll which, by its very nature, is not supposed to be dangerous. So although the spokesperson's claim is true, the premise is irrelevant to the conclusion.

Global versus Local Relevance.   Relevance as we have been speaking of it thus far might be termed *local relevance*, the relevance of an individual premise to a conclusion. But because conclusions themselves are located in a dialectical context where there are multiple issues and competing points of view, there is another kind of relevance which we shall call *global relevance*. A claim may be *locally irrelevant* (irrelevant to the conclusion as formulated) but, yet, be *globally relevant* (relevant to the issue that the conclusion addresses). We shall say more of this when we discuss *red herring* in Chapter 5.

We turn next to the fallacy of *hasty conclusion*.

Hasty Conclusion

Even when the premises of an argument pass the relevance test, they may not provide *sufficient* support for the conclusion. When this happens, it is some-times referred to as "jumping to a conclusion"; the conclusion itself is called *hasty conclusion*. You will also encounter the term *hasty generalization*, a special case of *hasty conclusion* in which a conclusion is drawn from an unrepresentative sample. We had an example of a *hasty conclusion* earlier, in Highly Disappointed's letter to Ann Landers. Consideration of additional exam-ples will help to bring out the specific features of this fallacy.

After visiting the Calgary (Alberta) Zoo, a disgruntled tourist wrote this letter to the *Calgary Herald*:

8   We arrived at the park gate at 7:25 P.M., at which time the cashier gleefully took our admission money. Upon entering the zoo and walking across the bridge, we heard the loudspeaker state that the zoo buildings were closing at 8:00 P.M. and that the zoo itself would close at 8:30 P.M. We went to the ticket counter and asked if we could get a pass for the following day. The answer was "no." It is easy to see that Calgary is anything but friendly, but, rather, out to rake off tourists for all they can get.

We can all sympathize with this tourist's disappointment and frustration. Let's assume the facts to be as reported. Still, this small sample of life in Calgary can hardly justify the strong claim the tourist made. This one incident does not show that Calgary is anything but friendly, nor yet that Calgary businesses are out to rake off tourists for all they can get. To determine this, we would need a great deal more evidence about how tourists are treated at other tourist destinations and, indeed, other data about the zoo. The evidence here is much too limited to support the strong (and no doubt strongly felt) conclusion. Indeed, the evidence doesn't even allow us to draw any conclusion about the zoo and its policies. Perhaps this incident was atypical. Imagine a scenario of the following sort: The person at the ticket center was new to the job and didn't understand the zoo's practice of giving passes to people in this situation. In any event, this argument illustrates two common patterns of *hasty conclusion*—the use of anecdotal evidence and of unrepresentative samples.

Anecdotal Evidence.   One typical form of *hasty conclusion* occurs when the arguer uses anecdotal evidence. Evidence is anecdotal, as contrasted with sys-tematic, when it takes the form of recounting an experience, often in story form, of one person or a few people. An example would be someone who argues like this: "Professors really have it easy. My parents have their cottage in the Adirondacks, and there's this professor who owns the cottage next to theirs. This guy is there from late May right through mid-September. Professors really have a pretty easy job, eh?" Let's suppose that the facts here are as stated and that the professor really is just loafing during the four-month period. The conclusion drawn from this one incident goes far beyond its probative power. To draw a conclusion about how hard or easy professors have it, one must take a much more systematic approach.

There is a difference between using a story to illustrate a thesis in a premise that has already been established and using a story to prove a point. We refer to the latter situation when we allude to the dangers of anecdotal evidence.

Unrepresentative Sample.   Another common way of coming to a *hasty conclusion* is relying on an unrepresentative sample. Sampling is a technique used by pollsters. It is a device for gathering information about an entire population from a small subset—a *sample*. A *representative sample* is one in which whatever features in the overall population deemed relevant to the issue at hand are represented in roughly the same proportion as these features are found in the population.

A sample of students taking first-year courses at your university could hardly be considered representative of all students at your university, much less of students in general, because it excludes upper-division and graduate students. Thus, such a sample would not be representative.

Sydney Harris, a syndicated columnist, in an article entitled "Jogging Is an Unnatural Activity for Human Beings," writes:

9   While exercise (such as running) is beneficial for the lungs and heart and the whole circulatory system, it is debilitating to the legs. That is why most physical fitness experts recommend swimming as the ideal all-around exercise, not walking or running: because in swimming the legs move easily through the surface and do not pound a hard surface.

While walking may do more good than harm, in terms of total bodily welfare, I cannot believe that jogging is anything but a bonanza for the podiatrist and the orthopaedic surgeons. Some medical specialists indeed have already begun to warn the public of the probable perils in jogging as a daily routine.

Harris clearly believes, and would like his reader to believe, that jogging is not a good method of exercising, on the grounds that it is debilitating to the legs and that specialists have begun to warn the public about the perils of jogging.

The problem with his argument is the evidence that it fails to take into consideration. In this argument, the untapped evidence is of two sorts. First, there is no doubt that jogging leads to injuries in many cases, but in how many cases? How many in relation to the total number of joggers? Under what conditions do injuries arise under conditions of intelligent mileage? If only a relatively few joggers are injured, and then only when they try to run too far too soon and don't rest properly or run with inferior shoes, then Harris's evidence, while relevant, doesn't add up to a good case for his claim.

Second, it may be that though there is a risk of injury to all joggers, the gains to them in better circulation, increased lung capacity, lower weight, improved self-image and greater energy outweigh the dangers. In that case, Harris's evidence fails to support his claim because it is partial in a different sense. We need to know that the risk is widespread (not restricted to a select group) and that the disadvantages outweigh the benefits. Harris fails to provide this further evidence. His conclusion is drawn without taking these factors into consideration, and so he is guilty of coming to a *hasty conclusion*.

The defining conditions of *hasty conclusion* are listed in the box.

HASTY CONCLUSION

1. The arguer presents a set of premises as a sufficient basis for a conclusion.
2. The premises, taken together, are not sufficient to support the conclusion because of one or more of the following:
   a. They do not provide evidence which has been systematically gathered by an appropriate method.[1]
   b. They do not supply a sufficient sample of the various kinds of relevant evidence.
   c. They ignore the presence of, or the possibility of, contrary evidence.

As in the case of charging *irrelevant reason*, you have two tasks to perform in making a case for *hasty conclusion*. First, you must properly show that there is an argument and properly identify its premises. That's condition 1. Then you must assert—and support your assertion—that the evidence is not sufficient. That's condition 2. You may do this in several ways:

1. You may show that what the evidence presented does show is less than what the arguer concluded.
2. You may indicate that the arguer failed to supply an additional sort of evidence, evidence that is needed to generate the conclusion. This may be more evidence of the same sort or evidence of a different type. The onus, by the way, is on you to show that this type of evidence is needed.
3. You may argue that the arguer has ignored or overlooked evidence that weighs against the conclusion and so the needed refutation of that evidence is missing.

Whatever the case may be, it is never sufficient for you to merely assert that more evidence is needed; you must defend your assertion.

Let's work an example showing how the two conditions are to be used. The following is a letter from another tourist, this one from Warren, Michigan. She is recounting her experiences during a visit to the area of Windsor, Ontario,

---

[1] We are grateful to Hendrik van der Breggen for calling our attention to an infelicity in the previous formulation of this condition.

which is just a quick trip across the Detroit River for Detroit-area residents. She writes:

10   On January 28, I entered your city to enjoy the winter countryside. Anticipating a day of relaxation and pleasure, I was driving along Cabana Road at a very slow and safe speed—keeping with the flow of the traffic—when an officer of your police force approached my car on foot. His vehicle was parked conveniently behind a pickup truck. He was pointing his finger at me. Both the passengers in my car and I were very frightened and thought that there must have been a crime or a health hazard in the area. No, he was flagging me down, not to warn me—since it was clear I was a visitor—but to issue a speeding ticket. (It was evident that he didn't bother to check my driving record—twenty-two years without so much as a parking ticket.)

Yes, you do have a beautiful country, but your police force is using a speed trap on this road. For I had just pulled away from being ticketed when this officer was hailing another poor unsuspecting motorist into this trap.

We think the writer commits *hasty conclusion*. Condition 1 is satisfied. The writer advances two incidents as evidence that the Windsor Police Force is using a speed trap in that area. She feels that she was caught in the trap, and she cites the case of another "poor unsuspecting motorist" who was also caught in that trap.

Condition 2 is satisfied. This evidence is insufficient to conclude that the police force is using a speed trap. Why? First, we must clarify the term speed trap. A *speed trap* is a location where police officers hide in waiting for cars that are speeding. It often contains two additional ideas. First, the police enforce the limit strictly; they do not "give" the motorist anything. If you are going 35 miles per hour in a 30-mile-per-hour zone, you will be ticketed. Second, those who are ticketed are not local drivers but others passing through the local area. Now, even if we suppose that these factors were in operation at the time of this incident and that the writer was not exceeding the limit (to assume the latter, we must bypass pretty bad reasoning), these two incidents would still not be adequate evidence. One would need to have data stretching over a much longer period of time, at least a couple of weeks, to show that the police had, indeed, set up a speed trap. If, during that period, it turned out that only Americans who sped were ticketed, then the evidence would be much stronger. As it is, the writer has some reason to suspect that a speed trap is in operation but stands at some distance from anything like adequate evidence.

A classic example is found in this excerpt from a book, *Off Madison Avenue*, by David Lyon, in which he defends advertising against its critics. At one point, he writes:

11   I think I can show you that on balance advertising carries a higher proportion of truth than you are likely to encounter in most of the dicussions you hear or the books you read. Consider the detergent commercial that you hate the most. You may, if you wish, question whether it actually does make clothes whiter than white;

you may doubt that it gets out more stubborn dirt than other washday products leave in; you may wonder whether it really leaves your clothes squeaky clean and ever so manageable. But there is one thing you may bank on with a considerable degree of confidence. It is a detergent. Doubt, if you wish, that Winston tastes good but doubt not that Winston is a cigarette.

Lyon's argument is weak. He claims to be showing that advertising carries more truth than most books and discussions. His lone premise for this claim is that advertised products do, indeed, belong to the product type which the advertisements assert they belong to. We don't doubt the premise is relevant, for it reminds us there is some minimal truth in advertising. But to establish the conclusion, he would have to show that there is even less truth in most books and conversations; and that he has not done. Indeed, Lyon ignores (in reaching his conclusion) the contrary evidence right under his nose: that most ads are guilty of *puffery*—inflated claims which are not literally true. The ratio suggested by his own analysis of the detergent commercial is 25 percent (one true claim for every three false ones). So he needs to establish that ordinary forms of speech and communication typically fall below this quotient. But he has not offered any evidence at all for that part of his argument.

It seems clear that as humans, we have a built-in tendency to jump to conclusions on the basis of limited evidence. Sometimes we will get a notion into our heads, cast about for a few scant bits of evidence, and settle immediately into our position. We thereby promote intuitions and half-truths to the status of full and incontrovertible truths without bothering to consider and weigh the evidence. That's the idea behind the saying: "Don't confuse me with the facts." Or we reason from our own personal experience (*anecdotal evidence*) to draw conclusions that run far in advance of it. Or we ignore evidence. Sometimes we suppress evidence. Or we simply fail to bring all the evidence to bear on the situation. We certainly only rarely hunt out evidence that goes contrary to our own predilections. Some of these tendencies may stem from our primitive heritage, when the world was simpler and also more dangerous. Strategies that may work perfectly well in an evolutionary setting (inference from a small sample) may well be disastrous in another.

As arguers and reasonable people, we need to be sensible in our demands for sufficient evidence. There is no handy gauge that registers how much evidence is enough. The onus is on the critic to cite, in each individual case under scrutiny, specific ways in which the evidence put forward is unsufficient. In effect, evidence advanced in an argument can be fairly challenged as insufficient only when the critic can cite some item of relevant evidence that would make a difference to the conclusion and has not been taken into account in the argument.

Often, too, the argument can be retrieved and made immune from the *hasty-conclusion* criticism by making a simple change in wording; by, for example, changing "always" to "usually," "in every case" to "in most cases," or "entirely" to "partially." This kind of qualification may be all the arguer needs to make the point. In such cases, the critic needs to be aware of the minimal force of the *hasty conclusion* charged and can even suggest the qualification that would immunize the argument from the criticism.

This advice can be turned around and put to good use when you are constructing an argument. You have no business thinking your opinion or claim is sufficiently supported until you have gathered enough evidence to answer reasonable challenges. You should be careful to qualify your conclusion so that its generality does not go beyond the limits justified by the evidence you have been able to assemble. These two moves—anticipating and trying to meet challenges, and qualifying the conclusion—will nip many a case of *hasty conclusion* in the bud.

Local versus Global Sufficiency. What we have been speaking of is one very important kind of sufficiency, the sufficiency of the evidence embodied in the premises to support the conclusion. But, as was the case with relevance, there is another kind of sufficiency important in argumentation, one that stems from the dialectical nature of argument. We call this *global sufficiency*.

Arguments typically occur in a dialectical setting; i.e., there are competing points of view on an issue and the argument is an attempt to show that one of these views is correct or deserves allegiance. If your argument is to succeed in its attempt to persuade rationally, it is not enough merely to present the reasons or evidence that led you to accept its conclusion. You must also respond to competing points of view on the issue and to the reasons why others might resist your conclusion. You can identify alternative viewpoints and argue that they are defective, or inferior to yours. You need to identify standard objections to your position and show how those objections fail. An argument that does not in some sense address these competing points of view, these dialectical matters, fails to satisfy the requirement of global suffency. If you can show that the arguer has failed to address such dialectical material, then you have shown that the arguer has not satisfied the global-sufficiency requirement and therefore is guilty of *hasty conclusion*.

In sum, when you are assessing an argument, you must consider how well it meets the requirements of both local and global sufficiency. Check to see whether some of its premises engage objections or attempt to refute alternative positions. Are there well-known competing points of view that might be acceptable but that have not been shown to be inadequate?

Problematic Premise

We have seen that the premises must satisfy the relevance requirement, and they must satisfy the sufficiency requirement. What more is there? Here the term "sufficiency" may be misleading. In one common sense of the term, if premises are sufficient, then you would think that's the end of the matter. However, what we mean by sufficiency is that the arguer has cited the appropriate types and amounts of evidence to support the conclusion. The relevancy and the sufficiency requirements both concern the relationship of the premises to the conclusion. But there are other criteria the premises must satisfy. One (acceptability) concerns the relationship of the premises to the audience. The other (truth) concerns the relationship of the premises to the world. We discuss the truth requirement first.

The goal of many arguments is to establish that the way things are in the world shows the conclusion to be true and hence worthy of the audience's belief. For such arguments, it is clear that they must live up to their own standard: The premises must be true. But whether a given premise is true is not something that logic or the study of argumentation can help you to determine (except in very rare cases of what is called *logical truth*), and so we do not propose here to treat the truth requirement separately. If you find that a premise is false, that is an important criticism and could be a good reason to reject the argument. But such criticism is not logical in character, and as that is what we are especially concerned with in this text, we turn to that sort of criticism next.

Whether or not the truth of the premises is at issue, if the premises are to move a particular audience along the route to the conclusion, they must be acceptable to the members of that audience. The perspective we take on acceptability is that of logic. Many audiences will find the sloppy and disordered argument unacceptable, preferring the well-written and the organized. These are matters of style, not logic; they need not affect the strength of the argument's support for its conclusion—i.e., its logical substance. What, then, makes premises acceptable from a logical point of view?

The basic idea governing the logical acceptability of premises derives from the purpose of arguments. Their point is to provide grounds (the premises) to convince a reasonable person to accept a claim (the conclusion) that person originally questioned or did not accept. If the person questions any of the premises, then that premise will have to be either discarded or supported. Once challenged, an unsupported premise cannot be a reason for this person to accept the conclusion. Since we are hypothesizing that the argument is addressed to a rational person, then we can assume that the arguer will be obliged to deal only with reasonable questions and challenges. The arguer, then, has an obligation to respond to any reasonable doubt or question about the argument. Should there be a reasonable question about whether any premise should be accepted, then the arguer has a duty to supply an answer; i.e., a reason why the premise should be accepted.

Thus when an arguer uses as a premise of an argument a claim that he or she fails to defend when it should have been defended, the arguer has violated the acceptability criterion. Here is an example:

In an article on the Op-Ed page of *The New York Times* (August 14, 1992), Carolyn See described some historical and current problems in the state of California, while arguing that "we've been dead before, plenty of times. But we always get over it." One claim she made was:

> When Ronald Reagan became governor in 1996, he began siphoning money out of what was then the country's finest public education system.

In reference to this claim, one might say: "The writer doesn't prove that charge about Reagan, and that's quite an assumption to make about California's system. Surely in each case some evidence should have been provided." This makes it a case of *problematic premise*.

Not every undefended claim makes an arguer guilty of this fallacy. Consider this claim about gun control made in a letter to *Time* magazine (November 1991):

12   "Guns don't kill people; people do" is a foolish argument. The range of firearms available in the United States market gives unimaginable killing power to just about anybody.

In the context of the current discussion about guns and their availability, we'd have no problem accepting the premise, even though the arguer doesn't defend it.

So when ought we, as the critical audience of an argument, accept its premises? Two considerations apply here, and they pull in opposite directions. On the one hand, the arguer's job is to persuade us, and so it is up to her to argue in defense of any premise she thinks we might not accept without a defense. On the other hand, we can't require that every premise be defended without getting into infinite regress. At some point, the arguer will have to produce as a premise a statement (and typically more than one) for which she provides no support. We call these the argument's *ultimate premises*.

When we come to these ultimate premises, we must make a decision: Is it reasonable to accept these premises without support, or do we think the arguer ought to have provided some support for them? In the latter case, we are making a logical criticism of the argument. We have found an unsupported premise or premises that we feel ought to have been supported. In this case, we say the arguer has violated the acceptability requirement.

We say a premise is *problematic* if it is introduced into the argument without defense and is unacceptable without this defense. Anyone who uses such a premise in an argument commits the fallacy we call *problematic premise*. Before listing the conditions of this fallacy, we shall flesh out our account of acceptability by discussing specific cases where undefended premises are acceptable.

It is reasonable to accept an undefended premise if it is generally known to be true, or at least represents knowledge shared, and known to be shared, by the arguer and the audience. Thus, for example, in parts of the world where Christianity has historically been the predominant religion, it would be permissible to use as an undefended premise that Christmas is December 25. In the United States, Central America, Japan, and Canada, you could assert, without needing to defend it, that the World Series is held in the fall; and in the United States, but probably not elsewhere, you could assert in an argument, without defense, that the first permanent colonists came from Europe.

Even when the premises of an argument are in an area of controversy and not in the domain of common knowledge, there are a few situations in which the requirement that the premises be defended can be waived and it would be reasonable for you to accept an undefended premise. These exemptions are listed in the box.

EXEMPTIONS

1. The premise in question has already been defended elsewhere, and all parties know this or could reasonably be expected to know it.
2. The arguer acknowledges that the premise needs defense and accepts the responsibility for providing that defense, if need be, later or on another occasion.
3. The premise is offered "for the sake of argument" in order to show what follows from it.

The situations listed in the box are situations where the requirement to defend in face of a question is suspended, deferred, or transferred, not where it is done away with.

The identity conditions for the fallacy of *problematic premise* are listed in the box.

PROBLEMATIC PREMISE

1. The arguer failed to present a defense for a premise offered in support of a conclusion.
2. In the circumstances in which the argument is presented, there is some specific reason why the premise should not be accepted without a defense.

We emphasize that to make a charge of *problematic premise* stick, you need to cite reasons specific to the particular argument in question. We have of necessity been discussing in general terms the sorts of situations where a premise ought to be defended. For any particular argument, unless you can give a specific reason—related to that subject matter and that argument—why the premise needs a defense, your charge will amount to no more than a general and unreasonable accusation that is itself problematic.

Let us bring these conditions and the discussion leading up to them to bear on some examples. First, we examine the text of an argument.

13   No man can be a total feminist because in order to be a total feminist, he has to know what it feels like to be discriminated against as a woman, and no man can have that experience.

Here is our reconstruction of this argument:

14   1. No man can have the experience of what it feels like to be discriminated against as a woman.

2. In order to be a total feminist, a man has to know what it feels like to be discriminated against as a woman.

3. No man can be a total feminist.

We have quarrels with both premises, a minor quarrel with the first, and a more fundamental one with the second. The first comes close to the truism that no man can be a woman. Still, there are cases where women have had sex changes and become men and so, as men, can report from direct experience what it was like to be discriminated against as a woman. Also, a man could masquerade as a woman in order to find out what it feels like to be treated as women are. This would be analogous to what John Howard Griffin did when he put black pigment on his skin and lived and was identified by others as a black person, an experience he reported on in his book *Black Like Me*. These two possibilities represent a minor objection to the first premise because it remains true that for most men, the experience of being discriminated against as a woman is inaccessible.

As for the second premise, it is not clear that a man (such as one who is black or handicapped or homosexual) cannot have direct experience of what it is like to be discriminated against in respects that are sufficiently similar to what a woman experiences to permit him to be a total feminist; that is, to sympathize totally with women. Moreover, it is possible that some men (perhaps not many) who have never been discriminated against themselves are nevertheless sufficiently sensitive and imaginative to have all the sympathy with women needed to make them total feminists. Our verdict, then, is not that the second premise is false but that it is pretty controversial. It may be true, but it needs some support to refute or block the points we have made. This is why we call this argument as it stands guilty of *problematic premise*.

Our second example comes from a letter to the editor of *The New York Times* about smoking. The arguer claims that since smokers die sooner than nonsmokers, and since there are so many smokers, smokers actually save taxpayers vast sums of money in social security and medicaid benefits. In support of his two premises, he writes:

15   Recent news stories tell us that 33 percent of all Americans smoke. An actuarial study by State Mutual Assurance Company concluded that a healthy nonsmoking 32-year-old man can expect to live 7.3 years longer than a healthy smoking 32-year-old-man.

Should we accept these premises? If we seriously want to challenge their truth, we have to do a good deal of work. We have to look up the studies, check their methodology, and possibly repeat them ourselves. Is the effort worth it? There is no particular reason to question the claim that this data was reported or that it was reliable. Furthermore, even if the figures are on the high side, the conclusions drawn from them (that smokers in America die earlier than do non-smokers, and that the earlier demise of the smokers saves significant amounts in social security and medicaid benefits) would still be warranted. So while we might challenge the strict accuracy of the arguer's figures, we have no basis for a charge of *problematic premise* here. (The argument, as it stands, does commit *hasty conclusion*. We will leave it to you to figure out how, if you haven't done so already.)

This concludes our discussion of *problematic premise*. We now turn to two important variants on this fallacy.

Variations of Problematic Premise

Begging the Question

We shall be presenting our treatment of a variety of common species of the three basic types of fallacy (irrelevance, insufficiency, unacceptability) in Chapters 5 through 9. Two exceptions, the fallacies called *begging the question* and *inconsistency*, will be treated here because they are paradigm instances of arguments where the acceptability requirement is violated.

As we have said, arguments come into being against a background of controversy and lack of consensus. Thus the very existence of an argument presupposes the existence of persons who do not, or are not disposed to, accept a particular point of view (the conclusion). Since the purpose of an argument is to lay down a route leading from premises that the audience already believes or is prepared to accept on reflection to the conclusion, it is clear that one may not use as a premise in one's argument the very conclusion one is seeking to establish. If someone requires support for the conclusion, she will be no more inclined to accept that proposition when it's in the role of a premise.

Yet arguers at times deploy in their arguments, as premises or support, statements identical or equivalent to the conclusion. Such a move cannot be allowed. If the conclusion is acceptable, then no argument is needed to support it; and if the conclusion as it stands is not acceptable, then it cannot be appealed to as a premise. Arguments violating this stricture that the premises must be acceptable independently of the conclusion commit the fallacy of begging the question. You will sometimes still find this fallacy referred to by its Latin name, *petitio principii* (*petitio*, for short).

A humorous illustration of the flavor of this fallacy—though it is not itself an argument—can be seen in the following exchange from an episode of the British sitcom *Fawlty Towers*:

16   COLONEL HALL: Who are you? I mean, I don't know your name.

BASIL: (to his wife, under his breath) What is it?

Sybil: What?

Basil: My name.

Sybil: (calmly): This is my husband, Basil Fawlty.

Basil: That's it!

Colonel Hall: What?

Basil: How do you do!

Colonel Hall: How do you do?

Basil: May I introduce my wife?

Colonel Hall: She just introduced you.

There is a circle here spawned by Basil's momentary lapse (forgetting his own name) in which Sybil introduces Basil to Colonel Hall. This act presumes that Sybil is known to Hall but that Basil isn't, which is what makes for the circular and inappropriate move when Basil then makes as if to introduce his wife to the Colonel. Something like this can occur in an argument when the arguer uses what he is supposed to be showing—the conclusion—as a premise of his argument.

A premise can be the same as the conclusion without having exactly the same wording. As long as the premise expresses the same proposition as the conclusion, the effect is the same. Here is the classic textbook example, from the nineteenth-century treatise *Elements of Logic* (London, 1862) by Richard Whately:

17   To allow every man unbounded freedom of speech must always be, on the whole, advantageous to the state; for it is highly conducive to the interests of the community that each individual should enjoy a liberty perfectly unlimited of expressing his sentiments.

The flowery phrasing of the argument serves to disguise that it begs the question. If we structure the argument and use some common sense, we can readily see the flaw.

18   1. It is (a) highly conducive to the interests of the community that (b) each individual should enjoy a liberty perfectly unlimited of expressing his sentiments.

   2. (b1) To allow every man unbounded freedom of speech must always be, on the whole, (a1) advantageous to the state.

What does it mean for a practice to be (a1) "advantageous to the state" if not that it is (a) "highly conducive to the interests of the community"? These two phrases express the very same notion in different words. And what does it mean to (b1) "allow every man unbounded freedom of speech" if not (b) "each individual should enjoy a liberty perfectly unlimited of expressing his sentiments"? The phrases "unbounded freedom of speech" and "a liberty perfectly unlimited of expressing his sentiments" are synonymous. The premise says that "each individual should enjoy" such a freedom, while the conclusion states, in effect, that every man should be allowed such a liberty. But these statements are merely semantic variations on the same theme. The premise and the conclusion are one and the same proposition expressed in different words. Thus the argument is guilty of *begging the question.*

Whately's example offends against the requirement of acceptability that the premise must not be the same as the conclusion either in the same words or in the form of a logically equivalent proposition. Our next example shows a violation of the more general stipulation that the acceptance of the premise must not require prior acceptance of the conclusion. This example is from David Ogilvy's *Confessions of an Advertising Man* (1968). Ogilvy was touting his own Rolls Royce ad, in the last paragraph of which he had written, "People who feel diffident about driving a Rolls Royce can buy a Bentley." He then went on to argue:

19   Judging from the number of motorists who picked up the word "diffident" and bandied it about, I concluded that the advertisement was thoroughly read.

We've reconstructed Ogilvy's argument, adding some points omitted from the above excerpt:

20   1. Many motorists picked up the word "diffident" and bandied it about.

2. The word "diffident" occurred near the end of Ogilvy's 700-word advertisement.

3. Research shows that readership of advertisements falls off rapidly up to fifty words of copy but drops very little between fifty and five hundred words.

4. Many motorists read Ogilvy's Rolls Royce advertisement thoroughly.

Now focus on the first premise. Is it acceptable? That depends on where Ogilvy thinks the motorists picked up the word "diffident"; there's no doubt he thinks they were influenced to use the word by reading his advertisement. That supposition, however, *begs the question* because if we accept the first premise— that the motorists picked up "diffident" from Ogilvy's ad—we have already accepted the argument's conclusion—that many motorists read the Rolls Royce ad thoroughly. Since the acceptability of the first premise depends on our already having accepted the conclusion, that premise cannot be used to prove the conclusion.

Another form of *begging the question* frequently occurs in arguments against abortion and in arguments against capital punishment. The word "murder" plays a key role in both. Consider these condensed arguments:

21   Abortion is the murder of an (innocent) fetus, so clearly it is wrong (immoral).

22   Capital punishment is legalized murder, so it ought to be abolished.

We agree that if these premises are acceptable, the conclusion follows. The problem arises in deciding whether to accept the premise. Is abortion the murder of the fetus? Is capital punishment legalized murder?

To answer these questions, we must consider carefully the meaning of the word "murder." It refers to the killing of a human being but, more than that, to killing that (unlike self-defense) is without justification and is therefore wrong. We can accept that abortion and capital punishment are murder only if we already accept that these actions are without moral justification and so wrong. Notice, however, that this is just what the above arguments set out to establish. Their conclusions are that abortion is wrong and that capital punishment is unjustified (and so should be abolished). You can see, then, that we must already accept these conclusions if we are to accept the premises used in these arguments to support them. We are asked, in both cases, to grant in advance the question at issue. Both arguments beg the question, for the acceptance of a premise must not require prior acceptance of the conclusion of the argument.

There is another sort of question-begging that follows a pattern. A critic makes a charge. The respondent replies to the charge by asserting a more general claim which, if true, would falsify the critic's charge; but the claim cannot be accepted until we know on other grounds that the critic's charge is false. For example, accused of plagiarism, a student defends herself by saying, "I am not a cheater; I never cheat." This claim may be true. But, in this context, it is not acceptable because that she never cheats is just what has come into question, and so it cannot be used as a premise to defend the conclusion that she was not in this case guilty of plagiarism.

Here's another example. The mystery writer Mickey Spillane once defended his book *The Erection Set* against a charge of being pornographic by arguing:

23   In the first place I wouldn't write pornography because it doesn't sell.

If he means to defend as a conclusion the statement that *The Erection Set* isn't pornographic and to support the conclusion with the assertion "I wouldn't write pornography," it is clear that his argument begs the question because to accept his premise, we must already have accepted the conclusion.

One does *not* beg the question if the general claim introduced to rebut a specific charge is argued for on further, independent evidence. So, for example, our friend accused of plagiarizing could avoid *begging the question* by giving lots of evidence that she is not a cheater, evidence that is entirely independent of whether she plagiarized in the case in question. This would not be the strongest kind of case against the charge, but it would not, with that addition, be guilty of *begging the question*.

We can now summarize *begging the question* and present its conditions. There are two species to be recognized. In one, the premises contain the conclusion, either expressed identically or stated in a logically equivalent form. This first version of the fallacy is usually found in long compound arguments. The question-begging premise tends to occur in a subordinate argument; the conclusion it begs is one or more steps removed. In the second kind of *begging the question*, the guilty premise is plausible or reasonable only if one already accepts the conclusion. The acceptability of the premise depends on our first accepting the conclusion it is being used to defend. The box states the conditions of the fallacy of *begging the question*.

BEGGING THE QUESTION

1. A claim is offered in an argument as a premise in support of a conclusion.
2. The claim is (a) equivalent in meaning to the conclusion or (b) in the context of this argument, acceptable only if the conclusion has already been accepted.

We tend to beg the question in our own arguments and overlook it in the arguments of others when we are dealing with issues whose truth strikes us as self-evident. It is difficult to think of reasons for a claim that seems obvious on the face of it. Hence we end up repeating the claim in different terms when we try to argue for it or using premises that of course show it to be true because they presuppose its truth. The message should be clear: When dealing with matters close to your heart that seem ever so true to you, be on your guard against question-begging reasoning.

When you develop your case to show that this fallacy has occurred, your first move should be to identify the conclusion and the offending premise. Your second move is to show (1) that the premise and conclusion mean the same or (2) that in this instance the premise cannot be accepted unless the conclusion is accepted first.

Inconsistency

Without trying to pinpoint the notion exactly, let's talk for a moment about inconsistency. On the one hand, it is debilitating. Psychological experiments have shown that when subjected to inconsistent treatment by researchers, laboratory animals get so frustrated that they become inactive. Human beings react in the same way. You have probably experienced the frustration of coping with inconsistent demands from parents and teachers. Given the erratic way in which we humans form our beliefs and the sometimes impulsive ways in which we act, it is not surprising that we hold inconsistent beliefs and act in ways that are inconsistent with what we have preached. Another complication is the fact that we sometimes change our minds, whether as a result of careful review of the evidence or because of the sheer force of a more attractive opinion that comes along and captures our fancy. In short, inconsistency is a frustrating but widespread phenomenon of human life. What we are interested in here is not simply the phenomenon but how and why it threatens the practice of argumentation and hence constitutes a logical failure.

Consistency plays a crucial role in argumentation. We may view a good argument as laying down a rational route from premises to conclusion. The argument, as it were, says to us: If you accept the premises (and you wish to be consistent), you must accept the conclusion. Argumentation, then, assumes that people are sensitive to the requirements of consistency. In short, though we may rightly tolerate some inconsistency in other areas of life, in the practice of argumentation we cannot do so without jeopardizing the whole enterprise.

Two statements are inconsistent when, from the truth of one of them, the falsehood of the other follows. For example, consider:

24   1. Aldo is unfailingly truthful.

2. Aldo lied to Louise about his age.

If the first statement is true, then the second must be false, and if the second is true, the first must be false; so the first and the second statements are inconsistent. Anyone who asserted the first ought to deny the second and vice versa. Moreover, if I have made use of the first in an argument, I have forfeited any right to use the second in that argument.

There can be other forms of tension between statements that fall short of this strict logical inconsistency. Compare:

25   1. Aldo usually tells the truth.

2. Aldo lied to Louise about his age.

There is no logical contradiction here. One does sense some tension, but that tension need not be ruinous or worrisome. Someone might use the first statement at one point in the argument and then turn around and use the second later without jeopardizing the process of argumentation nor the argument in which the tension occurred—provided some explanation of how the two statements were compatible in that case were available.

We say a person is inconsistent when he asserts or believes two propositions which cannot both be true at once. We also say a person is inconsistent if she asserts one thing yet acts in a manner that would not be justified if her assertion were true. Children often make such observations about the conduct of their parents, as this one did: "My dad gets bombed every night, double-bombed on weekends; my mother fills the house with smoke, then raises hell when I smoke and goes crazy if I have a drink. Where do they get off trying to keep me from doing things they say are bad for me when they don't practice what they preach?" This teenager is onto something. Her parents say that smoking and drinking are bad, yet Dad drinks and Mom smokes. Now, true, neither parent has *asserted* two inconsistent propositions, but their actions don't line up with their stated policy. If we take Mom's smoking as in some way endorsing the proposition that it is okay to smoke, then there is a kind of inconsistency. There is no logical obligation to dismiss someone's advice merely because he or she doesn't follow it, yet such failure to practice what you preach undermines the credibility of the one giving the advice.

The fallacy of *inconsistency* occurs only when an inconsistency undermines an argument. When two premises of an argument are inconsistent, for instance, we are getting conflicting signals from the arguer. She asks us to grant the conclusion on the basis of the premises she offers. However, we don't know which of the two inconsistent premises to accept, and we know we can only accept one. Alternatively, the premise is incompatible with the conclusion. Here again, we are in a bind: We can't accept both the premise and the conclusion. So the argument undermines itself. Finally, the premise may be incompatible with something else the arguer says, either on the same occasion or at some other time. Then we face the question, Which are we to accept, the premise or the incompatible assertion? The effect of inconsistency in an argument is to undercut the acceptability of a premise. We cannot then be justified in taking that premise as support for the conclusion. Inconsistency in arguments short-circuits the segment of the argument in which it occurs.

An illustration of this can be found in the memoirs of Vincent Theresa, a former mafioso, which included the following qualified defense of the brotherhood:

26   Not that mobsters are all bad. There are plenty of good things about them the public might be interested in. For instance, does the public know whether mob guys are patriotic or not? The truth is, most are. We don't think about undermining the government. We corrupt politicians, but that's only so we can do business.

Theresa is trying to persuade us that mob guys are not without redeeming features. One main premise is that the mob is patriotic, and this premise is defended by Theresa's contention that the mob has no intention of undermining the government. Theresa then tries to undercut the unspoken counterargument, that the Mafia corrupts politicians, by maintaining that the purpose of such corruption is only to "do business" (and, presumably, not to undermine the government). The trouble is that whatever the Mafia's intentions, corrupting politicians does, in fact, serve to undermine the government. When people find out that politicians are being bought off by the Mafia, they lose confidence in those politicians; and the knowledge that some politicians can be corrupted is bound to undermine one's faith in government. So we are asked to believe that most mob guys are patriotic; at the same time, we are given evidence that they are not. The result is that the argument goes nowhere. Either the premise that the mob is patriotic must be accepted, in which case we must reject Theresa's evidence that the mob corrupts politicians; or, and this is more likely, we must accept Theresa's evidence and deny that the mob is patriotic. We can't do both; we haven't, from the argument and Theresa's comments, any basis for choosing one or the other. We cannot accept the premise.

It is harder to see how inconsistency between assertion and action can undermine an argument. After all, an argument is a piece of discourse, a collection of assertions, while an action is not a statement in any unmetaphorical sense. Still, actions imply statements in that the principle by which any action is justified can be expressed as a statement. This explains why, when the principle of an adjacent action is incompatible with the premise or conclusion of an argument, we find ourselves at a loss which to accept: the premise and conclusion or the principle. A good example was cited by Trudy Govier in an article in the *Informal Logic Newsletter* (June 1981).

27   Several years ago Ontario and Federal government officials in Canada, having exhorted Canadians to spend winter holiday money at home in Canada, nevertheless abandoned our northern country for winter vacations in Florida and the Caribbean. We can imagine the following fairly plausible arguments the Canadian officials might have made:

28   1. To help Canada's balance of payments position, as many Canadian dollars should be kept in the country as possible.

2. The Canadian economy would benefit from increased spending in our winter tourism and entertainment industries.

3. Canadians should spend their winter holiday money at home in Canada.

Yet many of these same officials vacationed in Florida and the Caribbean. They must have been operating on some such principle as the following:

> PR1: It is not imperative that Canadians spend their winter holiday money at home in Canada.

Now the problem with this argument, given this principle, is that if we accept the principle, it tells against the conclusion of the argument. (In that case, incidentally, the stated premises cannot be adequate support for the conclusion.) On the other hand, if we accept the premises, we are led to accept the argument's conclusions, but then we must reject the principle. The same officials enunciated the argument and acted in conformity with the principle. Which are we to believe: their argument or their actions? The two are inconsistent, and we have no way of deciding which is acceptable. Hence the argument's premises are undercut and we cannot accept its conclusion in this situation. We say, in cases where conduct conflicts with argument in this way, that the fallacy of *inconsistency* has been committed.

The conditions for this fallacy are listed in the box.

INCONSISTENCY

1. In an argument, an assertion serves as a premise for a conclusion.
2. There is an inconsistency between (a) the assertion and some other premise or some other assertion made by the arguer or (b) the premise or the conclusion and some principle of an action performed or recommended by the arguer.

Here is an example that will test your understanding of the conditions and the fallacy of *inconsistency*. Syndicated columnist Joseph Sobran, in a column in the *Detroit Free Press*, took the liberal press in the United States to task for preaching in favor of women's rights and equality for women while, in their practice, failing to hire women in top management positions. After the defeat of the Equal Rights Amendment, *Time* magazine ran a cover story about women and equality. Sobran wrote: "The story was written by a man, with the aid of a woman or two. Never mind. It said all the right things. It ringingly affirmed that we are all equal." In the same issue of *Time*, Sobran reported, twenty-four out of twenty-six stories were written by men, and only one of the top twenty-four names on the masthead (and none of the top fourteen) belonged to a woman. Sobran also noted that at *Newsweek*, the top seven jobs were held by men, and only three of the top sixteen positions were held by women. He found that similar proportions applied to the "great liberal dailies." At *The New York Times*, two of the top sixteen and none of the top eight names on the masthead belonged to women and at the *Washington Post*, there was one female in the top seven and three in the top seventeen. Sobran continued:

29   Day after day, these publications favor us with articles and columns designed to raise our consciousness on the subject of women's role in society. Why are we so hypnotized by their pompous cant that when an editorial assaults us with it, we don't automatically look down the page to see how the preacher himself is behaving?

Our question is this: Has Sobran identified instances of the fallacy of *inconsistency*? Note first that unless the articles and columns in question contained arguments for equality for women, we could not speak of a fallacy here, though we could still make the moral judgment of hypocrisy (as Sobran does). Let us assume that some of these press sources do present arguments. Is the fact that an editorial argues for equality for women while the newspaper or magazine in which it appears is dominated by men at top editorial and management levels grounds for a charge of *inconsistency*? We believe the answer depends on the hiring practices and policies of the newspaper or magazine in question. Only if it has a policy of hiring women in order to achieve the balance of men and women at all levels of the organization, and is implementing that policy, would the principle of its conduct be consistent with its editorial position. Otherwise, a charge of *inconsistency* would be applicable. Each newspaper and magazine has to be examined on the merits of its own practices, but we are inclined to agree with Sobran that his statistics make a prima facie case for inconsistency between preaching and performance and, if the preaching is argument, that a case for the fallacy of *inconsistency* could be made.

Conclusion

A final point should be made to introduce the next part of the book. Treat the presence of a fallacy in an argument as a warning light, not as a stop sign. Rare is the argument that is destroyed completely by the presence of a fallacy. Even arguments that beg the question usually contain other, non-question-begging premises. And treat the warning light as an amber flash on your own mental dashboard, not as a strobe to beam into the eyes of the arguer whose argument you are assessing. Accusations of "Fallacy!", like personal character attacks, are the least efficient way to elicit a change in your opponent's reasoning or conclusions. Gentle, patient argumentation of your own promises much more success. Keep in mind what Proverbs has to say: "A soft answer turneth away wrath; but grevious words [like "Fallacy!"] stir up anger."[2]

EXERCISES

Directions. For each extract assigned, decide whether there are any arguments present, and, if so, whether they contain any of the fallacies you have studied so far. If you think there is no argument, explain what the function of the passage is. If you think any arguments are logically good ones, try to anticipate possible criticisms, and argue against such criticisms. If you think there are any fallacious arguments, write a critique supporting your judgment (see details below). If you think there is some fallacy not covered (yet), say so. While you may reasonably expect that these passages contain instances of the fallacies taken up in this chapter, understand that some passages may not contain arguments at all, some may contain arguments with fallacies you have not encountered, and some of the arguments may be fallacy-free.

For *each* fallacy you identify, do the following in your critique: (1) identify: the argument's conclusion, the premise(s) in which the fallacy occurs, who commits the fallacy, and the name of the fallacy (if it is not one covered so far, describe it); (2) formulate an argument to convince a neutral observer that the fallacy you allege has indeed been committed; and (3) say whether any fallacy completely undercuts the argument or whether the argument can be repaired, and explain why you think so.

1. *Background: Rolling Stone* carried an article about The Lemonheads (a rock group) that elicited this response:

    The Lemonheads are not worthy of their candy namesake. Proof positive that a pretty face and some chords will get a full page in your mag every time.

2. *Background:* This is an excerpt from a letter to the *San Francisco Chronicle* (July 13, 1992) about reproduction rights:

    Three cheers for those who ask the question, Don't men have reproduction rights? It takes both a male and a female to make a baby; it ought to take both to decide whether to keep it or not.

3. *Background:* In the early 1970s, a commission was established in New York City to investigate allegations of corruption in the police department. One of the witnesses before the commission was a police officer who, when apprehended for taking payoffs, "turned" undercover agent. He gave key testimony, claiming that all plain-clothes detectives took regular payoffs and that "there's no way one man can go in a division and remain straight." Following his testimony, the police commissioner told reporters:

    That is an absurd charge. I know for a fact that there are plainclothesmen who are not "on the pad."

4. *Background:* Michigan is one of many states which, at present, does not allow capital

---

[2] (XV, 1). Thanks to Hendrik van der Breggen for this reference.

punishment. In 1982, there was another round in the debate about whether or not to reinstate the death penalty. One letter opposing the idea came from Willis X. Harris, president of the Michigan Lifers Association (an organization of individuals who have been sentenced to life in prison). The following is an excerpt from his letter to the *Detroit Free Press*:

> We have capital punishment in thirty-eight states, and their statistics show no significant decrease in capital crimes. The first-degree murderer is the least likely to repeat and the most likely to repent his or her crime. Nationwide, corrections officials report that lifers make the best prisoners and are a stabilizing influence in their prisons. So clearly, capital punishment is not something we should be going for.

5. *Background:* Defending what he called "the Christian Right" against an article by Fred Clarkson in *Mother Jones* (November/December 1991), Robert Simonds wrote:

> According to Fred Clarkson, the Christian Right is a dangerous movement, taking advantage of our democracy to promote their evil agenda. We believe in democracy and its institutions, including public schools. One bedrock principle is to vote for people who believe as you do. Christians comprise 75 percent of all homes above the Mason-Dixon line and 85 percent of all homes south of the line. We should have 75 to 85 percent Christians in all offices, right? That's democracy!

6. *Background:* The excerpt below is from "In Defense of Culture: The Unravelling Tie that Binds," by Robert Solomon. Solomon is arguing that American cultural identity is threatened and that neither television nor contemporary music is capable of forging the cultural ties needed to bind Americans together. He writes:

> Consider the case of contemporary music: The Beatles are only a name to most 12-year-olds. Beethoven, by contrast, continues to provide the musical themes we can assume (even if wrongly) that all of us have heard, time and time again. This isn't snobbery; it's continuity.

7. *Background:* In a column called "Watergate: Who Can Ever Forget It?" (*Detroit Free Press*, June 1982), William Safire quotes this excerpt from a *Time* magazine article: "Certain effects have found their way into law as a result of Watergate. Congress established the Freedom of Information Act, for example." Safire responds:

> That act was signed into law by Lyndon Johnson on July 4, 1966. . . . *Time*'s minor historical error illustrates the tendency of journalists to attribute everything good for civil liberty in the past decade to the overthrow of the Nixon gang.

8. *Background:* In Chapter 10, we will argue that many advertisements do not offer arguments to support their claims. Some ads, however, do contain arguments, including the newspaper ad from which we quote this example. The ad was for a brand of so-called "natural" potato chips that were said to contain no additives whatever. The strategy of the ad was to contrast its "no-additives" ingredients with the ingredients of a competitor's brand, and so, making reference to the competitor's ingredients, the ad contained the headline, "Is this a 'potato chip' or a chemistry set?" Part of the ad's copy ran as follows:

> The ingredient list on the package of a new so-called [potato chip] reads as follows: "dehydrated potatoes; vegetable shortening; salt; mono- and di-glycerides; dextrose; ascorbic acid; sodium phosphates; sodium bisulfate; and BHA added to preserve freshness."
>
> Now a chemist probably understands this concoction, but where does that leave the rest of us? Are we supposed to eat what we can't even pronounce, much less understand?

9. *Background:* The argument below is adapted from a Canadian magazine article entitled "The Case against Abortion":

> In 1988, more than 152,000 women had their children killed before they could be born. These numbers are on the increase every year. By the end of 1995, we will have reached the 200,000 level. The percentages are similar in western Europe. They are greater in the Soviet Union. No one would be against abortion when the woman's life is at stake, but that situation is now exceedingly rare. The present mass feticide takes place almost always for convenience. Medical professionals tell us that 95 percent of abortions now performed kill the healthy offspring of healthy women. How has this quiet medical slaughter become part of modern societies everywhere?

10. *Background:* The debate about the aggressive behavior of men brought this letter to a newspaper:

> I don't want to hear any more of this talk about how barbaric and brutal men are. I work in the emergency room of Parkview Hospital. Allow me to tell you what I have seen lately. The other night, they brought in a man who had been beaten silly by his wife while he was sleeping. In another case, a man came in complaining of a headache that had lasted for several days. X-rays revealed a bullet in his head; later he found a note from his wife explaining that she had shot him while he was asleep and that he should go to the hospital. A young baby boy was brought in with bruises all over his body; his mother had beaten him. That's the kind of thing that makes me think this talk of men being the aggressive ones is overblown.

11. *Background:* A Roanoke, Virginia, prosecutor announced his decision to initiate legal proceedings against the driver of a school bus who lost control of the bus on a slippery side road and skidded into a child standing waiting for the bus. That prompted this letter:

> I am a law-abiding individual, I believe in our system. We must have laws, courts, judges, and jurors to determine guilt or innocence. But there comes a time when we must realize the human side of things as well. I am referring here to an incident involving a lady who was driving a school bus in Roanoke and accidentally hit and killed a child.
>
> This lady has tried herself over and over again. Nothing any court can do can punish her more than what she has done to herself. She has to live with this for the rest of her life.
>
> I feel for the parents who lost their sweet little child, but what we are doing in taking this case to court is not going to bring the child back. Leave this woman alone! Get on to the people who are the real criminals; those who break the law by robbing, stealing, killing, and so on. Don't waste our tax money on this innocent victim of an accident.

12. *Background:* The following is an excerpt from a review of *Nietzsche: A Critical Life* by Ronald Hayman. The review, written by J. M. Cameron, appeared in the *New York Review of Books* (October 1980). The excerpt begins by quoting a sentence from the book.

> This mistake is connected, I suspect, with Hayman's initial agreement with Nietzsche: "Nietzsche saw that we can have no objective knowledge about the facts which determine our condition." As it stands, this is surely false or without sense. We know many of the facts that determine our condition, even though there are philosophical techniques for inducing in us perplexities about their analysis.

13. *Background:* In his book *The Soviet Approach to International Political Communication*, Paul Herscheneto attributes the following argument to Soviet bureaucracy (p. 305):

There is a manifest evil in the world. All right-thinking people, regardless of party, abhor that evil. The main exponents of the evil are the enemies of the Soviet Union or the Communist Party. The Soviet Regime, or the party, unflinchingly combat it. Hence, all right-thinking people, regardless of party, must count the Soviet Union, or the Communist Party, as an ally, and act accordingly.

14. *Background:* There is an ongoing debate in Canada and the United States about doctors' incomes. This particular excerpt comes from a spirited defense of doctors and their incomes in a column entitled, "Stiff Medicine for Doctor Bashers," written by Nicholas Rety, a urologist practicing in Vernon, British Columbia. This passage from the column, which appeared in *Maclean's* (August 1981), criticizes those who think doctors make too much money. (Keep in mind that these are 1981 figures; also, the Canadian dollar was worth about 85 percent of the United States dollar at that time).

Robert Evans, a University of British Columbia economics professor, sneers indignantly that doctors' incomes are three times the average income of the general public. He gets wide coverage in the west coast media, yet he ignores the fact that theoretically, a worker of modest skills earning $12 an hour, with standard overtime benefits could almost equal the doctor's average annual income of $53,422 by working the doctor's sixty-six-hour week. Much public resentment is stirred up by such critics who, in truth, only comment on issues from a professor's chair with tenure (the ultimate in job security) and enjoy a year's sabbatical at public expense every few years.

15. *Background:* The following was sent to the *San Francisco Examiner* (July 19, 1992) by a doctor in San Jose:

Your article about Kate Michelman was well done and, I think, unbiased. However, I must take issue with the so-called "logic" of the abortion rights movement. Nature includes human gestation, and human gestation involves the development and growth of the human, always a person, no matter how small or how immature. The end, the adult, is in the beginning the zygote. The zygote is a person, no matter how many persons deny the fact. Some people even deny their own existence. Some people even deny that 2 plus 2 equals 4.

16. *Background:* The following was written to the *San Francisco Chronicle* in June 1992 concerning the race for President:

When I watched Bill Clinton on the CBS *This Morning* show, I saw a man who is sensitive, thoughtful, and very, very bright. A man who, not incidentally, is very, very right for the job of President of the United States.

Some years back, Madison Avenue sold us on the idea that it was necessary to be on the downside of 60 to head this country. Age is not all that important. Experience is. And Clinton has that in spades. Five terms as governor of Arkansas has given him the seasoning he needs. Four re-elections suggest that he has been doing a good job. Now he's ready for a larger playing field.

I see in Clinton a man with the intellect and vision to lead this country into the twenty-first century and the youthful vigor it will require to carry out his dreams and ours.

CHAPTER FIVE

◆

Fallacies of Diversion

Introduction

The fallacies in this chapter work by diverting attention from the proposition at issue. Each fallacy accomplishes this diversion in a different way, but the effect in each case is the same: to shift the focus of the argument.

Worth noting is the locale of these fallacies. They typically reside in adversarial contexts; that is, when one person is attacking someone else's position or defending his or her position from someone else's attack. Some examples of adversarial contexts are political campaigns, management-labor disputes, and public controversies over issues of vital importance such as capital punishment, abortion, and sexual harassment. In such cases, the arguer runs the risk of wanting too much to defeat the opponent, a desire that can work at cross-purposes to the goal of arriving at the most reasonable position. Watch for these fallacies, then, particularly in adversarial contexts.

Straw Person

A cardinal principle that governs all argumentation is this: *The position criticized must be the position actually held*. This principle is particularly prone to violation in adversarial contexts, where each side may want to make the other side look bad. The temptation to distort the opponent's view is strong. What we call the fallacy of *straw person* is the direct result of a violation of this principle.

Suppose you're having an argument with someone. The topic is one you feel strongly about. You are aware of several positions that you consider dead wrong. Now your antagonist makes a claim that sounds awfully close to one of those dreadfully mistaken views. In the heat of controversy, it is tempting to jump on your opponent for holding the view that you're familiar with and that you *know* (think) to be false. You don't have the patience to listen to the significant differences between your opponent's actual position and the one you are eager to criticize. Or, if you think your opponent's stand sounds downright dangerous, or morally outrageous, your emotional antagonism can completely blind you to significant differences between what was said and what it reminds you of. You may launch into a defense of democracy, or free enterprise, or the institution of marriage when your opponent didn't really mean to put any of those in question. Finally, if you're devious, you can deliberately misrepresent the views of your opponent and proceed to make your opponent look silly for saying something he or she didn't say at all.

In any case, when you misrepresent your opponent's position, attribute to that person an implausible or inaccurate version that you can easily demolish, and then proceed to argue against the trumped-up version as though it were your opponent's, you commit the fallacy of *straw person*. The fallacy also occurs when you wind up defending a position that is not really the one you're supposed to be defending. The following example from an interview with a TV news reporter illustrates the latter way of committing the fallacy. In the background here is the ongoing controversy about the relative merits of print journalism and electronic journalism (principally television news.)

1   INTERVIEWER: How do you feel about the description of broadcast news as shallow and too entertainment-oriented?

REPORTER: Well, I consider who's making the criticism. I spend a lot of time with print people, and once they get to know us, they understand we're as hardworking as they are.

The position that the reporter is defending is not the position he should be defending if he intends to deal with the criticism mentioned by the interviewer: that broadcast news is too entertainment-oriented. The reporter makes it sound as though the issue were how hardworking electronic journalists are. It's as if the question was "What do you say to the criticism that you broadcast journalists are not hardworking?" But that was not the question at all. The reporter's response was thus guilty of defending against a criticism that had not been made (that broadcast news reporters are not hardworking) and, in the course of doing this, failing to respond to the criticism that *was* made (that broadcast news is too entertainment-oriented).

The exchange we are going to look at now contains a sequence of instances of this fallacy. It appeared in the *Windsor Star* several years ago; the topic is capital punishment. First, we quote part of the letter to the editor that started the debate off. It is from Professor Lawrence LaFave, who is opposed to capital punishment.

2   The vast majority of Canadian police officers appear to favor capital punishment, especially when one of their colleagues is murdered in the line of duty. These officers are entitled to their opinion. However, the public should not take their views on this subject seriously, and the mass communications media (with special reference to the *Windsor Star*) should not continue to give so much space to their views.

Reading Comprehension Test

Without glancing back at the example, we ask you to respond to the items below.

1. Professor LaFave opposes letting police express their opinions. True _____ False _____
2. Professor LaFave thinks the public should disregard the views of police on capital punishment. True _____ False _____
3. Professor LaFave thinks media should not report the views of police on capital punishment. True _____ False _____
4. Professor LaFave thinks the pro-capital-punishment view of police should be censored. True _____ False _____

We think the correct answer is, in each case, "False." We will go through the statements one by one and give you our reasoning.

1. LaFave never says "Police should not be allowed to express their opinions," nor anything close to it. The only thing he says that might relate to whether police should be allowed to express their pro-capital-punishment views is his statement that they are "entitled to their opinion." That might be understood to imply that he thinks they should be allowed to express it. Certainly he nowhere says they *shouldn't* be allowed to.
2. This statement is tricky. LaFave does say "the public should not take their views on this subject seriously," but that does not mean they should disregard their views. For instance, you may not take the views of terrorist revolutionaries seriously and still think it important not to disregard those views completely. You don't ponder their ideology trying to decide whether to adopt it yourself, but you do make a point of noting it, particularly since it represents a threat to international security. In short, we would argue that not taking something seriously is not equivalent to disregarding it.
3. LaFave didn't encourage the media not to report police views; he merely urged them to reduce the amount of space devoted to reporting the police viewpoint.
4. LaFave said absolutely nothing at all about suppressing (or censoring) police opinions, nor did anything he said lead to such a suggestion. What we've said about "disregarding" goes for "ignoring" those opinions, too.

If you answered "True" to any of these questions, it may be that you did not read carefully enough. We cannot stress too much the importance of avoiding attributing to someone views they did not express. Unless you do, you won't be evaluating the actual assertions you're looking at. You'll be criticizing a different position, and you will thus commit what we call the fallacy of *straw person*.

It's hard to listen carefully to or read thoughtfully the arguments of someone who espouses a view you consider harmful or dangerous. Yet the practice of argumentation demands that you do so. Although there is a dimension of this task that depends on character and integrity, skill is also involved. You can learn to do a better job of hearing the position of someone you deeply disagree with by paraphrasing it. The reciprocity exercises we discuss later will help develop that skill.

The point of the recent exercise was not just to emphasize the importance of careful reading but to prepare you for the *Windsor Star's* editorial response to Professor LaFave. The *Star* began by quoting the segment of the letter we've been looking at and then went on to say:

3   Wrong, Dr. LaFave. Police officers are entitled to their opinion, as your letter says. But police officers and other groups are also entitled to express their opinions and have them reported. The media would be failing in their responsibility if they did not give space to the opinions of all groups. And on the subject of capital punishment, a good case can be made for greater attention to the views of police groups, which are close to the situation. Nor should such views be disregarded by the public.

The *Star* agrees with Dr. LaFave in his opposition to capital punishment and disagrees with the anti-abolition stand that he feels is the majority view of Canadian police officers. But the *Star* does not agree that the view should be suppressed, censored, or ignored. Democracy is a process of making choices after the facts are known, the alternatives discussed, and the opinions weighed.

We believe the *Star* is guilty of four counts of *straw person* in its rejoinder. The fallacy can be characterized in general in terms of the following conditions listed in the box, so we'll need to show that the *Star*'s response to LaFave qualifies on each point:

STRAW PERSON

1. A critic attributes a particular position to an opponent.
2. The opponent's position is not the one the critic attributed to him or her but a different one.
3. The critic criticizes that different position as though it were the position actually held by the opponent.

Typically, the attributed view will be a much easier position to attack than the actual position. That's where the "straw" part of "straw person" comes in; it is easier to rip apart a straw figure—an effigy—than it is to take apart a real one. The fallacy consists of not only distorting the arguer's position but subsequently attacking the distorted (and usually easier-to-attack) position.

In the case of the *Star,* we've already shown that the first two conditions of the fallacy are satisfied. We based our Reading Comprehension Test on four statements that the *Star* appears to have attributed to LaFave. The editorial says, "Wrong, Dr. LaFave," referring to the first three claims; and the second paragraph proceeds to disagree with the fourth claim. If you reread the editorial, you'll see that it supports claims it takes to be opposed to Dr. LaFave's position. That's one standard way of criticizing a position: Show its opposite to be true. Of course, this procedure also reinforces the erroneous impression that LaFave actually did hold the opposite view.

The parade of *straw persons* in this exchange did not end with the *Star's* editorial response to Professor LaFave. He then wrote a rejoinder to the *Star* calling attention to the distortions we have noted and adding:

4   The *Star* suggests I am antidemocratic. By its view of democracy, if an inmate of an institute for the feebleminded, innocent of physics, argued that he had refuted Einstein's theory of relativity, his statement ought to be granted as much press coverage as the same claim made by an eminent physicist. If ten out of ten physicians believe a man has measles, while eleven out of eleven street cleaners deduce he does not, then by *Star* logic, he (by a vote of eleven to ten) does not have measles.

LaFave's point here is that the *Star* is committed to a view of democracy that would give the incompetent as much voice as the expert and permit majority rule to decide in matters best left to specialists. Now LaFave is the one who's guilty of *straw person*. Before we argue that, we offer two observations.

First, look at our sentence following this last quotation from LaFave. In that one sentence, we have compressed his views and given an interpretation of what he's saying or actually committed to. We've tried to cut through the metaphors and express the point that it seems he meant to make. Slipping your fingers through the rhetoric and withdrawing the kernel of assertion is a skill you'll need to become proficient at.

Second, notice, too, that LaFave was *extrapolating* the view of democracy he attributed to the *Star*. He was drawing an inference from what was said. The position he attributed to the *Star* was one he took to be logically implied by what it stated. Specifically, he took three points: (1) the *Star's* insistence that it should give space to police opinions about capital punishment, (2) the *Star's* disregarding his own claim (argued elsewhere in his letter) that the police have no special competence to judge the merits of capital punishment, and (3) the *Star's* lecture on democracy. From these three points, he drew the inference that the *Star* endorsed a view of democracy that would allow majority rule to decide on matters requiring specialized knowledge and would give equal media coverage to the views of lay persons and authorities on subjects calling for such expertise.

This move, extrapolation from a stated position, is frequently used in argumentation as a way of exploring the merits of the position. In making it, to avoid the *straw-person* fallacy, one must stick to inferences logically warranted by the original position.

We contend that in his response Professor LaFave commits *straw person* because he attacks (by ridicule) an extrapolation not entailed by the *Star's* stated view about democracy. We say it's not entailed because we don't think enough is said in the brief response to be able to pin this view onto it. The *Star* may hold this view, but neither LaFave nor we can know that from the scant bit that's been said. In ridiculing a view of democracy that he had no adequate grounds for attributing to the *Star*, LaFave committed the very fallacy which he had rightly accused the newspaper of.

It should be clear that your capacity to detect this fallacy depends on your knowing the positions taken by others on matters you're interested in. If you don't know who holds what positions on the issues you're dealing with, then you'll find yourself persuaded by *straw-person* criticisms.

Earlier we said that all argumentation must abide by this principle: The position being criticized must be the position actually held.

Even a critic with honorable intentions may unwittingly alter the position he or she is attacking, which leads to another principle of logical self-defense: *When two individuals are on opposite sides of an issue, the accuracy of either's statement or any other representation of the views of the opponent must be checked*. In other words, be cautious of the move that begins, "Now my opponent believes that . . . but such a view is surely wrong because . . ." Our advice is "Find out for yourself what the opponent's position is; don't take the critic's word for it." If you follow these two principles and if you have some awareness of and information about the issues being discussed, you will avoid being diverted by *straw-person* rejoinders.

There is one final matter which we want to discuss in this connection— reciprocity. An exercise that we recommend goes like this:

The exercise works best if *A* and *B* are on opposite sides of the issue. *A* states his position, including, if you like, some of the reasons why he thinks his position is correct. Then *B* has to do two things: (1) restate *A*'s view *to his satisfaction,* and (2) restate *A*'s reasons for holding the position, again *to his satisfaction.* Then, and only then, is *B* allowed to enter a criticism of *A*'s view or his reasons for holding it. The process can then be repeated with *A* and *B* switching roles. To do this, *A* must now restate *B*'s critical conclusion (about her own position) *to B's satisfaction.* Then *A* must restate *B*'s reasons, *to B's satisfaction.* Only then may *A* respond to *B*'s criticisms. The process can go on indefinitely, with each side restating the views and the reasoning of the other to the other's satisfaction.

What the exercise demands is the ability—one not easily acquired—to set forth a position with which one does not agree, and the reasoning behind it, and to do this to the satisfaction of someone who takes that position. This is good dialectical training, and it provides an experiential reference point for nipping *straw persons* in the bud.

Ad Hominem

When you disagree with something, the logically appropriate response is to direct your analytic powers to that position, examine its premises, look for any fallacies, and/or look at its implications. We have just seen one way in which arguers divert attention from the issue and the position, by attacking a straw person—a distorted version of the arguer's position. Another common tactic in adversarial contexts is to ignore the issue altogether and, instead, attack the person who asserted it, either by casting aspersions on the person's character and background or, perhaps, by discussing his or her motives. In some cases, such an "attack" is, in fact, appropriate, and we'll discuss those cases. But in a great many instances, such an attack is beside the point. An irrelevant attack on the person instead of the position is the fallacy called *ad hominem* (literally, "against the person"). Here's an example of one version.

Abusive Ad Hominem

In the fall of 1989, Allan Bloom's book *The Closing of the American Mind* was published. In it, Bloom attacked rock music as an overtly sexual form of music that contributes to an overall climate of promiscuity. He mentioned Mick Jagger's "pouty lips and wagging butt" as examples of how rock promotes sexuality. In a review of the book in *Rolling Stone,* William Greider wrote:

5   Bloom's attack on rock is inane. Still, the professor is correct about one important distinction between the kids of the 50s and those of the 80s: in the 50s the kids talked endlessly about sex; today the young people actually do it. This seems to drive the 56-year-old Bloom—who is still a bachelor—crazy. Bloom denounces Jagger with such relish that one may wonder if the professor himself is turned on by Mick's pouty lips and wagging butt.

After his initial statement, which signals his strong disagreement. Greider's response consists of an attack that is largely personal. He makes no attempt to deal with Bloom's arguments. He might, for example, have argued that Bloom makes casual claims that are not well supported by evidence. Instead, his comments are little more than innuendo about Bloom's own sexuality. He is "still a bachelor." Because we have difficulty seeing how one's marital status would disqualify a person's views on rock music, Bloom's status as a bachelor would seem to have no bearing on his argument about rock music. Next, Greider indulges in a bit of lay psychoanalysis, hinting that perhaps Bloom secretly likes Jagger's butt and so is highly repressed. The implication here is that Bloom is homosexual. Even if this were true, it would not have any relevance to an appraisal of Bloom's argument. Bloom's argument is about the effects of rock music on sexuality in general; his own sexuality is not the issue. So this remark is irrelevant and makes no contribution whatsoever. Thus Greider is guilty of *ad hominem*. We call this an *abusive ad hominem* because it consists largely of personal abuse.

In an issue of *Harper's* magazine, James Kenneson had an article called "China Stinks," detailing his year's experience in the Chinese province of Szechwan. What Kenneson had to say about Szechwan was not flattering, and it brought this response in *Harper's*:

6   I regret that *Harper's* was used as a vehicle to spread the stench by James Kenneson, who wrote the article "China Stinks," which appeared in the April issue. I can't believe that such a distinguished magazine would want to nauseate its reader with such undigested material. *It is obviously the work of a constipated and jaundiced man* who has just spent a year in outlandish and poverty-stricken Szechwan, where these was no running water, toilet, or other *amenities of life to which Mr. Kenneson had been so accustomed in Indianapolis.* [Emphasis ours.]

Instead of addressing the response to the actual assertions that make up Kenneson's position, the writer attacks Kenneson personally (in the words we italicized). In effect, he is psychoanalyzing Kenneson, claiming that his own disappointment with conditions in Szechwan caused him to write an unsympathetic article. That may well be true, but it must first be shown that Kenneson's position is inadequate. If his facts were incorrect, his interpretations questionable, then the critic should be prepared to detail these for us instead of launching a personal attack on the author. Such an attack is irrelevant. We don't need to know or determine whether Kenneson was constipated, literally or metaphorically, as far as assessment of his position goes. We don't need to know whether he was accustomed to a comfortable life. This irrelevant attack on the person is another instance of the abusive *ad hominem* fallacy, since the critic's main focus is on the person of the arguer and consists of little more than heaping abuse on Kenneson.

Circumstantial Ad Hominen

By contrast, the circumstantial *ad hominem* fallacy occurs when, instead of abusing the person, the arguer refers to circumstances in the arguer's situation and uses that reference to discredit the arguer's position. In *Backlash* (1991), Susan Faludi discusses the apparent change in direction of Betty Friedan's thinking between *The Feminine Mystique* (1963) and *The Second Stage* (1981). After briefly recapping Friedan's position, Faludi asks, "Why was Friedan stomping on a movement which she did so much to create and lead?" (*Backlash,* p. 322). (If you are wondering about the appropriateness of "stomping on," you're onto an important concern, one we take up in Chapter 7 in a discussion of the role of language in argumentation.) After considering one explanation for Friedan's change in direction (that the backlash tendency makes it inevitable to "turn and bite one's tail"), Faludi writes:

7   But in Friedan's case, another possibility presents itself as well. A closer reading of *The Second Stage* suggests that the prime mistake the "radical feminists" made was not following her orders. . . . [H]er book is punctuated with the tantrums of a fallen leader who is clearly distressed and angry that she wasn't allowed to be the Alpha wolf (leader) as long as she would have liked. (*Backlash,* Crown Publishing Inc., p. 322)

Even if Faludi's claims are true, without a detailed critique of Freidan's position, these remarks amount to a circumstantial *ad hominem.* Instead of directly dealing with the logical strengths and weaknesses of Friedan's position, she attacks the person by referring to the circumstances that led to Friedan's position. Even if she were correct, this would not be relevant to an assessment of Friedan's claims about the movement. Friedan's reasoning and her evidence have not been addressed, and their validity cannot be determined simply by reference to the circumstances of her life. For another instance, consider this letter to *World Press* magazine (April 1992, p. 2):

8   Phillip Adams's comments that Americans have "enthusiasm for assassinating national leaders," "are high on individualism and low on ideology," "can no longer distinguish reality from the movies," and that "America is a society that is patently going bonkers" really sting. Is this why we have such a love affair with Australia, an affair that has made vacationing there such a large and rapidly growing industry?

Whether Americans are vacationing in Australia has no bearing on whether Adam's comments are truthful or insightful. His comments have to do with problems in American society (a penchant for assassinating national leaders and so on). But the letter writer is attempting to combine Adams's personal circumstances (he is an Australian) with the fact that Americans in large numbers now vacation in Australia to discredit his criticisms. The implication is, "If we're so crazy and we like your country, what does that say about your country?" This may work as effective put-down on television, but as a reply to Adams's criticisms, it is beside the point.

Ad hominem is characterized by the conditions listed in the box.

AD HOMINEM

1. The critic responds to the position of an arguer by launching a personal attack on the arguer, ignoring the arguer's position.
2. The personal attack on the arguer is irrelevant to any assessment of the argument.

To show how to use the conditions in the box, we use the following example:

In the fall of 1991, the United States Senate held hearings to determine whether Federal Judge Clarence Thomas should become an associate justice of the Supreme Court. A former employee of Thomas's by the name of Anita Hill, alleging that Thomas had engaged in activities that could be considered sexual harassment, said, among other things, that he had, in her presence, made reference to a pornographic film featuring a character named Long Dong Silver and had also asked out loud about a "pubic hair on my Coke." In a column following the hearings, a columnist for the *Detroit Free Press* wrote:

9   . . . not that there weren't figures at the hearing who rowed heroically against the stream. Senator Orrin Hatch of Utah, he of the shuddering little chin, fulminated against the "perversity" of the accusations against the nominee: *Imagine, a respectable man making reference to pubic hairs on Coke cans to a woman. Imagine, such a man watching films of Long Dong Silver.* [Emphasis ours.]

The senator really ought to get a life. . . . The porn industry would go broke in a week if it were patronized only by drooling perverts.

The columnist is guilty of *ad hominem.* Here is our reasoning:

First, the columnist responds to a position Hatch has taken by attacking Hatch rather than his position. Hatch's position is that Thomas is a man of such character that the remarks attributed to him could not and would not have been made by him. The columnist attacks Hatch first by referring to his "shuddering little chin," a feature that is meant to indicate weakness in his character. The next personal attack comes when he says that Hatch "ought to get a life," implying that he is naive and out of touch.

Second, the attack on Hatch is irrelevant to any assessment of his position. Hatch is defending Thomas, and certainly it would have been possible to criticize and evaluate his defense without making abusive remarks about his character. Thus those attacks were here irrelevant. And we would charge the columnist with *ad hominem*.

We need to make two additional comments. First, you may not have noticed the *straw person* the columnist slipped in. The issue here was not whether Thomas had watched pornographic movies but whether he had made unwelcome sexual remarks in the presence of Anita Hill. In this context, the issue of Thomas's watching pornography was not what should have been argued; rather, the point should have been that his references to pornography did not constitute sexual harassment. Notice how much more difficult this case would be to make.

Second, in becoming a candidate for the position of associate justice of the United States Supreme Court, Thomas's record as a jurist and his character are both fair game. That is, not only the alleged instances of sexual harassment but also his attitudes toward, and his personal use of, pornography are potentially legitimate issues. There are instances when reference to character is relevant.

As we have seen, an attack on the person can come in a variety of forms: a criticism of his or her personality or character, a derogatory crack about the person's ethnic or racial background, a condemnation of behavior ("People in glass houses shouldn't throw stones" is an example of that one), or speculation about motives or special interests. In fact, any response that attacks the person can be *ad hominem* if it steers attention away from the issue under debate and toward the person who proposed it.

Legitimate Attacks on the Person

However—and we want to put this "however" in flashing lights—finding a controversy in which someone has been personally criticized is not enough to charge the fallacy of *ad hominem*. In certain situations it is relevant to attack a person as a means of discrediting that person's views. That's why we require that condition 2 exist in order for an argument to be a fallacious argument *ad hominem*. It's difficult to come up with a rule of thumb for distinguishing legitimate from illegitimate criticisms of the person when the dispute is over a position. Each case will have to be judged on its merits. Instead of a rule of thumb or a general principle indicating when it is relevant to attack the person, and hence when such an argument cannot be considered an *ad hominem* fallacy, we describe three sets of circumstances under which an *ad hominem* argument may be legitimate.

Appeals to Authority, or to Expert Opinion.   If in the course of developing my argument, I ask you to believe something I say by arguing that an authority or expert on the subject says it's true, you may legitimately question the background or motives of that authority. If I'm asking you to accept the point just because she or he says so, then it's fair to challenge credentials and to be critical of the authority's interests. Suppose I tell you that Nikes are good basketball shoes and cite Bo Jackson's endorsement of them as my authority. If you point out that Jackson is employed by Nike to make their commercials, you don't commit *ad hominem,* even though you are questioning his motives in endorsing the product instead of evaluating the shoes on their own merits. For in the case we're imagining, Jackson's endorsement of the shoes may be judged, indeed should be judged, in the light of his tie with the manufacturer. He would have an interest in people's buying those shoes whether they were good ones or not. On the other hand, he might have chosen to endorse Nike's shoes over the other brands because of their superior merits, and this possibility should also be considered in evaluating the argument.

Candidates for Positions of Public Trust.   No matter what arguments they put forward for being qualified for the office sought, it is always legitimate to consider the character and background of political office seekers. Not every facet would be fair game for critical appraisal. It wouldn't particularly matter if the leader of a party turned out to prefer the Rolling Stones to Ravel. If, on the other hand, she has a history of coronary attacks or is suffering from an incurable disease, these factors would probably outweigh even the best arguments for electing her, and someone who made them known would not be guilty of *ad hominem.* In between these extremes are questions like, How relevant is the candidate's sexual behavior?

In the 1992 presidential campaign, a great deal of media attention was given to allegations that Clinton had been unfaithful to his wife. Many people were uncomfortable with this line of questioning because they were unclear about the relevance of this issue to the question of his suitability for the presidency. But on the whole, candidates for public office are vulnerable to personal attacks, and the reason is clear: In electing an official, we elect the human being, not just the mind that shapes the policies. The character of that human being is relevant, though most would argue that there is a line between aspects of character that are purely personal (liking broccoli) and have no effect on trust and other aspects of character, such as believability, that are relevant. Marital infidelity is in a gray area.

Cases of Credibility.   Courtroom proceedings furnish the clearest examples here. Suppose someone has testified in court. If that person is found to be a habitual liar, then this fact damages his or her credibility. The lawyer who points out this personality trait is attacking the person as a means of discrediting the testimony, not as an alternative to confronting it.

It should be clear what makes certain *ad hominem* arguments fallacious. An argument is an attempt to elicit our consent to the truth of a proposition by appealing to other propositions we accept and showing how the acceptance of those leads rationally to the conclusion. In argumentation we eschew appealing to force, flattery, or personality. If you disagree with a claim, logic demands that you inspect the reasons put forward to support it. You normally need know nothing about the person who happens to put forward the claim, whether he or she is rich or poor, college- or high school-educated, supports the Republicans or Democrats.

If arguing *ad hominem* is so often clearly fallacious, then why do people continue to do it and to be persuaded by it? We suspect it's because there's something emotionally satisfying about putting down someone you disagree with. It's irritating to admit that someone you dislike has made a valid point. Also, when you identify with a view, an attack on it seems like an attack on you, so it's natural to counter with a personal challenge of your own. Logical self-defense requires some detachment from your beliefs. It also requires that both arguer and critic embrace the Socratic ideal of pursing the truth, wherever the path to it may lead.

To conclude our treatment, we want to discuss the relationship between *ad hominem* and some other arguments frequently used along with it.

Poisoning the Well

We have mentioned abusive and circumstantial *ad hominem* fallacies. But sometimes people will talk about *poisoning the well*: This means trying to cast doubt in advance upon someone, usually by referring to that person's motives and in this way compromising his or her position. This is much like the *abusive ad hominem*. When the aspersions are irrelevant to the issue, it is a form of *ad hominem* fallacy.

Here is an example.

Let us suppose that Dr. Hubbard is a member of the American Medical Association (AMA), and let us suppose further that that organization has gone on record as being opposed to voluntarily assisted euthanasia. Now Dr. Hubbard develops his own line of argumentation in support of the AMA's position. Someone then responds to his argument by stating: "Of course you're supporting the AMA's position! You're a member; what else can you do?" Here the critic is trying to discredit Hubbard's argument by referring to certain circumstances in his life. But the fact that he is a member of the AMA and that that organization opposes voluntarily assisted euthanasia is irrelevant as far as assessing the merits of Dr. Hubbard's own argument. This is called *poisoning the well* because the arguer is attempting to discredit the position *in advance* by appealing to irrelevant features.

In *Backlash,* Faludi (again discussing Friedan) claims: "Anyone who disagrees with her is simply dismissed as one of those radical feminists who is 'still locked into the first stage thinking themselves' and 'threatened by my attempt to reconceptualize the movement' " (p. 321). If that is Friedan's position, then she is guilty of *poisoning the well* by attempting to discredit criticisms of her position in advance by castigating those who advance them.

Tu Quoque

Closely related to *poisoning the well* is the fallacy sometimes called *tu quoque*; which literally means "you're another" or "but you're doing it, too." Recall the example given in Chapter 4, about a group of members of the Canadian House of Commons who were discovered to have vacationed in Florida after officially taking the position that Canadians should be spending their tourist dollars in Canada. When people found out about this, many were outraged, telling their representatives, "Here you are doing the very thing that you object to!" If this remark was construed as an argument against the position taken by the government representatives, then it was a form of *ad hominem* argument. The fact that the representatives did not follow their own advice certainly suggests a kind of character flaw in them, a moral failure, but it does not, in and of itself, invalidate or detract from their position.

Remember, however, that in some contexts the inconsistency of actions and words may be an appropriate line of criticism. There are cases, for example, where someone acts in a way that is contrary to the way she has advised others to act, and her reasons for doing so are good reasons for others to do so as well. In such a case, she has undermined her own advice and undercut her own position. Here is one author's reasoning:

10 Say that I am a libertine priest. If I ask you to take my advice on my authority, but don't myself follow that advice, you are justified in thinking that my morals undermine my logic. They undermine my *authority*—which is why you were supposed to follow my advice. So, too, the stockbroker: If I advise you to buy stock *x* while I am dumping *x*, you are justified in doubting my logic because you doubt my probity.[1]

To conclude this section, we discuss another fallacy often found in political discourse: *guilt by association.*

Guilt by Association

This fallacy involves attempting to downgrade a person's position by attacking the person instead of the argument, but here the attack on the person is indirect. The person is attacked in terms of his or her alleged associations and relationships.

Suppose one of your friends works for a day-care center and another works for a family-planning bureau; because of these friends, your parents conclude that you're "one of those radical feminists" and a pro-abortionist. Suppose you express agreement with environmentalists' concerns about pollu-

---

[1] Charles A. Willard, *A Theory of Argumentation,* The University of Alabama Press, 1988, Tuscaloosa, p. 227.

tion from petroleum exploration in the Arctic, so your friends accuse you of being a "green freak." What has gone wrong? Certainly people who associate with one another have some common interest, but that doesn't mean all their beliefs are identical. Groups can have some beliefs in common without accepting everything the others believe.

These obvious truths tend to be ignored in the heat of debate. Especially in an adversarial context, you may be tempted to transfer some perceived discredit to an opponent, based on some association that person has with a supposedly discreditable individual or group. The attack is usually (though not always) *ad hominem* in form, since its objective is to refute or discount the opponent's position by attacking his or her person. But it is an indirect strike against the person, made by transferring alleged "guilt" that has accrued to someone else, or to some other group or doctrine, to the opponent, using the connection between them as a bridge. When the mere association is not reason enough to attribute any opprobrium to the opponent, we call this move the fallacy of *guilt by association*.

When the president of the Canadian Medical Association, Dr. Bette Stephenson, pressed for liberalized abortion laws, her stance provoked this letter in response:

11   Perhaps it is not the law which ought to be called into question but the arrogant attitude of the president of the medical society. Laws should be designed to afford reasonable protection for all human life. Statutes made and enforced by sensible, civilized societies should not provide for the thoughtless, wholesale slaughter of those considered to be less than human by some. Remember Dachau and Auschwitz.

By associating the doctor's position with Nazi concentration camps, where millions of Jews and other "undesirables" were murdered under Hitler's horrifying program of genocide, the writer invites enormous antagonism to the doctor's views. To make the association, the writer had first to create a straw person, which he or she did by describing Dr. Stephenson's proposals for more liberal abortion laws as entailing "the thoughtless, wholesale slaughter of those considered to be less than human by some." With this distortion in hand, the writer had only a slight jump to make to forge a link with Nazi extermination camps. But the link is complete fabrication. The president wasn't calling for thoughtless and wholesale slaughter. Furthermore, favoring liberalized abortion laws does not require believing that the fetus is less than human. One might, for example, take the position that the fetus is a human being but that the mother's right to life can, in some circumstances, take precedence over the fetus's. Finally, even if the doctor did believe that a fetus is "less than human," that's not the same as considering it subhuman in the way Hitler and the Nazis viewed so-called non-Aryans. The writer committed *guilt by association* by alleging a nonexistent association. Sometimes the fallacy occurs when the association does exist but isn't strong enough to support the connection based on it.

The conditions listed in the box cover *guilt by association*.

GUILT BY ASSOCIATION

1. The critic attacks the arguer on the basis of some alleged association between the arguer and some other person or group.
2. The alleged association either (a) does not exist at all or (b) does not provide relevant or sufficient support for the critic's attack.

We conclude our treatment of *guilt by association* with an example from Scotland. When Queen Elizabeth II visited there some years ago, there was a demonstration by antiroyalist students, which occasioned this news item:

12   Four hundred students chanted obscene songs and hurled insults at the Queen, jostling the royal entourage during a ceremony at the university. The scenes involving the Queen were the worst ever during her reign and were criticized by leading Scots. The chairman of the Conservative Party said: "The damage done to all Scotland's image across the world is incalculable."

The chairman's fears would have a foundation only if we assumed that people around the world would commit *guilt by association,* blaming all Scots for the rowdiness of a few students. In a world of good reasoners, his fears would be groundless.

Red Herring

You will recall the spiked-doll example we used to illustrate the generic fallacy of *irrelevant reason* in Chapter 4. Some consumers objected to a doll whose head, when removed (a feat which toddlers could manage), revealed a dangerous spike. They wanted the government to outlaw the product. A spokesperson for the company that manufactured the doll replied to this proposal by saying, "No legislation is going to protect a child against the normal hazards of life." We argued then that this reply was irrelevant: The issue was not protecting children against "the normal hazards of life" but protecting them against hazards that could readily be avoided.

In defense of the spokesperson, one might say that he surely did not believe his reply was irrelevant. Its irrelevance was so blatant that it would be uncharitable to believe he could have intended it as a reason for not passing legislation to protect children against shoddy, poorly designed toys. If we accept this defense, then we are left with the question, What was the point of the spokesman's reply? It seems plausible to interpret it along the following lines:

The toy company was under attack for a blatantly dangerous feature of its doll and faced pressure for legislation that would have forced it to redesign the doll and to recall all the spiked dolls already in the marketplace—both expensive prospects. No defense that would meet public acceptance seemed available. (The public would hardly be sympathetic with the argument that this was the cheapest way to attach the doll's head, or that complying with the proposed legislation would cost the company money.) In such a situation, it may have appeared that the best defense was to take the offensive: to set up a new issue—trying to protect children against the normal hazards of life—that has some tenuous connection with the old one, but where the company could hold a defensible position. Such a strategy (in effect, changing the subject) would distract attention from the hazards of the spiked doll and take the heat off the company. While the strategy might not appear ethical to an impartial observer, it would at least be clear of the charge of blatant irrelevance.

Whether or not we have accurately described the spokesperson's intent, his reply certainly could easily have had the effect of changing the subject and so distracting critics from the original issue. This move, intentional or not, is quite common in arguments in adversarial situations. It is called introducing a "red herring," and from this term, which is in widespread use, we take the name for the fallacy it represents. This move is logically fallacious for, although the introduction of a *red herring* makes sense as a tactic of defense when under criticism (defense by counterattack), it remains logically irrelevant to the original issue in dispute.

The origin of the term "red herring" makes it a good descriptive label for this fallacy. It comes from the sport of fox hunting, in which hunters on horseback follow a pack of hounds tracking a fox's scent. To divert the hounds from the hunt—either to save a good fox for another day's chase or to call off young hounds being trained—a real red herring (one that's been dried, smoked, and salted) is drawn across the fox's track ahead of the pack. The dogs are diverted by the fresher, stronger scent. The term's application to this fallacy is evident.

A typical *red herring* was used by then-Senator Paul Martin, well known for extolling the virtues of his hometown of Windsor, Ontario, on the occasion of defending Windsor against a slur in Arthur Hailey's novel about the auto industry, *Wheels*. Hailey wrote of "grimy Windsor" across the border from Detroit, "matching in ugliness the worst of its U.S. senior partner." According to press reports, Martin responded:

13   When I read this I was incensed. . . . Those of us who live there know that (Windsor) is not a grimy city. It is a city that has one of the best flower parks in Canada. It is a city of fine schools, hardworking and tolerant people. . . .

Martin's first point does tell against Hailey's appraisal, for it can be argued that a city with an attractive flower park cannot be completely grimy. To put it another way, the existence of a superb flower park would at least be relevant to the issue of how grimy a place Windsor is. But the Senator didn't continue building his case for Windsor's beauty (as he might have) by extolling its splendid rose gardens and miles of riverfront parkland. Nor did he mention the kind of empirical evidence that one would expect in considering the issue of grime (pollution counts, for example). Instead, he changed the subject. Fine schools and hardworking, tolerant people are no doubt an asset, but they have nothing to do with whether a city is grimy or ugly.

The Senator's shift here is a common type of *red herring* move. Martin began his defense of Windsor on topic, then shifted to an associated point, not strictly relevant to the attack. Perhaps Martin interpreted Haliey's criticism of Windsor's physical appearance as part of a general critique of the city. That would explain his more general defense. It wouldn't alter the fact, however, that Hailey's comment was restricted to Windsor's appearance. Nor would it make the Senator's second point any less a distraction, inviting a shift in the focus of the debate and raising another issue. The effect, whether intentional or not, was to move the argument onto different ground, to terrain more favorable to Martin. It's harder to document the allegation that the quality of life in a city is lamentable than it is to show that the city is physically grimy and ugly.

It is important not to think of this fallacy as necessarily one of intent. The difficulty we have in knowing the intentions of others would restrict our employment of the *red herring* tag. It would be an undue restriction because we often want to mark a distractingly irrelevant response whether or not the person was trying to change the subject. Nor should we think in terms of the effect a response has in diverting the opponent's attention to a different topic because that would mean we could charge *red herring* only when the opponent was duped by the irrelevant rejoinder. Hence, the presence of the fallacy would then depend on the cleverness of the opponent—an odd situation, since we'd want to say that the clever opponent exposed the fallacy or avoided it. We would not want to say, paradoxically, that the fallacy didn't exist because the opponent spotted it! Certainly a paradigm of *red herring* is an exchange in which someone deliberately introduces a diversion to try to divert the opponent's attention from the point under controversy, and as a result the opponent is distracted by the diversion and follows it up, leaving behind the original issue. We find it more useful, however, to use the label for responses to attacks in adversarial contexts that, because they are close but not strictly relevant to the topic, *invite* the opponent to digress, whether or not the distraction is intended or successful.

The conditions of the fallacy are listed in the box.

RED HERRING

1. In an adversarial context, an arguer makes a claim that is or implies a criticism of a position that his or her opponent holds or identifies with.
2. The opponent responds by introducing an issue that is not relevant to the original position, thereby inviting a shift of focus.

Sometimes it is difficult to decide whether a particular consideration is a *red herring*. During the hearings to confirm Clarence Thomas, Anita Hill implied that Thomas was guilty of sexual harassment. Thomas responded:

14   I would like to start by saying unequivocally, categorically, that I deny each and every single allegation against me today. . . . I cannot shake off these accusations because they play to the worst stereotypes we have about black men in this country.

Is this a *red herring*? Well, the judge responds directly to the charge; so there is no evasion. But of what relevance is the claim of stereotyping? Here the reader needs to know that one of the accusations made by Hill was that "he referred to the size of his own penis as being larger than normal."

We need to add one consideration before concluding our treatment of *red herring*. The fallacy of *red herring* is often the result of the problem of failing to be clear about the difference between local and global relevance. If the issue introduced into the argument has some relevance to the question being addressed, when that question is considered broadly, it has global relevance. On the other hand, if the issue injected is not relevant to this particular argument about the issue, it does not have local relevance.

Figure 5-1 *This chart shows how the fallacies of diversion are related.*

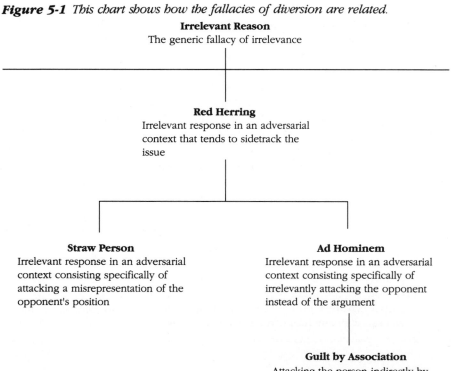

Irrelevant Reason
The generic fallacy of irrelevance

Red Herring
Irrelevant response in an adversarial context that tends to sidetrack the issue

Straw Person
Irrelevant response in an adversarial context consisting specifically of attacking a misrepresentation of the opponent's position

Ad Hominem
Irrelevant response in an adversarial context consisting specifically of irrelevantly attacking the opponent instead of the argument

Guilt by Association
Attacking the person indirectly by attacking some association of the person when that is irrelevant or insufficient to discredit the position

With this treatment of *red herring,* we complete our list of discussion of fallacies of diversion. When evaluating an argument in an adversarial context, you should be consciously on the lookout for these fallacies. It might be helpful in keeping them in mind, and also in keeping them distinct from each other in your mind, to be clear on how they are related. Figure 5-1 sets out their connections.

EXERCISES

Directions.   For each extract assigned, decide if there are any arguments present, and, if so, whether they contain any of the fallacies you have studied so far, If you think there is no argument, explain what the function of the passage is. If you think any arguments are logically good ones, try to anticipate possible criticisms, and argue against such criticisms. If you think there are any fallacious arguments, write a critique supporting your judgment (see details below). If you think there is some fallacy not covered (yet), say so. While you may reasonably expect that these passages contain instances of the fallacies taken up in this chapter, understand that some passages may not contain arguments at all, some may contain arguments with fallacies you have not encountered, and some of the arguments may be fallacy-free.

For *each* fallacy you identify, do the following in your critique: (1) identify: the argument's conclusion, the premise(s) in which the fallacy occurs, who commits the fallacy, and the name of the fallacy (if it is not one covered so far, describe it); (2) formulate an argument to convince a neutral observer that the fallacy you allege has indeed been committed; and (3) say whether any fallacy completely undercuts the argument or whether the argument can be repaired, and explain why you think so.

1. *Background:* In an interview (*Image,* July 19, 1992) conducted at her home in the hills of Mendocino, Alice Walker, author of *The Color Purple* and *Possessing the Secret of Joy,* complained about the spiritual emptiness of America: "America is a terrible place for spiritual growth because it is so full of material goodies that you can latch onto those things and think that is really what it's all about." In a letter to the editor, R. W. D. wrote in response:

   > Why should we listen to a lecture by Ms. Walker about what a rotten country America has become while she lives in splendor in her lush pad on a Medocino hillside?

2. *Background:* Bob Talbert writes a daily column for the *Detroit Free Press.* He covers a variety of local activities and issues. Like most columnists who receive letters from their readers, Talbert devotes an occasional column to these letters and his re-sponses. Here is a letter he received from someone who used the pseudonym "Sam Detroit," along with Talbert's reply:

   > The danger of writing a witty(?) column such as yours is that eventually, being in the public eye, hobnobbing with the celebrities, you begin to acquire a false sense of importance, which some psychiatrists call delusions of grandeur. Come down off your white charger and try writing an amusing article for a change. —Sam Detroit
   >
   > Wonder what psychiatrists would call hiding behind a pseudonym? —Bob Talbert

3. *Background:* With reference again to Arthur Hailey's charge that Windsor is ugly, here is the response of another Windsor politician, then Minister of National Revenue and Member of Parliament for Windsor West, Herb Gray:

I don't think Hailey's impressions are correct. The fact that thousands of people choose to live in Windsor even though they work in Detroit, and that even larger numbers of Detroiters come to Windsor for shopping and entertainment, shows that the negative aspects of life in Detroit, fortunately, are not found in Windsor.

4. *Background:* Back in the days of gas shortages in the United States, the *Pittsburgh Press* TV editor commented on the Indy 500, saying: "All of us who can't get gas will readily be able to see where a lot of it went." A reader responded by noting that the editor's comment contained "a serious research blunder. Indianapolis race cars use a methyl-alcohol fuel mixture, not gasoline." The editor responded:

> I don't care if they put water in those Indianapolis cars, the effect is the same— viewers who can't get gas sit at home watching cars racing around in circles, while auto enthusiasts from all over the country drive to Indianapolis to watch the event that does encompass a lot of gas-eating machines.

5. *Background:* This exchange took place during a panel debate in Detroit about whether the media create bad news. One member of the panel said: "You have the smallest sales of any major market that I have seen. So you're hurting yourselves when you endlessly report bad news because Detroit's image makes people want not to locate factories here." Another said: "The Sunday brunch at the Westin Hotel has doubled in size, but you never report things like that." In response the spokesperson for the newspaper stated:

> So you're saying that if we stop reporting bad news or if the media in general stops reporting crime, then overnight we'll get a tremendous infusion of business and the city's problem will be solved. But that is just plain naive thinking on your part— wishful thinking, in fact.

6. *Background:* Alan Dershowitz is a famous attorney whose book, *Chutzpah,* was reviewed by Stefan Kanfer. Dershowitz took exception to the review in a letter to the editor.

> Stafan Kanfer's *ad hominem* review of my book showed real chutzpah. Kanfer never informs the reader of its thesis: that American Jews still regard themselves as guests in someone else's land and must be more assertive in insisting on first-class status. Nor does he mention the book's chapters on Israel, the Holocaust, the Pollard case, separation of church and state, and other issues of pressing concern. Kanfer has the right not to like me, but he has the obligation to be fair to your readers and mine about the book he is reviewing. You apparently have a schlemiel for a reviewer.

7. *Background:* In a debate about apartheid, one arguer declared: "Apartheid is a crime against humanity. It is on the same level as genocide and slavery." One response to this was:

> As unjust and debasing as apartheid is, it is not on the same level as genocide. European Jewry, Armenians, and members of the Baha'i religion would hardly agree with the arguer's view. What she is saying is that Soweto is equal to Auschwitz. Where are the gas chambers and the ovens in Soweto? Although apartheid may also have been labeled a crime against humanity, in no way are genocide and apartheid on the "same level." Anyone who equates Soweto to Auschwitz demonstrates an abysmal lack of understanding of what Auschwitz was. Are the gas chambers running twenty-four hours a day in Soweto?

8. *Background:* In 1982, the issue of nuclear deterrence and the idea of a nuclear freeze

surfaced in North America with great force. Here is a quote from an opponent of a freeze:

> We have known that nuclear war is horrible for as long as there have been nuclear weapons. For the proponents of the freeze to act as if they had discovered something new is a sign of almost staggering ignorance of the history of the last thirty-seven years. For all of that time, the United States' paramount goal has been to maintain freedom and avoid a nuclear war. To imply otherwise is not only specious but insults the speaker as well as the listener. If no one is eager for a nuclear war, the demonstrators and senators are doing no more than uttering a cliché: "We do not want nuclear war." The nuclear-freeze petition signers are uttering a truism that is embarrassingly hackneyed. Of course no one wants nuclear war. Are the proponents of the freeze doing anything more than satisfying themselves by uttering a momentarily satisfying but empty banality? No. And that's what makes junk thought.

9–11. *Background:* In late February 1981, President Ronald Reagan flew from Washington, D. C., to his ranch in Santa Barbara, California, at an estimated cost to United States taxpayers of $52,000. This happened at a time when Reagan was attempting to get members of Congress to agree to slice the federal budget and to show fiscal restraint. Many were upset by Reagan's trip, arguing that Reagan should be expected to practice what he preaches; i.e., restraint. If he wanted some rest and relaxation, they said, Camp David in Maryland was closer to Washington and would cost less money to reach.

Below are several letters to the editor of the *Los Angeles Times* (March 8, 1981). They make reference to an earlier round of letters. Appraise the logical merits of each.

9. If President Reagan does the job for the country he proposes to do, he deserves everything we can give him, including a ranch on the moon with a ring around it! And free travel, too! What have the "complainers" gone without in order to help the inflation picture? An unnecessary trip? A new suit? Or perhaps a new automobile or TV set? How about one less trip to the racetrack?

10. This is an angry letter. I am referring to your printing seven letters faulting Reagan for taking time for rest and relaxation at his ranch. Who are these writers? . . . The answer is self-evident. They are, one and all, inconsequential people. No matter what they do, whether they live or die, it is of no consequence to the world at large. Not so with the president of the United States. What this man does, and the decision he makes, has direct bearing on the welfare of every single person on the face of this earth. And presidents are humans which means that their decision-making powers are directly affected by their personal mental and physical condition. They become fatigued, and harried, and impulsive and irritable, just like anyone else. But the consequences of these negative states, the decisions that come out of them, are of the greatest possible pertinence to us all. All right, then, if President Reagan has the need to spend his weekends in Tierra del Fuego, or even at the North Pole, fine. No matter what the expense, as long as he returns refreshed and restored to a state of calm and correct judgment, fine.

11. Has Reagan been so blinded by the glamour of Hollywood that he cannot see the stark reality of abject poverty? Has he no heart or soul that he can so readily cut out things like nutrition for young children when he freely spends $52,000 getting away from the very thing he fought so hard to obtain?

12. *Background:* In the 1972 Olympics, the black nations of Africa stated they would

boycott the games if Rhodesian athletes were allowed to compete. (Rhodesia was then the name of Zimbabwe.) The International Olympic Committee subsequently voted Rhodesia out of the games. In an editorial entitled, "Racism in Black Africa, too" (August 1972), the *Detroit News* stated:

> The black nations of Africa, citing racism by the white supremacist Rhodesian regime, almost wrecked the Olympic Games opening this weekend by using their political muscle to force Rhodesia out of the games. It was coincidental that the day they won their point, Uganda, one of the leaders of the movement, confirmed its own brand of racism by spelling out the details of its arbitrary ouster of Indians and Pakistanis who have for generations lived in Uganda.
>
> Racism is clearly a two-way street.

13. *Background:* In "Three Days of the Con Job" (*GQ,* March 1992), Joe Queenan relates his experiences at the First International Men's Conference held in Austin, Texas, and refers to a comment by Robert Bly warning that the movement was still in its infancy. Queenan writes:

> Of course it's easy for Robert Bly to say "Hold the publicity!" now that Bill Moyers has anointed him the Saint Thomas Aquinas of the late twentieth century on a widely viewed PBS special, now that Bly has had a number-one book on the *New York Times* best-sellers list, now that Bly has banked a few big ones by preaching an esoteric philosophy whose highly debatable central tenet is that the industrial revolution ruined everything for men, that things were a whole lot better back in the Middle Ages, when Dad stayed home. (Yes, Bob, it's true that Dad stayed home, but the Visigoths didn't.)

14. *Background:* In a letter to a Toronto paper, a writer commented on a favorable review of a feminist book. She took the occasion to state her reasons for rejecting the feminist view about relations between the sexes, saying:

> I will not subscribe to a philosophy that purports to represent some sort of vague liberation from alleged wrongs while, at the same time, advocating the destruction of traditions and democracy. . . . Let me just say that I vigorously oppose any ideology that arrogantly proposes to reduce my husband and my children and my family to superfluity because we don't fit some sort of elitist, sexist new order.

15. *Background:* This is an excerpt from a review of *You Just Don't Understand: Women and Men in Conversation"* by Deborah Tannen. (The review, by Mary Beard, appeared in the *London Review of Books,* August 1991, p. 18.)

> Judging the matter as it stands, I find it hard to interpret the man's actions as anything other than rudeness verging on exploitation. First he gets his sex, then he gets his breakfast cooked and paper provided. [That is how Tannen recounted the incident in question.] For her it is a matter of language again. In fact, she congratulates the woman concerned, who apparently realized that different genderlects were at stake here: "She realized that unlike her, he did not feel the need for talk to reinforce their intimacy." Any women who actually believed this ridiculous interpretation would no doubt also believe that washing-up and nappy-changing are somehow at odds with men's sense of their own language. She would probably accept, too, the inevitability of male abuse—just "getting attention" again, she would say.

CHAPTER SIX

◆

Fallacies of Impersonation

Introduction

Fallacies are sometimes said to impersonate good arguments. In fact, many fallacious arguments seem to be almost counterfeits of sound arguments.[1] The three fallacies we discuss in this chapter exhibit this feature. Three of the most common and useful kinds of argument in public discourse are (1) arguments from analogy, (2) appeals to fairness and precedent, and (3) arguments about causal claims. The fallacies we call *faulty analogy, two wrongs* (and its variant, "improper appeal to practice"), and *questionable cause* impersonate these three legitimate types of argument.

Faulty Analogy

An *analogy* is a comparison between two or more things that notes a likeness or similarity between or among them, some property that they share. It is the opposite of a *contrast*, or disanalogy, which compares two or more things and notes differences between them.

Analogies serve a variety of functions. For example, an analogy may be used to describe ("You look like death warmed over") or to explain ("To show that a fallacy has been committed is like producing enough evidence to convict the accused in a court of law") or to state in provocative language, as political columnist James Eayrs did when he wrote about the CIA-backed military coup against the Allende regime in Chile.

1   Like a group of bystanders unconcernedly gazing at a mugging, the world's democracies stood to one side last week as one of their number was brutally beaten to death.

[1] See the title of W. Ward Fearnside's and William B. Holther's book: *Fallacy, The Counterfeit of Argument*, Spectrum Brooks, Prentice-Hall, Englewood Cliffs, NJ, 1959.

An analogy can also be used to persuade, and it is such uses—arguments employing analogies—that we are concerned with here. Moreover, we'll restrict out treatment to just one type of such argument, what has been called the *argument from a priori analogy*.[2] We will call it simply the *argument from analogy*.

Here's an example of such an argument from a letter to the Winnipeg *Free Press*. It argues for an increase in the sales tax on alcoholic beverages.

2   I believe the citizens of this province, whether they be drinkers or dry, might consider it only fair that liquor sales revenue be further increased to cover the costs to society of the extra costs that seem to fall in the wake of imbibing. In other words, why cannot the full costs of the effects of drinking be met by the sales tax on alcoholic beverages, just as the costs of highway maintenance are met by the sales tax on gasoline? What would we expect this additional revenue from liquor to cover? For openers, about $10 million is the annual provincial loss though absenteeism from drinking workers.

Notice what the writer has done here. He has taken an accepted belief that the cost of highway maintenance should be met by a sales tax on gasoline and used it to pave the way for the proposal for an increased tax on liquor. The argument says: The two situations are alike, so if you accept the principle in the case of gasoline taxes, you should also accept it in the case of liquor taxes. One's acceptance of the conclusion based on this argument depends entirely on the adequacy of the analogy.

Does the analogy support the conclusion? To explain how to decide, we need to explain the general strategy of arguments from analogy.

Such arguments rely, first, on getting the audience to grant a premise that a certain claim may be made about one of the two things being compared. The assumption, usually not made explicitly, is that the claim is true about that thing because it has a certain property.

In the above argument, for instance, the writer is claiming that the sales tax on gasoline is used to contribute to the costs of gasoline consumption—namely, the wear and tear on highways caused by driving—and legitimately so. The writer doesn't say what makes it fair to use the sales tax on gas to pay for highway maintenance. What she may have in mind is that the amount a driver contributes to the wear and tear on highways is more or less proportional to the amount of highway driving he or she does, which, in turn, is more or less proportional to the amount of gas used. A tax on gas, then, puts the bite on drivers roughly in proportion to the highway wear and tear they contribute. That seems fair, and it gives plausibility to the writer's initial reliance on the fact that the gasoline tax is used to pay for highway maintenance.

---

[2] See Trudy Govier, *A Practical Study of Argument*, 3d ed., Wadsworth, Belmont, CA, 1992, p. 227. Another type, the argument from empirical analogy, is used to support the likelihood of as yet unperceived similarities, using perceived similarities as premises.

Having proposed that a certain claim may be made about one of the two things being compared, the arguer then asserts (implicitly or explicitly) that the second thing is like the first, and on the basis of that alleged analogy concludes that the same claim may be made about the second thing.

Sometimes the likeness is explicitly contended, and sometimes it's even defended. But often, as in the above argument, it is simply taken for granted. The writer in our example doesn't claim explicitly that gasoline and liquor consumption are alike. Nevertheless, her argument relies on the comparison, for otherwise there would be no point to mentioning that the costs of highway maintenance are paid for by the sales tax on gasoline.

For an argument from analogy to be a good one, the second thing being compared to the first must be not just like it, but like it *in those respects in virtue of which the claim made about the first thing is acceptable*. The property that makes the premise acceptable must be shared by the second thing, if that acceptability is to transfer to the conclusion.

Let's review the booze-tax argument with these points in mind. For the argument to be cogent (for the existence of the former tax to be a reason for having the latter tax), what makes it reasonable to accept a tax on gasoline consumption must be true also of liquor consumption. The legitimacy of the gasoline tax relied on its fairness; i.e., the rough proportionality between a vehicle's gas consumption and its contribution to highway wear. Is there a rough proportionality between a person's liquor consumption and his or her contribution to the social costs of alcohol abuse?

We'd argue that there is not such a correspondence. First, by no means all who consume alcohol contribute to the social costs of alcohol abuse: Most drinkers don't abuse alcohol. Second, the causes of alcohol abuse cannot all be laid at the feet of people who drink too much. Sometimes social and economic conditions beyond their control play a part. So what makes a gas tax fair—costs borne in rough proportion to responsibility for them—does not carry over to a tax on alcohol. The costs of alcohol abuse would not be born in rough proportion to responsibility for them.

To summarize, the writer's argument from analogy fails. It requires that, like gas consumption and wear on highways, liquor consumption be roughly proportionate to its social costs. But that's not the case. So the two are not similar in the respect needed to support the conclusion. Such arguments, we say, exhibit the fallacy of *faulty analogy*.

Here is another example of an argument from analogy. In reply to an article by Thomas Middleton in *Saturday Review* calling for stricter gun-control legislation, a reader wrote:

3   I wish to protest the article written by Mr. Middleton. Can Mr. Middleton be so naive as to really believe that banning ownership of firearms would significantly reduce murders and robberies? Did banning booze significantly reduce drinking?[3]

---

[3] Thanks to Brian Savard for bringing this example to our attention.

Setting out the structure of this argument helps make the role of the analogy explicit.

4   1. Prohibition did not significantly reduce drinking.

MP   a. Banning ownership of firearms is analogous to banning booze.

2. Banning ownership of firearms won't significantly reduce murders and robberies.

Here's a case where the analogy was not explicit, so we made it explicit by adding the missing premise. Does the comparison support the suggested conclusion? That depends, recall, on whether what is true of the first analogue, which makes the initial claim plausible, is also true of the second analogue. We'll call that key feature the *relevant property set*.

What were the relevant properties of the situation in the 1920s that caused the failure of Prohibition to reduce drinking significantly? To answer the question, we need some background knowledge, a normal requirement of argument evaluation. In our view, Prohibition failed for a number of reasons: (1) it didn't have the support of most people, so a lucrative market existed for alcohol; (2) smuggling on a large scale could not be prevented; and (3) the illicit manufacture of liquor sprang up and couldn't be stopped. Hence, the relevant properties seem to be that there was a large, lucrative market for the product and illicit importation and manufacture of it could not be prevented.

Does the ownership of firearms in our own time share any of these properties? Is there a similar demand for firearms for the purpose of murder and robbery? Is large-scale smuggling or the illicit manufacture of firearms likely in the event of a ban?

The answers to these question aren't obvious. Most murders, we read, are committed by people known to the victim, such as friends or family members, and are not planned but, rather, are spontaneous acts that occur in the heat of the moment. If that is true, then it is hard to imagine a "demand" or market for firearms for the purpose of murder. Robbery, though, is another matter. Are firearms used in armed robberies (instead of other weapons, such as knives or clubs) because of the ready availability of firearms or because robbers insist on using firearms and would seek them out illicitly if they were banned and not generally available? We don't know the answer to that question; nor, we suspect, does anyone, since guns have long been readily accessible to robbers. In the absence of evidence about the extent of the demand for firearms for murder and robbery, it's hard to speculate sensibly about whether large-scale smuggling or illicit manufacture of firearms would occur in the event of a ban.

We conclude, then, that the argument from the analogy of the failure of Prohibition is not a strong one. It does not fail because the relevant properties are clearly not shared by the two things being compared, as was the case in the liquor-tax argument. It fails because it is *open to question* whether the relevant properties are present in the guns-for-murder-and-robbery situation. The appeal to an analogy between the two situations is problematic, and, as a result, it cannot succeed in lending support to the conclusion. Once again, *faulty analogy,* though this time for a different reason.

Generalizing from the above two arguments and others like them, we get the conditions listed in the box for the fallacy.

FAULTY ANALOGY

1. The analogy occurs in an argument from (a priori) analogy.
a. In the premise of an argument a predicate is attributed to a first thing (a person, act, event, situation, and so on) allegedly because of a set of properties it has (call these the *relevant properties*).
b. In another premise (tacit or stated), the first thing and a second thing are claimed to be similar in the respect that both have the relevant properties.
c. The conclusion of the argument is that the same predicate is, or should be, attributed to the second thing.
2. The analogy fails to support the conclusion because:
d. It is false or problematic that the predicate does, in fact, apply to the first thing because of the relevant property set.

OR

e. It is false or problematic that the second thing does, indeed, share the relevant property set.

Faulty analogy of the sort we identify in this chapter is, thus, a failure to meet the acceptability requirement of good arguments. There is a false or problematic assumption about the similarity of two cases or situations at the heart of the fallacy.

The analogy may be explicit (as in the gas-tax example) or implicit (as in the firearms-ban example). The relevant property is rarely made explicit.

The first step in showing that an argument contains *faulty analogy* is to establish that you are, indeed, dealing with an argument from analogy, which means establishing that conditions 1*a*, 1*b*, and 1*c* pertain. For example, suppose a student, Maria, argued:

5   Luis handed in his paper a day late and didn't get penalized. I handed my paper in a day late and I was penalized 5 percent. It's not fair. I shouldn't get penalized for being late if Luis didn't.

Here the predicate of being "excused from any late penalty" is attributed to Luis's paper. No ground for this predicate is explicitly offered by Maria, so presumably she thinks it is the property of being "no more than one day late." (Here we have satisfied condition 1*a*.) Maria goes on to claim that her paper is similar to Luis's in being a day late. (Pointing that fact out satisfies condition 1*b*.) Maria's conclusion is that her paper should also be excused from any late penalty, which is the predicate attributed to Luis's paper. (We thus show that condition 1*c* is met in this case.) So Maria's argument is an argument from analogy.

The second step in showing that an argument contains a faulty analogy is to identify the property that is being transferred to the second thing with the help of the analogy. That is the predicate referred to in condition 1*a*. In our example, Maria wants the predicate of being "excused from any penalty for lateness" applied to her late paper the way it was applied to Luis's.

The third step is to identify the relevant property of the analogy. The relevant property consists of the features of the first analogue that supposedly make the initial claim acceptable. Our example is typical in that this property is not stated. Presumably, Maria advanced her argument because she thought the relevant property was that the paper was *only* one day late. But since she was penalized and Luis wasn't, it is possible that there was another property in play. Perhaps Luis got a one-day extension in advance; or perhaps he had a good excuse for being a day late. In general, Maria is assuming that there is no relevant difference between her circumstances and Luis's.

The fourth and last step is to show that condition 2*d* or condition 2*e* applies, keeping in mind that your claim must be supported by good reasons if your charge of fallacy is to be warranted. It seems to us problematic that there is no relevant difference between the two cases, given that Luis was not penalized for lateness and Maria was. That is, we doubt that Maria's situation was similar in all relevant respects to Luis's. Why? Because we find it less plausible that the professor was being blatantly unfair to Maria than that there was some relevant difference between her situation and Luis's that Maria did not know about. So we think it is possible that Maria committed the fallacy of *faulty analogy* in her argument. In the absence of knowing further facts about the case, we can go no further. You might disagree. "Isn't it just like professors," you might think, "to side with the professor in this case and assume the student who has a complaint is wrong?" Maybe we are being biased in favor of our (imaginary) colleague, but you will have to admit that it is at least possible that the cases were different and that Maria's argument was, therefore, fallacious. We will settle for that.

In typical cases, the faulty analogy seems persuasive because the two things compared are, indeed, similar in some respects. To make a case for your claim that the fallacy has been committed, you needn't argue that the two things are in no way alike. *Any* two things will be alike in some respects and different in others, so it won't even be relevant to argue that there are some respects in which the two things are dissimilar. What you must show is either that they are not alike in the relevant respect or that the reason the predicate in question applies in the first case is not due to the relevant properties.

We want to illustrate how, and how *not*, to make a case for an allegation that an argument contains a faulty analogy. To serve as our example, we have adapted a letter to *Time* magazine that was written when the United States was still actively engaged in the Vietnam war.

6   Contrary to your article, the events that are taking place in South Vietnam's presidential election offer the best opportunity for the United States to make a "decent" exit from southeast Asia. Under the existing circumstances, the United States should declare that South Vietnam is unable to sustain a political democracy, that there is no reason for us to remain there, and that we should withdraw our remaining forces. By doing this, we would leave the image of a patient who died despite the extraordinary efforts of a good doctor.

First, we lay out the structure of the argument.

7   1. By withdrawing from southeast Asia with the declaration that South Vietnam can now be seen to be unable to sustain a political democracy, the United States would be acting like a good doctor who, despite extraordinary efforts, lost the patient.
2. No one would blame a doctor whose patient dies despite the doctor's extraordinary effort.
3. No one could blame the United States for withdrawing from South Vietnam under the circumstances.

First we will review an *unsatisfactory* attempt to show that the letter writer is guilty of *faulty analogy*.

8   The United States and South Vietnam cannot be compared to a doctor and her patient because a doctor is paid for her services, and the United States did not receive any pay from South Vietnam.

Although it's true that the United States did not receive any pay, this attempt to defeat the analogy seizes upon a nonrelevant feature of the analogy and over-looks the pivotal ones. Even if the United States had been paid by South Vietnam, the analogy would fail for the following reasons:

9   In order for the analogy to apply, the analogue of the patient's life would have to be a democratic South Vietnam, and the analogue of the doctor's extraordinary fight to save that life would have to be the United States' extraordinary efforts to create (or sustain) a democratic South Vietnam. The record is clear, however, that the United States was willing to tolerate clearly undemocratic regimes in South Vietnam so long as they were fairly stable. Both the Diem and the Thieu regimes, though patently undemocratic, were sustained and supported by the United States with little effort to make them more democratic. The analogy fails, then, in the respect relevant to support the conclusion: The "doctor" did not make an extraordinary effort to save the "patient's" life.

It also fails because the doctor-patient metaphor has certain built-in assumptions not warranted here. It assumes that South Vietnam was a single patient, but that assumption is questionable. The war there could have been interpreted as a civil war, with the United States in the role of a doctor treating conjoined twins, one of whom does not want to be separated.

Finally, whether the United States can reasonably be termed "a good doctor" in terms of this analogy is open to question. A "good doctor" here would be one who sought to make a democracy a workable form of government. In fact, United States foreign policy throughout the 1950s and 1960s can be interpreted as more anti-Communist than pro-democratic. Witness United States support of the undemocratic regime of Batista in Cuba, Somoza in Nicaragua, the military dictatorship in Greece, and so on.

We said at the outset of this section that the fallacy called *faulty analogy* refers to bad *arguments* from analogy. We also noted that analogies function outside arguments, for instance to describe or to explain. A particular analogy might be a poor one for any of those other purposes, too, but that does not make it a logical fallacy because in those cases there is no argument.

Analogies are so widely used in reasoning that they figure in several different patterns of argument. The fallacy we turn to next is a good example of such a species of argument from analogy.

Two Wrongs

The fallacy we're calling *two wrongs* (short for "two wrongs make a right") is a logical fallacy, employed primarily in ethical arguments and appealing to very strong emotional and psychological factors. This deceptively simple maneuver is one most children are capable of using. Remember when you father or mother criticized you as a child for poking your brother or sister and you defended yourself by saying, "But she [or he] hit me first!" The idea is simple and attractive, isn't it? You were wronged (your brother slugged you, and that's something he shouldn't have done) and that act, you reasoned, made it okay to return the favor by hitting him back. The fallacy of *two wrongs* seeks, in effect, to elevate the instinct to retaliate into an argument. Let's look at a few examples.

The first one needs a bit of background. A group of militant native Canadians took possession of a small park on the outskirts of Kenora, Ontario. They claimed that they had exclusive rights to its use. The occupation made national headlines because the native people involved were armed, so there was the possibility of violent confrontation. An agreement was eventually reached and the occupation ended peacefully. It stirred a great deal of comment in the press. The following passage is adapted from a letter to the Winnipeg *Free Press*, defending the actions of the Indians against criticisms that had been previously aired:

10   The occupation of a 14-acre park by the native people in the Kenora area is completely justified. After all, what's a mere 14 acres when they have been robbed of 14 million square miles (the entire North and South American continents)?

Notice the pattern here. It started with criticisms of the action. There then followed a defense that took the form of citing some other wrongdoing, the implication being (in this case it is explicitly stated) that the action criticized was justified. The formula is a recurrent one. If we set out the elements of this compact argument, we get:

11   1. The native people were robbed of North and South America.

  a. The native people were wronged long ago.

  2. The native people were justified in occupying the 14-acre park in Kenora.

Clearly, an implicit premise or assumption operates behind the scenes here, but what is it? The writer's reference to "a mere 14 acres" suggests that he or she is thinking of some version of the principle that persons who suffer wrongdoing are entitled to compensation. The idea would be that 14 acres is little enough compensation, given the magnitude of the original wrong done to the native North Americans. In claiming that the Indians were justified, the writer would no doubt concede that the seizure of the park by just any group would, in normal circumstances, be wrong. Thus, the complete idea behind the argument is this: An action that would be wrong if taken in ordinary circumstances is permissible under certain circumstances. The ordinary judgment that would be applied to such an action in normal circumstances is overruled, or does not apply, so it is alleged, because in this case the agent has already been wronged by the person whom the action is affecting. The first wrong justifies the second one and makes it right; in other words, "two wrongs make a right."

When such arguments seem plausible, it's because they appeal to our sense of justice and fair play; they model legitimate arguments. They go wrong, however, when they involve a misapplication of the principles of justice, when they involve unwarranted assumptions, or both.

In the case of the argument about the Kenora occupation, the wrongs done to Indian peoples in the Americas by invading Europeans does not justify the occupation of the Kenora park by local Indians. Even if the forebears of the non-Indians living in Kenora today stole land from the aboriginal residents, that does not justify the park takeover because the mere suffering or a wrong from someone does not, by itself, warrant acting outside the law to try to redress that wrong. If that principle were embraced, then private feuds would be constantly disrupting peaceful society. There must be additional factors present, such as that the Kenora band had tried every legitimate means to get its land back and was refused any sort of fair hearing, plus perhaps that the occupation of the Kenora park seemed the most effective way of drawing attention to their grievance and getting a fair hearing. But the writer appeals to no such additional factors in this case. Do not infer from these points that we are saying that the Kenora park occupation was wrong. Our objective is not to judge that issue. Our argument is only that the writer's defense of that takeover, based as it is solely on an appeal to a past wrong, does not succeed. It remains an open question whether the takeover was justified on other, or additional, grounds, such as those we've just mentioned.

We need to say something here about an ancient principle of justice, the *lex talionis* ("an eye for an eye, a tooth for a tooth"), which has been mistakenly used to try to justify "two-wrongs-make-a-right" reasoning. The point of that law (which defined a sort of combination of retribution and compensation) was that *no more* than an eye could be taken for an eye. It placed a limit on compensation or retribution. Furthermore, *lex talionis* was undoubtedly intended metaphorically, not literally. Its message was that the compensation or retribution should be equivalent, not identical, to the damage. Finally, the law did not stipulate that the person who suffered the wrong should be the one to exact retribution from the wrongdoer. It was left to judges to interpret the extent and seriousness of the wrong done and to decide what would be appropriate compensation; and then it was left to the officers of the court to enforce the judgment.

The next example arises from the on-again, off-again debate about whether to restore capital punishment. Taking issue with an earlier defense of the abolitionist viewpoint, someone wrote to the local newspaper along the following lines:

12   Mr. E. stated that "capital punishment is legal vengeance based on emotion instead of logic." Really! What kind of "reason and logic" do killers who snuff out the lives of innocent people use?

I don't think any murderer can produce a logical reason for taking a life. So why should society be hesitant to give him the same treatment he meted out to others?

The writer's meaning is less than fully clear. Is she arguing that just as a murderer cannot produce a logical reason for taking a life, so, too, society should not have to apply reason and logic to its actions? Probably not. Perhaps her point is that capital punishment is society's emotional response to murder, but that is all right because murder itself is an act of emotion, no logical (i.e., nonemotional) reason for taking a life being imaginable. The writer's reasoning in this case would seem to be that an emotional reaction to murder, namely the desire to impose capital punishment, is justified since murder itself is a crime based on emotion. The trouble with this reasoning is that it does not yield defensible results consistently. Emotional acts are often best defused by coolly unemotional responses. Our "gut" reactions to wrongs we and others suffer, our impulse to strike back at the wrongdoer, is often counterproductive or futile, not to say illegal. So our writer must find some other argument to defend capital punishment. The manner in which murders may be carried out cannot justify reacting to them in the same manner.

The next two examples bring out variations of the pattern we've been looking at. They're close enough in spirit to the *two wrongs* fallacy to be considered here.

A state official, who shall remain nameless, came under criticism because the agency for which he was responsible had bungled the storage of surplus eggs, and over 27 million eggs had been allowed to spoil. In an interview, the official took issue with his critics by saying:

13   I wouldn't call that a *surplus*. It was only two days' consumption for the whole state. They think that's a lot, but how many billions, and I mean billions, of potatoes were dumped in Idaho years ago? Nothing was said about that.

The two-wrongs motif is evident here. The official was criticized for wasting eggs (a misguided action), and he defended himself by pointing to another bad situation (the potatoes dumped in Idaho). His argument differs from the two we've seen already because he did not appear to be arguing that the earlier wrong somehow justified the present one. Instead, he seemed to be saying: Nobody jumped all over Idaho when it wasted all those potatoes, so why are you jumping on me now? The official's point seems to have been that he and his agency were being subjected to unfair criticism. Our sense of justice and fair play were being appealed to (similar cases should be treated similarly).

Suppose the two situations were, indeed, similar. Then the official would have had a legitimate grievance. But what follows? Not that the agency responsible for surplus egg storage was being wrongly or unfairly criticized. It truly goofed in allowing 27 million eggs to spoil. All that follows from an appeal to fair play is that the cases should have been treated similarly, which could as well be taken to mean the Idaho potato dumpers should have been criticized as that the egg agency should not be. That the potato wasters weren't criticized *then* doesn't mean we should repeat the oversight *now*; the way to correct the situation is not to compound or double the wrong by withholding criticism here. How strange the principles of justice and consistency would be if they required us to blind our eyes to obvious wrongdoing simply because similar wrongdoing had escaped detection and criticism in the past. Our defensive official was guilty of a variant form of the fallacy of *two wrongs*.

A second variant of this fallacy is exemplified by a situation involving a philosophy professor at an Ivy League college. To supplement his income, Professor *X* took on a second teaching job at another university, thus violating his contract with the first university; he did not inform either institution of his dual role. Apparently an extremely able and mobile person, he managed to do a competent job at both institutions. Alas, however, he was discovered and promptly lost both jobs. According to a report in *Time* magazine, he admitted a mistake, but not a fault. In a fifteen-page letter, he reminded the president of the Ivy League College that (here we paraphrase):

14   I can show you a professor who spends her time doing extensive consulting, another who writes best-sellers, a third who has written an introductory textbook, and a fourth who writes a column for a popular magazine, none of which contributes to scholarship or teaching but all of which pay substantial amounts of money and require large amounts of time.

Professor *X*'s argument was that since he can point to other faculty members who, without blame or penalty, do outside work that takes time from their teaching and scholarly work, his taking an outside job should not have been blamed or penalized either.

This argument illustrates a feature often present in "two-wrongs" arguments. Professor *X* was making argument from analogy when he compared his holding two jobs to another faculty member who consults, one who writes novels, one who's written a textbook, and a fourth who writes opinion columns, in order to try to show that his conduct was not more wrong than the others'. "Two-wrongs" arguments are often, perhaps always, special cases of arguments from analogy. The arguments may then turn out to be guilty of the fallacy of *faulty analogy* as well as the fallacy of *two wrongs*.

Is Professor *X*'s argument from analogy a good one? It requires the assumption that holding two jobs at once is on a par with doing those other sorts of outside work that take time from teaching and scholarship. We question that assumption. (Admittedly, we have a personal stake in doing so!) First, Professor *X*'s contract explicitly prohibited him from taking another job, whereas the activities he mentions are not generally prohibited under terms of a faculty contract. Second, introductory texts can be contributions to teaching, and they can also include conceptual innovations that are contributions to scholarship, so people occupied with them aren't necessarily doing outside work. Also, such writing, or authoring a magazine column, cannot be compared, in terms of the time and effort required, with holding a second job. So we think the relevant properties that make writing textbooks and newspaper columns legitimate do not apply to holding a second job in violation of a contractual agreement. We think Professor *X* commits *faulty analogy*.

Quite apart from that, however, Professor *X*'s reasoning is fallacious on other grounds. If faculty members are violating their contracts by doing outside work, then they should be dealt with in the appropriate way. If such wrongdoing has gone undetected and unpunished, that is no reason for tolerating it in Professor *X*'s case. These other wrongs can't be used to justify his conduct. Professor X also commits *two wrongs*.

Clearly, *two wrongs* is a fallacy to look for in an adversarial context, when someone is attempting to defend some action (or course of action) against criticism. The conditions for the fallacy are listed in the box.

TWO WRONGS

1. Someone's action has come under blame, criticism, or some sort of sanction.
2. Someone tries to defend the person criticized by citing an allegedly similar set of one or more actions (the wrongness of which is granted or at least not challenged) performed without blame, criticism, or sanction.
3. The lack of blame, criticism, or sanction for that other set of actions is either irrelevant or insufficient to establish the impropriety of blaming, criticizing, or otherwise sanctioning the initial action in question.

The two-wrongs argument is fallacious, at least in the paradigm versions, when it offers no reason for us to put aside our standard condemnation of a given action other than the fact that the agent previously received an injury from the victim of his or her current action. By itself, such a ground must always be insufficient evidence, and it may also be irrelevant, at least in a society like ours, where vengefulness is not a virtue and where the right to punish offenders has been taken out of the hands of the injured individual. Thus the two-wrongs argument will either fail to meet the relevance criterion of good arguments or it will fail to meet the sufficiency requirement. We place *two wrongs* next to *faulty analogy* because its typical pattern of argument involves a claim of an analogy between two similar-looking treatments.

Variations on the basic pattern of the *two-wrongs* fallacy don't go quite so far as to try to justify the wrong. They are attempts to excuse, or to mitigate blame, or to block criticism. But the appeal they make solely to an earlier wrong remains insufficient or irrelevant to the conclusion. The occurrence of the earlier, admittedly wrong act does not, by itself, make the present, similar act excusable, nor blame for it less in order, nor criticism of it less appropriate.

To show that *two wrongs* has been committed, you need to identify the two actions involved in the argument and to sort out just what line of defense is being offered. Does the argument attempt to justify the act, excuse it, mitigate blame, or block criticism?

We've already indicated why a two-wrongs argument is an impersonator. Its air of respectability comes from its apparent similarity to various principles of justice. The defense of the Kenora Indians' occupation imitated the principle of retributive and compensatory justice, which says that when a wrong has been done, the victim deserves compensation. The spoiled-eggs example traded on the principle of justice that holds that similar cases should be treated similarly. Both of them misapply the principles of justice in the naïve belief that the interests of justice can somehow be served by either compounding or ignoring wrongdoing.

Improper Appeal to Practice

You've surely heard (or used) this line of defense before: "But everybody else does it." To rebut or defuse a criticism of an action, someone will appeal, not to *one* other case, but to a whole set of cases. This person is claiming, in effect, that the action in question is common practice. A variation of the appeal to common practice is the appeal to tradition or past practice to justify or deflect blame from conduct: "But this is the way it's always been done!"

These two appeals to practice to justify an action or to mitigate criticism are not necessarily fallacious, but they easily can be. The fallacious ones look much like the sound ones and, by this impersonation, can get past the inattentive critic.

Consider this example, which is an extension of the excerpt from Vincent Theresa's reminiscences discussed earlier, in Chapter 2:

15   There are plenty of good things about [mobsters]. . . . most are [patriotic]. We don't
think about undermining the government. We corrupt politicians, but that's only so
we can do business. We cheat on taxes, but let's face it, there isn't a damn business
executive who doesn't.

Theresa here offers a defense of the Mafia's cheating on taxes: All business
executives cheat on their taxes. Put aside the fact that this claim is simply false.
The gist of Theresa's defense is that cheating on taxes is a common practice, at
least among business executives, and that therefore it is not culpable. Our
contention is that this appeal to practice is improper. It won't do, for the reason
that no one contends that the practice of cheating on taxes is a legitimate one.
Those who do it are placing their personal interests (money) above their legal
(and moral) obligation to pay for the services the state provides for them and
their fellow citizens. They are trying to get a free ride. The arguments against tax
evasion are not undermined by the fact that lots of people cheat on their taxes
(and not just business executives). The numbers of people doing it does not
make it right. Hence, the appeal to common practice is fallacious. Theresa
commits here the fallacy we term *improper appeal to practice*.

The Theresa example involved an appeal to a practice that, no matter how
widespread, is conceded to be wrong. There is another kind of appeal to
practice, one where the arguer contends that although the action was once
considered wrong, the fact that it is now widely practiced is grounds for ceasing
to consider it wrong. Especially when there is no objection to modifying a
practice, the new version may in time come to represent the norm and be
granted legitimacy. Such arguments have been used to defend actions as diverse
as premarital sex and canceling classes on the Friday afternoon of a holiday
weekend.

We do, and indeed must, figure out how to function in our society by
learning its customs. We may not appreciate the importance of these customs
because we've grown up with them and they therefore seem the only possible
or reasonable way to behave. If we move to a different culture, however, we may
find ourselves at a loss as to how to behave toward others until we find out what
conduct is considered appropriate there. (One of the things that infuriated
colonized peoples about the conduct of their imperialist oppressors was their
lack of respect for local customs and the imposition of their own customs.)

This kind of appeal to practice, therefore, can be relevant, in the absence
of any controversy about the propriety of the actions. The appeal, however, is
not, by itself, sufficient, for one must also show that the practice is currently
accepted and is not being challenged. When a practice is in the midst of change,
or if there is a dispute about its continuance, clearly an appeal to that practice
would *beg the question*.

For example, if a woman argues that she should not include a promise to
obey her husband in her wedding vows on the grounds that such a promise is
inconsistent with the role she wants to play in the marriage, she is implicitly
challenging not only the tradition of including this promise in the wedding vows
but also practices built into the marriage role which that tradition reflects. It

would be irrelevant in that situation for her traditionalist parents to argue that she should follow the standard service and make the promise to obey on the grounds that this is part of the traditional and customary wedding service. In appealing to the tradition, they are assuming its legitimacy, when that is just what she denies. For this sort of *improper appeal to practice*, what makes the appeal improper is that it *begs the question*.

Here is another example to illustrate an *improper appeal to practice*. The following fragment from a letter to the editor opposing gun-control legislation is typical:

16 The people of this country are accustomed to living in a state of individual liberty. Part of our heritage is the privately owned firearm.

This heritage (or the myth that there is such a heritage) is precisely what proponents of stricter gun-control legislation want to put an end to. The writer's appeal to tradition takes for granted what is at issue, so it begs the question. What he needs to do is produce reasons that will answer the present objections to continuing the tradition.

We can, then, distinguish the following different types of appeal to practice used to defend an action against criticism.

Case 1. There is the appeal to a practice that is conceded to be wrong. This appeal is improper because it is irrelevant.

Case 2. There is the appeal to a practice that is in the midst of change or under dispute. This appeal is improper because it *begs the question*.

Case 3. An appeal to practice is used to argue that values or expectations have changed. If the arguer establishes that the new practice is generally accepted and unchallenged, then the argument in that respect is not fallacious. (But if the arguer fails to show that the practice has become established, then it's a case of *improper appeal to practice* due to a *hasty conclusion.*)

The conditions of *improper appeal to practice* are listed in the box.

IMPROPER APPEAL TO PRACTICE

1. Someone defends an action against criticism by arguing that the conduct is widely practiced, is a customary practice, or is a traditional practice.
2. Either there is, in fact, no such practice, or, in these circumstances, the existence of the practice is not relevant or not sufficient to justify or excuse the conduct being criticized.

An *improper appeal to practice* will, in some instances, be a violation of the acceptability criterion of good arguments; in others, it will be a violation of the relevance requirement; and in yet others, it will be a failure to satisfy the sufficiency criterion.

We conclude this section with an example that we find difficult to analyze. Some years ago, the city of Regina, Saskatchewan, was debating whether to build a new city hall. The city council favored the idea, but not all taxpayers shared its opinion, as the following, adapted from a letter to the editor, attests:

17   A new city hall will cost many million of dollars, and that cost will increase the property rate as well as other taxes.

      In the opinion of many taxpayers, it is undemocratic for the mayor and city council to bypass the public on this important issue. Past councils would never have gone ahead with the scheme until the people had approved of it in a special ballot.

In the last sentence, the writer appeals to past practices of city councils. Let's assume that she is right, and there was, in Regina, a custom that when big civic expenses that would increase the property tax rate were proposed, the city council put the question on the ballot. In that case, this argument is a strong one, we think, though not yet complete. For the writer would also need to show that no one on previous councils had raised any objection to the city's practice and therefore there was no particular reason to amend it. (One could imagine a council member making such an objection. A city council is, after all, elected by the citizens to run city government and plan for the city's future. That will often involve making commitments for expenditures. If council members have the legal authority to do this, then, by virtue of having been elected, they have the moral trust of the electorate to make such decisions. It might be argued, then, that a city council would be abrogating its responsibility and wasting time and money if it delayed a decision until the next election or held a special referendum.) So, as it stands, we think the writer's argument is a case of *improper appeal to practice*. In this case, however, the flaw seems minor. It might easily be repaired by providing assurances that the practice of putting major expenditures on the ballot had not, explicitly, been objected to.

      An *improper appeal to practice* is a cousin of the *two-wrongs* argument. Both involve seeking to deflect criticism by citing as precedent the actions of others. Such an appeal is sometimes appropriate and sometimes not, and that is what makes it easy to commit these fallacies and hard to identify them.

Questionable Cause

Think, for a moment, of some of the hotly contested public issues of the past few years. Should pornography be illegal? Should economic recessions be fought with tax cuts or with government spending? Should something be done about the violence on TV?

      To be able to give intelligent answers to these and scores of similar questions, we must make judgments about *causal relationships*; i.e., about what influences or brings about what.

For example, does capital punishment serve as a deterrent to murder (cause people not to kill when they otherwise would)? Does the open availability of pornography decrease the incidence of sexual crimes (cause people who would otherwise commit sex crimes to be satisfied instead by viewing pornography)? Does legal access to abortion encourage its use as a form of birth control (cause women to be careless about birth control because they know they can always get an abortion)? Do tax cuts increase spending (cause people to spend the money they would otherwise have used to pay their taxes) and hence increase production and employment (cause manufacturers to make more goods and to hire more workers to do so) as well as government tax revenue (cause an increase in taxes from increased sales and income)? Does increased government spending have that effect (cause more money in salaries and income from goods and services sold, which causes extra spending, which causes extra manufacturing and employment, which cause more tax income), or does it merely increase deficits (cause more money to go out than comes in)? Does violence on TV lead to violent behavior in viewers (cause people who watch it to emulate it)?

Much of the discussion about public policy, and the persuasive argumentation directed at the citizens connected with it, must consist of or presuppose arguments about causal claims.

A *cause* is an event that produces another event, its *effect*. We refer to causes in various ways: We say that one event *leads to another, produces it, brings it about, makes it happen, forces it, stops it, prevents it, stems it, increases it.* The list could go on to some length. No one or two or three terms can be depended on to signal a causal claim or a causal argument. You will have to judge from the context whether a causal claim, or an argument, is involved.

A systematic account of causal reasoning is beyond the scope of this text. Indeed, the theory of causal inferences is still debated in philosophical circles. As it happens, however, detection of some of the kinds of mistakes typically found in causal reasoning that characterize public-policy discussions (as contrasted with debate among scientists about their sciences) does not depend on theoretical subtleties. Moreover, causal fallacies are best understood through the examination of concrete examples. We will work through a healthy sample of representative errors in arguments employing causal claims, introducing any needed theoretical background information as we go. These errors, we shall say, constitute cases of the fallacy we call *questionable cause.*

Arguments "to" and "from" Causal Claims

It's useful to distinguish two types of arguments involving causal claims. Some are intended to show that one thing is the cause of another. Their conclusions are therefore causal claims. We call them *arguments to a cause.* Others use a causal claim as a premise and argue from there to some further claim, often a recommendation for an action or a policy. We call these *arguments from a cause.* Of course, the two may be combined. Someone argues first that X causes

Y (an argument to a cause), and then uses that conclusion as a premise to argue that something should be done to prevent *X* on the grounds that *Y* is undesirable or that something should be done to bring about *X*, on the grounds that *Y* is desirable (both arguments from a cause).

Keeping clear about the distinction between arguments *to* a cause and arguments *from* a cause can help you spot flaws. For instance, it may be true that *X* is *a* cause of *Y* (for example, that handguns are *a* cause of murders), but not the only one. Hence, an argument based on the assumption that *X* causes *Y* and concluding that preventing *X* (restricting access to handguns) will therefore prevent *Y* (bring an end to murder) is clearly a case of *questionable cause* because other causes of *Y* will still be operative even if *X* is stopped.

Although most arguments in the public domain involving causal claims push recommendations that an action be taken or that a policy be implemented (and thus are arguments *from* causes), their flaws are usually due to some error in reasoning *to* a causal claim. Therefore, in the inventory of examples that follow, we focus primarily on arguments to causal claims and the typical ways in which they can go wrong.

Particular and General Causal Claims

Arguments to causes can further be divided into two groups. The first group deals with the causes of *particular events*, events that are unique in time. Belonging to this group are arguments about the causes of the Persian Gulf war or of the breakup of the Soviet state in 1991, the cause of atmospheric ozone depletion in the 1980s and 1990s, the cause of a girlfriend's or a boyfriend's sudden coolness, and so on. The second group deals with general causal claims, claims about the causes of recurring events, such as the cause of cancer, revolutions, inflation, sexual assault, resistance to women's equality, and so on.

As a rule, support for particular causal claims invokes general ones and consists of showing what general causal laws apply in the particular case in question. For example, in looking for the cause of one person's lung cancer, the researcher would seek to find what general cancer-causing factors were present in that patient's medical history. This model is less clearly applicable when dealing with historical events. In arguing about what caused the more or less simultaneous collapse of Communist governments in Eastern Europe at the beginning of the 1990s, there are no known general "laws" or history available to explain the phenomenon.

Particular Causal Claims.   The following examples will illustrate some of the variants of *questionable cause* possible in arguing to the causes of particular events.

Back in the spring of 1975, Canada changed from the Fahrenheit to the Celsius scale for measuring temperature. Among the many who complained about the change was a gentleman from Cape Breton, Nova Scotia, who wrote to his local newspaper:

18   Ever since we changed over to Celsius, the weather has been unusually irregular.

The man's assumption was that the switch from Fahrenheit to Celsius caused the irregular weather. We can smile at this inference, but the kind of mistake he made is not always without dangerous possibilities.

What is wrong with this argument is that the mere existence of a before-and-after sequence is never, by itself, sufficient basis for a causal claim—for a number of events immediately precede any effect, yet not all can be its cause or causes. We know the inference about the irregular weather was silly because we are familiar with the kinds of hypotheses meteorologists employ to try to explain weather changes, and we know that the influence of the units of temperature measurement is not among these hypotheses.

Such arguments are said to commit the fallacy called *post hoc, ergo propter hoc* ("after this, therefore because of this"). What gives this reasoning its appeal is that, typically, a cause of an event immediately precedes it. Looking for an event just prior to the one whose cause is being sought is therefore quite appropriate. The fallacy occurs when the arguer moves straight from the fact that X came immediately before Y to the conclusion that X caused Y. It is necessary, further, to have some hypothesis connecting the two events and, finally, to rule out alternative hypotheses as less plausible.

The following chain letter has been in circulation for at least the past fifteen years (versions of it came to us in the mail twice, more than ten years separating the two occasions, and we have heard of others getting it, too). Perhaps you have seen it.

19   "Trust in the Lord with all your heart and knowledge, and He will light the way." This prayer has been sent to you for good luck. The original copy came from the Netherlands. It has been sent around the world nine times. . . . You are to receive good luck within four days of receiving this letter. This is not a joke. Don Elliot received $60,000 but lost it because he broke the chain. While in the Philippines, General Walsh lost his wife six days after he received the letter and failed to circulate the prayer. Please send this letter (twenty copies) to people you think need good luck and see what happens on the fourth day after. . . . Take note of the following: Constantine Diary received the chain in 1933. He asked his secretary to make twenty copies and send them out. A few days later, he won the lottery of $4 million in his country. Carlos Broodt, an office employee, received the chain, forgot it, and lost his job. He found the chain and sent out twenty copies. Nine days later, he found a better job. Aaron Barachilla received the chain and threw it away; nine days later he died. For no reason whatever should this chain be broken . . .

No harm done in sending the prayer and letter on, right? After all, why take a chance? Well, this sort of superstition can readily intimidate those who have no defense against the *post hoc* version of *questionable cause*. Actually, even a prior consideration is the reasonableness of these claims. How could anyone have access to all this information? How could anyone follow the progress of the chain? But just for fun, assume that these ridiculous claims are correct.

What we are given are a few cases of "good luck" and a few cases of "bad luck," all consisting of before-and-after sequences. The numbers, however, have no significance unless we compare them to the total number of people involved in the chain (and if it's been going since at least 1933, that would mean billions of people). Also, no connecting hypothesis is offered, unless perhaps it is the implicit suggestion that God rewards those who circulate the prayer and punishes those who do not, a suggestion of dubious theological merit. No reason is offered, or obvious, for why God would take such an interest in a chain letter. This is a good example of how *post hoc, ergo propter hoc* can underlie superstitious beliefs.

The following example is from an editorial published back in the days when universal seat-belt installation was a novelty and safety officials were trying to persuade drivers to get into the habit of using them.

20   In Australia, where seat-belt use is mandatory, hospital occupancy, one of the highest prices society pays for traffic accidents, has been reduced by 25 percent.

The implication here is that the use of seat belts caused a decrease in hospital occupancy. It is clear why wearing seat belts might cause a decrease in serious injuries, thereby reducing hospital occupancy. Since this intervening principle is obvious, the principle of charity tells us to assume the editorialist had it in mind and so did not commit the *post hoc* version of *questionable cause*. But what about the reduction in highway speed limits that occurred widely at about the same time, partly as a result of a worldwide fuel shortage? That, too, could have been responsible for a reduction in the number of accidents and so reduced hospital occupancy. The editorial doesn't mention whether a speed-limit reduction could have been a factor in Australian statistics at the time.

A more careful statement on the same subject was reported in a Toronto newspaper a couple of years later, six months after seat-belt use had become mandatory in Ontario.

21   Staff Superintendent John Marks of the metropolitan Toronto police said in an interview, "There is absolutely no doubt that the seat-belt law is working.

"The sharp drop in death and injury statistics has more to do with seat belts than it does with lower speed limits. Our jurisdiction does not include the major provincial highways, where speed-limit reductions have played a major part in lowering accident statistics."

Here, Staff Superintendent Marks acknowledges the alternative hypothesis and explains why it was unlikely to have been a factor in causing the drop in deaths and injuries in auto accidents.

Another kind of mistake in arguing to causes consists of treating an explanatory hypothesis as an account of the cause of an event, without sufficient evidence. Here's an example from a *Time* magazine story some years back. The city of El Paso, Texas, was then about one-third the size of Dallas, but the number of El Paso residents found in state mental hospitals was one-seventh the number of Dallas residents in such institutions. Other things being equal, one would expect roughly similar proportions, so how might the difference be explained? A University of Texas biochemist offered this explanation:

> **22** El Paso's water is heavily laced with lithium, a tranquilizing chemical widely used in the treatment of manic depression and other psychiatric disorders. Dallas has low lithium levels because it draws its water from surface supplies.

An intriguing hypothesis: El Paso citizens were ingesting amounts of the tranquilizer lithium with their drinking water, which helps to prevent or remedy the symptoms of mental disorders for which they might otherwise have sought treatment in state mental hospitals. But more investigation is needed. Were there other cities with high lithium levels in their water supplies? If so, how did their mental hospital admission rates compare to those of El Paso? Also, how did admissions from Dallas compare with those of other cities with similar lithium levels? Furthermore, could there be alternative explanations? Does life in Dallas tend to put great pressure on its citizens? Does the considerably smaller El Paso have a more serene pace? Without investigating further the correlation between lithium intake and mental hospitalization and without checking alternative explanations, the biochemist is guilty of *questionable cause.*

As it happened, *Time* magazine had come across a competing hypothesis.

> **23** State mental health officials point out that the mental hospital closest to Dallas is 35 miles away from the city, while the one nearest El Paso is 350 miles away.

We shall not commit *questionable cause* ourselves by asserting that the health officials' explanation provides us with the cause of the higher incidence of mental hospital admissions in Dallas. But since the biochemist ignored that possibility, he can be charged with the fallacy.

Here's another example, from a London, England, newspaper:

> **24** A 16-year-old youth, dressed in white overalls, a collarless shirt, high boots, and a bowler hat, kicked a younger boy unconscious, smashed his ribs, and disfigured his face. Why did he do it?
>
> In the opinion of the British judge who sentenced the attacker to a term in reform school, it was simply because he had watched a "wicked film" Stanley Kubrick's *A Clockwork Orange.*
>
> The judge noted that the young man had launched his attack while wearing clothes similar to those of the "violence-crazed" characters in the film.

The judge did not argue in *post hoc* fashion. He reasoned from the fact that the crime resembled acts committed in the film and that the youngster was obviously imitating, in his manner of dress, the style of characters in the film. Still, the judge made a causal claim of a sort that is difficult to substantiate: a claim about the cause of a person's behavior. We cannot play this youth's life back over again to see what would have resulted had he not seen Kubrick's film. Moreover, as the liveliness of the current debate attests, there exists no established general causal claim about violence in films or TV causing violent behavior in their viewers. Finally, the judge's claim that the youth had committed the crime "simply because" of seeing the film is unclear. Does he mean that the film was the sole cause or that it was one of the contributing causes? The wording suggests the former interpretation, and if that is what the judge intended, then we think he did commit *questionable cause*.

The clothing, style, and manner of the attack do suggest a connection with *A Clockwork Orange*, but we must consider alternative hypotheses. Perhaps the movie started a clothing fad, and it was due to the fad, not to his having seen the movie, that the youth was dressed in that particular way. Perhaps the violence of his attack could be explained as plausibly or more plausibly in terms of factors unique to that youth. Did he have a history of outbursts of uncontrollable temper? Was he himself beaten or otherwise abused at home? Was he acting under peer-group pressure to meet some misconceived standard of manhood? Had the judge offered his opinion merely as a possible and reasonable hypothesis, he would have been on safe ground. But because he asserted it as an unqualified causal claim, without citing evidence ruling out equally plausible alternative possibilities, he was guilty of *questionable cause*.

What the *A Clockwork Orange* and the El Paso lithium examples have in common is the premature elevation of one possible explanation to the status of *the sole* cause. In both cases, alternative hypotheses were available and should have been investigated. A more thorough check might have revealed one of three possibilities: (1) one or more of the other plausible hypotheses correctly described the cause; (2) the factor proposed, together with one or more of the other possible causal variables, all operated as independent but mutually reinforcing causes; (3) the hypothesis proposing the causal factor did, indeed, describe the sole cause. So *questionable cause* may be seen to be a species of *hasty conclusion* in the two examples above, the hasty jump to the third possibility without checking out the first two.

General Causal Claims.   The following passage is from an article published a few years ago:

25   Psychiatry kills. It kills because of the ruthless, unprovable treatments used on those entrusted to its care. . . . These are just a few of the facts. The bodies of no fewer than twenty-one people have been discovered in shallow graves in California, all killed with machete blows and knife thrusts by one man in a period of less than two months. The murderer, a Mexican American, had previously been committed to a mental hospital. Sixteen people were shot to death by a student from the top of the Texas University Tower. The student had previously received psychiatric treatment. The Manson family killed seven in brutal murders in California. Manson had previously received psychiatric treatment.

The article went on to list many more instances of people who had received psychiatric treatment and later engaged in some form of violent, antisocial behavior.

Note that the article was not assuming that the cause of the behavior in each case was the psychiatric treatment that the people had received. On the contrary, the author used these examples to try to establish a *correlation* between psychiatric treatment and violent behavior.

CORRELATION

A *correlation* is a systematic covariance between two variables (properties or events) such that the occurrence of, or a change in, instances of one tend to be accompanied by the occurrence of, or changes in, instances of the other.

Showing that a correlation exists between psychiatric treatment and murderous behavior is the correct move to make if one wants to establish the general causal claim that such treatment can cause such behavior. If events of type x cause events of type y, then when instances of x occur, instances of y will tend to be found. Hence, to discover whether x's cause y's, the first thing to look for is such a correlation.

A correlation does not entail 100 percent co-occurrence. In the above example, the claim is not necessarily that psychiatric treatment always causes people to become violent. More likely, and more typical of general causal claims of this sort, what is being argued is that psychiatry *can* cause violence. Nor is the article claiming that psychiatry is the *only* cause of violence. In fact, it's a claim of the same variety as the assertion that smoking cigarettes in sufficient quantity causes lung cancer. Pointing out such counterinstances as that novelist Somerset Maugham smoked four packs a day for most of his life yet died a natural death at the age of 91 does not refute the general claim. Nor does showing cases of people who received psychiatric treatment but did not commit murder refute the former claim.

Furthermore, just as the fact that there are other causes of cancer besides smoking does not show that smoking isn't also a cause of cancer, so the fact that there are other causes of violent behavior besides psychiatric treatment would not show that psychiatry is not an additional cause of violence.

Does the article, then, establish that psychiatry is a cause of violent behavior? Clearly not. To show precisely why not, however, we must say more about the method of establishing this kind of general causal claim, and it will help to use the example of the established general claim that tobacco smoke is a cause of lung cancer.

To establish that claim, researchers first had to demonstrate, by carefully systematic studies, that the incidence of lung cancer is significantly higher among smokers than among nonsmokers. By "significantly" is meant, roughly, that the difference is too striking to be explained by chance. It is reasonable, therefore, to hypothesize a causal link between tobacco smoke and lung cancer. To corroborate this hypothesis, however, researchers had to rule out factors other than tobacco smoke that are associated with smoking and, therefore, may have been the actual causal agents (for example, the fumes from cigarette paper, match, or lighter). They also had to rule out factors that might cause both smoking and lung cancer independently, factors such as stress. Experiments were run in which these factors were present but the tobacco was absent, and the correlation with lung cancer disappeared. The experiments were refined until it was established that the nicotine and tar in cigarette tobacco are the causally operative factors. Researchers have not yet succeeded in discovering the precise mechanism at work (largely because they do not yet know enough about cancers generally), but it's considered a well-established causal claim that tobacco smoke is a causal factor in contracting lung cancer.

By comparing it with the article arguing that smoking is a cause of lung cancer, we can now take stock of the deficiencies in the article arguing that psychiatric treatment is a cause of violent behavior. They are:

1. The psychiatric treatment-murder correlation was inadequately established. The evidence was anecdotal, not systematic. What should have been done (the sort of study done to establish the tobacco smoke-cancer correlation) is this: Obtain representative samples of those who have and those who have not received psychiatric treatment. Check each group for its incidence of subsequent violent behavior. Only if there is a statistically significant difference between the two groups, with the treatment sample showing a higher incidence of violent behavior, has a correlation worth further consideration been established.

2. Additional correlations that might have turned out to signify causal connections were not ruled out (in the cancer example, tar and nicotine were isolated as the causal factors; and cigarette paper fumes, match fumes and stress, were eliminated). For instance, what led the people cited in the psychiatric-treatment article to seek or be referred for psychiatric treatment? Chances are that some underlying disorder first showed symptoms that resulted in their receiving psychiatric treatment and that in spite of the treatment, this disorder later also caused the murderous behavior. The article produced no evidence to rule out such an additional correlate as a causal factor in the violent behavior.

On these two counts, then, we consider the article guilty of *questionable cause* in arguing to the general causal claim that psychiatric treatment can cause violent behavior.

Arguments "from" Causal Claims

We have been concentrating on these examples as arguments to causes. However, in almost every case, the argument was intended as background for a further inference based on it. The gentleman from Cape Breton was suggesting that perhaps Canada ought to return to Fahrenheit degrees; the point of the argument about seat belts was to commend their use; the London judge went on to urge the censorship of movies like *A Clockwork Orange*; and the psychiatry article argued that people ought to avoid psychiatric treatment. (We're not sure whether the Texas biochemist was making any recommendations about the introduction of lithium into water supplies.) It's possible, now, to compile a rough catalog of mistakes found in arguments from causes, using the above examples to illustrate them.

An argument from a particular causal claim is faulty if:

1. The recommendation is based on a pure *post hoc, ergo propter hoc* inference without even any connecting hypothesis proposed. [See the Cape Breton gentleman's anti-Celsius argument (Example 18) and the chain letter (Example 19).]
2. The recommendation is based on a hypothesis offered to explain a spatiotemporal connection, but alternative, equally plausible hypotheses exist and have not been ruled out. [See *A Clockwork Orange* (Example 24) and El Paso lithium (Example 22).]
3. The recommendation is based on a claim supported only by a spotty correlation, one that hasn't been systematically established. [See "psychiatry kills" (Example 25).]
4. The recommendation is based on a claim supported by a correlation only, without other correlations checked out and found not to account for the cause. [See "psychiatry kills" (Example 25).]

An argument from a general cause can be faulty for a reason not yet fully discussed: The recommendation is based on mistakenly taking what is merely one cause among others to be the only cause or the main cause. There are two quite distinct versions of this mistake. The first version occurs when one among several independently operative causes is taken to be the only or the main cause. In the following example, the writer was concerned about gang violence in high schools:

26 The real problem was pointed out recently by assistant police chief Brown. He pointed out that the main cause of all this gang violence is the high incidence of single-parent families, resulting in a lack of discipline at home.

Even supposing that lack of discipline is one contributing cause of violent gang behavior—and that is certainly conceivable—it doesn't follow that introducing discipline will eliminate gang violence. For it is very likely that the phenomenon has other causes as well: lack of employment prospects, breakdown of the community, easy money to be made from dealing drugs, competition for drug markets, and so on.

The second version consists of failing to see one cause as merely one component in a set of causal factors, all of which operate together to bring about the effect. Here is an example, adapted from a letter to the *Detroit Free Press*:

27 This is written in reply to the dogma espoused by the *Free Press* and other gun-control proponents—the claim that the availability of firearms is the root cause of all the killings in the land. I was born in 1913 and was 15 years old before I was anywhere within a hundred miles of anyone who had been shot with a pistol, and that was a thief who was shot by the police. Everyone we knew had guns in their home and knew how to use them. . . . If the availability of guns is the cause of the killings, why weren't we all murdered back in those days? Guns were everywhere.

The *Free Press* editorial position had been that the availability of handguns was one factor that fitted together with others to result in murders and that if handguns were removed from the scene (the aim of gun-control legislation), that causal set would be broken up and a major cause of murders removed. The letter writer, however, took the *Free Press* to be holding that the availability of handguns *by itself* led to murders: This was the position he or she was arguing against. This is a case of a *straw-person* fallacy because the writer is criticizing the *Free Press* for a position it did not take. It seems to us that the writer's *straw-person* attack was probably due to his or her confusing two different types of causal factor: "necessary" and "sufficient" causal conditions.

Necessary and Sufficient Conditions

Philosophers and scientists have developed a convenient terminology for distinguishing two ways in which a factor can contribute causally to an effect: They distinguish between necessary and sufficient causal conditions.

A *sufficient causal condition* is an event or factor the presence of which brings about another event. "X is a sufficient causal condition for Y" implies "If X occurs, Y occurs." A burned-out bulb, for example, is a sufficient causal condition for a light not to go on. So is a broken switch, or a burned-out fuse, or a power failure. The occurrence of any one of these is enough to cause the light to fail.

A *necessary causal condition* is an event or factor whose absence prevents another event from occurring. "X is a necessary causal condition for Y" implies "If X does not occur, Y will not occur," or, what comes to the same thing, "If Y occurs, X must have occurred." So, for example, an unbroken electric circuit is a necessary condition for a light to go on. If the light does go on, electricity must be flowing through an unbroken circuit, and if *this* condition if absent—if the current is broken—then the light is prevented from going on.

NECESSARY AND SUFFICIENT CAUSAL CONDITIONS

X is a necessary causal condition of Y provided that Y will not occur unless X occurs.
X is a sufficient causal condition of Y provided that any time X occurs, Y will occur.

Many causes consist of a collection of factors where each one is causally necessary and all together are, jointly, causally sufficient to bring about the effect. To speak of "a cause" in such a situation is to refer to one of the necessary conditions. Return now to the letter to the *Free Press* about its stand on handgun control. The *Free Press's* position was that the ready availability of handguns was a necessary causal condition contributing to the increased frequency of murders. The availability of handguns, it held, was a necessary condition, but not alone a sufficient condition, for the increase in the murder rate. The writer mistakenly took the *Free Press* to be arguing that the widespread possession of handguns was a sufficient causal condition for the murder rate increase.

The second version of treating one cause as the only cause can be described as confusing a necessary causal condition with a sufficient causal condition.

We hope our discussion of these examples serves as a useful indication of some of the main complexities to be found in causal arguments, of the varieties of causal claims found in daily discourse, and of the sorts of critical questions to which the logical reader should subject causal claims. A summary of the general conditions of the fallacy we've been discussing can be found in the box.

QUESTIONABLE CAUSE

1. A causal claim occurs in someone's argument, either as a conclusion or as a premise.
2. The person argues *to* the causal claim as the conclusion but fails to provide adequate support for it; OR the person argues *from* the causal claim, as one of the premises, without supporting it, and there are grounds for questioning the acceptability of the causal claim.

To detect instances of *questionable cause*, the first and most important step is to ferret the causal claim (or implication) out into the open. Once that is done, the rest is a matter of looking at the sort of evidence that has been proposed for it. To defend your charge, it is not necessary that you prove the causal claim to be false. You need only show that the case for the causal connection hasn't been adequately made. An argument that can or might be strengthened by further evidence can still be guilty of *questionable cause* in its present form. In either case, the fallacy is an instance of a failure to satisfy the criterion of sufficiency for good arguments.

EXERCISES

Directions: For each extract assigned, decide if there are any arguments present, and, if so, whether they contain any of the fallacies you have studied so far. If you think there is no argument, explain what the function of the passage is. If you think any arguments are logically good ones, try to anticipate possible criticisms, and argue against such criticisms. If you think there are any fallacious arguments, write a critique supporting your judgment (see details below). If you think there is some fallacy not covered (yet), say so. While you may reasonably expect that these passages contain instances of the fallacies taken up in this chapter, understand that some passages may not contain arguments at all, some may contain arguments with fallacies you have not encountered, and some of the arguments may be fallacy-free.

For *each* fallacy you identify, do the following in your critique: (1) identify: the argument's conclusion, the premise(s) in which the fallacy occurs, who commits the fallacy, and the name of the fallacy (if it is not covered so far, describe it); (2) formulate an argument to convince a neutral observer that the fallacy you allege has indeed been committed; and (3) say whether any fallacy completely undercuts the argument or whether the argument can be repaired, and explain why you think so.

1. *Background:* The following is an old story, but it is still fun to analyze. The Chicago Bears had just lost for the sixth time in seven games during the 1981-1982 NFL season when a local football fan filed a complaint in small claims court. She charged that the Chicago Bears were guilty of false advertising and consumer fraud. She is reported to have reasoned as follows:

   The Bears advertised a professional football game, but they don't play a very professional game. They make too many mistakes and don't live up to their advertising. It's like, if Dolly Parton came on stage and suddenly got laryngitis and couldn't sing, I'd get a refund. If the Rolling Stones came to town without Mick Jagger, that would be misrepresentation.

2. *Background:* Some years ago, a New York City police officer was fired from his job when he was convicted of adultery. He filed a $1.6 million lawsuit against the New York City Police Department for damages. Part of his reasoning was:

   Extramarital relations are rather commonplace in Nassau County and New York. The laws against adultery have not been enforced in fifty years, insofar as any person is concerned, including, but not limited to, the former governor of New York.

3. *Background:* When the Catholic bishops of the United States made a public statement against abortion, syndicated columnist Harry Cook criticized their position on the grounds that they were not qualified to speak about abortion since the bishops were men, unmarried, and childless. Below, we paraphrase the response to that column sent in to a newspaper by one reader:

   Cook said that the Catholic bishops are unqualified to speak about abortion because they are male, unmarried, and childless. That is like saying that a physician who has never had tuberculosis is unable to treat a patient with tuberculosis. The latter is nonsense; so is the former.

   The bishops made several pronouncements in their annual meeting, not just the one against abortion. Yet Harry Cook raised no objection to the bishops' criticisms of the arms race, despite the fact that none of the bishops ever attended a military school or the Army war college at Ft. Leavenworth. On Cook's reasoning, their lack of expertise in military matters would make them unqualified to make any statements alleging that the arms race is immoral.

4. *Background:* Recently, there was a newspaper report about the trial of a woman who had been arrested for going topless at a local beach. It brought a response from a sympathetic reader, which we represent below:

   I'm disgusted by the hypocrisy of laws that lead to the prosecution of women because men cannot deal with their sexual frustration and so require women to keep their breasts hidden from view at the beach. I used to live in Europe, where such laws would be subject to ridicule. When I came to the United States, I, too, was arrested for innocently sunning myself topless.

   State paternalism laws are designed to protect individuals from themselves, even if they don't want to be protected, because restricting their freedom serves a greater good. An example is seat-belt laws, which are good because wearing seat belts saves lives and reduces the state's medical expenses by reducing the severity of injuries. Similarly, paternalistic laws restricting interest rates and controlling drugs are justified by the fact that the good they do outweighs the harm of limiting individual liberty.

   But no such paternalistic justification supports the law against public nudity at the beach.

And the same system that prosecuted me and that poor woman last week permits pornography between the covers of magazines and provocative displays of nudity in strip clubs. Like I said: hypocrisy!

5. *Background:* The drive by Native Americans for compensation for past injustices prompted the following letter to the editor:

If we are going to correct past injustices, how far back should we go?

For example, my people, too, were forced off their ancestral lands, where they had lived for untold generations. They, too, were dispossessed by white invaders from Europe who settled on their land. Shouldn't my people get compensation as well? And if the government of the European Community refuses to provide it, then the invaders (the Angles, Saxons, Vikings, Jutes, and Normans) should leave England to the aboriginal Celtic tribes. (The Celts banished to Wales should at least be relieved of income tax.)

6. *Background:* In 1991, there was a heated dispute that originated when a chemistry professor published a paper in the *Canadian Journal of Physics* (Vol. 68, 1990), a respectable peer-refered scientific journal, on the subject of what causes the problems of teenagers and young adults. The professor's argument, in brief outline, went something like this:

There is a significant correlation between teenagers and young adults who have problems and the lack of full-time parent in their homes when they are growing up. Most women who work outside the home do so to protect themselves against the possibility that their husbands will leave them, not because the feminist movement is correct. Most women are equipped by nature to be nurturers, whereas most men are not. Without the socioeconomic pressure to work, most women would choose to remain in their natural roles. The growth of feminism is merely a symptom of unstable families and therefore of an unstable society. Feminism could not sustain an economically stable society.

7. *Background:* Farley Mowat (author of *Never Cry Wolf*) was asked on his seventieth birthday what he thought about the prospects of the human species. He replied in the following vein:

Humans today are acting like yeast in a brewer's vat, multiplying mindlessly, all the while greedily consuming the limited subsistence of our world. If we continue to act like the yeasts, we will perish as they do, having exhausted our resources and poisoned ourselves in the lethal brew of our own wastes.

8. *Background:* The following news report appeared in several newspapers in the United States:

WASHINGTON—Heart disease is the leading cause of death in the United States, accounting for 35 percent of deaths in 1990, according to the National Center for Health Statistics.

Cancer was the second largest killer, at 23.4 percent, followed by strokes, causing 6.7 percent of deaths.

Homicide moved from tenth place in 1989 to ninth in 1990, and AIDS retained its position as the eleventh leading cause of death, though AIDS deaths increased at a slower rate than the previous year.

9. *Background:* During one of the periodic protests against rock 'n' roll, a number of ministers and priests organized musical bonfires in which teenagers were asked to toss records they felt unleashed their carnal appetites. One minister observed:

There's a rhythm to our bodies, and when we hear music with a similar rhythm we respond to that beat. Too much of this can affect you in the wrong way. Out of 1,000 girls who became pregnant out of wedlock, 984 committed fornication while rock music was being played.

10. *Background:* A new regulation requiring payment of a $50 fee for an entry visa to Canada (by visitors from countries whose citizens must have visas to enter Canada) brought the following critical response:

> This regulation is another nail in the coffin of Canada's dying tourist industry. The people most affected are tourists from countries in Eastern Europe and the third world, who need visas to visit Canada. By the time they buy snapshots and pay for return courier service to the nearest Canadian embassy, they'll have had to spend more like $150. The cost will deter people from visiting their Canadian relatives, even though they are now free to travel for the first time in recent memory.

11. *Background:* An alderman from the city of Windsor, Ontario, proposed to the council that cats be licensed just as dogs are. In an editorial, "The Last Free Spirits," the *Windsor Star* argued:

> Cats are free spirits, the last really independent creatures around. You can no more license cats than you can license the wind. Dogs may submit to bureaucracy. Cats won't. The same spirit tends to rub off on cat owners. They have enough trouble being pushed around by their cats without being asked to submit to man-made laws. Besides, there's an economic factor. They've never had to buy licenses, so why start? No . . . it just won't work.

12. *Background:* A study done by Jane Maulden, a researcher at the University of California at Berkeley, and reported on in the August 1990 issue of the journal *Demographics*, discussed the effects of a marital breakup on the health of the children.

> Maulden studied 6,000 childrens' health histories. In families in which divorce had occurred, the children averaged 0.13 more illnesses per year after the divorce than before. Such children ran a 35 percent risk of developing health problems over a three-year period, as compared with a 26 percent risk among all children.
>
> Nearly one-third of the illnesses reported were accounted for by ear infections and pneumonia. Others included allergies, asthma, chronic skin conditions, chronic lung problems, and urinary infections.
>
> Maulden said that "children are likely to experience very significant stress because their living standards change dramatically. . . . They probably also lose many of the resources that contribute to good health: a safe, comfortable environment relatively free of environmental hazards and the risks of infection; good food; and constant adult supervision."

13. *Background:* The plan in the United States to commemorate Elvis Presley with a postage stamp provoked the following letter:

> It's ridiculous to honor Elvis with a postage stamp. In the 1960s, drugs hit the American scene like a tidal wave. Rock 'n' roll entertainers, Elvis among them, encouraged drug use by example and promoted it in their music. Today, we see the social wreckage that resulted. Lives were destroyed and are still being destroyed. The human and economic costs have been enormous. That money could have been put to much better use—for example, to help the poor. It's a crying shame to whitewash the past with this stupid stamp.

14. *Background:* The abortion debate is the occasion for innumerable arguments. The following argument is adapted from a letter written by someone who took issue with the claim of columnist Clair Hoy that the fetus is an innocent human being:

Hoy misunderstands innocence. Innocence is not absence of guilt; it's freedom from guilt. Freedom from guilt implies the ability to choose to do wrong. A fetus is no more innocent than I am innocent of speeding on the highway on my bicycle. I'm incapable of going that fast. But a fetus is incapable of any freedom of action whatsoever. So a fetus cannot be innocent.

15. *Background:* A newspaper editorial once made the claim that abortion should be a matter entirely between the woman concerned and her doctor and that this needn't violate the consciences to those women and medical practitioners who are opposed to abortion. That opinion drew the following response:

> Your concept of conscience in indeed narrow.
>
> One who is opposed to smoking, for instance, is not content to leave the matter between the child and the tobacconist. Indeed he or she seeks to have glamorous advertising of the product banned and tries to make smoking as difficult as possible (e.g., banning it in schools, in food establishments, and so on) to create a deterrent to immature as well as casual smokers.
>
> Similarly, one who is opposed to abortion cannot possibly leave this matter between an often immature or panic-stricken woman and a doctor often too busy and too materialistic to oppose her wishes.

16. *Background:* An excerpt from an advertisement for numerology contained the following claim. (It's not relevant, but Dionne Warwick has since dropped the final *e* from her surname.)

> We have found that numerology is a very useful tool in producing good luck. For example, each letter in the alphabet has an assigned number. Singer Dionne Warwicke took the advice of her numerologist and added an *e* to the end of her name. Her numerologist told her that this would bring about the correct, fortunate combination.
>
> She immediately skyrocketed to fame. She has told the story about her numerologist on the Johnny Carson show twice.

17. *Background:* Newspapers across the country picked up this report of a study carried out by a group of doctors led by Dr. Philippe Van de Perre of the national AIDS control program in Kigali, Rwanda, and originally reported in the *New England Journal of Medicine* (August 1991):

> A study was carried out on 212 healthy women whose blood was tested for AIDS when they gave birth and at three-month intervals thereafter.
>
> Sixteen of the women later tested positive for HIV-1, the AIDS virus, indicating they had acquired it after giving birth. Of their sixteen babies, nine developed the infection.
>
> Five of these women, and their babies, were found infected three months after the births. In the other four infected babies, the infection was first discovered six, nine, fifteen, and eighteen months after the babies' births.
>
> Because all of the infected infants were breast-fed, it was concluded that the colostrum initially secreted by the breasts, and breast milk, "may be effective routes for the transmission of HIV-1 from recently infected mothers to their infants."
>
> "When a safe alternative to breastfeeding is available, women at risk . . . should refrain from breast feeding their babies," Dr. Van de Perre said.

18. *Background:* In a column in the *Toronto Star*, Michelle Landsberg once advocated a policy of permitting parental leave in the work place (a policy that would allow either the mother or the father of a newborn child to have nine months' leave from the job at 90 percent pay). After presenting her reasons for thinking the policy would be a

good thing, Ms. Landsberg anticipated an objection: "But aren't thousands of lazy men and women going to idle away the months, having babies at our expense?" Her rejoinder follows. (By the way, the "baby bonus" referred to in the column was a monthly federal payment to every family in the country for each child under the age of 16.)

> No. That is just what was predicted when Canada brought in the baby bonus, and our birthrate has steadily fallen. In Sweden, after a decade of parental leave, the birthrate has dropped below the replacement level, and only 12 percent of Swedish men take the leave.

19. *Background:* Ms. Landsberg's column (see Exercise 18) elicited the following rejoinder:

> Rejoice! Michelle Landsberg is back with her amusing emotional illogicalities, jumping to her *post hoc, ergo propter hoc* conclusions as usual.
>
> She solemnly declaims that introduction of the baby bonus caused a reduction in the birthrate as if there were a causal relationship between them. If you believe that, you'll believe that burning witches at the stake restored milk to cows.

20. *Background:* We have adapted the following from an "opinion" piece in a newspaper:

> Two genetic researchers analyzed 170 couples who were married seven years before and fifty-two of whom had since divorced. They found a statistically significant correlation between a couple's similarity of forearm length and the endurance of their marriage. It seems if you want to reach out and touch someone, on a lasting basis, it had better be someone who can reach out and touch you at the same time.

21. *Background:* The following account summarizes a study reported on in the journal *Archives of General Psychiatry* (December 1991) by Dr. Michael Bailey, assistant professor of psychology at Northwestern University in Evanston, Illinois.

> The study provides the strongest evidence yet that homosexuality has a genetic basis (though not that social conditioning may not also be a factor).
>
> The study examined fifty-six male identical twins, fifty-four fraternal twins, and fifty-seven adoptive brothers. Identical twins are genetic clones, having developed in the womb from a single egg that split after being fertilized by a single sperm. Fraternal twins develop simultaneously from two separate eggs fertilized by two separate sperm, making them only as similar as nontwin siblings.
>
> Fifty-two percent of the identical twin brothers of gay men were also gay, compared with 22 percent of the fraternal twins and 11 percent of the genetically unrelated adoptive brothers . . . "which is exactly the kind of pattern you would want to see if something genetic were going on," Dr. Bailey said. "The genetically most similar brothers were also the ones most likely to be gay, by a large margin."
>
> The degree of the genetic contribution to homosexuality could range from 30 percent to over 70 percent, depending on varying assumptions about the prevalence of homosexuality and about how well the sample represents twins in the general population, according to Dr. Bailey.

CHAPTER SEVEN

♦

Fallacies of Language and Meaning

Introduction

If your keep your ears perked, you can hear bizarre-sounding statements these days. Here are a couple we've heard:

1   The patient did not fulfill his wellness potential.

2   It was a therapeutic misadventure of the highest degree.

Do you know what these statements mean? Possibly not. Simply put, both statements were used as roundabout ways of saying "the patient died." Our best guess is that the people who formulated these statements were not much interested in clarity of expression or rational persuasion. More likely, they were using language here to *conceal* meaning. And that's not at all unusual.

Much attention has been focused in recent years on the state of language in North America. Writers like Edwin Newman, William Safire, and Robert MacNeil have written about the state of language use, calling attention to doublespeak, psychobabble, jargon, and other varieties of verbal trumpery and campaigning for improvement in language skills. They have insightfully documented the many ways in which people use language to cloak meaning and avoid responsibility.

In this chapter, we, too, will be concerned with language, primarily insofar as it affects the practice of argumentation. We are not concerned with details such as the aberrant use of the word "hopefully" that seems to have gained currency. Rather, we are concerned with abuses that weaken the practice of argumentation. Before we look at these abuses however, we want to say a few words about how to process the language of argumentation.

One of the first steps in evaluating an argument—and this applies to other forms of reasoning as well—is determining when the meaning of a claim or a term under consideration is unclear. Before you can judge whether a premise is relevant to a conclusion, or before you can determine whether a given claim is acceptable, you need to know what it means. And you have to know how to clarify the claim if it is unclear. Finally, you have to deal with other types of problems that arise because of the language used.

Argumentation, as a practice, depends upon language, and so participants in the practice must learn proper respect for language. A master woodworker keeps her tools clean, sharp, and oiled and uses them properly. The same should be true for anyone engaged in the practice of argumentation. Words are the symbols used in argumentation to express basic points (the conclusion) and the basis for them (the premises). When you engage in the practice of argumentation, the onus is on you to use words in such a way as to convey your meaning clearly and unambiguously. Thus we might say that the use of language in argumentation is subject to two basic principles.

1. Be clear. Since the purpose of argumentation is to bring about rational acceptance of the conclusion on the basis of the premises, the arguer has a responsibility to be clear in formulating the material of the argument: the premises and the conclusion. We cannot be persuaded rationally by a claim whose meaning is unclear to us.
2. Be responsible. Since argumentation aims at rational persuasion, it is important that the arguer use language responsibly. The arguer needs to say what he or she means and should mean what he or she says. It's important to be responsible. If an arguer uses a term with an emotional or judgmental component to it, he must first earn the right to use it by showing that the evidence needed to support that dimension is available.

The first group of fallacies we discuss are violations of the first principle; the remaining fallacy, *the freeloading term*, violates the second.

A WORD ABOUT LOGIC AND RHETORIC

Our concern in this text is with the logic rather than the rhetoric of argumentation. *Rhetoric* is the art of putting thoughts into language in evocative and forceful ways. A piece of discourse can be rhetorically effective yet logically weak. The classic example of this situation would be the speeches of Adolf Hitler which were, if we are to judge by their effect, compelling to German audiences at the time, and yet from a logical point of view they are shot through with weak assumptions and problematic premises.

On the other hand, an argument can be logically cogent but rhetorically ineffective, for example, if it fails to take proper account of its audience. Conclusions should be adequately supported, and the resulting arguments should be presented so as to be convincing to their audiences. In our experience, logicians tend to underestimate the importance of the audience and the context to the comprehension and evaluation of argumentation. Rhetoric as a discipline has important insights about argumentation that logicians need to embrace. Ideally, our arguments should be both logically compelling and rhetorically appealing.

Once you become attuned to the way language is used and abused, you will discover that discourse can sound quite impressive and mean next to nothing. Here's an example from a press conference given by Alexander Haig, the former Secretary of State, in which he said, "I think the issue is that we do have a tendency to indulge in episodic preoccupation, if you will, with one another on the strategic horizon." *Possibly*, if we knew more about the context in which this statement was made, we would see some shred of meaning here, but we confess to being stumped.

Let us cite another example. Suppose that in a report about a company's financial situation, you read the following:

3   The problem with the gradient parameters is functional rather than systemic and hence can be expected to impact negatively on the emergent matrix.

Sounds impressive, right? Would it surprise you to learn that we constructed this sentence (if you can call it that) by consulting something called "The Jargon Generator," which has appeared in various formats and publications? This list contains three columns, each containing ten meaty, polysyllabic words, such as "parameter," "gradient," "functional," and so on. By combining words from each column, we produced the sentence above, which—unless your guard is up—you might allow to pass by without challenge, probably on the grounds that the person who wrote it must have known what he or she was talking about. The lesson here is this: *A sentence that sounds impressive does not necessarily make sense*. The amount of semantic inflation in our linguistic culture these days— where there is talk of "wellness potential," "downward adjustments," and "negative enhancement"—means that there will be times when you will have to run the risk of being thought stupid by saying, "Pardon me, I didn't quite understand what you just said. Could you repeat it in simpler terms?"

The opposite situation also occurs: Discourse that sounds opaque or dense can actually be quite meaningful. Here is a passage from Soren Kierkegaard's *The Sickness unto Death*:

4   What is the self? The self is a relation; the self is not the relation but rather that in the relation which accounts for it that the self relates itself to its own self.

The language Kierkegaard uses here is convoluted, to be sure. To grasp its meaning, you have to work with this text, seeing it in its context and in relation to the larger point. Even though, at first glance, it might seem to be nothing but words, it has an intelligible core. Though it would take us outside the scope of this text to defend our exegesis of what Kierkegaard means in the above text, we take him to be saying that the self is not a thing, not a substance, not anything like an object at all. The self is more like a relationship than it is like a thing.

Though you must learn to rely on your own sense of when something is clear and when it isn't, you cannot rely completely on your first impressions to decide whether some obscure discourse is nonsense. Read the argument carefully, consider the context, and try to find the sense in what was argued, develop hypotheses about what it might mean, and then check them out.

In looking over an argument (and this same advice applies to most other kinds of reasoning as well) to determine its clarity, we suggest the following policies:

Policy 1

Focus on the crucial claims and terms in the argument. Time is short. You cannot possibly dwell on each and every word of an argument you are considering. Instead, practice scanning an argument to identify its crucial terms.

How will you find them? Start with the conclusion, the single most important claim in the argument, for that is what the writer is trying to persuade you of. Look first at the conclusion and its important words or terms (usually the subject and the predicate). Next in line will be the main premises or reasons offered to support the conclusion and the terms prominent in them. In short, simple arguments, the crucial terms are usually easy to find. Consider this example:

5   Ellen is so responsible. She's always looking out for other people.

In the conclusion, the crucial terms are "Ellen" and "responsible." Presumably the context will make it clear who Ellen is, but the term "responsible" might create a problem. In the premise, the crucial term is "looking out for," and again you would want to make sure that you knew what the arguer meant here.

In longer arguments, it is much more difficult to determine which terms are crucial. It requires the capacity to process units of the text while retaining the sense of what you've read. We still believe that it's good advice to look at the conclusion, identify the important terms in it, and ask yourself whether they're clear. Next, you need to look at the premises that contribute directly to the conclusion, zero in on their important terms, and see whether they're clear.

Policy 2

Ask yourself: Is it clear? Once you've identified the crucial terms, you need to ask yourself whether they are clear. Do you understand their meaning? Don't confuse this question with others, such as: Is the claim true? Is there enough evidence for it? It is possible to grasp the meaning of a claim even though you regard it as false. In fact, if you don't understand the claim, you don't know what you're disagreeing with. If the answer is, "Yes, I understand these terms," then you provisionally take it as clear. Proceed to ask how well the evidence supports the conclusion. If the answer is, "No, I'm not sure what some of these terms mean; I don't really grasp what's being said," then there are a number of possible explanations. It might be that there's a problem of meaning in the passage; below we discuss the most common of these problems. It's also possible that the reason the terms are unclear is that your own brain isn't in gear: Either you're in a mental fog (not paying sufficient attention) or you don't know enough about the subject. In other words, sometimes the explanation for a claim's not being clear lies in the receiver.

Here are some tests for clarity:

1. A statement is clear to you if you can restate its meaning in other words that express the same meaning.

If you didn't have the right lexicon to decode the pair of statements that opened this chapter, you probably would not know what they meant. That's okay, because those statements are intentionally opaque; they are attempts to conceal meaning, to give the appearance of having said one thing while, in fact, saying something else. "The patient did not fulfill his wellness potential" sounds perhaps like he did not get as well as expected. It sounds nothing at all like "he died," and even if you were familiar with phrases like "wellness potential," it's unlikely you'd know what was meant here.

2. A statement is clear to you if you know the conditions under which it would be true and the conditions under which it would be false.

One way that we can be sure we've understood a statement is to offer potential verifiers and falsifiers. To illustrate this point, contrast:

6   Coke has a slight flavor of clove.

with

7   Coke is it!

You probably know what experiences would verify the first statement. Assuming that you are familiar with the taste of clove, you would open a bottle, sip, and pay attention to the taste for that hint of clove. If you tasted it, that would serve to verify the statement; if not, that would serve to falsify it. Neither experience would be definitive, but the ability to imagine the relevance of each helps us grasp the meaning. You could also smell or taste clove, and then try some Coke to see whether there's any similarity.

What about the second statement? What would serve to falsify or verify it? What does "it!" refer to? Does "it!" mean the best soft drink, the soft drink you'd like to have right now, a perfectly acceptable soft drink, or what? It's not at all clear and, consequently, neither is the statement.[1]

3. A statement is clear if competent users of the language would come up with approximately the same responses when asked to state the meaning.

There is a different and even better sort of test of clarity—but more difficult to apply. It stems from the idea that language is an intersubjective experience.

---

[1] A recent article in the *Detroit News* (March 14, 1993), written by Paul Fahri of the *Washington Post*, confirms our impression that this attempt to mystify is deliberate. He writes, "The new Miller line ('It's it, and that's that') is part of a lamentable trend: the use of the nonreferential 'it' that makes many slogans absolutely mystifying. A few years ago, Coca Cola bragged that 'Coke is it!' without providing so much as a hint what it was that Coke is."

Meaning is an intersubjective phenomenon. When several people read or hear a statement and all get pretty much the same meaning from it, that indicates a clearly formulated statement. Ask someone else what they get from the statement, and if you both get the same meaning, that's one indicator that it's clear.

We suggest these three strategies as potentially helpful methods for determining whether the meaning of a statement—your own or someone else's—is clear. Constant vigilance is the price of clarity. You have to be ready to press for clarity at all times in your own thinking, reading, and writing no less than in that of others.

If the discourse is unclear, and that unclarity is—to the best of your ability to judge—not due to defects in your own knowledge or thinking, then you need to do what you can to make it clear.

Policy 3

Where possible, seek clarification. If you have a problem grasping the meaning of a claim in an argumentative text, there are steps you can take.

If the claim you're investigating was made by someone not present, then the task is much more difficult, but if you can talk to the person, there are several things you can do to get clarification:

1. You can ask the individual to reformulate the claim in a different way by asking, Could you please state your point in different words?
2. You can ask for an explanation of a crucial term by saying, for example, "I'm not sure what 'obfuscate' means. Could you tell me?" Or "I'm having trouble understanding what you mean by 'freedom' in this context. Could you please explain it to me?"
3. You can ask for an example or illustration by saying, for example, "You said that 'love means never having to say you're sorry.' Could you give me an example to help me understand?" Or you might present an apparent counterexample and ask the person to respond to that. "What about when you hurt someone you love? Does that mean you don't have to apologize?"

If you can't get the necessary clarification from the arguer, then the best you can do is to hypothesize what the unclear statement means, then test your hypothesis and compare it against alternatives. You should, of course, check unfamiliar terms in the dictionary, but that's no help when you encounter familiar terms used in puzzling ways. If the statement remains opaque, then consider the hypothesis that the problem is the arguer's rather than yours.

Fallacies Related to Meaning

If attempts to clarify the term fail, that may signal a problem with the meaning of the claim. Below, we discuss four common problems related to meaning. Three of them—ambiguity, equivocation, and vagueness—are instances of lack of clarity; the fourth—which we call *the freeloading term*—occurs when the arguer uses a term before having earned the right to use it, thus violating the principle of responsible language use.

ABOUT DICTIONARIES AND DEFINITIONS

Consulting a dictionary is clearly mandated when you are just plain unfamiliar with a word, or when, though you are familiar with it, you sense that it is being used in a new or odd way. People sometimes abuse or misuse words, and the best possible way to check against this is by having a good dictionary and using it. Don't try to guess what an unfamiliar word means; look it up. On the other hand, you cannot expect a dictionary to shed sufficient light on or resolve issues that involve the meanings of important concepts, or ideas.

The current debate about what constitutes pornography, for example, exists because people have very different concepts of pornography. No appeal to a dictionary can settle the issue. If it could, then it would have been settled a long time ago. A good dictionary can report the uses of the word "pornography," but it is unlikely to help settle a dispute. What is needed to resolve or clarify such disputes is careful analysis and argumentation.

To *equivocate* is to use a term in one sense in one part of your argument and then, without signaling it, to turn around and switch meanings, using it in a different sense elsewhere in the same argument. Such argumentation is fallacious. For equivocation to occur, a term must be susceptible of having more than one meaning. Thus equivocation is a cousin of ambiguity. Webster defines *ambiguous* as "capable of being understood in two or more possible senses." We distinguish between the occurrence of ambiguity in discourse and the fallacy of *ambiguity* in argumentation.

Ambiguity

Ambiguity occurs when a word that is susceptible of two or more meanings is unclear in the context; that is, the context does not provide sufficient information to determine which meaning is intended.

There is nothing wrong with words having multiple meanings. Most English words do, including the word "word." This feature of our language can be used to great effect, as, for example, when Public Broadcasting Service newscaster Jim Lehrer, in an address to the graduating class at Southern Methodist University in 1989, said:

8   I urge you to please keep in mind what the diploma you are about to receive does *not* mean. It does not mean you are educated. Quite the contrary. It means, I hope, that you have been opened up to a perpetual state of ignorance.

The shock value and, indeed, the real force of Lehrer's admonition depend on the multiple senses of the term "education." In one sense of the term, the graduates certainly had received an education; they had completed a course of studies at an institution of higher education. The degree they were about to receive was "proof" of that. But Lehrer wanted to remind them that there was another sense in which they were still far from educated; they had just begun to learn. To do this, he relied on the multiple meanings, the ambiguity, of the word "education." He was not guilty here of the fallacy of *ambiguity* because there was no argument trading on the ambiguity.

The fact of multiple meanings creates a problem only when the speaker or writer exploits the feature, whether in argument or elsewhere. The fallacy of *ambiguity* occurs when the ambiguity is an impediment to understanding or assessing an argument. The defining conditions of the fallacy of *ambiguity* are listed in the box.

AMBIGUITY

1. A term with two different meanings is used in the argument.
2. In the context, it is not possible to decide which meaning is intended.

In the 1992 presidential campaign, Bush said on one occasion that homosexuality was "not normal." This is an ambiguous claim. It could mean either that homosexuality is not the normal situation, which is true; or it could mean that homosexuality is an abnormal, an unnatural, condition, which is false if it suggests that homosexuality is not found in other parts of nature. Now, were this claim part of an argument, we would be in a position to charge *ambiguity*.

Equivocation

As we indicated above, equivocation occurs when the same word or phrase undergoes an unsignaled shift in meaning during one piece of discourse or argument. Here is an example:

In 1982, before the Chicago Bears became a National Football League powerhouse, a disgruntled fan brought a suit against the Bears, charging them with false advertising. Her argument went, in part, like this:

> They advertise themselves as a professional team, but they do not play a very professional game. Look at all the mistakes they make each game.

The argument is based on equivocation on the word "professional." The conclusion of this argument is that the Bears are not a professional team. The evidence is that they do not play like professionals. The writer can get to this conclusion only be exploiting the two senses of the term "professional"—in effect shifting its meaning. In its first occurrence, "professional" means something like "receiving payment for its performance or services," as contrasted with amateurs, who are not paid. The Bears certainly were a professional team in that sense in 1982. But "professional" also means "performing well and skillfully in the manner expected of those paid," which is the meaning the writer invokes in the second occurrence. In this sense, a professional team may not play like professionals; that is, they may play poorly. That doesn't mean they aren't still professional in the first sense. The reasoning here exploits this shift in meaning; it seems plausible to the degree that we fail to notice the equivocation. The implicit conclusion—"The Bears should not call themselves a professional team"— requires that "professional" mean "paid money for their services." But the premise "The Bears do not play a very professional game" is plausible only if "professional" is taken to mean "highly skilled." That's the switch that makes this a case of *equivocation*. If "professional" is taken throughout in the sense in which the premise is plausible, then the conclusion doesn't follow. On the other hand, if "professional" is taken throughout in the sense in which the conclusion would follow, then the premise (taken that way) becomes false.

The defining conditions of the fallacy of *equivocation* are listed in the box.

EQUIVOCATION

1. A term is used in two different senses, either in two different premises, or in a premise and the conclusion of an argument. That is, the statements in which this term occurs are intelligible only if the term they share appears in a different sense in each.
2. If the term is used consistently throughout the arguments, then either the premise in which it occurs is acceptable but the other premise (or conclusion) is not or the conclusion is acceptable but the premise is not.

Here is another example:

When men of draft age went to Canada in the late 1960s to avoid serving in the United States Army, which was then engaged in war in Vietnam, some argued that Canada should not allow them to immigrate. Then-Prime Minister Pierre Elliot Trudeau took the opposite view, arguing that "I think the only ultimate guide we have is our conscience, and if the law of the land goes against our conscience, I think we should disobey the law." In response, an editorialist for the *Windsor Star* argued:

9 The point of the matter is that Trudeau has the business of law and conscience mixed up. Not conscience, but law, is the ultimate guide. Without law there could be no conscience. When a man thinks a certain law violates his conscience, it is only because there is some other law on the same subject that he believes should be followed.

As support for the claim that law, not conscience, is the ultimate guide, the writer puts forth the assertion that "When a man thinks a certain law violates his conscience, it is only because there is some other law on the same subject that he believes should be followed." We think the editorialist uses "law" equivocally here. In the first part of his statement, we take "law" to be referring to statutory law. (An example here would be a law in the South that forbade blacks from riding in the front of a bus). Note that the second half of the statement contains a reference to "law" that makes sense only if we take the editorialist to be referring to something like moral law. So if the first reference to law is to be true, it must be taken to refer to statutory law. The second reference must be to something like moral law. The arguer thus shifts the meaning of the term "law" within this statement, thereby committing *equivocation*.

The litmus test for equivocation is to look for a term that occurs twice. In order for a term's meaning to shift in the course of an argument, the term must appear in at least two places. Put differently, when one term occurs repeatedly or plays a central role in an argument, you need to make sure that it is being used the same way each time it occurs.

Vagueness

The next fallacy related to meaning that we take up is *vagueness*—a problem related to but different from ambiguity.

Vagueness creates a problem for us as arguers much the way that a blurry image presents a problem to us as perceivers. Suppose you are walking along a path through a park at night. You see a shape looming in the distance, but you don't know what it is; you just see an indistinct shape. That may present a rather serious problem, depending on where the park is located and what local conditions are like. Is it a mugger, someone exercising, or nothing at all? The lack of clarity about what you're seeing makes it difficult to determine its significance. Similarly, when someone makes a claim and the meaning of that claim is unclear (and the lack of clarity is not due to any fault in you as the interpreter), that is the situation we call vagueness.

The following letter illustrates how vagueness creates problems:

10   I am currently in the tenth grade, and I agree wholeheartedly that physical science is not learned well. The chief problem, as I see it, is teaching methods. We are taught simply to memorize a formula and then regurgitate it in a test or examination. As a result, we forget almost everything we learn until the next year. Furthermore, even if there is a thinking question on a test, a clever student can pull the wool over the teacher's eyes. I often hand in projects I consider to have little or no scientific merit. They usually receive top marks. In short, the educational system needs a thorough overhaul, not only in the physical sciences but in all areas of study.

One difficulty here is in knowing exactly what the writer means by "a thorough overhaul" of the educational system. Is the arguer referring to secondary education? to primary *and* secondary education? to college education? He or she has been speaking here mainly of teaching methods and problems related to teaching. Does the writer also believe that the organization of the curriculum is problematic? Does the writer believe that school should be a year-round affair, as it is in Japan? Should there be admission standards at the elementary and secondary level? All of these are conceivably within the meaning of "a thorough overhaul." It is difficult to assess the writer's argument here because we are not exactly sure how to take the conclusion.

Another example, from a letter to the *Detroit Free Press*, concerns the question of whether capital punishment should be carried out in Michigan (which presently does not allow it). The writer states:

11   It looks like the politicians don't want the voters to decide whether we should have capital punishment. I believe the voters should have more to say about everything. For this reason, I say that if the legislature and others do not put capital punishment on the ballot, we should throw them out of office. The most important thing to do is vote and show that you can throw them out. I am angry because for a long time I have believed that the criminal element is running this country.

Clearly, the arguer thinks that capital punishment should be on the ballot in Michigan and that any politicians opposing this idea should be thrown out of office. What is not clear here is the last statement. What does the writer mean by "the criminal element"? Does the writer mean that organized crime (or the Mafia) is running the country? Are we to take the writer's meaning to be that the President and the Congress are part of that criminal element or, at the least, have been bought out? And what does it mean to be part of the "criminal element"? The context does not help us to answer these questions—which points the finger at the claim as vague.

Our next example of *vagueness* is taken from an article in *USA Today*. The eminent American historian Henry Steele Commager here discusses the issue of how historians will view the current stock of presidents.

12   I don't know about future historians, but historians today generally think poorly of most of our recent presidents. . . . We can't blame Ford because he was appointed to the job to rescue the nation. But in any list of presidents, Nixon must be at the bottom. There is no question about that. He was the only really dangerous president we ever had. He was the only really contemptible president we had.

The claim that Nixon is at the bottom of the list is supported by the claim that he was the only really dangerous President the United States ever had. The problem here is that it's not at all clear what it means to say that Nixon was "really dangerous." The problem isn't that we don't know, in general, what "really dangerous" means. We know what it means to say that drunk drivers are really dangerous, that experimenting with crack cocaine is really dangerous, that trying to defuse bombs is a really dangerous enterprise, and so on. But that knowledge is of no help in determining Commager's meaning. This inability to determine meaning makes it impossible for the reader to evaluate the premise and, as a result, the argument itself. The vagueness of the claim impedes our understanding of the premise and is thus objectionable.

Vagueness should be distinguished from *ambiguity* and *equivocation*. In both *ambiguity* and *vagueness*, there is a lack of clarity stemming from the language used. In *ambiguity*, the possible meanings can be pinned down to two, but the context doesn't allow you to decide which of the two is intended. *Vagueness* is more open-ended; there is a range of possible meanings, none of which is clearly indicated by the context. In a case of *equivocation*, the terms undergo a shift in meaning within a given context. The problem here is not that the terms lack a clear meaning but, rather, that they have been used in two clearly different senses.

Vagueness should also be distinguished from the phenomenon known as *euphemism*, which substitutes indirect and usually softer language for harsh expression. A classic example is the reference to someone as having "passed away" rather than died. Thus construed, euphemism is not so much a lack of clear meaning as it is an attempt to soften the impact. It creates a problem when the reader is unfamiliar with the euphemism or when it shades off in the direction of not merely softening but concealing meaning. The substitution of a phrase like "detention center" for "concentration camp," for example, not only softens meaning but actually conceals it.

Euphemism should be distinguished from what we call *obfuscation*—the deliberate use of unclear or misleading language to cloak or conceal meaning. One of the statements that opens this chapter—"It was therapeutic misadventure of the highest degree," when what is meant is that the patient died—is not euphemism, which attempts to soften meaning, but, rather, a deliberate attempt to conceal meaning.

We also need to distinguish between *vagueness* and *jargon*. *Jargon* is special, sometimes technical, vocabulary often associated with a discipline, profession, or craft. This language is unclear to the uninitiated, and the problem with its use is not so much logical as rhetorical; i.e., it is used inappropriately. This excerpt from a letter from the John F. Kennedy School of Government at Harvard illustrates what we're talking about:

13 Dear Colleague:
I need your assistance in a study I am conducting of the voluntary or selective marginal situation: a sought-after situation that entails being on the margins of two social positions, attitudinal dispositions, or ideological commitments, but a full member or adherent of neither, and which enables individuals to differentiate themselves from others who share their social positions, values, and attitudes.

Without further elaboration, it is difficult to know what exactly is meant by this phraseology, but the terminology may be stock-in-trade for the audience at whom it is directed; e.g., sociologists or communication theorists. Outside such a context, it would certainly be objectionably vague.

We are most concerned with vagueness insofar as it affects argumentation, but we want to call your attention to two other places where vagueness often resides: in clichés and advertising.

Consider the meaning of this cliché: "Everyone has a right to his or her opinion." What does this mean, exactly? Is the right in question here a legal right? No. There are no such laws, though there are laws regarding the expression of opinion. Is the right in question a moral right? If I attempt to deny your opinion, or your right to it, have I offended a moral law? That doesn't seem right. Is it some other kind of right? Clichés have enough truth and meaning to get by in some circumstances, which is why they are in wide use. But they are often not clear enough to survive scrutiny, and certainly not strong enough to stand as the premises of an argument, without further clarification.

As for advertising, consider the current slogan for Pepsi-Cola: "Gotta have it!" This was introduced with much hoopla during the telecast of Superbowl XXVII in January 1992. One presumes that it means that the person in question has to have a Pepsi-Cola. But wait, can this be serious? What kind of "have to" is this? Is Pepsi-Cola addictive? No, not really. Is this a matter of "wants"? Okay, so the person wants a Pepsi, so what? Really, the slogan amounts to words that in this expression have very little meaning but that can be used as a kind of focal point for all kinds of fancy effects and imagery, as the rest of the commercial shows.

To sum up, the conditions of the fallacy of *vagueness* are as shown in the box.

VAGUENESS

1. An argument contains a premise, or a conclusion, whose meaning is indeterminate, in that context.
2. The indeterminateness of the statement makes it impossible to assess its acceptability as a premise or its significance as a conclusion.

Vagueness is called by many names, and calling attention to it is not unheard of in ordinary argumentative discourse. Witness its occurrence in the following letter to the *Toronto Star* (May 1989):

14   Re: When is poverty a case of relative inequality?
I must express how unclear the term "relative inequality" remains to myself as a Canadian. After all, Britain and the United States have governments very similar, and citizens of all three countries must feel many of the same pressures. The best idea of our human condition has little to do with economics and much more to do with the quality of living. Teachers should be paid proportionally more, as should child-care workers, professors, and all hardworking people. It seems to me that British Social Security Minister John Moore's statement about relative inequality is misleading. We should be thinking about relative equality. Little is relative about inequality.

In effect, the writer is arguing that the term "relative inequality" is vague, and objectionably so.

The Freeloading Term

Years ago, the philosopher Bertrand Russell introduced what he called the "emotive conjugation." Here's one example:

15   I am firm.
You are obstinate.
He is pigheaded.

This conjugation reveals an important truth about human behavior. We are often more lenient in appraising our own behavior than in appraising that of others. So when I refuse to go along with your suggestion that we go to a movie, I am being "firm"; but when you refuse to go along with my suggestion that we go to a movie, you are being "obstinate." This illustrates a point of interest to logicians: how the same behavior can be described from various points of view.

Labels are crucial, in life no less than in argumentation. The term "firm" has a commendable air to it; the term "pigheaded" has nothing to recommend it. We like people who are firm and dislike those who are pigheaded. The logical point to note is that words and terms are *loaded*, in the sense that many of their uses—not all—carry with them an evaluative component. Many words are, by convention, loaded with emotional and psychological freight. As long as the arguer earns the right to rely on these associations by providing the requisite evidence for their applicability, there is no problem. However, such terms are easily abused, often thrown into an argument without any justification being given. They appear to lend support to the conclusion, but really they are present in the argument the way freeloaders are—they haven't paid their way. More precisely, the arguer hasn't paid for them. When this happens, we have the fallacy we call *the freeloading term*.

The following ad, sponsored by a tobacco-industry lobby, appeared in a national newsmagazine. The lead question was; "Do cigarette companies want kids to smoke?" The copy in the ad then went on to read:

16   No. As a matter of policy. No. As a matter of practice. No. As a matter of fact. No!
All of us need a time of "growing up" to develop the mature judgment to do so many things. Like driving. Voting. Raising a family. And knowing enough to make an informed decision about all sorts of adult activities.
In our view, smoking is an adult custom, and the decision to smoke should be based on mature and informed individual freedom of choice.

The use of the phrase "adult custom" to *classify* (label, describe) smoking puts smoking in the class of things like planning and taking a vacation or going out to dinner (things that kids don't normally do). Once the ad has succeeded in describing smoking this way, it has done a lot to win the reader over to the ad's unexpressed conclusion, that "society has no business interfering with people's right to smoke." Should that classification remain unchallenged? Has the advertiser earned the right to use the term "adult custom"? In view of the pleasant connotation of the term "custom" and the unpleasant realities that surround the habit of smoking—both in terms of its impact on health and the environment and the developing groundswell of antismoking sentiment—we think the term "adult custom" is not justified here. If we consider other adult customs, we find that they carry either a neutral or a positive association to their meaning. Dating, for example, is an adult custom, as is buying goods on credit. On the other hand, murder is a practice pretty well restricted to adults, but would it be called a "custom"? Given these problems with the term "adult custom," the advertisement (if taken as an argument) commits the fallacy of *the freeloading term*.

The conditions for this fallacy are listed in the box.

THE FREELOADING TERM

1. The arguer labels something—a person, an act, an event, or a situation—using a term that has an evaluation built into it.
2. The evaluation plays a role in supporting the conclusion.
3. The arguer uses this term without any support or without adequate justification.

Here is another example and our application of the conditions listed in the box. This letter, adapted from one that appeared in a community where there is a university, is largely self-explanatory.

17   Three weeks ago, I overheard a conversation at the bus stop. One male university student was loudly relating the day's fun in the laboratory. It seems this morally depraved "student" had been amusing himself by dropping a half-anesthetized cat from the laboratory bench. The student, now reaching an amused and feverish pitch in his voice, loudly noted to all in the bus shelter that the cat had not landed on its feet. Perhaps professional help is in order for this pitiful human specimen?

Platitudes and assurances from the head of the biology department, who said "I assure you there was no suffering" when informed of what had been overheard, produces no solace for our suffering feline.

Surely something must be done to stop this sort of thing from happening again.

There are a number of dimensions to this argument, but for the moment, direct your attention to the first paragraph, where the arguer suggests that professional help is in order for the student, whom the arguer classifies as "this pitiful human specimen." The basis for this classification is the testimony of one student about the events that took place in the laboratory. The same reasoning is used to justify the claim that the student in question is "morally depraved." In our view, both of these claims demonstrate the fallacy of *the freeloading term* because they satisfy the three conditions.

Condition 1 is satisfied. The writer uses the terms "morally depraved" and "pitiful human specimen" to describe the student, and both of these terms have evaluations built into them; both suggest an adverse judgment on the student.

Condition 2 is satisfied. If we accept these terms, then we are more likely to accept the writer's conclusion that something must be done to alter the treatment of animals in the laboratories.

Condition 3 is satisfied. The writer uses these terms without sufficient justification. First, we need to be clear just what it means to call someone *morally depraved*. This is the strongest possible rebuke to level at someone; it means that they are totally lacking in moral sense. What justification does the writer have for this charge? Let us suppose that the student did, indeed, drop the cat from a bench; i.e., the student did knowingly inflict some amount of pain on the cat. Is that sufficient evidence to warrant the application of the term "morally depraved"? We think not. We don't defend what the student allegedly did. Such behavior certainly indicates a moral flaw, but we don't think this one incident provides adequate justification for this moral condemnation, which is the strongest possible censure. If this student is "morally depraved," what term is left to describe Hitler? Thus we conclude that the arguer was guilty of the fallacy of using *freeloading terms* when he or she used the terms "morally depraved" and "pitiful human specimen." The arguer does not have enough evidence for the application of these condemnatory terms.

The crucial point is that if an arguer uses highly charged evaluative language that is problematic or controversial to advance a conclusion, he or she must justify its use. On the other hand, you, as critic of argument, must be fair and evenhanded, which means not jumping on every instance of spicy language. First, stop to think whether the language plays a central role in the argument. And, of course, writers often use such language in perfectly valid ways. For instance, elsewhere in the letter we have just been discussing the writer stated:

18   I should not be leveling my indignant salvo entirely on the biology department.

Two terms here carry an evaluative component: "indignant" means "angry because of unjust treatment"; and "salvo" means a "burst." But the use of such terms is unobjectionable here. After all, the writer is referring to herself or himself and should know whether or not these terms are appropriate.

To conclude, we want to underscore the importance of being responsible in your use of language and in your selection of terms. As we have said, labels are important; they do a lot of work for us. Remember how the word "custom," when used to describe the smoking habit, can go a long way toward suggesting that smoking is really rather innocuous. That being so, it is important to make sure that the labels don't do too much work for us. We must use them with due regard for the evidence and justification sometimes required.

The continuing debate about abortion provides good illustrative material. The terms that have gained currency—in this debate "pro-choice and "pro-life"—both carry evaluative freight. The idea imparted by the word "pro-choice" is that the other side is *against* choice; the idea buried in "pro-life" is that the other side is anti-life. In each case, we believe, the impression created by the label is false. Even if you disagree, you have to concede that the judgments buried underneath the labels can be contentious and need to be supported, but once the label gains currency, the need for such justification is lost.

If we examine these fallacies from the view of the RSA triangle, we find that *ambiguity, equivocation,* and *vagueness* are violations of the acceptability requirement. You ought not to accept as a premise or a conclusion a statement whose meaning you do not understand. Use of *the freeloading term* is typically a violation of the acceptability requirement also, although even if the arguer provides some support for the term (and hence is not guilty of violating the acceptability requirement), that support may not be relevant (meaning a violation of the relevance requirement has occurred), or it may not be sufficient (and hence a violation of the sufficiency requirement has occurred).

EXERCISES

Directions: For each extract assigned, decide if there are any arguments present, and, if so, whether they contain any of the fallacies you have studied so far. If you think there is no argument, explain what the function of the passage is. If you think any arguments are logically good ones, try to anticipate possible criticisms, and argue against such criticisms. If you think there are any fallacious arguments, write a critique supporting your judgment (see details below). If you think there is some fallacy not covered (yet), say so. While you may reasonably expect that these passages contain instances of the fallacies taken up in this chapter, understand that some passages may not contain arguments at all, some may contain arguments with fallacies you have not encountered, and some of the arguments may be fallacy-free.

For *each* fallacy you identify, do the following in your critique: (1) identify: the argument's conclusion, the premise(s) in which the fallacy occurs, who commits the fallacy, and the name of the fallacy (if it is not one covered so far, describe it); (2) formulate an argument to convince a neutral observer that the fallacy you allege has indeed been committed; and (3) say whether any fallacy completely undercuts the argument or whether the argument can be repaired, and explain why you think so.

1. *Background*: The November 4, 1991, edition of *Time* magazine contained a section devoted to "alternative medicine." Practices such as acupuncture, homeopathy, biofeedback, and holistic medicine were discussed. Here is one letter in response to that article:

   > As a practicing physician for the past thirteen years, I was very disgruntled to read about alternative medicine in a magazine of *Time's* stature. The days of snake-oil medicine should be over, not undergoing a revival. People will eventually come to realize that the best health care is provided by the physician and not by alternative gimmickry.

2. *Background*: In the spring of 1970, the United States, which was then at war with North Vietnam, invaded Cambodia. This was the trigger for student protests on university campuses across the United States. These protests were sometimes met with force and violence, as at Kent State, where four students were shot and killed by the National Guard. Such events led to a discussion of repression. As cited by Howard Kahane in *Logic and Contemporary Rhetoric* (1971), columnist John Roche stated at the time:

   > Every society is, of course, repressive to some extent. As Sigmund Freud pointed out, repression is the price we pay for civilization.

3. *Background*: From the ongoing debate about abortion comes this letter:

> Pro-abortion groups never refer to the true meaning of abortion. They use the phrase "termination of the pregnancy." They shy away from the term "killing unborn babies." Perhaps the true meaning would not enhance their case.

4. *Background*: Dr. Henry Morgantaler is a Montreal physician who supports the right of women to have abortions. In a speech in Edmonton in 1985, he claimed that:

> Terminating a pregnancy is not the same as terminating a life. Pro-lifers contend there is a baby at the moment of conception. That's absurd.[2]

5. *Background*: This excerpt is adapted from a review of John Le Carre's *The Little Drummer Girl*.

> Once in a while, a book comes along that shatters the existing parameters of a literary genre and sets the tone for a new trend by drawing on diverse elements of change that have not, by themselves, achieved a cohesive new identity. This is such a book, and it should therefore be read by all who care for the format of literature.

6. *Background*: The following passage about crime and how to deal with it comes from a sociology textbook, *Theoretical Criminology*, by George B. Vold and Thomas J. Bernard.

> Criminals are organically inferior. Crime is the resultant of the impact of environment upon low-grade human organisms. It follows that elimination of crime can be effected only by the extirpation of the physically, mentally and morally unfit; or by their complete segregation in a socially aseptic environment.

7. *Background*: Here is one woman's response to the question of whether prostitution should be legalized:

> Most of us have prostituted ourselves, morally or physically, in one sense or another, at some time in our lives, without prosecution, having had to answer only to our consciences. Why, then, is sexual prostitution between consenting adults illegal?

8. *Background*: The Senate hearings (in October 1991) for the confirmation of Clarence Thomas as a Supreme Court justice raised the problem of sexual harassment in the workplace. To the claim that men can also be the victims of sexual harassment, one writer responded:

> Anyone who chooses to address the issue of sexual harassment in such a way as to portray men as victims is wrong. Sexual harassment is a method men use to control women and is part of the continuum of violence against women. A number of recent studies have shown that up to half of the women employed in any work force have been sexually harassed.

9. *Background*: The internationally known physicist Carl Sagan once hosted a series (*Cosmos*) on the Public Broadcasting System in the United States. After *Time* magazine printed an article highly favorable to this series, the following letter was written:

> Sagan promotes Sagan, and *Cosmos* promotes Sagan. As he postures before lingering cameras and delivers overly dramatic monologues, he skillfully blends fiction with a smattering of fact, leaving viewers perplexed. This type of presentation imbues science with the razzle-dazzle of show biz and reduces it to bubble-gum mentality. Most scientists have more integrity than to cheapen themselves and their profession by resorting to such show-biz routines. I think it's time that viewers flicked their dials and left Sagan where he really belongs: "Lost in Space."

---

[2] Thanks to Hendrik van der Breggen for bringing this example to our attention.

10. *Background*: Some shareholders of the Mobil Corporation proposed to the board of directors that Mobil adopt the so-called Valdez principles proposed by the Coalition for Environmentally Responsible Economics (CERES). They defended their proposal by saying that the principles provide public accountability instead of self-policing on an issue that increasingly affects everyone." The Mobil board of directors responded by recommending a vote against this proposal, arguing:

> Adoption of the Valdez principles is unnecessary and would be superfluous in relation to Mobil's already existing and long-standing commitment to environmental protection. . . . A stated objective of this shareholder proposal is what the proponents call "public environmental responsibility"—to be achieved, apparently, by thorough monitoring by a private outside organization called CERES. However, Mobil is already publicly accountable for our environmental performance—to shareholders, to many government agencies, and to the public at large.

11. *Background*: Should smoking be allowed in public places such as restaurants? One Windsor, Ontario, alderman—the Mr. Porter referred to by this writer—thought that smoking should be allowed only in especially designated areas. His position provoked this response:

> Recently, one of our aldermen proposed that nonsmoking sections should be provided in restaurants. I wonder why Mr. Porter is so against smokers.
>
> I remember I had a cigarette in my hand when I met him during his campaign, and he didn't object to my smoking when he was interested in my vote. In my opinion, the question of smoking is my own private business, even in a restaurant. And don't forget, Mr. Porter, the government makes a big profit from us smokers.
>
> Mr. Porter, your proposal is discrimination. I remember the last time I felt the same way. The year was 1944, and I had to sit in a certain section in a restaurant because I was a Jew.

12. *Background*: This writer objects to the organized killing of pigeons.

> We would like to praise those who protested the pigeon slaughter. We are appalled to think that anyone could be so insensitive and inhumane. To starve and then slaughter these poor creatures is unthinkable. Of those who say that "these protesters have no right to interfere with our freedoms," we ask, How can cruelty to animals be considered a cherished freedom? And how about the remark made by the man who said that he shoots skeets but prefers live birds because they are more unpredictable. Whatever happened to live and let live? Murder for sport is still murder.

13. *Background*: In an article in the *Windsor Star*, a local columnist argued against pornography. Distinguishing between "erotica," which she defined as sexual expression between people who have enough power to be there by choice, and "pornography," she wrote:

> It may be that what the country needs, besides more employment, is more erotica. What we don't need, and should not tolerate, is pornography. Pornography makes half the human race feel like malleable objects at best and like helpless or debased subjects at worst. Surely if pornography insults or injures half the population and may possibly incite or negatively influence the other half, then it has no place in our shops and homes.

14. *Background*: In a letter to *Mother Jones* (April 1992), Robert Simonds, president of the Citizens for Excellence in Education (CEE), responded to an earlier article suggesting that the Christian Right is a very dangerous movement.

Children are being brutalized by left-wing groups presently in control of our schools. How? Through atheistic and immoral programs such as Planned Parenthood; by forcing boys to hold bananas in class while girls practice putting condoms on the bananas; and by teaching children that homosexuality is as normal and fulfilling as heterosexuality. CEE wants parents—Christian or otherwise—to be elected to school boards. CEE has never "endorsed" a candidate. We educate and encourage parents to run for office.

15. *Background*: This is an excerpt from an editorial written by an anesthesiologist in a professional journal in the aftermath of the Clarence Thomas-Anita Hill confrontation:

As nearly as I can tell, sexual harassment takes place when the actions of one employee offend another employee. When this happens, the person who is offended is supposed to tell the offender to stop. If he does not stop, then harassment has taken place. The problem is that it is the person who is offended who defines what the offense is. What a mess! And it goes further still. You see, I do not want to be embarrassed by having someone tell me to stop doing something that I thought was perfectly innocent and appropriate because if they do, I have already committed an offense even if I didn't know it was an offense when I committed it. What a mess!

16. *Background*: In March 1993, Dr. David Gunn, a doctor who ran an abortion clinic in Pensacola, Florida, was murdered. A man named Michael Griffin was charged with the crime. In a nationally syndicated article titled "Why Weep for an Abortionist When the Score is 30 Million to 1?" Joseph Sobran argued:

The man who shot (Gunn) was not even a member of an anti-abortion organization. . . . Nevertheless, Peter Jennings and his colleagues made the most of it, leading off the evening news and filling the front pages with the murder of the poor "doctor." The moral was supplied by Kate Michelman of the National Abortion Rights Action League, who decried "anti-choice terrorism." Terrorism? Why not just call it murder? The killer's intent was to kill, not to terrify.

CHAPTER EIGHT

◆

Fallacies of Intimidation

Introduction

We call the three fallacies discussed in this chapter *fallacies of intimidation* because the types of arguments in which they occur tend to be perceived as putting pressure on their audience to accept the conclusion. Arguments from authority, for example, may seem to pressure us by appealing to our respect for experts and, generally, those more knowledgeable than we are. Arguments from popular opinion lean on our tendencies to "groupthink" and to be impressed by public opinion. By making dire projections about the future, arguments from the buildup of a chain of causes, from precedent, or from a combination of the two can stampede us into prematurely accepting a conclusion.

Improper Appeal to Authority

We deem it a condition of individual autonomy and rationality that we acquire the capacity and motivation to investigate and evaluate the claims we are invited to adopt on the say-so of others. People who decide for themselves what to think are regarded as more fully realized human beings than are people who accept unquestioningly what others say. We are urged to be filters of opinions rather than sponges who soak them up indiscriminately. The capacity to interpret and assess arguments gets part of its rationale from this ideal because argument is a tool that can be used to test the quality of the support for a claim.

Yet it would be a mistake to picture the autonomous, self-guiding, belief-scrutinizing individual as a person who sets off completely independently, an isolated rational agent building up a system of beliefs by carefully checking and confirming each "belief" candidate before adding it to the store of trusted claims or discarding it as unverified or false. For one thing, the very classification and testing systems such a person would have to use would themselves at some point just have to be accepted, at least for the time being; otherwise there would be an infinite regress of testing tests and testing concepts. For another, it is simply physically and mentally impossible for one person to verify everything. No single individual can have the time or the intelligence to do the job.

Even scientists, the people best qualified to test empirical facts and theories, must routinely take on trust the word of *other* scientists in order to carry out their experimental research. Some scientific reports have dozens of coauthors, each of whom has checked out one specialized aspect of the report's claims so that each must rely on the say-so of the others to produce the collective results.

Or consider more down-to-earth information: phone numbers; weather forecasts; the times of high and low tide; product information; medical diagnoses; drug dosages; the scheduled times of TV shows; bus, train, and plane schedules; the dishes available in a restaurant; the music to be played at a concert; the way to assemble a barbecue; when to service a car; the meaning of a word or how it's spelled; or the biography of a celebrity. This list could continue indefinitely, and each of these items of information usually comes to us from someone else.

We call this reliance on another person's observations, calculations, inferences, or judgments an appeal to *authority*. If what we have described above as our common situation is true, then, since we manage our cognitive lives reasonably well under these conditions, there appears to be no objection, *in principle*, to appealing to another's authority as the basis for a belief. Furthermore, we expect to find the authors of arguments citing the authority of others as support for their premises. In sum, the practice of appealing to authority in arguments is, in principle, perfectly legitimate.

The kind of appeal to authority we are considering here is an appeal to authority in matters of belief or opinion. Such an authority is different from a political or administrative authority (the authority of a police officer to stop you if you're speeding or of a teacher to require that you complete an assignment in order to pass a course). The latter are sources of commands or instructions regarding conduct, which is a different matter. In our references to "authority" hereafter, we shall be speaking only of the appeal to other sources to back up beliefs.

The fallacy of *improper appeal to authority* occurs when the appeal is made in an argument under conditions that make such an appeal unreliable. We think it's most helpful to recognize these conditions as failures to meet the requirements of acceptable appeals to authority in arguments. There seem to be four general conditions that have to be satisfied if an appeal to authority is to be legitimate. We call them (1) *appropriateness*, (2) *capability*, (3) *consensus*, and (4) *credibility*. As you will see, these conditions are not "on/off" or "yes/no" tests or requirements. Instead, they indicate dimensions along which an appeal to authority can range from totally improper at one extreme through degrees of increasing legitimacy up to complete propriety at the other extreme.

Appropriateness

There are some kinds of assertions it is inappropriate to back up by an appeal to authority. You don't rely on a doctor to tell you that you have a headache, that you have dizzy spells, or what you dreamed last night. You don't rely on a food expert to tell you that you like the taste of broccoli but dislike mushrooms. No one else can choose your favorite colors or the music you enjoy. It is inappropriate to rely on another person's say-so to back up most claims about a person's subjective state.

Similarly with matters of religious faith (belief in God), highly speculative subjects where there isn't enough evidence to make a determination (the existence of unidentified flying objects, the possibility of extrasensory perception), or matters of personal judgment about which informed sources disagree (the relative significance of Bruce Springsteen and Michael Jackson in the world of popular music). All these are subjects where appeal to someone's say-so, even an expert's, is an inappropriate way to settle a disagreement or establish a claim.

Consider some hypothetical cases. Suppose, for example, that someone claims that "chemical additives in food are more harmful than helpful to human health." This is a claim about the nutritional value of chemical additives, a claim that belongs to the science of nutrition. A competent nutritionist should be able to tell us whether it is true or false, so it would be appropriate to try to support (or refute) such a statement by an appeal to authority. Or suppose someone asserts that "van Gogh painted *The Starry Night* at St. Remy, in Provence, France, in 1889." This statement belongs to the field of art history and, more specifically, to the specialty of the provenance of van Gogh's paintings. A lot is known about where van Gogh painted various works, so it would be appropriate to cite a source to back up or deny this claim.

Suppose, however, that the statement was that van Gogh "had been able to locate more cathartic emotion in a vase of sunflowers than Gauguin, with his more refined Symbolist sense of allegory, had been able to inject in dozens of figures"?[1] What sort of statement is this? It is an aesthetic judgment, one that presumes to rank van Gogh's work above Gauguin's in terms of its amount of purifying emotion. Art historians and critics sometimes engage in this type of argument, making illuminating observations along the way. But they often disagree with one another about many of these contentions, for such judgments involve too much of an element of variable personal preference. So to back up the above claim by pointing out that art critic Robert Hughes thinks so (which he does) would be a violation of the appropriateness condition for appeals to authority.

Do the cola commercials that seem to appeal to the authority of Bill Cosby or Wayne Gretzky meet the appropriateness condition? We would argue that they don't because what is at issue is taste preference, a totally subjective affair.

Capability

An appeal to authority can be legitimate only if the source knows what he or she is talking about. There are two aspects to knowing what you're talking about.

Competence.

If the claim in question belongs to theoretical physics, only a theoretical physicist would be in a position to know whether it's true. If the claim is about dairy

---

[1] Robert Hughes, *The Shock of the New*, Knopf, New York, 1981, p. 276.

farming practices, then only an experienced dairy farmer, or perhaps an agriculture scientist who specializes in dairy farming, can know whether it's true. A professional tennis player knows a lot about playing tennis, but not necessarily about cameras (sorry, Mr. Agassi). Being a rock star doesn't give one the competence to judge the disappearance of the rain forests (sorry, Sting).

Notice what we tend to do when we get one recommendation from one doctor and a different recommendation from a second doctor. If the doctors are equally capable, we have no way to decide between them. One may be a general practitioner and the other a specialist in the area of medicine to which our condition belongs. In that case, we tend to give the specialist's advice greater weight. What we are doing, quite correctly, is relying on the authority whose credentials indicate greater capability. (More on this point below.)

Opportunity.

No matter how competent the specialist, he or she is not capable of making an authoritative judgment about a particular claim without having had the opportunity to check it out. A biochemist might have the competence to carry out or understand tests of the nutritional value of certain food additives, but unless she's actually done the tests or read reports of such tests, she is not capable of making a judgment that should be treated as authoritative about the nutritional value of particular additives.

Consensus

If an arguer backs up a claim with an appeal to one authority and you know of another authority who holds the opposite view, which authority are you to believe? When the numbers on both sides are roughly equal, and their capabilities are on a par, we have no way to decide which opinion to accept. Suppose, however, that a patient has been thoroughly examined by five doctors who specialize in the area of the patient's complaint and four of the five independently recommend one treatment and only one of the five recommends a different treatment. The patient will likely follow the advice of the majority of doctors, and rightly so. It is always possible for one authority to make a mistake, but the chances that four out of five will be wrong and only one out of five will be right are not high. We are not saying that judgments backed by a majority are always right, but, other things being equal, it is best to believe the majority opinion.

Other things being equal, the broader the consensus among knowledgeable sources about a particular point, the greater the force of their authority as support for that point. Conversely, the greater the disagreement among capable sources about some point, the weaker the force of an appeal to the authority of any one of them is.

Other things are not always equal, however: Sometimes there is good reason for questioning the majority opinion or even going along with the opinion of a lone dissenter. When a theory is being challenged, for example, or when a new technology is being used for the first time, the prevailing opinion of the experts can turn out to be mistaken. Each case must be judged on its own merits.

Credibility

Imagine the following situation:

The claim in dispute is straightforwardly empirical and so setting it by an appeal to authority would seem clearly appropriate. Moreover, the arguer has appealed to the authority of a scientist who specializes in the field under consideration and who, in fact, has researched the question extensively. In other words, the arguer's source has both the competence and the opportunity to make a reliable judgment about the claim. Finally, the claim is a simple one, so there is no reason to expect that there would be any dispute about it among scientists who investigate it. For example, suppose the question is whether the ingredient called "Retsyn" in Certs breath mints has any bacteria-killing efficacy. Isn't this a case where an appeal to authority would be entirely appropriate?

Well, you can't be sure. Suppose the scientist being quoted is employed as a biochemist by the company that manufactures Certs. Furthermore, suppose the biochemist is quoted in a press release aimed at answering the criticisms of a consumers' group that claims "Retsyn" is a completely useless ingredient. Suppose further that the biochemist has just bought a house, is paying tuition fees for his two college-aged children, and has the prospect of a generous pension if he remains with the company until retirement. Should you accept the appeal to his authority in support of the claim of the efficacy of "Retsyn"? Clearly not, since the biochemist is under too much pressure to toe the company line and not be candid. The point is not that he is surely lying. The point is instead that because of his conflict of interest, we cannot be confident he is being completely candid. As a scientist devoted to the pursuit of knowledge, he has an interest in telling the truth even at the risk of losing his job; as an employee who needs the income and wants the security, he has an interest in keeping his job.

In general, then, an appeal to authority is proper only if it would be unreasonable in the circumstances to challenge or to question the reliability, honesty, trustworthiness, or dependability of the source. This requirement is what we call the *credibility condition*.

The fallacy of *improper appeal to authority*, therefore, occurs when the appeal is made in an argument under conditions where the appeal is inappropriate, where the authority cited is incompetent or has not had the opportunity to determine the truth of the claim, where there is no consensus among the authorities, or where the credibility of the authority is in question. These conditions are summed up in the box on page 172.

Although it is not a separate condition of the fallacy, we would add that unless the authority appealed to is identified in some way so that conditions *b* and *d* can be checked, an appeal to authority will be suspect. If the appropriateness or consensus condition is not met, an appeal to authority will be a fallacy violating the relevance requirement of good arguments. Failure to meet the credibility or the capability condition violates the sufficiency requirement.

IMPROPER APPEAL TO AUTHORITY

1. An arguer appeals to the authority of some source to support a premise or to support the main conclusion in an argument.
2. There is good reason to think that any one or more of the conditions for a proper appeal to authority is not sufficiently satisfied. These conditions are:
   a. The appeal must be appropriate.
   b. The authority must be capable; i.e., the authority must be competent and must have the opportunity to determine the truth of the statement.
   c. There must be fairly wide consensus among authorities in that area about such matters.
   d. The authority must be credible.

Let us put the general discussion to work on some examples of arguments in which appeals to authority are found. On the subject of the viability of nuclear energy as a source of power, the writer of the following letter to a newspaper came out against it:

1   It might be profitable for some journalists to check up on what one of the pioneers in the field of atomic physics had to say about atomic energy some forty years ago. Toward the end of his life, Professor Milliken of the University of Chicago wrote his autobiography, which appeared about the time that atomic-energy plants were being projected. In his book, he makes the flat statement that as a major source of power, atomic energy has no future—"It is out." He does not elaborate, but he must have had solid reasons for this opinion, which he must have stated elsewhere, probably in professional journals.

Note, first, that the writer's appeal to Professor Milliken is guarded. He says that "it might be profitable" to consider Milliken's views. Reading this letter, we can't be sure just what the author wants to establish by this appeal to authority. Does he simply want Milliken's views considered, or does he want them considered true? Read further. The writer goes on to surmise that Professor Milliken "must have had solid reasons" for his opinion that atomic energy "is out." Thus, the writer seems to think that atomic energy has no future. He takes this view because it was Professor Milliken's view, and he invites us to do the same.

Interpreted this way, the writer is making an *improper appeal to authority*. He does not even mention Milliken's reasons for believing that atomic energy is out; sufficient for him is the fact that Milliken, an authority, held that view. We can see that the appeal is fallacious if we isolate the claim: Atomic energy has no future as a major source of power. What sort of statement is that? To begin with, it is not a statement from the domain of theoretical physics, Milliken's field of competence. Nor is it a statement that would belong to some branch of technology or applied science. In fact, it's a complicated statement that involves judgments about technology, business and industry, ecology, and lifestyles. If anything, as a claim about how a country should organize its energy production, it is a statement of social policy. As such, it necessitates numerous reasoned value judgments of a social nature, and on such issues, the prospect of a consensus is slim indeed. So the writer has violated both the capability and the consensus conditions, and hence has made an *improper appeal to authority*.

In the next example, notice how the respect that people have for intelligence and achievement can too easily lead them astray. The writer is responding to an earlier letter that had accused some Christians of being dogmatic and narrow-minded.

2   One naturally wonders how the writer would class the late Sir Winston Churchill, whose words convey what he thought about Holy Scripture: . . . According to Churchill, everything written in the Bible is literally true.

The argument seems to be that it is not dogmatic and narrow-minded to claim literal truth for statements in the Bible because Churchill said the Bible expresses the literal truth. This appeal to Churchill's authority violates both the capability and the appropriateness conditions.

First, it is doubtful that Churchill was an authority on the Bible. He was widely admired as a statesman and influential as a politician; however, these are not qualifications for authority in biblical exegesis. You might make a case that Churchill was an authority on history (he did publish several historical works), but his field of specialization was English-speaking peoples and, more narrowly, World War II. He was not a biblical historian. Second, many of the statements made in the Bible belong to theology, not history. For example, the claims that God gave the Ten Commandments to Moses or that Christ is the son of God presume religious belief. Such claims are matters of religious faith, not empirical knowledge (or so we would argue). Religious beliefs of this sort cannot be *empirically known* by anyone, or if they can, there is at least no one in a position to vouch for their truth whose authority on their behalf can then be appealed to. Hence, although Churchill had some authority in one area of history, attempting to transfer that authority to a different area was an improper appeal to authority. Moreover, the writer attempted to make this transfer to an area where appeals to authority are inappropriate.

Here is another example of an appeal to authority in another letter to a newspaper:

3   May I bring to your attention the following statement made by Dr. Joseph DeLee? He was one of the most eminent obstetricians of this continent, and he devoted his entire life to the improvement of obstetrical care. He said, "At the present time, when rivers of blood and tears of innocent men, women, and children are flowing in most parts of the world, it seems silly to be contending over the right of an annullable atom of flesh in the uterus of a woman. No, it is not silly; on the contrary, it is of transcendent importance that there be in this chaotic world one high spot, however small, which is against the deluge sweeping over us. If we of the medical profession uphold the principle of the sacredness of human life and the right of the individual, even though unborn, it will prove that humanity is not yet lost and that we may ultimately obtain salvation."

The writer appears to be using Dr. DeLee's authority as an eminent obstetrician to support the view that abortion is wrong. Dr. DeLee was undeniably at one time an authority on obstetrics, as a check of *Who Was Who in America* shows.[2] He was, for example, the author of four books on obstetrics, one of which, *The Principles and Practice of Obstetrics*, originally published in 1913, went through seven editions. Dr. DeLee was an authority on obstetrics, but that does not qualify him as an authority on the subject of the morality of abortion, an issue that belongs in the field of ethics. Thus, the competence condition has been violated by the writer.

Furthermore, it is not clear whether the proposition that abortion is wrong can be a matter of knowledge. Since it is hotly disputed whether there can be any moral knowledge, there is no justification for taking it for granted that there can be an appeal to authority on this topic. So the author has violated the appropriateness condition as well.

In the letter from which the following excerpt is taken, the writer was criticizing an earlier article about Down's syndrome that had appeared in the *Windsor Star*:

4   I believe the *Star* is doing a great service to the mentally retarded in the Windsor area by its recent articles on the subject of retardation. However, I wonder why David Gibson was quoted in this most recent article. His statements are not supported by other researchers in North America, Great Britain, or Europe.

In an editor's note, the *Star* responded.

5   Dr. David Gibson is a Canadian expert in his field. He is president of the Canadian Psychological Association, professor of psychology at the University of Calgary, editor of the *Canadian Psychologist*, and has spent more than thirty years in active work with the mentally retarded.

Having listed Gibson's impressive credentials, the *Star* then adds:

6   There are those equally learned in the same area who disagree with him, an occurrence that is commonplace in most professions.

The crucial phrase in the *Star's* attempt to defend its appeal to Gibson is in the last sentence. Since the *Star* gives no reason for citing Gibson's views rather than those of his "equally learned" dissenting colleagues, it violates the consensus condition. Where there are degrees of authority within an area, there is stronger justification for an appeal to a widely recognized authority than to one less well

[2] Vol. 2, Marquis, 1943-1950.

known. However, where opinion among the top authorities is divided, as was apparently the case here, no appeal to authority can carry persuasive force.

As you can see, an appeal to authority in an argument can violate more than one of the conditions of proper appeals. The violation of any one condition undermines the argumentative force of the appeal, but some violations are more grievous than others. If the appropriateness condition is not met, there is no way to patch up that part of the argument. A source's competence, opportunity, or credibility can come under question, but in some cases, the critic's worries can be allayed by presenting additional evidence showing these doubts to be without foundation in the case in question. If the source is not competent to serve as an authority, no evidence of opportunity can strengthen the appeal, but if competence is established, then the question of opportunity can be addressed. Violations of the appropriateness and the competence part of the capability conditions are the most damning of charges against an appeal to authority.

The key to appraising any appeal to authority rests on your capacity to delineate carefully the general field or area to which the statement in question belongs. You must then make a judgment about whether this is, indeed, an area in which any appeal to authority can be appropriate.

By the way, when you challenge an appeal to authority, you are not thereby questioning the claim itself. Your point is that the argument fails to support the conclusion, not that the conclusion is false. Hence, if your point is that there has been an *improper appeal to authority*, it would be irrelevant for you to direct your criticism against the acceptability of the claim. Here's an imaginary exchange to illustrate this mistake:

7   PSYCHOLOGY MAJOR: Everything we do has some motivation, conscious or unconscious. Freud said so.
      LOGIC STUDENT: That's an improper appeal to Freud's authority. Lots of behavior, like tying your right shoelace before your left one, is just happenstance or habit.

We're not endorsing the psychology major's appeal to Freud, but the logic student's rebuttal takes the wrong tack. When someone appeals to an authority, that person is giving a kind of reason for the claim. To say an appeal is improper is not to say that the claim is false but that the reason given for the claim—that the "authority" said so—*is not a good one in this instance*. So the relevant critique is to show why it is not, which is where the conditions of the fallacy are intended to help out. The logic student should have said that the psychology major's appeal to Freud here was illegitimate because authorities in psychology disagree about whether all behavior is motivated and they disagree about the truth of the theory of unconscious motivation. In our terms, the consensus condition has been violated in this case.

Rule: When charging *improper appeal to authority*, focus on the appeal to the authority, not the truth of the claim.

Appeals to authority are perilous. They are sometimes arguments of last resort. The thirteenth-century philosopher and theologian St. Thomas Aquinas even went so far as to say that "the argument from authority is the weakest of all arguments." Don't try to trip us up on the principles we've just listed because (you guessed it), we aren't appealing to Aquinas's authority. You don't have to take his word for it—or ours, for that matter. With the conditions for proper appeals to authority in hand, check out arguments from authority for yourself.

Popularity

The noted American philosopher and psychologist, William James, provides an example of specious reasoning that illustrates the fallacy we take up next: *popularity*. An anecdote from James's *Pragmatism*[3] serves to illustrate the kernel of this fallacy.

James and a group of his friends had gone camping in the mountains. While James was away from the campsite on a walk, the remaining members of the party got into a heated dispute. James tells us what he found upon his return.

8   In the unlimited leisure of the wilderness, discussion had been worn threadbare. Everyone had taken sides, and was obstinate; and the numbers on both sides were even. Each side, when I appeared, appealed to me to make it a majority.

James, of course, did what philosophers are famous for: He drew a distinction that he thought resolved the issue. But suppose he had sided with one group rather than the other, would that have made its view the correct one? If you think so, then beware the fallacy of *popularity*, which consists of thinking that if most, or the majority, of people believe something, then it must be true. For many, the popularity or widespread acceptance of an idea is an index of its truth, while lack of acceptance is often construed as an index of its falsity.

In its purest and most blatant (and rarest) form, the fallacy of *popularity* occurs whenever an argument proceeds from the popularity of a view to its truth, thus:

9   1. Everyone believes P; therefore
       2. P is true.

Instead of "everyone," the argument may refer to "almost everyone" or "most people" or "majority." The flip side of the argument also occurs.

10   1. No one believes P; therefore
        2. P is false.

Instead of "no one," the reference may be to "almost no one" or "very few" or "nobody I know of."

---

[3] Meridian Books, Cleveland, 1955, Lecture 2.

This move is so outrageous, when baldly stated, that the fallacy of *popularity* rarely occurs in such a blatant form. You often have to dig below the surface to find it. For example, Ari expresses the belief that smoking marijuana is harmful and urges Bart to stop using it. Bart counters, "Oh, come off it! Nobody believes that nowadays!" Bart has not actually said that because nobody believes it, it is false; but that is the clear implication. Hema says that people should not engage in sexual relations until after they are married. Shi responds, "That's conservative claptrap, and everyone I know agrees with me." Shi seems to be saying that his claim gets its support from the agreement of his circle of friends. The best way to counter such a move is to ask, point-blank, "Hold on, are you saying that because everyone (or no one) in your group believes it, therefore it is true (or false)?"

Here's an example of the fallacy, from a letter to a newspaper in which Concerned argues that laws should be more strictly enforced and that the courts should be handing out stiffer penalties:

11   Every other person with whom one discusses this problem will say that the time has arrived when the lash will have to be reintroduced in our courts.—*Concerned*

Concerned stops short of saying that since this is what most people believe, it is true. But if that is the implication, the fallacy of *popularity* has been committed.

To argue that a claim is true simply because a certain number of people *think* it's true is outrageous. However, we doubt that most people who are guilty of the fallacy of *popularity* are following this line of reasoning. Instead, we expect they reason (implicitly) as follows: that many people believe something is a good reason for thinking it is true or, at least, believing it, too. That's because, so the reasoning goes, there would not be popular acceptance of that belief unless there existed, independently, good reasons for thinking it to be true. "Where there's smoke, there's fire." Hence, so the thinking goes, the popularity of the belief is some evidence of good reasons for accepting it. The key premise in this argument is that the widespread acceptance of a proposition provides good reasons for believing it.

We are not saying here that the popular acceptance of a belief is *never* reason for believing it. Suppose you find that everyone in a community you are visiting believes the fish in a nearby lake are contaminated. That would, by itself, be a reason for you to believe that the fish truly *are* contaminated. The point is not that their believing it makes it true but, instead, that everyone's believing it is an indication that there is evidence for the claim. So popular belief is not always an irrelevant reason for accepting a proposition.

However, the mere acceptance by numbers of people of a belief cannot be relied on as a good reason for you to believe it. If people were generally in the habit of arriving at their beliefs in a reasonable way (by considering all the relevant evidence, weighing it, and so on), then a consensus of opinion would be as impressive in ordinary life as it is, say, in the case of science. But evidence that people actually do this is meager. Instead, people are persuaded by bad arguments; they're duped by fallacies; they judge first and think afterward; they fail to search out and review the evidence; they face the limits of time and energy. If all this is true, the appeal to popular consensus, even as an indicator of what is probably true, is fraught with pitfalls.

Of course, in arguing against the reasonableness of popular opinion as a basis for belief, we are not supposing that the appeal to popularity is always intended as a reasonable argument. Much of the time it's a tool of intimidation, an attempt to browbeat a person into accepting some claim. Still, it gets some of its influence by hiding behind the facade of good argument. You need to see it as the facade it is.

In the absence of any strong connection between the quantity of people who hold a position and its truth or probability, the appeal to popular acceptance is a fallacy. The conditions for it are listed in the box.

POPULARITY

1. Someone claims or implies that a proposition is true or credible and offers as support that it is widely accepted. Or someone claims or implies that a proposition is false or not believable and offers as support that it is widely rejected, or not widely accepted.
2. In the circumstances, the popularity, or unpopularity, of the proposition is not an adequate reason for accepting or rejecting it.

For several reasons, people find the appeal to popular acceptance attractive. In the first place, going against the grain of popular opinion can be experienced as threatening. (We haven't forgotten the "one in every crowd" sort who loves to disagree with everyone.) Peer pressure is difficult to resist.

Second, two perfectly respectable principles provide masquerades for *popularity*: majority rule, and popular sovereignty. A brief discussion of each of these may help you to detect *popularity* when it gets passed off as one of the others.

Majority Rule

This is the principle that what the majority of members of a decision-making group agrees to is what should stand as the decision of the whole group. The principle does not imply that the decision thus arrived at is true, or right, or the best one, but only that this is an effective way to carry on the group's affairs. (It could be replaced by a principle that calls for 75 percent in favor, or unanimity, before motions are passed.) The majority-rule principle is a *procedural* one; it is a procedure for decision making. Behind *popularity*, in contrast, lies a *criterial* principle. The appeal to popular acceptance offers the fact that most people embrace a claim as the criterion of its truth or plausibility. By failing to distinguish the procedural principle from the criterial principle, people can make the mistake of invoking majority rule as the justification for a belief.

Popular Sovereignty

Related to majority rule (and sometimes used to help justify it) is the political principle of *popular sovereignty*, the principle that says that law should be based on the will of the populace. The foundation for this principle is the idea that the people are sovereign and their views and attitudes should be reflected in the laws of the land. This is an important principle because if the laws of a country stray too far from widely shared beliefs about the sorts of conduct and policies that ought to be legislated, people will begin to lose sympathy with the laws; and respect for the law is needed for a well-ordered and flourishing society. (Even as a political principle, popular sovereignty needs qualification: Popular opinion on some issues changes more rapidly than the law can or should; also, it can be argued that legislators should have a role in influencing popular opinion as well as representing it.)

The principle of popular sovereignty should not be confused with, and cannot justify, appeals to popular acceptance as a basis for beliefs. The former makes no claim for the wisdom of the people or the worth of their preferences but only for their right to influence policy, to have their interests served. Appeals to popular acceptance, in contrast, take the further step of supposing that what the majority (or any large number of people) believes is true or plausible.

Against this background, consider the following statement, which was made after the 1992 elections. During that election in Colorado, a proposal to remove the protection of gay and lesbian rights in state legislation was passed.

12   The citizens of Colorado have spoken and decided: Gays and lesbians do not deserve the protection of the law.

Is this an instance of the fallacy of *popularity*? Or is it really an appeal to the principle of popular sovereignty?

If the author is simply pointing out what the majority of Colorado voters on the issue wanted, then there is no fallacy; indeed, there is no argument. But if the author is contending that gays and lesbians should not receive legal protection against discrimination because the majority of Colorado voters declaring themselves on that issue said so, then she is guilty of the fallacy of *popularity*. The Colorado vote decided that their state would be prohibited from doing something; in other words, popular sovereignty was exercised. But the vote does not prove that the majority was correct in its opinion. It would be quite consistent to acknowledge the authority of the vote while maintaining that the majority was wrong.

As a concluding note, we add that something like an appeal to popular acceptance is found in many advertisements.

13   Chrysler Minivan—the best-selling van in America.

14   More than 250,000 hairdressers the world over believe in what L'Oreal Hair Coloring can do for you. What more can we say?

A quarter of a million hairdressers can't be wrong! Here the assumption is that popularity is a criterion or index of the quality of a product, an assumption not far removed from taking popularity as an index of the truth of a belief. That assumption is questionable (Honda outsells Mercedes by a wide margin, but which are the better-built cars?) although not necessarily false in these particular cases. However, because advertisements have their own special logic, we will not multiply examples here, preferring to leave our confrontation with advertising until Chapter 11.

Slippery Slope

A common and perfectly legitimate way to assess a policy or a proposed course of action is to draw inferences about its likely consequences. If the proposal can be shown to have undesirable consequences, then that becomes a strong (though not decisive) reason for not embracing it. (It is not decisive because the alternatives might have even worse consequences.) Much debate and argument about social policy therefore takes the form of making causal projections. So long as the causal claims that lie at the heart of such projections are well founded, there is no logical problem. However, it often happens that in haste to discredit a policy, the critic fails to provide close argumentation to support the causal claims. When the causal projection is weak because one or more links in the causal chain are dubious, and either not defended or insufficiently justified, then one form of the fallacy we call *causal slippery slope* is the result. There are two typical forms of argument employing such causal forecasts. In one, the whole series of causal steps is included.

15   1. If we do/allow A, then B will result.
2. If B happens, that will cause C.
3. Once C occurs, then D is inevitable.
4. If D happens, it will bring about E.
5. But E would be a terrible eventuality.
6. Therefore we should not do/allow A.

For example:

16   If abortion is legalized, it will become widespread. If it becomes widespread, respect for human life will weaken. If respect for human life weakens, our form of civilization will be jeopardized. It would be folly to risk weakening our form of civilization; therefore, abortion should not be legalized.

In the second form, just the first and last chapters of the causal story are included in the argument.

17   1. If we do/allow A, that will lead in due course to Z.
2. Z would be catastrophic.
3. Therefore we should not do/allow A.

For example:

18   The legalization of abortion will be the first step along a road that can only end in the weakening of our form of civilization. Surely we don't want to jeopardize our form of civilization. Therefore, we must not permit abortion to be legalized.

The argument is fallacious when there is a link in the causal chain that is open to objection and not defended (a violation of the acceptability requirement) or when, although a controversial link is defended, the defense is questionable (a violation of the relevance or the sufficiency requirement).

The following examples illustrate both forms of the fallacy. First, the long form.

United Auto Workers' president Owen Bieber, in a letter to *Newsweek* magazine, objected to the praise a *Newsweek* article had given to Japanese automakers who were building plants in the United States.[4] Pointing out that only 30 percent of Japanese cars were manufactured in the United States at the time, Bieber wrote:

19   To make matters worse, Japanese auto firms, collectively, put less than 40 percent of American parts in their transplant cars, compared to 90 percent for the Big Three. They have shunned traditional United States parts makers—including those that meet or exceed their quality and cost standards—preferring to import key components from Japan or buy them from an estimated 250 Japan-based suppliers that have migrated here. This "buying within the family" is destroying a major United States infrastructure at a cost of tens of thousands of jobs. It threatens to turn the United States into a "branch plant" economy in which we supply basic materials and relatively unskilled labor while many of the most important technologies and higher-order skills remain in Japan.

Bieber is arguing that even for their United States manufacturing plants, Japanese automakers choose to either import parts from Japan or buy them from Japanese parts companies in the United States. These practices are responsible for massive job losses in the United States at the auto-parts manufacturing level. These job losses then cause the loss of technological and higher-order manufacturing skills. The absence of home-grown technology and skills would cause the United States to have to import them from Japan. As a result, all that the United States would have left to supply would be basic materials and relatively unskilled labor; it would have become a "branch plant" economy. In short, Bieber argues that the present manufacturing practices of Japanese automakers in the United States will start a causal chain, leading down a slippery slope that will end, finally, in the United States becoming a "branch plant" economy supplying raw materials and unskilled labor to Japanese manufacturing overlords. Tacit in Bieber's argument is the assumption that such an eventuality is highly undesir-

----

[4] Quoted in Douglas Walton, *The Place of Emotion in Argument*, Pennsylvania State University Press, 1992, p. 242.

able. From that missing premise and the causal chain he alleges, Bieber implies the conclusion that Japanese automakers should not be permitted to continue their present objectionable practices in the United States.

We think there are problems at a couple of points in the causal chain that Bieber projects. First, "tens of thousands of jobs" is a vague number but sounds like a lot. Precisely how many job losses can be traced to the practices of Japanese automakers in the United States? Accepting Mr. Bieber's figures, it looks like that "40 percent of American parts in their transplant cars" is 40 percent more than would be there if the cars were all made in Japan with 100 percent Japanese-made parts. Admittedly, if only American cars were selling in the United States, then 100 percent of the work needed to build those cars would be in this country. However, that suggests that the problem is competition from Japanese auto sales (whether imported or made in the United States), not the Japanese auto-parts sourcing practices. Moreover, the parts supplied by Japanese companies operating in the United States are made with United States labor, using technology located in the United States. So we think Bieber's claim that Japanese practices in American car making are producing unemployment in the United States auto industry partly misidentifies the cause of the unemployment and is partly just wrong.

Second, we question whether the loss of jobs in the United States, considerable though it may be, amounts to the destruction of the American auto-parts manufacturing infrastructure. That is a very strong claim and requires defense.

Third, we think that Bieber just gets carried away when he suggests that the destruction of the auto-parts manufacturing industry in the United States amounts to turning the entire United States economy into a "branch plant," merely supplying relatively unskilled labor and basic materials to foreign-owned manufacturers. We grant that the auto industry is a large component of the American industrial giant, but it is not the only one; and even if it were vastly reduced, it's far from clear that other industries would not emerge to take its place. The catastrophic outcome Bieber foresees, if it ever occurs, is not going to be caused just by the truncation of the United States auto-parts industry by Japanese branch-plant practices in the United States.

For all these reasons, then, we think Bieber is guilty of the *slippery slope* fallacy in his letter to *Newsweek*.

The next example illustrates the short form of this fallacy. When the use of seat belts in cars was being made mandatory, one of many who objected wrote to the newspaper as follows:

20   If they can make us swallow this infringement on our personal rights, what's next? A seat-belt law for the bedroom so we won't fall out of bed and hurt our little selves? Boy, when Big Brother watches us, he really watches us, doesn't he?

The argument here seems to be that the seat-belt requirement is the first step down an incline leading to a veritable *1984* ("Big Brother watches us"). But how, precisely, is this horror to come about? The intervening steps are not mentioned, except for a sarcastic reference to seat belts in the bedroom. We are given the first and the last chapters but nothing in between. Most will agree that if the legislation were the first in a series of steps leading inevitably to the confiscation of all individual rights, then it should be rejected. From our vantage point many years later, of course, we can see that the writer's prediction has not been borne out, but even at the time the projected outcome was dubious, and the author offers us no reason to expect it.

Though it does not bear directly on the charge of *causal slippery slope*, we think it worth pointing out the potential mischief of the classification of the seat-belt law as "an infringement on our personal rights." In one obvious sense, the law does take away a person's right: the right, if you will, to choose whether to use a seat belt. On the other hand, it may be argued that no citizen has the right to take an unnecessary risk when the consequences of that risk must be borne by the rest of society. Since the evidence shows that the probability of severe injury and death is decreased when seat belts are used, it could be argued that refusal to wear them constitutes an unnecessary risk. Second, the costs of automobile injury and death—police and court expenses, hospitalization, un-employment—have to be paid by the family or shared by other citizens. If this argument can be cemented, then the phrase "infringement on our personal rights" is of dubious application here, and we have a case of the fallacy of *freeloading term* in this argument, as well.

The conditions necessary for the fallacy of *causal slippery slope* are listed in the box.

CAUSAL SLIPPERY SLOPE

1. Someone claims that if an action or policy is permitted, it will set in motion a chain of events that will eventually, through a series of more or less fully elaborated causal steps, lead to a particular outcome.
2. The person claims or argues that this outcome is undesirable and that therefore, the initial action or policy that will set in motion the chain of events leading to it should not be permitted.
3. At least one of the alleged links in the causal chain (whether defended, just claimed, or assumed) is questionable or false.

In the short form of *causal slippery slope* arguments, just a jump from an initial action or policy to a final outcome is alleged. In the longer form, many or all of the intervening steps are described. But in neither the short nor the long form is sufficient evidence for the progression provided. The fallacy thus violates the sufficiency requirement of good arguments.

Not every arguer who relies on the projection of a causal series into the future is guilty of a *causal slippery slope* fallacy. Such reasoning is, in principle, perfectly legitimate. After all, if the causal links are plausible and the outcome is genuinely unappetizing, then the conclusion is well-supported. For example, the following argument from a magazine article about fitness seems to us eminently reasonable.

21   If you don't get into the habit of exercising regularly when you're young, you are less likely to keep exercising during your late twenties and your thirties when career, home, and family take up more of your time and interest. You'll then tend to become sedentary and physically unfit. That will set you up for various heart and lung diseases during your middle years. No one wants to have a heart attack at the age of 45 or 50. To lessen that possibility, you ought to get into the habit of exercising regularly when you're young.

The writer's argument seems cogent to us. The launching pad for the causal projection (not getting into the habit of exercising regularly when young) is followed by a series of claims qualified by "less likely" and "tend to" so that the argument becomes a probabilistic one rather than one delivered with ironclad assurances.

Causal slippery slope should be distinguished from a form of legitimate argumentation it resembles: the *appeal to precedent*. Decision-making bodies, especially in government, must take into account the effects of the policies they set. One of these effects is the setting of a precedent. Consistency and fairness require that if one case is treated in a certain way, similar cases should be treated similarly. For example, if your city council grants the Ukrainian community a parade permit for its national celebration, that sets a precedent. Other groups with similar requests will expect to be granted the same permission, and rightly so.

There is no logical misdemeanor in objecting to some plan or policy on the ground that it establishes an undesirable precedent. Such an argument will often be truncated, thus resembling the short form of the *causal slippery slope* argument, but in full regalia it would follow the form outlined in the box.

THE ARGUMENT FROM PRECEDENT

1. If we do/allow *A*, it will set a precedent that will justify doing/allowing similar actions (*B, C,* and so on).
2. *B, C,* and so on are undesirable.
3. Therefore we should not do/allow *A*.

The acceptability of such an argument depends primarily on whether the undesirable actions, *B, C,* and so on, are similar in relevant respects to the initial action, *A*. If they aren't, then no precedent justifying *B* is established and the argument fails. The fallacy in that case is not *causal slippery slope*, for no causal chain has been projected, but *faulty analogy*. The first premise is unacceptable because the respects in which *A* and *B, C,* and so on are similar do not suffice to support the claim that if *A* is justified, then so are *B, C,* and so on. As we said, arguments from precedent are based on the requirement of consistency: that similar cases can be treated similarly. These arguments break down when two allegedly similar cases are not similar in the relevant respect. Arguments on the *causal slippery slope* pattern are based on the prediction of causal interactions. They break down when the evidence to support the causal chains predicted is weak or worse.

Here's an argument we heard a professor make once that uses an appeal to precedent and founders due to *faulty analogy!*

22   A student has asked me for an extension on her essay because her baby-sitter quit suddenly and she has to spend a couple of days finding a new one. It is time she had planned to devote to working on my essay. But I can't give her an extension. If I do, I'll have to give an extension to anyone who asks for one, and that would make a joke of having a deadline in the first place. It's important to have deadlines, both to force students to get down to work, to help them get projects completed before the end of the semester so all their work won't pile up at the end, and to give me a chance to grade and return the essays before the end of the semester. So I had to tell her, "I'm sorry, but you'll have to take a late penalty."

The professor was worried that granting an extension in this case would commit her to granting one in every case and that setting such a precedent would undermine the whole practice of deadlines. Her argument makes the assumption that this particular student's reason for asking for an extension was similar in relevant respects to any other possible reasons other students might have. That assumption strikes us as indefensible. Not many college students have children and rely on baby-sitters. Moreover, that kind of excuse is, to our minds, a legitimate one; so if any other student asked for an extension on similar grounds, the professor should grant it. We agree with the reasons for having essay deadlines, but deadlines are not incompatible with, nor will they be undermined by, extensions for legitimate reasons. The professor feared granting an extension would set a bad precedent, but her fear was based on the assumption of a *faulty analogy* between the grounds for the request she received and any future request she might receive.

Many textbooks use the term *slippery slope* to denote a quite different type of argument from either causal-chain projections or the appeals to precedent that we have been examining, and we should draw it to your attention. Here's an example:

23   The official spring break starts on Monday, but to take advantage of the weekend before, many students leave school early Friday afternoon, skipping their afternoon classes. It's no big deal to miss a class or two. But if you're going to miss your afternoon classes, you don't miss that much more if you skip the morning classes, too. So you might as well leave school Thursday night and get the extra day. But then, why not leave early Thursday afternoon, to give yourself more traveling time so as not to be exhausted when you get to your destination? After all, Thursday afternoon's classes are for different courses from Friday's. So you're really just missing one class from each course. In fact, you might as well skip Thursday morning's classes, too, since they belong to different courses as well. But that means it makes sense to leave for spring break on Wednesday evening of the week before the official vacation, and that is what you should do if you're planning to go away for a vacation.

The reasoning in this argument is that since it is no big deal to miss one class, you can skip a second class without serious consequences. If you then add just one more to the number skipped, it still isn't serious, and so on. The trouble with this reasoning is that before you know if you have missed not one but four or five classes, and that means you have a lot more work to make up than if you missed just the one.

One writer has called this fallacy *slippery assimilation*[5]; others have it in mind when they use the term *slippery slope*. It's also called *sorites*, or "the heap," because according to this argument, you could never make a heap of sand from a single grain because no single additional grain will make enough difference between what was there before it was added and what was there after to make a heap.

Slippery assimilation seems to rely on a kind of *faulty analogy* of this form: if *A* is scarcely different from *B*, *B* is scarcely different from *C*, *C* is scarcely different from *D*, *D* is scarcely different from . . . and so on to *Z*, then *A* is scarcely different from *Z*. Try that reasoning next time you're stopped for speeding 30 miles per hour over the limit. "Look, Officer, one mile per hour over the limit is too close to call and not worth giving me a ticket for. But two miles per hour over the limit is only one mile per hour more than one mile per hour over the limit, so two miles per hour over isn't worth a ticket either. And the same is true for the difference between three miles per hour and two miles per hour over the limit. And so, eventually, thirty miles per hour over the limit is only one mile per hour more than twenty-nine, so it follows from this line of reasoning that you shouldn't give me a ticket for going thirty miles per hour over the limit." Good luck!

To end this section, we want to warn you about a further complication. Some arguments include aspects of both the causal slippery slope argument and the argument from precedent. Thus someone might argue that a given policy will *cause* people to appeal to the *precedent* it sets, and following that precedent will *cause* undesirable consequences. An example is an argument such as the following, one you might have heard from one of your professors:

24   If I give you an extension for your essay so you can do a better job, the word will get around; and others will ask for extensions on that ground, too, since everyone can do a better job given more time. And then I will have to grant extensions to everyone who wants one because there would be no difference between their claims and yours, and it's unfair to give you a benefit not extended to everyone in a similar situation. The more extensions I give, the more people will want them, and soon most members of the class will get extensions. But if nearly everyone can get an extension, then, in effect, the deadline won't mean anything; and that would be a

[5] Trudy Govier, *A Practical Study of Argument*, 3d ed., Wadsworth, 1992, pp. 296-298.

bad result because people need deadlines to force them to get down to work. So I'm sorry, but I can't give you an extension so you can do a better job.

We may be biased, but we think this argument is a good one. It combines claims about what actions will be caused by others with claims about what precedents will be set by an action. (If you disagree, write and tell us what's wrong with it.)

By this point, you should be able to see that *slippery slope* arguments are tricky. There is a collection of similar, yet distinct, patterns of argument here. Each can have logically good instances and logically bad instances. And they can be combined, with the resultant combination patterns capable of logically good and logically fallacious instances, too.

EXERCISES

Directions: For each extract assigned, decide if there are any arguments present, and, if so, whether they contain any of the fallacies you have studied so far. If you think there is no argument, explain what the function of the passage is. If you think any arguments are logically good ones, try to anticipate possible criticisms, and argue against such criticisms. If you think there are any fallacious arguments, write a critique supporting your judgment (see details below). If you think there is some fallacy not covered (yet), say so. While you may reasonably expect that these passages contain instances of the fallacies taken up in this chapter, understand that some passages may not contain arguments at all, some may contain arguments with fallacies you have not encountered, and some of the arguments may be fallacy-free.

For *each* fallacy you identify, do the following in your critique: (1) identify: the argument's conclusion, the premise(s) in which the fallacy occurs, who commits the fallacy, and the name of the fallacy (if it is not one covered so far, describe it); (2) formulate an argument to convince a neutral observer that the fallacy you allege has indeed been committed; and (3) say whether any fallacy completely undercuts the argument or whether the argument can be repaired, and explain why you think so.

1. *Background*: The following argument is from a letter to the editor. The author took himself to be contributing to the ongoing debate about abortion laws.

   Very soon, there is going to have to be some way to limit the number of births in some countries. If people don't do it voluntarily, then governments will have to pass laws that somehow have that effect. Otherwise, it won't be long before we will be in the situation nature was in before humans came along, when the only law was the law of the survival of the fittest.

2. *Background*: An editorial in the *Brandon Sun* made reference to a decision by the Manitoba government to require people to pay the tax on a car wash even if it is one of those "free" car washes you get when you fill your gas tank. The *Sun* made the following points:

   The Government has announced that a "free" car wash will be considered to be worth $1.50, and you will have to fork over the provincial tax on $1.50 even though you don't have to pay the $1.50 itself for your free car wash. It's not a lot of money, but think of the implications. Once the revenue department realizes what it has done, the possibilities for expansion are mind-boggling.

Couldn't they tax our savings? It's money we are not spending on something taxable. Do-it-yourself projects could be assessed for tax purposes, for aren't they products and services you sell to yourself? Come to think of it, that car wash you do in your driveway should be taxed, too. Shouldn't it?

While they're at it, why don't they go all the way and assume a taxable value on dreams?

3. *Background*: Some years ago, the Reverend Jesse Jackson began a campaign to force American businesses to open up greater opportunities for African Americans. He argued that it was time to right some of the wrongs done to African Americans down through the history of the United States. He threatened to organize a boycott of Coca-Cola unless blacks were granted more distributorships and management positions. One commentator replied along the following lines:

> Reverend Jackson's arguments for his economic campaign are generally persuasive. He should, however, steer clear of the extortion hinted at in the Coca-Cola boycott threat.
>
> In fact, there are several things Reverend Jackson might steer clear of, among them exaggeration in his figures. Some of them are astounding. Jackson claims that 60 million black slaves were killed while slavery was in force in America. But only 650,000 slaves were transported to America. Jackson cites as his source W. E. B. Du Bois, a renowned black scholar, also a Communist. Either Jackson misquotes Du Bois or Du Bois is no scholar because no reputable scholar would endorse the myth of 60 million slave deaths.

4. *Background*: When the Faculty of Physical Education at the University of Windsor changed its name to the Faculty of Human Kinetics, the local newspaper editorialized about the name change in the following vein:

> Whatever will be next?
>
> Undertakers are now *morticians*. People selling real estate have become *realtors*. Janitors are now, if you please, *maintenance personnel*. Garbage men, we all know, are *sanitary engineers*. Reporters have become *journalists*, and bartenders call themselves *mixologists*.
>
> The latest edition, we have just learned, is that physical education students at the University of Windsor are to be known as *kinesiologists*, and the faculty of physical and health education will be called the *faculty of human kinetics*. We kid you not.
>
> The dean of student services has called the change *academic snobbery*. We recommend that the university senate institute a new degree—Academic Snobbism (ASS). And we nominate the good dean for an honorary DPE degree—Defender of Plain English.

5. *Background*: The following contribution to the abortion debate was specifically intended to be on the question of whether it can ever be justified for a pregnant woman to have an abortion to save her life.

> Chief Rabbi Immanuel Jacovits of the United Hebrew Congregation of Great Britain and the Commonwealth was awarded the Templeton Prize for progress in religion in Vancouver recently. The rabbi is a pioneer in Jewish medical ethics. In accepting the prize, he pointed out that Jewish medical ethics takes a "fundamentally different attitude to the unborn child" than that taken by Catholics and conservative Protestants. "The fetus does not have an absolute right to life," he said. "We would regard it as a grave offense to the sanctity of human life to allow a mother to perish in order to save her unborn child."

Rabbi Jacovits is entitled to his opinion, but in this case he couldn't be more wrong. The distinguished author and journalist, the late Malcolm Muggeridge, said in an address to a "Festival of Life" in Toronto on behalf of the pro-life movement: "Either life is always and in all circumstances sacred, or it is intrinsically of no account. It is inconceivable that it should be in some cases the one and in some cases the other. If we take that power into our own hands, we've come to the end of the road that began 2,000 years ago."

6. *Background*: Following the Gulf war in 1991, there were numerous reappraisals and reconsiderations of United States policies. In one of these, United States political analyst Theodore Draper pointed out Saddam Hussein's charge that Kuwait was exporting more than allowed by the OPEC (Organization of Petroleum Exporting Countries) quota. A critic who took Draper to be implying that Hussein had a legitimate grievance against Kuwait responded as follows:

> If, as Saddam Hussein maintained, Kuwait was exceeding oil quotas set by OPEC and so driving down the market price of crude, the quota was honored in the breach by most other members of the OPEC as well. So is it right to say that Kuwait was inviting invasion by its ungentlemanly conduct? Surely not.

7. *Background*: In a *Time* magazine essay on the decline of ethics, reference was made to the controversy over a recent Vatican document calling for legal restraints on medical manipulation of human birth, including in vitro fertilization, surrogate motherhood, and the abortion of flawed fetuses. *Time* reported that moral traditionalists of all faiths welcomed the pronouncement and continued:

> But many liberals sided with Michigan lawyer Noel Keane, a pioneer in arranging surrogate agreements, who reportedly declared, "I think the church is a little out of touch with reality."

8. *Background*: When seat belts first became standard equipment on motor vehicles and people were being encouraged to get into the habit of wearing them, the following list of statements appeared in the *Canadian Public Safety* magazine:

> *a.* The average driver is not an expert.
> *b.* Racing drivers are experts.
> *c.* Racing drivers wear safety belts.
> *d.* Racing drivers agree that public highways are more dangerous than racetracks.
> *e.* You drive on public highways. Why, therefore, don't you wear safety belts?

9. *Background*: Sometimes the best way to make a point is through humor. That seems to be the approach in the following letter to the editor:

> Roger Singh's letter about the deficit is powerful and persuasive. He signed it "MD," even though it isn't about medicine. In another letter on the same page, William B. Jason cleverly makes fun of driver education programs in high schools. No medical issues come up, but he, too, mentions that he has an MD degree. We have also been getting a series of essays on women's rights by Arthur Manuel, "MD."
>
> Why do doctors feel obliged to add their medical credentials when writing about nonmedical subjects? I have a couple of hypotheses. Maybe doctors mistakenly believe people don't think well of their writing skills, so they have decided to appeal to the pity that we soft-hearted Americans feel for underpaid professionals. Or maybe doctors believe people think that just because their handwriting is illegible, doctors are illiterate, and they're trying to shatter that myth by writing letters to the editor signed "MD."
>
> I hope readers will write to say which conjecture is right. I should mention that I am a high school graduate.

10. *Background*: In a newspaper article about the views of Christian theologians on the doctrinal support for pro-choice and pro-life views, the following points were made:

> One issue near the center of the debate is whether the fetus is a human being.
>
> Pro-choice theologians claim it is not because life begins at birth, with breathing. They refer to the creation story in Genesis in which man becomes a living creature when God breathes into him and to I Kings, where a dead child comes to life after God breathes into him.
>
> Also in Christian scriptures, the Incarnation, or the "Word made flesh" was celebrated at Jesus's birth, not at a speculative time of conception.
>
> Moreover, the commandment "Thou shalt not kill" does not forbid abortion because it was not an unqualified injunction against killing all living things. The ancient Israelites were supposed to kill animals for food and sacrifice and to kill their enemies (e.g., the Philistines) in war.
>
> And the book of Exodus said that if a man harmed a pregnant woman and caused her to miscarry, he faced a fine; but if he killed her, he would be put to death. So, pro-choice scholars argue, the Old Testament Mosaic law valued a mother's life over that of her fetus.
>
> But pro-life theologians have their own sources. For example, on the claim that life begins with breath, they counter that there are different accounts in the Old Testament about where the soul resides. One is breath, but another is blood. Animal flesh with blood still in it could not be eaten because of the belief that blood is the substance of life.
>
> As for the argument that living persons have more rights than "potential" persons, St. Paul clearly says that we are not to take advantage of others' helplessness.
>
> So the appeals to one side or another heat up as legislatures and courts start to change the status quo and restrict a woman's legal right to an abortion. Some of the top theologians and ethicists are being enlisted on either side of the debate.

11. *Background*: In the debate over fighting in professional hockey games, one argument often heard runs as follows:

> If you don't allow fighting, you're going to spoil the game. Hockey isn't a namby-pamby game like cricket or shuffleboard. Hockey players are skating fast and hitting hard. Somebody's always bound to run into another fellow too hard or with his stick up or whatever, and the other guy's got to defend himself because he has to go back and play the guy that hit him next week. Plus, if you get a reputation for being soft around the league, you're done for. You have to be able to stand up for yourself, and that means fighting. If you cut out the fighting, then players will retaliate in other ways, like with the stick work, which can get really dangerous and cause bad injuries. Fights aren't dangerous—nobody ever gets hurt. That's the way hockey has always been, and that's the way it's got to stay or else you change the game, and for the worse.

CHAPTER NINE

◆

The Causes of Fallacious Reasoning

Introduction

In the previous six chapters, we discussed some thirteen different fallacies, listed their defining conditions, and analyzed examples of each fallacy. A question that hovers over our entire treatment of fallacies is, Why do people reason fallaciously? Since the purpose of this text is to help the reader both to detect fallacious reasoning and to argue better by avoiding it, it might be useful to say something about what causes someone to reason fallaciously. Since, to our knowledge, there is little solid theoretical understanding of this phenomenon, what we have to say will necessarily be speculative.

There is apparently no one reason why people argue fallaciously. In Chapter 3, we said that one of the reasons was that people allowed their emotions to dictate their thinking. Though certainly part of the story, we believe this view does not go deeply enough into the problem. It presupposes a simplistic dichotomy between reason and emotion.

In the first place, the act of reasoning is rarely carried on in a situation that lacks an emotional dimension. Since reason and emotion are abstractions from a single integrated experience or reaction, any attempt to segment or fractionalize them is ill-conceived. Few of us are, like Mr. Spock on *Star Trek*, totally dispassionate, aseptic, and cooly analytical. When we think about an issue, we do so because it interests us; it strikes chords in us that may well spark our emotions. Typically, where we have a personal stake, we have made not only a cognitive but an emotional commitment. Sometimes it is precisely because we have such a commitment that we undertake a careful and rational review of the arguments. Sometimes that review will cause us to change our conclusion. In some cases, therefore, our emotions are actually funding our cognitive endeavors. Nor are emotions entirely bereft of cognitive content. For example, when one is alarmed about a situation (say the possibility of a nuclear holocaust), one is alarmed precisely *because* one realizes (grasps intellectually) the horror of the situation.

A second and more important reason for distrusting this dichotomy between reason and emotion is that it obscures the deep and rightful influence of our rationality on our emotional reactions, and vice versa. Why does one have just these emotional readings and responses? The answer seems to be that they serve a function. To illustrate, suppose that you're walking along a busy city street, and all of a sudden you hear what sounds like gunshots. At this point, you may experience fear. This emotional response may be entirely rational and may well serve the function of putting you on guard, making you ready to flee if the danger approaches or to defend yourself if that becomes necessary.

The psychological literature dealing with the causes of bad reasoning and the debate about its origin pivots around two competing explanations. The first explanation believes that the basic cause of bad reasoning is cognitive malfunction—a psychological explanation. The second view is that the basic cause is affective bias—a psychodynamic explanation.[1] What seems clear at this stage is that we are unlikely to see a clear resolution. The ordinary reasoner must stand on guard, vigilant on both the affective and cognitive fronts.

In the next two sections, we will present illustrations of how ethnocentric and egocentric attachments (which are notoriously emotion-laden) can impede the process of argumentation. In the last section, we look at one final fallacy closely connected to egocentricity and ethnocentricity—*dubious assumption*.

Ethnocentrism and Egocentrism

The view we are presenting here can be summarized in this way: Many fallacies are due to either egocentric or ethnocentric attitudes. We must therefore understand what is meant by the terms "ethnocentric" and "egocentric." These terms were first introduced by the Swiss psychologist Jean Piaget, who was researching the process of intellectual development in children. However, our understanding of them enjoys the benefit of the intervening years of work, developing the theory.

Ethnocentrism is a tendency to see matters exclusively through the eyes of the group or class with which one identifies and/or is identified. Most prominent among such groupings are those by religion, culture, nation, gender, race, and ethnic background. An ethnocentric commitment, therefore, is one that we make, either explicitly or most often implicitly, to a group of people; and an ethnocentric attitude, as applied to culture, is one that assumes (probably never explicitly) that our culture is somehow better than others' culture *or else* that what is true of our culture is also true of others' culture.

Ethnocentric attachments are perfectly legitimate, indeed inevitable. It is when such a commitment leads to an ethnocentric attitude that we become blinded to certain realities, become unduly influenced in our thinking, and see only certain sorts of items as evidence, overlooking all contrary evidence. In doing all this, we become prone to fallacious reasoning.

---

[1] Richard Nisbett and Lee Ross, *Human Inference: Strategies and Shortcomings of Social Judgment,* Prentice-Hall, Englewood Cliffs, N.J., 1980, chap. 10.

Egocentrism is a tendency to view the world primarily from the perspective of one's own ego and to allow one's interests to define one's world. Here we are thinking of the more specific kinds of attachments and differentiating interests and involvements that individuals have as individuals. Such attachments often result in a failure to recognize another point of view, to see the possibility of an objection to one's view, or to look at an issue from someone else's point of view.

For example, if your brother is a nurse, he probably belongs to a nursing association that promotes the interests of nurses. He probably tends to hold the viewpoints and perspectives of that association more or less as a matter of course. He is defensive when that point of view is challenged. Suppose, on the other hand, that your sister is a physician. She probably belongs to a medical association that promotes the interests of physicians. She tends to be defensive when her point of view is attacked. The same might apply to auto workers, electricians, professional athletes, accountants, and so on.

By *egocentric commitments*, we understand more specific and individuating interests and involvements that we have as individuals, as contrasted with the more universal features (gender, nationality) at work in ethnocentric thinking. Differentiating between the two can be tricky in specific cases. Our point in discussing them here is simply to alert you to their possible presence in your own reasoning.

Ethnocentric Thinking

One area in which ethnocentric commitments work to limit clear reasoning is the area of nationalistic sentiment, which can impede the careful review of evidence and positions (both pro and contra) that argumentation requires.

Here is an example:

In December of 1991, when he was at Pearl Harbor to commemorate the fiftieth anniversary of the bombing of that harbor, President Bush is reported to have referred to the United States of America as "the best country in the world." This sentiment—often considered patriotic—was also widely expressed during the war against Iraq in the Persian Gulf. Such an attitude is ethnocentric. In some cases, it would be difficult, if not impossible, to cite evidence to support it. What evidence could one use to support one's deep-seated belief that "my country is better than your country" or that "this is the greatest nation in the world"? What determines excellence in nations? Stop and think for a moment about the difficulty of answering such a question. What criteria would you use? How would you decide what criteria to use? To answer this question, we would most likely look at the areas in which we believe our country excels and immediately conclude that these are the criteria that make for excellence. Our neighbors, on the other hand, would select a different set of criteria. Now who will adjudicate these criteria? And by what standards?

To illustrate this point, inhabitants of modern industrial nations often look down their noses (sometimes without realizing it) at more "primitive" cultures because, they say, these cultures are "backward" and lack our improvements.

When asked what they mean, they might say that these cultures don't have VCRs and fax machines. But how or by whom was it decided that these material things should be the criteria of culture? The answer is: those who value home entertainment and rapid communication. But such an appeal begs the question because these criteria are as much at issue as are the ones being argued about. Ethnocentrism typically blinds the reasoner to the need for digging out and providing evidence.

Perhaps nowhere is ethnocentric thinking more obvious than in the use of stereotypes. You probably know the typical cultural stereotypes: Germans are industrious; native North Americans are lazy; Scots are stingy; the English are aloof; men are rational, agressive, and out of touch with their feelings; women are emotional and illogical, unable to compete, but nurturing and in touch with their feelings; blacks are musical; Latin Americans are lazy; Asians are clannish and competitive. Stereotypical thinking is notoriously resistant to the influence of contrary evidence, as you may know if you have ever experienced the frustration of trying to combat it. You point out examples, say, of generous Scots. The response is predictable: "But those are the exceptions! The rest of them are stingy!" So now instead of an empirical generalization, we have the highly qualified view that "some Scots are stingy." In this qualified form, the claim has lost much of its interest, for presumably the same can also be said of Germans, Canadians, and so on down the line. Once a judgment is qualified, it loses its interest.

On this matter of national identity, we can do no better than to feature the words of an American who visited Toronto and wrote this letter to a local newspaper:

1   When an acquaintance found out I was American, her first comment was, "But you're not loud and obnoxious." I am getting increasingly offended at such remarks. Such backhanded, ignorant comments do no credit to Canadians.

There are 280 million people in the United States. It is ignorant to assume that we all share the same characteristics. I am not responsible for the personalities of my fellow Americans, nor am I necessarily representative of them. In turn, I do not assume all Canadians are rude and thoughtless drivers in spite of the evidence I see on the streets of Toronto every day. Your culture has elements I find admirable and elements that I don't like. I don't feel compelled, however, to inform every Canadian that I meet of the cultural traits I don't like or understand. To do so would only foster hostility and divisiveness and would serve no purpose. Each culture, including yours and mine, has both positive and negative aspects. The assertive and outgoing nature of my culture is neither better nor worse than your reserved and law-abiding nature; it is simply different.

Another place where ethnocentric thinking has been harmful is in racial matters. In the spring of 1992, Los Angeles was experiencing riots and civil unrest in the aftermath of the "not guilty" verdict in the trial of the Los Angeles police officers accused of beating Rodney King. It was not unusual to hear whites quoted to the effect that the officers had had their day in court and been acquitted, whereas African Americans and other persons of color would typically claim an abuse of justice. In this connection, consider the words attributed to John Mack, president of the Los Angeles Urban League, who said:

2   I worry about the reactions we will get from the white community. Just because there are irresponsible black people out there exploiting this situation is no reason to assume that all black people are looting and burning. In the same way, it would be dangerous for the black community to assume that the actions of a few white officers stand for the beliefs of the entire white community. Now is not the time for generalizing.

Our only real disagreement with Mack would be with his suggestion that there is ever a time for such generalizing.

Finally, as we move through the 1990s, it is apparent that gender issues and sexual politics will be high on the agenda for discussion and argumentation. To illustrate the many hazards that lie in wait for us, consider the highly publicized trial in late 1991 of William Kennedy Smith for sexual assault in Florida. Without entering into the details, we will observe that many people arrived at conclusions about Smith's guilt or innocence without benefit of the evidence made available at the trial. A great many women "knew" (read "assumed") that he was guilty of the sexual assault; a great many men "knew" that the complainant was fabricating. In most instances, the reasoners were going, not on the evidence about this specific case but, rather, on their gut readings, intuitions—in short, stereotypes.

It is not stretching matters to infer that gender bias, a form of ethnocentric thinking, is at work here. Here are some samples of reasoning that suggest this conclusion to us:

3   I don't want to hear any more about how brutal and barbaric men are. I work in an emergency room in Queens, and the last five men to come in had been attacked. Three had been beaten up by their wives, one had been banged around by his girlfriend, and the fifth had been beaten by a drunk woman who lived next door. She said his TV was on too loud. The case is closed as far as I'm concerned.

If the author is suggesting that women are capable of violence, then he or she has a case. But who has ever denied that? If, on the other hand, the author is implying that the problem of women's violence against men is comparable in magnitude to men's against women, then this case is far from adequate.

Just the opposite kind of thinking is on display in this statement by the drafters of the White Ribbon Campaign in Canada, a campaign born in the wake of the 1990 massacre of seventeen female engineering students in Montreal by one deranged man. The organizers of the campaign stated that "men's violence against women is not aberrant behavior. . . . The white ribbon symbolizes a call for all men to lay down their arms in the war against our sisters." The statement was written by men, so it seems that bad thinking about gender does not run solely along gender lines. We would argue that the claim that "all men" should "lay down their arms in the war against our sisters" implies that all men are guilty of violence against women. The claim that men's violence against women is not aberrant behavior is very close to claiming that it is typical. Without downplaying in any way the impressive evidence that most violence is committed by men (on other men as well as on women), that evidence does not show that the typical man is violent against women, or even violent at all.

Here again, we present what we take to be a more thoughtful view of these matters.[2]

4   We all know we are unique individuals, but we tend to see others as representatives of groups. It's a natural tendency, since we must see the world in patterns in order to make sense of it; we wouldn't be able to deal with the daily onslaught of people and objects if we couldn't predict a lot about them and feel that we know who and what they are. But this natural and useful ability to see patterns of similarity has unfortunate consequences. It is offensive to reduce an individual to a category, and it is also misleading. Dividing women and men into categories risks reinforcing this reductionism.

Egocentric Thinking

Thus far, we have been looking at ways in which ethnocentric commitments can lead to fallacious reasoning. But investments in nation, race, and sex are not the only sponsors of fallacious reasoning. In addition, each of us carries around a stock of more individual attachments: to organizations, clubs, professions, causes, and other interest groups. Our attachment to these can be quite as strong, as our attachment to culture or religion.

And we need to mention the dangers of these attachments, particularly when it comes to causes. We have a natural tendency to rush to the defense of something or someone we love or value or identify with. Loyalty is an important trait. Unfortunately, however, it can interfere with our rational appraisal of the evidence and with our ability to face and respond to cogent criticism.

Perhaps no more vivid example of how egocentrism impedes clear thinking can occur than when loyalty causes someone to rule out in advance the very possibility of any basis for criticism. The Watergate scandal is a classic example of this. In July 1973, David and Julie Eisenhower, son-in-law and daughter of then President Nixon, appeared on a late-nite TV talk show. The United States Senate's Watergate hearings were taking place, and the conversation turned to them. When asked who he thought the most important witnesses were, David Eisenhower replied:

5   The most important witnesses are the people who know most about it. The importance or nonimportance of the witnesses is irrelevant if you believe as Julie and I believe that the President was not involved. They're all important, but the question is, can they be believed?

[2] Deborah Tannen, *You Just Don't Understand*, Ballantine, New York, 1990, pp. 16-17.

It's not hard to understand what happened here. Naturally loyal to his father-in-law, David appears to have made up his mind in advance of hearing the evidence (which special prosecutor Archibald Cox and the Senate committee had only begun to accumulate). Nixon may have told them himself that he was not involved, and Julie and David were not prepared to accept the possibility that there could be evidence indicating otherwise. It was their egocentric commitment to Nixon that caused them to come to a *hasty conclusion*, one based on insufficient (even if personally compelling) evidence that Nixon was not involved in the scandal or the cover-up.

Questions that may have occurred to you as we went through our discussion are: "Why are we not guilty of *ad hominem* reasoning when we point out ethnocentric or egocentric thinking in someone else's reasoning? Aren't we attacking their persons rather than their arguments? Isn't that just what you warned us against in Chapter 5?"

The answer is "no" because, at least if you are going about it in the right way, you are *not* attacking the person; you are looking for explanations for why the person reasoned fallaciously. This presupposes that you have not ignored the person's reasoning but rather have investigated it and shown it to be fallacious. It's not a matter of attacking the person rather than the argument; it is not a matter of attacking at all. It is a matter of coming up with the best possible explanation for why people reason fallaciously. Our interest is less accusatory than diagnostic. The point is not to level accusations or attempt to psychoanalyze but, rather, to come to grips with why people commit fallacies in order to reduce our own tendencies to reason fallaciously.

Our treatment of the question of what causes people to reason fallaciously has been framed in terms of egocentric and ethnocentric attitudes. To conclude, we suggest three strategies for dealing with this kind of material.

First, the very best way to avoid fallacy in our own argumentation is to become aware of our own egocentric and ethnocentric attachments.

Second, remember the exercise we termed *reciprocity*, introduced in Chapter 5, which requires you to find someone who takes a different point of view, one to which you are opposed. The text is this: See if you can lay out her reasoning in such a way that it is both recognizable and satisfactory to her. If you can do this without misrepresenting that position, then you have avoided one of the main pitfalls of egocentric thinking.

Third, solicit feedback and criticism of your argument from others. They are often in a position to see how your ethnocentric and egocentric commitments have influenced your reasoning.

Dubious Assumption

In the two previous sections, we put the spotlight on two attitudes that dispose people to fallacious reasoning. We did not introduce any new fallacies because the logical miscues that ethnocentric and egocentric thinking sponsor are fallacies already included in our catalog. For example, when an egocentric commitment leads the arguer to assert, without defense, a premise that really ought to be defended, the appropriate charge is *problematic premise*.

However, discussion of egocentric and ethnocentric habits of thought as sponsors of fallacy does bring into the open how much our reasoning depends upon deep, hidden, and difficult-to-unearth elements. The final fallacy in our inventory is *dubious assumption*. This fallacy is often the result of an egocentric or ethnocentric pattern of thinking, but it is not limited to such contexts.

To begin with, we need to clarify what we mean by the term "assumption" because our use of it will vary somewhat from standard usage. For example, by an assumption, people often mean something that hasn't been proved, as when someone says, "Wait a minute. You're making a big assumption when you say that." What she means is that you haven't really proved or argued for the claim you're making. When the arguer has used in her argument a statement that she does not defend and your judgment is that it needs to be defended, then the proper charge is *problematic premise*.

To illustrate, consider the following example, in which the writer urges a reappraisal of Canada's foreign-aid program:

6   Canadians are continually being urged to give money to feed starving children in India. While it is distressing to think of their suffering, it has to be remembered that as much *as three quarters of all aid sent to India goes into the pockets of corrupt politicians and black marketeers.* [Emphasis ours.]

Referring to the italicized portion, one might want to say, "The writer doesn't prove that charge, and that's quite an *assumption* to make." But the assertion we put in italics does not stand behind any other claim the writer makes; it's an allegation that stands by itself. A case can be made that the charge is serious enough and controversial enough to require that it be defended, meaning that it is really a case of *problematic premise*.

When we speak of an *assumption* hereafter, what we have in mind is a piece of reasoning taken for granted by or underlying an assertion or a position, as when someone says, "The assumption underlying the policy of tax breaks for corporations is that the economy will continue to expand." The idea here is that although it is never explicitly stated that the policy is premised on continued economic expansion, if that were not the understanding, the policy would make no sense, would be inappropriate. A simpler example might be when a friend asks when you and your partner are coming over for dinner. He's assuming you still have a partner. Roughly, then, we use the term "assumption" as shown in the box.

ASSUMPTION

An assumption of a statement is an unstated proposition that must be true if the statement is to be true, intelligible, or appropriate in the context in which it is made.

So-called double-bind questions present a clear instance of assumptions in operation. Someone asks you, "Have you stopped cheating on your math exams?" or "Are you still doing dope?" How do you answer such a question if you've never cheated on a math exam or done dope? You're in a double bind because if you say "no," you imply that at one time in the past you cheated or did dope. If you say "yes," you're affirming not only that you used to cheat or do dope, but that you are still doing so. The problem here is that the question involves an illegitimate *assumption*. From the logical point of view, the appropriate response is to challenge the assumption that underlies the question. In double-bind questions, then, the appropriateness of the question depends upon the truth of the proposition being assumed. Unless the assumption is true, the question is inappropriate.

However, we are most interested in how assumptions enter into arguments. We shall be looking at how the premises of arguments can be laden with questionable assumptions. In this connection, it is natural to include missing premises as a species of assumption. What is the missing premise/assumption in the argument below?

7   Ellen is so irresponsible with money. Why, she spent half of the first month's salary from her new job on a leather jacket, of all things!

The inference employs some such missing premise as this:

8   Anyone who buys a leather jacket before anything else is irresponsible with money.

Here the assumption takes the form of a missing premise—an unstated link needed to get from the stated premise to the conclusion—that is taken for granted. It is necessary for the intelligibility of the argument. If the arguer wasn't committed to this proposition, didn't have this proposition (or one very much like it) in mind, the conclusion would not make any sense.

The conditions necessary for the fallacy of *dubious assumption* are listed in the box.

DUBIOUS ASSUMPTION

1. Someone employs an assumption in an argument where (a) the assumption is an unstated proposition on which a stated premise depends for its truth, intelligibility, or appropriateness; or (b) the assumption is a missing premise.
2. The assumption is open to reasonable challenge.

To illustrate, we present this historic example from the Watergate hearings in the 1970s.

During the hearings, John J. Wilson, a lawyer for a White House staff member, was heard making reference to the committee member from Hawaii, Senator Daniel Inouye, as "that little Jap." This remark, spoken into a microphone Wilson assumed was off but which was live, created a furor when it was widely reported in the media. Attempting to defend himself, Wilson wondered aloud what the hoopla was all about, saying, "I wouldn't mind being called 'a little American'." The clear implication of this defense was that Inouye shouldn't mind being called "a little Jap." An alert reader of the *Detroit Free Press* neatly exposes the *dubious assumption* underlying Wilson's argument: "What is Senator Inouye *but* an American? Apparently Wilson believes that 'American' is spelled *W-A-S-P*." In other words, Wilson's statement cloaks the assumption that *real* Americans are those who derive from the original colonists; i.e., white Anglo-Saxon Protestants, for that appears to be what's behind his thinking that Inouye (an American) is really Japanese, while he, Wilson, is really an American. The ethnocentric attitude embodied in this thinking is evident.

For another example, we refer to the hearings held in October of 1991 in the Senate to determine whether Clarence Thomas would become as associate justice of the Supreme Court. During the hearings, a professor of law at the University of Oklahoma—Anita Hill—claimed that during the 1980s Thomas (who was then her employer) sexually harassed her. Commenting on this affair, one columnist began by describing both individuals and then said:

9   Never mind that she may have been sexually harassed. Never mind that she says her boss used his position to direct repeated unwanted sexual remarks toward her.

The point is that a woman's accusation against a powerful male is still worth very little in this nation.

Not so long ago, Douglas Ginsburg was nominated for the Supreme Court. Then it was discovered that years ago, he had smoked marijuana. His nomination was withdrawn. The same power structure thought that was the right thing to do. Smoking marijuana would present a bad image for the court.

Too bad the abuse of women doesn't give one the same image.

For this last comment to have any bearing on the issue, the author has to assume that Thomas—like Ginsburg—was guilty of an indiscretion (in Thomas's case, sexual harassment). But that is a *dubious assumption*, because the question at issue was whether any form of inappropriate behavior had occurred. Ginsburg admitted to having smoked marijuana; Thomas denied the allegations against him. This is a fundamental difference between the two cases.

The final example of *dubious assumption* comes from a letter to *The New York Times* regarding gender-specific pronouns. This writer claims that the obvious solution is to use the plural ("If people are late, *they* . . .").

10   Of late I have noted a covert operation designed to redress grammatical imbalance by letting woman embrace man. Last year, for example, the *Times* columnist Anthony Lewis wrote: "Every time an American moves or changes jobs, she is likely to find herself with a different health-insurance carrier." Just recently, a (male) professor, discussing computerized college testing . . . noted that "the student will immediately receive a score earmarking her prospects for life." In neither case was there a specific female antecedent anywhere in sight. What you had was linguistic politicking at its sneakiest.

The conclusion that these uses represent a "sneaky," "covert operation" of linguistic "politicking" follows only if the authors' uses of the female pronoun were not just a bias-free convention, were intended to be surreptitious, and were elements of a distasteful operation both were party to. All three assumptions are unsupported and open to question. Many writers, in an effort to achieve bias-free prose, alternate male and female pronouns when there is no specific antecedent to refer to. The practice is entirely open. The attempt to redress a long history of sexual inequality is indeed a political act, but does not therefore deserve the pejorative label "politicking." And the suggestion that Anthony Lewis and the professor are agents working together in some sort of covert operation is, in the absence of no other evidence, implausible. So we conclude that the writer is guilty of *dubious assumption*.

In conclusion, it follows from what we have said in this chapter that a significant step in the avoidance of fallacious reasoning is self-awareness. If you want to avoid being led into fallacious thinking, you need to become aware of your own ethnocentric and egocentric commitments. Indeed, you need to understand the basis of these commitments and engage in critical thinking about them. Good logical critical thinking cannot and does not occur in a vacuum; both the force of personality and the complexity of the issue inevitably enter into any assessment of a process of reasoning. Logic alone is not enough, but awareness of the criteria of good argument, plus practice, plus self-knowledge and knowledge pertinent to the issue—all of these must be integrated into the evaluation of argumentation.

EXERCISES

Directions: This exercise is somewhat different from previous ones. Not all the passages here are arguments; some are included in order to illustrate egocentric and ethnocentric thinking. Some contain the fallacy of dubious assumption. There may be other fallacies as well, or passages with arguments but no fallacies. Some of these passages have appeared before; they are repeated here because there is something more to be learned about them specifically from this chapter.

1. *Background:* A student at New York University, challenged about having submitted a plagiarized paper, argued:

   > Why shouldn't I buy a term paper? I'm an English major; I've been assigned a paper on physics, a subject I don't know anything about and don't care to know anything about.

2. *Background:* This passage comes from a journal devoted to temperance education. Such publications were widespread during Prohibition in the United States.

   > Girls should never touch alcoholic liquors. The reasons are obvious. It is for them to steady the young men and so maintain their dignity, beauty, and intelligence.

3. *Background:* This passage comes from a Canadian history textbook.

   > A good number of the coureurs de bois married Indian women and abandoned all traces of civilization; some even lowered themselves to the level of savages and

became as ferocious as the redskins when it came to torturing or killing enemy captives.

4. *Background:* In November 1991, *Time* magazine featured a story about alternative medicines—reflexology, homeopathy, and so on. That elicited this letter to the editor:

> As a practicing physician for the past twenty years, I was very disgruntled to read your issue devoted to alternative medicines.
>
> The days of snake-oil patent medicines should be over, not undergoing a revival. People will eventually come to recognize that the best health-care provider is the physician and not some quack, or practitioner of alternative gimmickry.

5. *Background:* In the fall of 1991, Clarence Thomas, a black federal judge was nominated by then-President Bush for the position of associate justice of the United States. During the Senate hearings, a former employee of Thomas's—Anita Hill—came forward with allegations about Thomas's sexual behavior in 1987, while he was her boss at the Department of Education. A columnist referring to these hearings wrote as follows:

> Sen. Orrin Hatch of Utah, he of the shuddering little chin, fulminates against the perversity of the accusations against the nominee. Imagine, a respectable man making references to pubic hairs on Coke cans to such a woman. Imagine such a man watching films of Long Dong Silver.
>
> The Senator really ought to get a life. Many otherwise successful men are grotesque stumblebums when it comes to approaching women. And the porn industry would go broke in a week if it were patronized only by drooling perverts.

6. *Background:* This is an excerpt from an essay entitled " 'PH' Stands for Political Hypocrisy" that appeared in *Academy*. In the essay, Cathy N. Davidson recounts her experience after her letter about political hypocrites appeared in *The New York Times*.

> Yes, I also received some honest-to-goodness hate mail.
>
> One person cut my letter out of the *Times* and sent it to me anonymously with the word "bullshit" stamped on it in red. (Imagine someone so disgruntled with the world that he goes out and buys his own "bullshit" stamp!)

7. *Background:* After Denmark legalized pornography in the 1970s, the following editorial appeared in The *Windsor Star:*

> Latest crime statistics from Denmark provide a striking illustration of the beneficial effects of that nation's experiment in pornography and should provide a powerful argument for those favoring the legalization and open availability of pornography here in Canada.

8. *Background:* The following is from the same editorial as the one above.

> Whatever weight attaches to the moral or good-taste arguments against pornography, it seems doubtful they will prevail in the long run over increasingly liberal attitudes in modern society, particularly when the liberal position is buttressed by proof that legalized pornography leads to a decline in sexual crimes.

9. *Background:* The following conversation is reported by the Russian scientist Zhores Medvedev to have taken place in the mid-sixties between himself and a Russian bureaucrat named Filippova when Medvedev was seeking approval to attend an international congress of scientists to be held in the United States:

"Comrade Medvedev, do you read the papers?"

"Of course I read them," I replied.

"Obviously you don't read them very well. You ought to know that they [the United States] are sending U2 planes over and dropping spies by parachute. And you've been getting ready to go and visit them?"

"It's not going visiting; it's a congress. And anyway, it's an international congress, not an American one!"

"Well, so it's international, but if this international congress were in West Germany, would you still want to go?"

When I tried to show that if Soviet scientists took part in international congresses, it would help raise the prestige of Soviet science, Filippova at once rejected my arguments: 'We don't need the recognition of American pseudoscientists; we got our sputniks up first.'"

10. *Background:* Writing in *Time* magazine,[3] Robert Hughes had this to say about "political correctness":

> But here we come up against a cardinal rule of the PC attitude to oppression studies. Whatever a white European male historian or witness has to say must be suspect; the utterances of an oppressed person or group deserve instant credence, even if they're merest assertion.
>
> The claims of the victims do have to be heard because they may cast new light on history. But they have to pass exactly the same tests as anyone else's, or debate fails and truth suffers.

11. *Background:* Here is an argument about the high salaries of professional athletes and what should be done about them.[4]

> How important are professional athletes to society? Not very. They're mere entertainers. They often present bad role models for children—just think of Pete Rose, or Steve Garvey, or Jose Canseco. And given the attention they get, they tend to distract us from serious social concerns. At the very least, then, the salaries of these prima donnas should be drastically reduced to reflect their social insignificance.

12. *Background:* From an article entitled "Men, Inexpressiveness and Power" comes the following:[5]

> Sexism is not significantly challenged simply by changing men's capacity to feel or express themselves. Gender relationships in this society are constructed in terms of social power, and to forget that fact . . . is to assume that men can somehow unproblematically experience "men's liberation"—as if there existed for men some directly analogous experience to the politics created by feminist and gay struggles. Men are not oppressed *as men* and hence are not in a position to be liberated *as men.*

13. *Background:* This is a letter that appeared in the *Toronto Star* about how first-world nations treat third-world nations:

---

[3] "The Fraying of America," February 3, 1992.

[4] Adapted from an exercise in Vincent Barry and Joel Rudinow, *Invitation to Critical Thinking,* 2d ed., 1992, p. 207.

[5] Jack W. Settel, in Barrie Thorne et al. (eds.), *Language, Gender and Society,* 1983, p. 123.

A recent item in the *Star* reported that French and Belgian troops had intervened once again to protect Mobuto Sese Seko, the dictator of Zaire. Mobuto came to power in a CIA-backed coup thirty years ago and has since murdered thousands of people while stuffing billions of dollars into foreign bank accounts. One thing certainly has not changed with the "New World Order"—the third world's people and resources continue to be looted in order to benefit elites both there and in the West.

14. *Background:* From an article about the importance of maintaining standards of good writing in journalism comes the following:

It is vitally important that standards of English be upheld, and some of us are at least aware of this. But even the ablest among us, harried by the demands of rapid-fire journalism, are not immune to lapses. Consider the fact that Irving Howe, on the front page of *The New York Times Book Review*, writes about "main protagonists." Now, the protagonist is the main actor in something and has, since Greek times, always been in the singular. Thus "protagonists" is incorrect (unless you refer to the protagonists of two or more dramas), and "main protagonists" is redundant, to boot—a double-barreled error.

15. *Background:* In the mid-seventies, the NBC-TV program *Weekend* featured a segment on racial tension in the city of Toronto, devoting particular attention to incidents involving immigrants from Pakistan and East India. In the program, the claim was made that "Toronto is a time bomb of racial tension." The following is a portion of a response from one Canadian newspaper:

Canadians are understandably upset at the charge by an NBC program that Toronto is a time bomb of racial tension, but Canadians should also be acquainted with the facts, should look at the gross exaggeration of the charge, and should not be too upset. A weekend visit to Toronto would provide the answer,

If anyone wanted to spend a few days in Toronto searching out prejudice, it would not be difficult to find. This is obviously how the NBC-TV program came up with the scare report that Toronto is a time bomb of racial tension. To find the true picture would take longer and be more difficult. . . . It would have been better if they had asked those of their countrymen who have firsthand knowledge of what the situation is. Let them ask thousands of Americans who crowd to Toronto on holidays, enjoying a clean, tension-free city where it's safe to walk the streets at night.

SECTION III

Argumentation and Mass Media

CHAPTER TEN

♦

Dealing with News Media

Introduction

Much of the information available to us for assessing the arguments we encounter comes from the information media: TV, radio, newspapers, magazines. Yet the media shape the message. In order to interpret this information intelligently, you ought to have a general understanding of how information is picked up by and filtered through the different news sources as well as up-to-date knowledge of the practices and policies of the particular outlets from which you get your information: your local newspaper(s), radio, and TV; national network news and current-affairs programs; *Time* and *Newsweek* magazines; and perhaps a "national" newspaper such as *The New York Times*, the *Los Angeles Times*, the *Christian Science Monitor*, or the *Washington Post*. Intelligent critical appraisal of the information supplied by the news media requires an informed understanding of how they operate. We hope this chapter will help you become an active critical consumer of the news.

   With this purpose in mind, we provide two items in the present chapter. The first is a checklist of questions that a critical consumer of the media needs to be in the habit of asking when reading the newspaper or listening to or watching the news. The second is a list of projects intended to lead you closer to the understanding we just spoke of.

Checklist of Questions

In the list that follows, we present a cluster of questions under each heading and, after the questions, a brief explanation of why they should be asked. You should be able to answer these questions after a careful reading or viewing of any news report. Unless you can, there is a good chance you will digest misinformation. In that case, your needs as a media consumer for an accurate and reasonably complete picture of ongoing events won't be met. The danger is that you'll base your assessment of arguments on this false understanding of events.

All Media

Headlines and Picture Captions

1. Is the angle or point of view created by the headline borne out by the news report? Or does the headline tend to lock the reader into an interpretation that is not supported, or even contradicted, by an independent survey of the details of the news report that follows?
2. Do the picture captions suggest interpretations of photographs that are not warranted by the photos alone or by the accompanying news report?

The first question should be asked because headlines are labels. They lead the reader to interpret the events reported in the light of the judgment they express. If the headline contains the word 'tragedy,' for example, we read the news story as the account of a tragedy. Sometimes the events reported bear out this interpretation. But not always. The headline writer (usually the editor assembling the page, not the journalist who wrote the story) can inadvertently or deliberately give a slant to a story that is not warranted by the text. The headline might give undue prominence to just one aspect of the story, for example. Or it might incorporate an editorial judgment upon the events reported when those events are consistent with alternative judgments. It takes a conscious effort to wrench yourself free of the headline's orientation, but if you do, you may suddenly see the events reported in an entirely different light.

The second question should be asked because photo captions can give a totally inaccurate interpretation of the event pictured. If the photo shows a few dozen people milling about but the caption reads, "Strikers riot at plant gate," the incautious reader will believe he or she has seen a photograph of a riot, not a picture of a few dozen people milling about.

Completeness

1. Is the account full, clear, and coherent? Are there inconsistencies, puzzling assertions, questions left unanswered?
2. Are there technical (or pseudotechnical) terms or statistical data that you don't fully understand?
3. Are the details too skimpy to form a clear picture of the event?

The first question should be asked because news reports are usually gathered and written in a hurry to make deadlines. Coherence and completeness are casualties of the rush. Events might still be unfolding when the reporter must write the story. Parts of the report might be secondhand; sources might give conflicting accounts.

The second question should be asked because reporters, like the rest of us, are sometimes smitten by meaningless jargon. Stories may omit technical explanations as too cumbersome. Journalists may assume more knowledge on the part of their audience than it possesses or, conversely, may not themselves understand what they are reporting.

The third question should be asked because readers and viewers tend to kid themselves about how much they really learn from news reports. Do you have a reasonably complete picture of the events? If so, could you describe and explain them to someone else?

Our point here is not to berate the press for incomplete news reporting but to caution the reader against assuming that more than a limited, partial, often highly incomplete understanding of reported events is gleaned from even the best news reports.

Sources

1. Does the story come from a public relations handout? A news conference? A leak? A "background" interview with an official who refuses to be identified?
2. Does it come from a wire service? These include the Associated Press (AP), the cooperative news-gathering service in the United States; United Press International (UPI), a United States-based international commercial news-gathering service; Reuters, the British news-gathering service; and Agence France Presses (AFP), the French news-gathering service. Does it come from a newspaper's or a TV network's own news service?
3. Does it come from a reporter's own observations, research, interviews? If so, how could the writer whose story you are reading, listening to, or watching have obtained the information he or she is presenting?

The first question should be asked because every large corporation, union, government department, institution (including college and university) has a public relations officer who writes "news" releases publicizing the outfit and putting its interests in the most favorable light. Often these releases get into the media unverified, or only slightly rewritten. News conferences can be stage-managed to overdramatize, divert attention, obfuscate. Leaks and "backgrounders" almost always serve the interests of the politician, party, or group that gives them and not the interests of the public.

The second question should be asked because all wire services tend to avoid controversy and overrepresent "establishment" news sources. Also, foreign wire services write for their own national points of view, while United States wire services tend to focus almost exclusively on American interests, ignoring other countries' points of view. The same is true of American newspapers and TV networks.

The third question should be asked because some events are not accessible, and reports can be based on rumor, stereotypes, or political prejudice. Reports from some locations (for example, wars) might be censored, managed, or both. (The coverage of the 1991 war in the Persian Gulf is a prime example of this.) Study the habits of accuracy and the personal biases of local reporters and columnists on whom you frequently rely for information. Some reporters cover a "beat" (such as city hall, business, or education) for years and acquire great knowledge of its inner workings and politics, but some also establish a cozy working relationship with those who give them the news, and that may result in self-censorship or biased reporting.

Background

1. What is the immediate context into which the story fits? Is it about an event that connects with other recent or less recent events? Is it a development of earlier events? If so, is it a response or a reaction to them? How did it come about?
2. Why is it being reported *now*? Why is this event being reported *at all*?
3. Is it an "update" report on an ongoing event, or a fuller account of events reported earlier in less detail?

The first question should be asked because most, if not all, events make sense only when viewed against the background from which they have emerged. (The background events may be as recent as the previous day, or they may go back over a period of years.)

The second question should be asked because the "reporting" may itself be part of the event that makes it news; hence, what occasions the report may help explain the significance of the events reported. Also, events can be staged to promote particular interests (for example, the "photo opportunities" that occur during election campaigns). Some activities are reported only because they involve people in high office or whom the media has elevated to the status of celebrities. Any time the President, Madonna, or "Magic" Johnson does anything, for example, it's in the news. But is it important?

The third question should be asked because news reports often presuppose that readers or viewers are familiar with prior accounts or earlier developments. If you aren't, you may have to do some research if you want to understand the news reports you're reading or viewing.

Balance

1. Does the story report the views of all the individuals or groups who have an interest in the dispute or controversial issue?
2. Does the story present events or issues from one perspective when others are available? Can you identify that perspective? What other perspectives are there? How might those same events be reported from those other perspectives? Does the report try to get you to draw a conclusion or share a judgment? Is its angle justified?

The first question should be asked because each adversary or party to a dispute tends to picture his or her side in the right and the other in the wrong. A fair judgment requires that all claims be considered. Sometimes reporters are lazy and file a report after checking with just one side. Other times, the reporter has tried to obtain the views of all parties involved, but some were unavailable or wouldn't be interviewed. Either way, the critical reader needs to note the fact that perhaps only one or two of many perspectives has been represented.

The second question should be asked because as columnist Tom Wicker once noted, the practice of objectivity is an act favoring the status quo.[1] Every report has some angle, if only that no interpretation, no background, no judgment should be given (which creates the image of a world of unrelated "neutral" events, events on which we must bring our "personal" and "subjective" judgments to bear). Most language is evaluative, judgmental, by virtue of the words used and the words not used. You have the choice of either unconsciously accepting the reporter's outlook or identifying it for what it is and thereby gaining the option of rejecting it.

Connections

1. Will the events reported affect you directly? Might they touch you indirectly? What should you do as a result of the information given? Should you watch for further developments? Should you change your mind about a previous opinion? Should you behave differently in some respect in the future?
2. Do the events connect with other, similar events and thus form a pattern? What is their significance? What do they mean? What do they portend?

The first question should be asked because forewarned is forearmed. You can put the information you receive from the media to good use if you think about its implications while you ingest it. Try to anticipate the possible consequences of what has been reported and estimate how likely any of these consequences are.

The second question is perhaps the most significant question in this checklist of questions. The mosaic of information from the media to some extent creates or reinforces an overall picture of the world. It reflects a theory, or interpretation, or understanding, about the nature of society—society's function and purpose, its possibilities and its confines. (This is not done intentionally; it's not controlled. We aren't suggesting manipulation.) Either you accept that theory by default, or you develop and bring your own theory into play, using it to place and connect and exhibit the significance of events reported in the media.

Importance

1. How important is the event reported compared to other stories elsewhere in the news the same day? Does it merit its prominence? What is its importance relative to other events that day?
2. Was the event staged or created exclusively for the media?

The first question should be asked because the front page of the newspaper, or the "top" of the news broadcast, have to be filled somehow. And these are the most prominent locations for news. Hence, someone has to make a

---

[1] As reported in Robert Cirino, *Power to Persuade: Mass Media and the News*, Bantam, Toronto and New York, 1974, p. 202.

judgment about the news stories available at that time and decide which are the most important. By the same token, some story or other has to be put inside the last page or before the last commercial; and these locations convey the message "not as important as the other stuff." Only an infinitesimal fraction of the events occurring on any given day even get covered. Each day, editors and producers must make decisions about what events to cover and what stories to put in the paper or on the news and how to feature them. You don't have to agree with their decisions. You, the reader or viewer, can choose to exercise your own judgment about the relative importance of day-to-day events.

The second question should be asked because events like press conferences, or even demonstrations, are pseudo events in the sense that they are put on just for media coverage. (This is true now for most sporting events, which are, like TV dramas, sitcoms, soaps, and the current fad of re-creation shows, organized in order to deliver an audience to advertisers. Would the Olympic Games continue to be held without TV?)

Television

Television differs from radio and the print media in two ways: the visual ingredient and the power of television. Film not only seems to bring one closer to events; it is also an enormously more powerful medium than words for creating an impression about the events reported. Remember, however, that TV news film is *always* edited. Film footage is chopped up and then pieced together by a producer and editor who must make judgments about what to show, what to leave out, what shots to juxtapose, what order to present events in, where to interpose still photos, how to pace the story, how much time to allot to it. Each filmed news item is a work of journalistic art; that means it's part creation. (We're not saying the film is faked.)

Narration

Does the voice-over suggest an interpretation that the film does not by itself bear out?

This question should be asked because narration can convince you to "see" what is not there in the film.

Video/Film

1. Does the video use props? Is it posed? Was it actually shot at the events, or is it old film from the station's or network's library?
2. Does the video emphasize certain aspects of the event (such as its violence), giving them undue prominence?
3. Is the story on the news only because of its visual interest?
4. What bias or perspective did the editing of the story produce? What impression did you get about the events you were viewing? On reflection, is that impression warranted?

The first question should be asked because of the power of visual impressions. It's mandatory to know whether the image you're left with really captures the event reported. If you see "file footage" flashed on the screen, stop watching and just listen to the voice-over. Otherwise you are getting impressions from the video of a different event.

The second question should be asked because video of a single fight at a demonstration can be used to give the impression that the entire demonstration was violent (even when the announcer's or reporter's voice-over states otherwise).

The third question should be asked because, other things being equal, of two equally important stories the one with interesting film will get into the news and the one without video will be cut. A corollary of this TV truism is that most TV news stories come from urban centers because that's where camera crews are stationed.

The fourth question should be asked because editing can influence not only your interpretation of the meaning of what you see and your value judgments about it but also your impression of what actually occurred. The camera *can*, in effect, "lie."

Some people believe television news is more reliable than news from other sources because the viewer can actually observe what is happening and that's a check on journalistic bias. As we have noted, such a belief is based on a misconception. Camera angles are chosen with care. What is taped is thoughtfully selected. TV news segments are edited with the craft and care of a TV commercial. We think the evidence shows that TV news producers, editors, and correspondents honestly want to deliver complete, accurate, balanced, and responsible coverage of the important events of the day. They spend a great deal of money and take great pains to do so. But we also believe that the consumer of media information who surrenders her or his judgment into their care has thereby given up the autonomy of a responsible citizen.

CHECKLIST OF QUESTIONS

All Media

1. Headlines and Picture Captions
2. Completeness
3. Sources
4. Background
5. Balance
6. Connections
7. Importance

Television

1. Narration
2. Video/Film

The checklist in the box and the accompanying rationales for the items on it suffer at least two defects: They are sketchy, and the opinions they reflect are not fully defended. We must leave it to you to apply questions to the concrete case of a particular day's newspaper or news broadcast or, better still, to a series of both. See what particular questions our necessarily schematic ones generate. Also, make your own critical judgment about whether our outlook toward the information media bears up under examination.

These questions are not intended as veiled criticisms of the news media nor as recommendations for changes in their policies or practices. Neither are we saying that they should *not* change in various ways. On that issue we pass. Our perspective is that of the consumer of news, not that of the journalist. Our basic question was this, Given the way the news media operate and are likely to continue to operate whether we like it or not, how can the information consumer make the most judicious use of what the media offer? Where is caution needed? What mistaken assumptions or naive beliefs need to be overturned? The goal is the intelligent use of the media as they now operate.

Projects

The questions on our checklist came from our acquaintance with how the media function and from a point of view that is skeptical of the capacity of the mass media to provide a totally adequate diet of information. The limitations and bias of the checklist are not serious failings in a device designed to pique your curiosity rather than sell you a bill of goods. However, asking yourself those questions is at best only half enough. To be able to use the media intelligently, you have to investigate two general topics: (1) how the various media actually operate day in and day out, and (2) the ideological role of the media.

Finding Out How the Media Operate

The first thing to do is to read everything you can get your hands on about the media. The reading list at the end of this chapter should get you started learning how the news media operate in the United States.

Once you know how the media operate in general, try to find out about the outlets that you come into contact with personally: your local newspaper and local radio and TV stations. Invite the editor or managing editor of the paper and the station manager or news manager of the radio and TV station to talk to your group. (They're usually delighted to come.) Your speakers will probably prefer to give at most a short talk and then answer your questions, so prepare your questions in advance. In addition, you might visit the newspaper and the radio and TV newsrooms. Talk to reporters, editors, newswriters. (You might have to assign small groups to different tasks.) See if you can follow a reporter or a camera crew around for a few days. All of this should give you fascinating insights into the whole news operation, though it will also tend to distract you from the basic question for the defensive consumer: In what ways does all this affect the information I get as I sit reading the paper or watching TV?

A third way to learn about the media is to make a systematic study of all the local newspapers and newscasts over a period of at the very least a week. Compare stories within each medium. Get an out-of-town newspaper or two during the same period. Watch different channels and listen to different radio stations. Also, compare the different media. Study TV, radio, news magazine, and newspaper treatments of the same story. Such observation of the media in action is useful for reality-testing the picture you might get from your reading, the talks, and the question-and-answer-sessions. We have observed that many (not all) newspeople tend to be unreflective about their working assumptions.

Discovering the Ideological Role of the Media

By the "ideological role" of the media, we don't mean only or primarily the political views influencing information packaging by the media. We are referring more generally to the overall world view the media propagate, usually unintentionally.

To become aware of the media's ideological impact, investigate their "working categories." These are the conceptual groups into which the media sort the realities they report and consequently, into which the information we consumers receive about those realities is parceled.

Newspapers divide information into an explicit, conventional set of categories, such as news, editorial matter, features, entertainment, business, sports, family, to list a few. Do the events in the world actually sort themselves out in this way? What effect does this organization have on the image of reality we consumers receive when we read the paper each day? (Some critics claim that so much space is devoted to sports in newspapers because newspapers are run by men. True?)

Newspapers try to keep a strict separation between factual information, which they put into their "news" columns, and opinions about that information, which they put into "editorials" or reports labeled "analysis" or "opinion." But is such a distinction between fact and opinion supportable? What are the defining features of each? And what effect does working in terms of this division have upon the picture of the world the newspaper conveys?

What is news anyway? What makes an event news, or "newsworthy"? Does the definition of "news" differ from one medium to the next? For example, do the picture possibilities influence what counts as news for television stations? What assumptions or other factors might affect editors' judgments about what is newsworthy? How does the news media's operating with this category called *news* affect the picture of the world received by the news consumer?

A second way to become aware of the media's ideological impact is to look for their own conception of their role and the standards they try to meet in filling it. For example, many editors, producers, and reporters see themselves as having a responsibility to "mirror" society. Your research should quickly uncover expressions of or reactions to this belief. What are the practical consequences of the idea that the function of the news is to mirror events in the world? What is the cash value, so far as influencing the content and form of information the media carry? Is it really possible for the media to "mirror" society in any intelligible way? And if this mirror metaphor is a myth, and yet journalists work in terms of it, then what is the effect on the information they produce?

A value taken very seriously by media people, in both rhetoric and practice, is objectivity. The idea is that the news media should not doctor the information they convey or serve as apologists for any political point of view. But what is a workable definition or set of conditions for "objectivity" in the media? Can the media be objective in any realistic sense? If not, how does their belief that they should try (and that they usually succeed) affect the information received by the consumer?

Or again, what should a reporter's role be? We've heard it argued that a reporter should be (1) impartial, (2) an adversary of whoever is in a position of power (a protector of the common people's interests), and (3) an advocate of a publicly acknowledged point of view. Which view prevails? Are there differences among the various media here? Are there differences among the individual reporters whose work you read, hear, or see? And, as always, what is the effect on the message?

The third factor that might affect the picture of the world emanating from the media consists of what we call, without begging any questions, *hard determinants*. We are thinking here of things such as financial resources, technological restrictions, and the other effects of technology; the concentration of media ownership and the economic interests of the media owners; and the education and training of reporters and editors, to mention just a few factors. Each of these determinants, and others this list might suggest, should be studied for its effect on the overall outlook shaping the information processed by the media. We urge you to look for concrete connections here, not generalizations before the facts. It's easy to say, for example, that because the owners of private media outlets are business people, the news is therefore likely to be slanted in favor of the business point of view. But is that true? How, in detail, do the owners have any influence on the information or editorial slant of their media? Indeed, do they have any influence at all? What influence specifically? You'll have to pose questions like these if you hope to learn anything about the influence of these hard determinants on the flow of information.

We complete this section by drawing to your attention a couple of claims about the ideological role of the mass media, in the classical sense of the word "ideology," which is the point of view of a social group so thoroughly interest-bound that its members are not able to see any facts that would serve to undermine their belief that their position in society is natural or fitting. One of these claims is the thesis of the recent book *Manufacturing Consent*.[2]

1   The mass media of the United States . . . serve to mobilize support for the special interests that dominate the state and private activity, and . . . their choices, empha-

2 Edward S. Herman and Noam Clomsky, Pantheon, 1988, p. 1.

ses, and omissions can often be understood best, and sometimes with striking clarity and insight, by analyzing them in such terms.

The second claim is more general. It was defended in a recent journal article entitled, "The Unspeakable: Understanding the System of Fallacy in the Media."[3] We paraphrase the defense as follows:

2   The dominant interests of any social order (such as large capitalist corporations in liberal democracies) control the production and distribution of social goods so as to promote those interests (for example, to maximize private capital), and the mass media of any social order systematically exclude public expression of information to the degree that it contradicts the necessity and value of this fact.

What these two claims allege, each in its own way, is that the mass media are ideological in the sense that their activities serve to support or reinforce the dominant power groups in society. It follows that the media cannot be relied on as sources of criticism or even critical appraisal of the basic structures of society or of those individuals or interests whose power is identified with those structures. If these claims are true, then whatever information we get from the media, and however useful it is to us, we must seek out other sources for the information needed if we want to take a truly independent look at how our society operates.

Both of these claims have been the targets of energetic criticism, as you might well imagine. We do not have the space or resources to investigate these criticisms. However, we do regard it as important for you to know of their existence because their proponents are responsible scholars. No thorough examination of the ideological role of the media would be complete without a study of these radical critiques and a well-informed assessment as to their plausibility.

We have tried to produce suggestions for research and examples of the sorts of questions to ask in order to learn about the media. Many more such questions than the ones we've listed here need to be answered. If our checklist questions and project ideas stimulate you to investigate, but, more important, to think about the significance while you seek information, then they will have served the purpose of making you a more reflective consumer of media information.

Suggestions for Further Reading

Altheide, David, and Robert P. Snow, *Media Logic*, Sage, Beverly Hills, Calif., 1979.

Cirino, Robert, *Power to Persuade: Mass Media and the News*, Bantam, New York, 1974.

Diamond, Edwin, *Good News, Bad News*, M.I.T., Cambridge, Mass., 1980.

[3] John McMurtry, *Informal Logic*, 10.3, pp. 133-150.

Doig, Ivan, and Carol Doig, *News: A Consumer's Guide*, Prentice-Hall, Englewood Cliffs, N.J., 1972.

Epstein, Edward Jay, *Between Fact and Fiction: The Problem of Journalism*, Vintage Books, New York, 1975.

————, *News From Nowhere*, Random House, New York, 1973.

Gans, Herbert J., *Deciding What's News*, Vintage Books, New York, 1979.

Herman, Edward S., and Noam Chomsky, *Manufacturing Consent*, Pantheon, New York, 1988.

Manoff, Robert Karl, and Michael Schudson (Eds.), *Reading the News*, Pantheon, New York, 1987.

McGinniss, Joe, *The Selling of the President 1968*, Pocket Books, Simon & Schuster of Canada, Richmond Hill, Ontario, 1970.

McMurtry, John. "The Unspeakable: Understanding the System of Fallacy in the Media," *Informal Logic*, X.3, pp. 133-150.

Mendelson, Harold, and Irving Crespi, *Polls, Television, and the New Politics*, Chandler, Scranton, Penn., 1970.

Siebert, Fred S., Theodore Peterson, and Wilbur Schramm, *Four Theories of the Press*, University of Illinois Press, Urbana, 1974.

EXERCISES

A. Newspapers

1. Obtain a daily newspaper, and analyze the stories on the front page, using the Checklist of Questions as a guide.

2. Formulate a hypothesis about the "news values" of that newspaper based on the sample you obtained. Check your hypothesis by going on to examine a series of front pages of that newspaper. Modify your hypothesis as needed in the light of that additional investigation.

3. Compare a single day's edition of different daily newspapers, using the Checklist of Questions as a basis for the comparison. Do any differences in orientation suggest themselves?

4. For any news story or set of stories, identify (a) what you learned that is new to you; (b) what claims you are invited to treat as information that you think require further confirmation, and state why you think that way; (c) what background knowledge you had to have in order to understand and assess the information provided to the extent that you could; and (d) what further background information you would need in order to understand or assess the information more fully. (The point of the last task is to show how the news media must presume some knowledge on the part of the reader, viewer, or listener.)

5. Isolate one factor, and study one day's edition of a newspaper from that point of view. For example, consider juxtaposition—the spatial juxtaposition of different news stories, or of pictures and stories, or of advertising and news. Or consider placement —where on a page each story is located relative to other stories and the significance of that placement; and where in the newspaper different stories, and different *kinds* of stories, are located and the significance of that placement. Other factors to

consider include length of story, headline size, story type (political, human interest, economic, and so on).

6. Follow the coverage of a significant event over a period of a week. What does that tell you about any single day's coverage?

B. Television

7. Tape the evening network news from two or more networks, and compare the coverage. Consider factors such as overlap and lack of it, sources, length and depth of a report, order of stories, and angle taken.

8. Study one single report—choose a longer one, perhaps of two or three minutes in length. Can you identify the way the report has been structured by the producer? Compare one network's treatment of a given story to another's, from this point of view.

9. Focus on the visuals used with a single story. What role do they play in the impression the viewer receives? Would different visuals convey a different impression? Compare the visuals used by another network in reporting the same story.

10. Focus on the interplay between the visuals and the voice-over. Have one group watch the visuals only, with the sound off, and write up their account of the events reported. Have another group analyze the sound track only, without seeing the visuals, and write up their account of the events reported. Compare the two accounts.

11. Consider the juxtaposition of stories in a single broadcast and the juxtaposition of news and commercials.

C. Intermedia Comparisons

12. Compare the news reported on a given day in your local daily newspaper with the local television news for the same day. Do the same for other days. Do any generalizations about differences in the nature of the information from the different media emerge?

13. Make the same comparison between a newspaper like *USA Today* or *The New York Times* and a network news broadcast.

D. Other

14. Make a list of the topics or issues covered over a period of days in daily newspapers and television, both local and national. Then make a list of topics or issues that were not covered and might have been—that is, ongoing events that could have been covered by the media and weren't. What inference can you draw?

15. Make a list of the points of view of special interest groups that are presented in news reports in daily newspapers and television, local and national, over a period of time. Then make a list of points of view or interests that were not represented and might have been—either in the stories that were reported or in stories that were not reported. What inferences can you draw?

See pages 292-294 for two model critical analyses of actual newspaper stories.

CHAPTER ELEVEN

◆

Advertising: Games People Play

Introduction

Why a chapter on advertising in an informal logic text? Here are five reasons.

First, advertising is an important part of the cultural and "information" environment. Perhaps the most powerful cultural force in contemporary North America, advertising helps shape perceptions, beliefs, expectations, and, to some degree, values. We might say that advertising, as a cultural force, teaches consumers three lessons.[1]

1. Every problem has a solution.
2. Every problem has a solution *now*.
3. Every problem has a solution now—the purchase of a new product or service.

Consider, however, the following alternatives to these three lessons:

1. Some problems are pseudo problems and, hence, have no solution; others are genuine but do not have a solution.
2. Sometimes the solution to a problem is a long time in the making.
3. Sometimes the solution to the problem does not require new technology; in fact, sometimes technology is itself part of the problem.

Because of the strong grasp that advertising has on people's minds and attitudes, it is important to approach it with vigilance and in full possession of one's reasoning powers.

The second reason for a chapter in advertising is that at least some of the time, advertising mimics argumentation. Many ads come on as though they were dispensing reasons to a rational agent. Think of ads that contain the line "Here's why." For example, an advertisement for Saab that appeared in *U.S. News and World Report* occupied two facing pages. The left page was headlined "21 logical

---

[1] Here, we are indebted to Neil Postman.

reasons to buy a Saab." The right page was headlined "One emotional reason." The ad listed twenty-one reasons, in the form of premises supporting a conclusion, for buying a Saab, but the implication was that it would only take one emotional reason to equal the twenty-one logical reasons. The Saab ad illustrates how advertising has the appearance of argumentation. As we shall see, this is a facade. Furthermore, it makes explicit the point that most advertising works not at the rational level but at a deeper level. There is some truth to the idea that advertising has a "logic" of its own, and it is important to understand that logic and to see the difference between it and the logic of real arguments.

The third reason why advertising should be part of an informal logic text is that today's consumers have a great deal of experience with and (supposedly) knowledge of advertising. They have seen perhaps 100,000 commercials by the time they reach their sixth birthdays, and they will continue to see many more. Most people have opinions about advertising: about what they like and what they hate, about what is good and what is bad, about what's effective and what isn't. Also, while surveys show that most people are cynical about advertising, the problem is that their cynicism is blind. They regard advertising as a bunch of "bull." Ask them to point out the "bull"—that is, to locate it and argue that it is "bull"—and the most they can do is remember that bull-in-the-china-shop TV commercial for Merrill Lynch. The function of this chapter on advertising is to help critics learn to focus their skepticism and become more forceful in articulating their reasons for it.

The fourth reason for this chapter is that in order to see what is wrong with advertising, you have to master the skills that are central to the critical thinking enterprise. Here, then, is a great two-for-the-price-of-one proposition: Learn the tricks of the advertising trade at the same time that you learn some of the skills that are the repertoire of the proficient reasoner.

The fifth reason is that advertising is a phenomenon almost everyone will confront regularly for the rest of their lives. It won't just go away. Learn how to confront it critically.

Myths about Advertising

There are many widely embraced myths about advertising. Until you identify and confront these myths, your thinking about advertising and your commerce with it will be hampered.

"I Want Truthful Advertising"

Many people believe that they want truthful and straightforward advertising. They think that hype and puffery and exaggeration are being foisted upon them by a crowd of con artists. However, it is far from clear that given a choice between straightforward, factual advertising and Madison Avenue glitz people will choose straightforward ads. Consider this research reported in *Time* magazine:[2]

> In pooh-poohing the need for sterner Government rules against deceptive advertising, agency chiefs like to argue that today's consumer is too smart to be hoodwinked. That comfortable belief has now been shaken by a study presented at a recent gathering of the American Marketing Association by Seymour Lieberman, president of Manhattan-based Lieberman Research Inc. His key finding: deceitful ads can be far more persuasive than promotions that tell the simple truth.
>
> Lieberman enlisted the aid of the Kenyon & Eckhardt agency to create one deceptive and one truthful television commercial for each of six fictitious products. A panel of 100 largely middle-income consumers watched the truthful commercials and another group of the same size, income and educational level saw the dishonest versions. Both sets of commercials used the same actors, and except for the misleading bits, the same language. Yet in four of the six tests, the cheating commercial placed well ahead of the honest promotion in coaxing the audience into a buying mood.
>
> More people were persuaded to buy the mythical Pro-Gro plant fertilizer when the commercial stressed that it contained protein—though protein is of absolutely no help to plants. A bunion remedy, D-Corn, drew more buyer interest when it was touted as having four times as much methylglyoxal as its competition; yet no evidence was offered to support the notion that increasing the amount of methylglyoxal might be in the least beneficial. When Lite-Bite Peaches were outweighed on a scale by a rival brand, the consumer panel got the deliberately misleading—but overwhelmingly persuasive—impression that Lite-Bite contained fewer calories. Lieberman hopes that the ad agencies will use his findings to help guide them in avoiding misleading advertisements, but says that so far he sees few signs of interest.

Further evidence of the same sort can be found in Carl Wrighter's informative book about advertising, *I Can Sell You Anything!* In the excerpt below, Wrighter tells about how a straightforward factual approach was originally used to advertise Pampers, but the product just didn't sell until it was given the Madison Avenue twist:

> Several years ago a friend of mine was working on Pampers, the disposable diapers. Now, Pampers was so drastically different from anything else in its category that the agency decided to play it straight. They set up a legitimate test situation, and went about showing, without any tricks or gimmickry, that this product was clearly superior. Then they put the thing into a test market (a small area of the country in which Pampers also ran advertising) and the product proceeded to die. Flopped on its ass. Lay there like a dead mackerel. Within a few weeks the manufacturer was getting phone calls from the grocers and supermarket chains, demanding that the product be removed from the stores, as it was taking up

---

[2] May 14, 1973.

valuable shelf space. The agency panicked, so they fell back on the old standby, the so-called "slice of life" commercial, which, in essence, I described earlier. The all-knowing mother; the bumbling, insignificant father; and the bright but uninformed next-door neighbor. They did a commercial, and then showed it to a group of ladies. Well, the ladies laughed at it. "Nobody talks that way," they said. "Do you think we're stupid?" Guess what the punch line of this story is? The commercial went on the air, and the product went through the roof. Couldn't make it fast enough. Within a matter of a few months, Pampers was responsible for more than 90 percent of all sales in its category. Blame the advertising. Blame its effect on people. It contained, as a matter of fact, less information, less fact in the slice of life than in the straight, honest approach, yet everyone responded to it. Was it because the advertising was reflecting life, or changing life styles? Was it that the group of ladies lied; that, indeed, people really do talk that way? Probably it was a combination of all of them. The point is, people were affected, motivated to go out and buy something. That's how deeply advertising affects us, and our lives.

Neither of these bits of evidence is conclusive, but taken together they suggest a disturbing possibility about consumer behavior.

"All Advertising is Dishonest, Deceptive, or Both!"

Many people subscribe implicitly to the belief that all advertising is deceptive and uninformative, forgetting the many ads they respond well to and rely on for information. For example, rock fans do not object to ads that inform them of an upcoming concert by their favorite group or a record sale they want to cash in on. We have been so conditioned by TV commercials that when we think about advertising, we automatically think of prime-time television advertising, where the amount of distortion and hype is proportionately greater than it is in other areas. A careful reasoner doesn't generalize beyond what the data base permits. It is important to keep in mind that the term "advertising" covers a wide territory, all the way from prime-time television commercials to ads in your local paper, billboards, and circulars delivered by hand to your house or apartment.

"They're Always Trying to Sell You Something"

Many people think that advertising has one, and only one, aim: to sell a product. Not so. Some advertising aims only at positioning a company in the minds of the viewers. Dow has for some years been running a campaign whose purpose is not to sell any specific product but simply to enhance the company's image. Other advertising aims at selling not a particular product but a *category* of products, as is explained in this memo to an account executive:

> Although he doesn't want this to be a headline, David would like the copy to be the one with the "ten" reasons why you ought to buy an AVS [audiovisual system]. David's strategy is that he is *not* trying to sell with this ad; he is trying to build the AVS category. The sale will come later.

Modern advertising is more subtle in its approach and more wide-ranging than the old hard sell.

"Ads Are a Slice of Life"

Many people seem to think that ads are just thrown together. The truth is that an immense amount of research, planning, and editing goes into the average TV ad. They may look natural and lifelike (verisimilitude is the name of the game). Perhaps you recall the ad for Lite-Beer from Miller (one of the most successful ad campaigns of all time) that featured a pool player—his name was Steve Mizerak—who performed a trick shot during the ad. It took almost twelve hours and 177 takes to get the shot you saw on TV. The applause we hear when he finally makes the shot is genuine. What we see is the five seconds of success, not the twelve hours of frustration.

For excellent insight into the amount of stagecraft that goes into the production of a prime-time commercial, we strongly recommend *30 Seconds*, the story of "Reach Out," the AT&T (American Telephone & Telegraph) campaign for long distance.[3] In the original commercial, there was a short segment featuring a ballet dancer. It lasted for about five seconds. The producers of the ad interviewed at least 183 women for that part! Every TV ad (and this also applies mutatis mutandis to print and radio ads) is like a thirty-second movie. It has a plot, actors, directors, a script, retakes, editors, and lots of interesting footage on the floor of the editing room. In spite of their apparently casual nature, ads are rigorously designed and carefully tested so as to achieve a precisely intended effect.

"People Aren't That Stupid!"

Someone always says "people aren't that stupid" about what is to us one of the most irritating TV commercials of all time—Wisk's "ring around the collar." But there it is, year after year, the same slogan. We know that people in the advertising business aren't stupid, so what follows? The conclusion we must draw is that a lot of people in the target audience continue to be influenced by the Wisk ad. Almost no ad reaches its final destination without having been screened many times by various groups. Even if you find the ad stupid or insulting, that doesn't mean it won't reach others and it does mean that the advertisers have implanted the name of the product firmly in your unconscious (if not your conscious) mind.

The "Logic" of Advertising

We said earlier that many advertisements have the facade of arguments. They look like premises leading to a conclusion and like exercises in rational persua-

³ M. J. Arlen, 1980.

sion. In fact, we are persuaded by the school that holds that advertising is best viewed as psychological persuasion—an attempt to use psychological strategies to implant the name of a product in our unconscious minds. Hence criticism of advertising as a form of argumentation is misconceived. Learning how to decode ads and making ourselves aware of the strategies that advertisers use is more useful than looking for fallacies in the arguments.

To understand advertisers' strategies, we must first understand some of the constraints under which advertisers operate, because it is these constraints that by and large shape the advertising message. When advertising is viewed in context—as essentially a response to a marketing problem—a great deal becomes clearer.

What is the situation in the marketplace? First, we have the inherent similarity of most brands. Because of the nature of modern business, most of the products in a given category differ from one another only in marginal or subjective aspects. Bayer may be correct in its insistence that "not all aspirins are alike," but the difference between Bayer and its competitors (forgetting the cost factor) is very slight. The same is true of soaps, soft drinks (taste is the factor here), stereos, and so on. Here is how Rosser Reeves described this situation:

> Our problem is—a client comes into my office and throws two newly minted half-dollars on my desk and says, "Mine is the one on the left. You prove it's better."[4]

If all products are essentially the same, the only way to succeed is to make your product *appear* to be different. The practice of advertising thus resembles the efforts of the Sophists, philosophers in ancient Greece of whom it was said that they attempted "to make the weaker appear stronger."

On this point, it is worth recounting a story about the legendary adman Claude Hopkins, who handled the Schlitz account in the 1930s.

> Hopkins had no trouble proving that Schlitz beer was better than all others. He visited the factory, watched the beer being made, and came up with the slogan "washed with live steam." When told that this was standard procedure, Hopkins wasn't worried. "The vital fact was not what the industry did but what the individual brewers said they did, and the steam bath had never been advertised," he explained.[5]

A second factor shaping advertising is laws that prevent advertisers from saying what they know, or should know, to be false; these same laws, however, go hand in hand with regulations that license exaggeration—what is known in the trade as *puffery*. You may have heard the phrase caveat emptor, "let the buyer beware." What this means is that no law and no agency will protect the consumer from his or her own ignorance, stupidity, or tendency to draw unwarranted inferences. If men really think that wearing a particular after-shave

---

[4] As recounted by Martin Mayer, *Madison Avenue U.S.A.*, Harper, New York, 1958, p. 53.
[5] As recounted by Ellen Roseman, *Consumer Beware*, 1974, p. 127.

will cause women to find them more attractive, they have only themselves to blame if it doesn't work. If women choose to believe that wearing a particular color lipstick or eye shadow will have the effects on men that are shown in the ads, it's their problem if it doesn't happen.

A third factor shaping advertising is the cluttered environment in which ads must compete with other ads for attention. In the United States alone, some 28,000 nationally advertised products compete with each other for attention. In one hour of prime-time television, you might see twelve minutes of commercials, some of them only fifteen seconds long. The net effect of all this advertising is clutter. Not only does the advertiser have to make the product appear better than its competitors; she must find some way to make the ad stand out from the rest of the ads or it will never be noticed. Consider this description of that cluttered environment:

> There are some 28,000 nationally advertised branded products for sale in the United States, a number that may take on added meaning when we recall that only some 3,000 stars are visible to the eye on a clear night. The advertiser's task is to make one of these stars stand out from the others, but since every star has its own advertising campaign, the overall effect is only to make the whole sky a little more luminous.
>
> The uncountable advertising campaigns going on simultaneously make us inescapably aware of advertising but virtually immune to any given advertisement. A study cited by Stephen Fox in *The Mirror Makers* claims that the average family is "exposed" to 1,600 ads each day. Of course, not all of them are TV commercials; according to the 1984 edition of the *Statistical Abstract of the United States*, the largest single chunk of the $67 billion of advertising expenditures in 1982—27 percent—went for newspaper ads. About 6 percent went for magazine ads, a little more went into radio, 20 percent was spent on "miscellaneous" items (such things as matchbook covers), and only about 21 percent went for TV ads. Just the same, it is as if more than half the stars in the sky entered our field of vision in the course of an ordinary day.[6]

A fourth factor shaping advertising is the expectation or mood of the audience receiving the message. Here we need to mention the "hype" factor in North American life. As a society, we have become so accustomed to exaggeration in advertising that we expect it, we take it for granted. In fact, we have become skeptical of straightforward talk. How else to explain the Old Spice ad in which the sailor comes to town, slaps on some Old Spice, and soon every women in the room is eyeing him voraciously?

Given these four factors and other constraints—not the least of which is the mentality and laziness of the average consumer—it is not surprising that manufacturers and advertising agencies have developed a number of strategies and gimmicks that either take advantage of or work around the constraints to

---

[6] Robert Heilbronner, "Advertising as Agitprop." *Harper's*, January 1989, p. 72.

create impressions and to weave the illusion of product desirability and superiority. What are these strategies?

Some Tricks of the Trade

The history of advertising is fascinating. We strongly recommend that you read Robert Glatzer's *The New Advertising: The Great Ad Campaigns from Avis to Volkswagen*.[7] This fine history of advertising shows that there are discernible trends in the business. For example, an advertiser today cannot field a national campaign without a theme song, even if it has to pay Michael Jackson a princely sum of money to use it. That was not true in the 1950s. Music has become a staple in advertising only since the advent of television.

The basic advertising strategies—on which there are innumerable variations—have been developed and refined just in this century, largely by these advertising giants.

1. Rosser Reeves did not invent the unique selling proposition (USP), but he did perfect it. The idea behind USP is to build an ad around a feature of the product that is unique or is at least perceived as unique. This strategy is easy to implement if you're lucky enough to be handling the original Polaroid account, for example. Focusing on what makes the product unique is one way of making it stand out. This strategy is also the basis of the so-called preemptive claim, about which we shall have more to say.

2. David Ogilvy rose to prominence in the late fifties on the basis of highly successful national campaigns like the "Man in the Hathaway Shirt" and "Schweppervescence" with Commander Whitehead. Ogilvy prided himself on the literacy of his ads, and by today's standards they are amazingly so (his ads are full of print). By today's standards, however, influenced as they are by the Doyle Dane Bernbach approach (discussed below), Ogilvy's ads look cluttered, busy. Ogilvy is important because he recognized and perfected two basic strategies, which he outlines in the passage below:

   > Dorothy Sayers, who wrote advertisements before she wrote whodunits and Anglo-Catholic tracts, says: "Plain lies are dangerous. The only weapons left are the *suggestio falsi* and the *suppressio veri*." I plead guilty to one act of *suggestio falsi*—what we on Madison Avenue call a "weasel." However, two years later a chemist rescued my conscience by discovering that what I had falsely suggested was actually true.[8]

3. Doyle, Dane, and Bernbach (DDB, as they are known in the trade) perfected the soft sell, often using self-deprecating humor in their advertising. They were responsible for the landmark print advertisement for Volkswagen that

---

[7] The Citadel Press, New York, 1970.
[8] David Ogilvy, *Confessions of an Advertising Man*, Dell, New York, 1964.

featured a picture of a Volkswagen and, below it, the word that all car buyers fear, "Lemon!" The ad went on to reassure readers that quality control at Volkswagen was such that this lemon would never reach a dealer. They also broke the basic rule of advertising when, for an Avis ad in the 1960s, they admitted, "We're only #2." But—and here is where they showed their genius—they added the rider, "We try harder."

4. We cannot conclude this brief account of advertising history and the tricks of the trade without mentioning what is known as the "Campaign of the Century"—the ad for Marlboro cigarettes created by Leo Burnett. The main appeal in this ad was psychological, finding an appropriate macho image for what had, until then, been a women's cigarette. The makers of Marlboro wanted to confront the widespread perception that filter cigarettes were for women. They chose the ultimate macho image—the cowboy. The tattoo was grafted on later, when the wife of one of the executives commented that wherever you find a man with a tattoo, you find mystery and adventure. The result of all this was the Marlboro Man. You can read more about the Marlboro Man in Glatzer's book.

These, then, are the main advertising approaches, and most ads are imitations of them; that is, advertisers have developed endless refinements and variations of these basic themes.

One more preliminary point: It is vital to realize that at the heart of all advertising lies the *proposition*, the basic idea behind the ad. This proposition can always be stated in one or two sentences, even if those sentences never appear in the ad itself. Whether supplemented by visuals or made more palatable by a catchy tune, the proposition is the anchor for all the gimmicks in the ad. Its function is to provide you with the product's reason for being (it will make you look younger for example), which then becomes your reason for believing. That is why you often hear the phrase, "Here's why. . . ." For the ad to be effective, the claim must be carefully thought through, researched for accuracy and impact, and ultimately presented in an engaging way for the consumer. So lots of work goes into the formulation of the proposition and the claims that spring from it.

The gimmicks about to be discussed are the ways in which advertisers attempt to put the Proposition across. To spot these gimmicks, you have to know what to look for and what to listen for. You have to focus clearly on just what has been said and why, but, more important, you must think about what has *not* been said and *why not*.

Semantic License

Though visuals and music came to the forefront with the advent of television advertising, it is still true that words—especially as combined in putting across the Proposition—are the cornerstone of advertising. Words can be manipulated for effect. Here are some of the main ploys with words.

Use of Open-Ended Meaning.   Words have a penumbra of meanings, and advertisers are experts at exploiting the difference between what you think the word means and the meaning they are prepared, if necessary, to defend if challenged. Take a word like "tradition." When a company refers to its "tradition," the word may mean nothing more than that it has a past. That's true, isn't it? Every company has one, however brief. But when the consumer hears the word, she or he chooses a richer meaning; namely, an outstanding history of excellence. And perhaps the company has such a tradition. Perhaps. Or take a word like "power." It means the capacity to engender an effect. "STP: power to clean, and power to burn." That means that STP has the capacity to burn (if it didn't, you'd be in big trouble) and the capacity to clean; it doesn't mean that it will clean your carburetor (if you think it will you need a course in auto mechanics). Essentially, what STP wants to imply here is that STP will clean your engine.

Weasel Words.   Words that we are so used to seeing and hearing that we don't notice them are called *weasel words*. They are qualifiers. They weaken the meaning of the claims in which they are imbedded. But research shows that somehow we tend to factor out the qualification and hear only what comes after it. These qualifiers are cunning and nimble creatures, hence the term *weasel*.

Help means "contributes to the overall picture." That Crest helps fight cavities is surely true; so does the toothbrush you use and the amount of effort and regularity you put into dental hygiene. These are all factors in the outcome. But when it reads "*X* helps fight cavities," what we hear is "*X* fights cavities." We factor out the weasel. That's why weasels are so popular; and once you begin looking for them, you see them all over. Keep in mind that there is absolutely nothing wrong with advertisers appropriately qualifying their claims. Isn't that one of the hallmarks of a careful reasoner? But it is our typical overlooking of such qualifiers that advertisers are relying on when they use weasels.

Can means "is possible," not "will." For example, an advertisement for L'Oreal reads: "Now you can actually restructure your nails from wimps to strengths." (And watch for the *double* whammy in "*X* can help. . . ." You can't get much more qualified than that: It says hardly anything! But it works.)

Up to means "the maximum is." "Up to twelve hours"—means that the absolute maximum is twelve hours, but you may find you get much less. "Lose up to 50 pounds in just four weeks" means that you may be one of the very few to lose this much weight. Revlon Anti-Aging Moisturizer advertises "continuous moisture protection for up to eight hours." The thing to remember is that if it gives protection for half an hour, and no more, well, the "up to" has covered that nicely.

Like, when used as a preposition, is called a *transfer-word*, meaning it switches your attention from the product or service to something that the advertiser wants to associate with the product. Wrighter explains the way in which Ajax exploited this weasel in the campaign with the slogan, "Ajax cleans like a white tornado." A tornado is powerful! But this one isn't dark and damaging like a real tornado. It's white (like a white knight), and it's available in a bottle. So the advertiser gets you thinking about how all this power has been harnessed in a bottle and how you can let this benevolent energy loose in your house. All of this has been accomplished simply by the use of the transfer-word "like." Of course it's all fantasy! Just remind yourself that if one thing is *like* another thing, then the two things are not identical . . . which brings us to the next weasels we'd like to discuss.

Virtually, if you look it up in the dictionary, means something like "in essence but not in fact." Those seats in the car you're going to buy are "virtually" handcrafted; i.e., they are *not* handcrafted! That oven that is "virtually self-cleaning" is—guess what—*not* self-cleaning.

Introducing, now, here's are all ways of saying "new" without saying "new." Because the word "new" is such a turn-on, and because its use is regulated by law, advertisers have an inventory of weasel words designed to get you to hear "new" when it cannot be said.

Watch out for those weasels!

Mystery Ingredients: Platformate, Retsyn, MFP.   Another strategy used in ads is the mystery ingredient. This is a variant on the misleading implication (covered later in this chapter) because the audience will most likely draw the inference that the mystery ingredient, or the ingredient with a mysterious name or set of initials, (1) is unique and (2) makes some substantive contribution to the product's performance. This inference is almost always wrong. Remember Ogilvy and the *suggestio falsi*.

The classic ad of this type was one for Shell in the 1960s that compared the mileage achieved by cars using Shell with Platformate against cars using Shell without Platformate. The car using Shell with Platformate always outperformed the one without. This created the idea that Shell has discovered some new magical or mystery ingredient. What they did not say was that Platformate was only their name for an additive that could be found in most competitors' gasolines—under a different and no less magical name, of course.

Certs used to advertise the fact that it contained "a sparkling drop of Retsyn." As Wrighter discovered, Retsyn is a kind of vegetable oil! Maybe you can figure out why that makes Certs a good choice. But how many people were influenced to buy Certs because of this mystery ingredient?

MFP is Colgate's registered name for their flouride compound. Thus, Colgate can safely claim that "only Colgate has MFP" because Colgate has reserved the exclusive legal right to use those letters! This claim does not imply (though many will infer that it does) that Colgate is the only toothpaste with flouride. Other toothpaste brands contain flouride, but they call it something else, like Flouristat (Crest's name for their flouride ingredient).

Confronted with a mystery ingredient, the consumer would be wise to assume that this may be merely the name for an ingredient found in the competitors' brands as well.

Semantic Claims: the Rain Tire, RCA XL-100, UnCola.   *Semantic claims* are claims that are not about the product so much as about its name or title or label. The reason for believing them has nothing to do with the product itself but with the name of the product. Thus, the Rain Tire is merely the name Goodyear gave to its tire. The company could have called it the Wet Tire or the Milechaser or the Roadrunner, but they chose to name it the Rain Tire. The name implies that the tire is designed to perform especially well in the rain, with the added implication that if it is designed to do well in the rain, it will do even better on dry roads. It's all in the name. What's in a name? A rose by any other name may smell as sweet, but a product's name is carefully chosen for the ambience it creates. And it behooves the consumer to remember that a name is no reason to buy a product.

RCA named one of its TV models XL-100. Think about this combination of letters and numbers. For one thing, *XL* sounds like "excel," as in "excellent." Then, too, *XL* connects with extra large, and this might imply, for some, that they are getting a bargain. The number 100 is like 100 percent, the top score. You can't do much better than that! They could have given it the name DUD 48, but that doesn't have quite the same appeal.

UnCola is the descriptive name that the makers of 7-Up use for their soft drink. The implication is that 7-Up is the only alternative to cola drinks, but if 7-Up made this claim it would be demonstrably false. What about Sprite? What about Mountain Dew? What about Orange Crush? What about milk or water? These are all alternatives to colas.

Empty Comparisons. When advertisers make comparisons, they know what they're doing. Either they compare themselves to themselves ("better by far than last year's model" or "the best we've ever made") or they compare themselves to some vaguely specified competitor or to no one at all ("XXX works better"). What the consumer should ask is, Better than what? What is being compared with what and on what basis? Clairol advertises that its Curl-Technics (hair rollers) "hold your hair better than ordinary rollers." But is that an apt comparison? First, we need to know what counts as an ordinary roller. Next, we must ask, Is this the most appropriate comparison? Is Clairol's product competing with ordinary rollers or with something more high-tech? The ads claim at the end that the product will give the consumer luscious curls, fabulous waves, beautiful body "easier than you imagined." Here they are comparing the ease of use of the product with an imaginary standard—the consumer's imagination.

Another comparison that advertisers often make is to nonuse of the product ("You'll fall asleep quicker with Snooze"). What is meant here is that you will fall asleep quicker if you use Snooze than you will if you don't use anything, not quicker than if you use a competing brand (like Doze).

Parity Claims. A *parity claim* is a claim that your product is as good as the competition's. The problem is that the claim is worded so as to afford the consumer grounds for thinking that the product is being touted as superior. The claim that "nothing works better than *X* to relieve pain" translates literally into "*X* is as good as any other product of its type." Currently there is an ad for Noxzema Clear-Ups that says; "No other acne medicine is stronger." That's a parity claim. Others may be and probably are equally strong. There is also an ad for New Gillette Soft & Dri that claims that "No other solid keeps you drier." That's a parity claim. The real meaning is that Soft & Dri is as good as other solid deodorants. No claim is made that it is better.

Worth mentioning here is that any company has the right to offer an opinion about its product. They're entitled to the view that the product is "the finest" or "the best." But remember whose opinion this is. Remember that the company has a vested interest, and ask yourself whether it's wise for you to adopt that opinion.

False or Misleading Implications

One of the commonest of all ploys is phrasing a claim in such a way as to state something that is literally true but invites a false inference! Ogilvy referred to this as *suggestio falsi*. When an advertiser is in a position to make a strong claim for a product, it is normally in his interest to make that claim. Hence, if a claim is merely suggested or left for the consumer to infer, that is probably because the direct statement of it would be false.

Cholesterol has become a health concern, and as a result many products advertise themselves as "cholesterol-free." The implication here is that competing brands contain cholesterol. But you would be wise not to draw that inference. For example, breakfast cereals amost always contain no cholesterol, so the fact that Crunchies are "cholesterol-free" does not differentiate them from their competitors, which are also without cholesterol.

The most important instance of this strategy is the preemptive claim, referred to earlier when we discussed tricks of the trade. Claude Hopkins, who advertised Schlitz beer with the claim "washed with live steam" was using a preemptive claim. What he did was take a standard feature of the manufacturing process and make it the centerpiece of an ad. Naturally, given the competitive context of advertising, the consumer will think that this feature is unique, will think that Schlitz is the only beer washed in "live" steam (what other kind of steam is there, we wonder). But to make that claim would have been false. Thus, in this approach, the advertiser *preempts* the truth. And there is this delicious side effect. Any other advertiser who wants to point out the truth ("Our beer is washed in live steam, too") will look like a copycat!

Suppressed Evidence

You've probably heard the old saw, "What you don't know won't hurt you." The proper frame of mind when you deal with advertising is, What they don't say may hurt you. That is, ads often fail to present evidence that would, if it were known to the consumer, alter her opinion. Hence the alert consumer needs to develop an eye for what hasn't been said! He or she needs to think about what sort of evidence would be relevant to the decision as to whether to purchase that (type of) product and then check that ideal list against the evidence that has been offered.

For example, cost is always a factor in deciding about a product, but it is not always mentioned. And, in thinking about drugs such as weight-control products, possible side effects should be considered, and these are almost never mentioned.

False implication and suppressed evidence often work in tandem. They make quite a one-two punch. A classic example of how false implication and suppressed evidence can work together is a Volvo ad that appeared in the late 1960s. When Volvo first began to take the North American market seriously, it produced an ad designed to create the impression of a car that was durable. The ad read, "Nine out of ten Volvos sold in the last ten years are still on the road." Now what did this claim imply? That Volvo was a durable car, of course, with 90 percent of them lasting for ten years or more. But wait—that is not what the ad said. It didn't say "90 percent of our cars last for ten years or more." It said "90 percent of the cars sold in the last ten years are still on the road." If you assume equitable distribution in sales over this ten-year period, then you wind up with a conclusion of super-endurance. But should you make that assumption? Of course not. Here is a piece of suppressed evidence (clearly suppressed—not just missing): The bulk of Volvo sales in North America had occurred within the previous five years. Seven out of ten Volvos sold in the United States in the previous ten years had actually been sold within the previous five years. When they unearthed this piece of information, two logic students approached a Volvo vice president and pointed out the misleading nature of the implication. He responded: "Look, it's true, so it can't be misleading." But the truth *can* be misleading. Suppose one of your friends reported, truthfully, that Professor Jones was polite in class today. The clear implication of this claim is that Jones is not *always* polite in the classroom. If he *is* always polite, then the reported truth, in this case, is misleading.

Appeal to the Psyche

Thus far we have covered three strategies that deal with verbal content, the claims and words and propositions. These are aimed at your mind. But advertisers, as we discuss next, know full well how to appeal to our fears and desires. The conventional wisdom is that ads appeal primarily to our emotions. Though we have come to think that this belief is based on a serious misunderstanding both of advertising's thrust and of the nature of human emotion, it is a belief that advertisers themselves endorse and encourage with ads like the Saab ad referred to earlier. If you think about that particular ad, which showed a Saab cutting through the rain, you need to answer the question, What emotion is being appealed to here? If you answer that it appeals to one's desire to have a sporty or nifty car, well, that may be true. But to call that desire (and it is a rather specific desire) an *emotion* seems wrong. Carl Wrighter seems to have a better handle on the situation when he writes:

> But perhaps the third function of advertising is the one we really ought to examine; it is the function of persuading. Here's where we part company with Webster, because the closest thing in that definition is "to arouse a desire to buy or patronize." That ain't persuade, honey. It doesn't even come close. You see, advertising is really a science, and it is mostly a science of human motivation and behavior. When we get ready to pitch a new soap at you, we know more about what you do in your bathroom than your own wife or husband [knows]. Not only that, we know why you do it, how you do it, and what makes you do it. We know what

kind of appeals you will respond to, what kind of emotions you will fall prey to, even the very words which will strike a chord on your heart strings. In short, persuasion in advertising is done not so much by dispensing information publicly as by attacking your weak spots emotionally, and having our products soothe your savage ego. Perhaps this is why Webster left it out of his definition; it is almost impossible to pinpoint.

Paraphernalia: Graphics, Visuals, and Music

So far, we have been considering the "copy" of ads—the claims, words, and phrases that together, constitute the written component. But advertising is more than copy. In print advertising such as that we find in magazines, there are the graphics; and television commercials present us with challenges in the form of visuals and music.

About the Graphics.   In print ads, the graphics have to be the "grabbers." Recall the picture in the Volkswagen ad with the word "lemon," the Man in the Hathaway Shirt, the tattoo on the Marlboro Man, and, today, the naked men and women featured in Ralph Lauren ads.

About the Visuals.   In television demonstrations and dramatizations, there is a lot going on visually. Commercials are, in effect, minimovies, with megabucks going into the shots. So keep in mind that what you see has been thoroughly scripted and edited!

About the Music.   Several years ago, a promotional ad for *Time* magazine featured the Byrds' singing, "Turn! Turn! Turn! There is a time for every moment under the sun." Shots of covers of *Time* were spliced in. No doubt you will remember the inventive use made by California raisins of "I Heard It through the Grapevine." And it's not only rock 'n' roll that's endangered. In recent years, advertisers have raised the classics portfolio, using arias from various operas to sell wine and other products. The hope is that the feelings associated with the music will transfer to the product.

Some Sample Analyses

On the pages that follow, we present our analyses of two print advertisements. In each case, we had to concoct the advertisement because of the difficulty we experienced in obtaining the permission of the company to reproduce the ad we would have liked to critique. Apparently the old saw, "Say anything you like. Just make sure you spell the name correctly," does not apply in advertising. Though invented, our examples use techniques that can be found in any number of actual magazine advertisements. In writing up our critiques, we did our best to abide by the principle of discrimination, which requires that we focus our analysis on the main problems with the ads.

Advertisement for Shield

Here's the first ad, for an imaginary toothpaste called Shield:

GOOD NEWS!
NOW THERE'S A SHIELD AGAINST TOOTH DECAY!
Introducing Shield

Evidence shows that today's Shield actually reverses tooth decay! That's right. That's because today's Shield contains an active ingredient that can actually help reverse the earliest stage of the tooth-decay process that leads to cavities. Clinical tests show how before the use of today's Shield, acids in your mouth can begin to attack weak spots in your enamel. Left unchecked, these spots can become cavities. But Shield goes to work on these soft spots, acting like a preventive shield to help stop tooth decay from starting.

Remember: Only Shield has the Ultra-Fluoride Formula,* especially formulated to help prevent tooth decay.

If this news sounds too good to be true, we suggest you ask your dentist because only your dentist can give your mouth better treatment than today's Shield.

*Registered trade mark.

The principal problem with this ad for Shield is that the language implies that Shield is new. The term "today's," which appears four times in the ad, is a weasel, a way of saying "new" without saying "new."

There is an axiom that if an advertiser can make a strong claim for a product, then she or he will do so. If the advertiser resorts to suggesting or implying the claim, then a careful thinker must conjecture that the claim is false. Here, the language *implies* that Shield is new; it does not state it. To support this misleading implication, the ad refers to "evidence" and "clerical tests," but even here no claim is made that these findings are new. Thus, at the heart of this ad, we find misleading implications about both the product and the research supposedly supporting it.

The term "reverse" is also central to the ad. It is open to various interpretations, the standard one of which is misleading. We are encouraged here to think that Shield can actually work on a decaying tooth and restore it to its orginal pristine condition. That would be one sense of the term "reverse." However, if you take the time to look the word up in the dictionary, you will find that it can also mean "to turn to the opposite direction or tendency." Can Shield do this? Can Shield (which contains flouride) stop "the decay process"? If so, then it can claim to have turned the process to the opposite direction, and, in that sense, it can be said to reverse tooth decay.

To answer these questions, we need to look carefully at what the research does show. Note that the ad contains no less than three weasels: "help," "work," and "like." Note also that the phrase "the earliest stage of the tooth-decay process" is vague. Depending on the reference of that phrase, the number of instances we are talking about could be very few or numerous. In effect, what the ad says is nothing more than that flouride can be helpful in arresting cavities at a very early stage of their development. This is the justification for the term "reverse"—but note that this highly qualified claim could very likely be made by any toothpaste with flouride.

There is also a psychological strategy here in the form of an appeal to fear in the claim, "Left unchecked, these spots can become cavities." But of course they may not become cavities. In any event, the ad is playing in the fear that parents have about their children's dental health. Parents don't want their kids getting cavities; and here Shield is, to some degree, playing on that fear and on the parents' desire for a simple and effective solution—Shield!

Reference to their fluoride ingredient under the name "the Ultra-Fluoride Formula" is meant to further these implications. Remember that it is nothing more than the company's name for the fluoride ingredient in its toothpaste. Many toothpastes contain fluoride, but they call it something else. The *name* is unique, and so the advertiser can rightly assert that you can't get it—the Ultra-Fluoride Formula—in any other toothpaste. What they want you to think is that you can't get fluoride in any other toothpaste. But of course they can't say that because it's false.

Finally, we should call attention to *the parity claim* in the ad ("only your dentist can give your mouth better treatment than today's Shield"). What this means, literally, is that no toothpaste is better than Shield, that Shield is just as good as any other fluoride toothpaste (the inherent similarity of brands was discussed earlier in this chapter), but the claim is worded so as to create the impression that Shield is somehow *better* than any other toothpaste.

Having combed through the copy and found the tricks, we now know that we have been given no reason to purchase Shield rather than any other fluoride toothpaste. Once we have stripped away the fancy semantics and the misleading implications, all this ad says is that Shield contains fluoride, which can help stop tooth decay in the very early stages of development. Though the implication is that the product is new, the fact that the copy does not say so but rather implies it suggests that the only thing new may be the advertisement—and perhaps not even that is new.

Advertisement for NuThin

Next we ask you to imagine an ad for an appetite-control product that we'll call NuThin (see next page). The ad consists of before-and-after pictures of four women who supposedly used this product and who report various amounts of weight loss.

The main pitch in the ad for NuThin is contained in the four "before-and-after" pictures of women who lost weight on the plan. The ad is clearly targeted at women; and its main appeal is to the psyche. As one student wrote in a critique of the ad: "The 1980s and 1990s are a time when 'thin is in'." The basis of this advertisement is therefore a psychological appeal to women's desire to be thin and their fear of becoming fat. For those who are already overweight, the psychological appeal is to their desire to lose weight quickly without having to do the hard work that is required to diet and exercise. But that is fantasy. No product can cause weight loss unless it is used properly.

To see what is going on in this ad, it is necessary to read the accompanying copy carefully. Note the presence of the weasels "can" and "help" qualifying the force of the claim. Next, note the statement "These results are not necessarily typical," which means that they are *not* typical, and that this is not a representative sample of the results achieved on the diet plan. The ad goes on to say that "Weight losses range from no loss at all to substantial weight loss." But since when was "no loss at all" a loss? What this means is that the product may not work for you, but they have cleverly disguised this fact.

Next, the ad says that "Clinical studies show that the average loss is about a pound a week." This statement is crucial. (For the moment, overlook the vague reference to "clinical studies.") It means that the weight losses by the women pictured were *way above average*. Remember, too, that for everyone above the average, there are others below it! Thus for every Eva DeNagy (Fremont, California) who lost 30 pounds in twelve weeks, there are four to five women who either lost no weight at all while using NuThin or else gained weight.

Combined with the psychological appeal in this ad is *suppressed evidence*. What is the chemical composition of NuThin? We know that it is a drug, and that it's been "clinicially tested." And we know that all drugs have potential side effects, *but we are not told about any of them here*. This is suppressed evidence,

There'll be a new you with NuThin !

BEFORE

AFTER

"I lost 50 pounds in 18 weeks with NuThin."
Clair Huston   Tuscaloosa, AL

BEFORE

AFTER

"I lost 43 pounds in 15 weeks. Thanks NuThin!"
Eva DeNagy   Fremont, CA

BEFORE

AFTER

"With the NuThin plan, I lost 35 pounds in just 13 weeks!"
Deborah Allen   Albany, NY

These results are not necessarily typical. Weight losses range from no loss at all to substantial weight loss. Clinical studies show that the average loss is about one pound a week.

Put the NuThin Diet Plan to work for you. You, too, can lose weight like these women.

for surely this knowledge would be available both to the firm that manufactures the product and to the advertiser. Also suppressed are any details about the "clinical studies." What clinics were involved? What did the studies show? All of this must be known to the advertisers, but they did not pass the information along to us.

The appeal to the psyche and the suppressed evidence in the ad are supplemented with semantic license. A semantic claim occurs twice in the name of the product alone. *Nu* is "new," and the claim of *Thin* is obvious.

Such an ad gives us no reason to use this product rather than another product in its category; and, indeed, in view of the rather qualified claims made for it and the amount of evidence about its chemistry and possible side effects that is suppressed, we would urge a cautious approach to the product.

Television Advertising

Television advertising is a realm unto itself and much too complicated to be dealt with fully in the short space available here. What TV ads have going for them is their visual impact, the impression they leave of reality and immediacy. Two types of television advertising warrant attention here: (1) the demonstration ad and (2) the dramatization ad. We'll make brief comments on each.

Demonstration

In a demonstration, we supposedly see the product in use and witness some benefit the product brings. The thing to ask here is, Exactly what is being demonstrated? To this end, you may find it useful to turn off the sound and simply watch so that what you see will not be influenced by the voice-over. Several years ago, STP used an ad that showed very clearly that a person cannot hold onto the tip of a screwdriver that has been immersed in STP. That is all that was demonstrated. While the commercial was being shown, however, the viewer was told, in part, that "STP reduces friction in your engine." The demonstration did not lend any substance to this claim. After all, skin and metal are very different. Unless you keep the "show" (demonstration) separate from the "tell" (voice-over), the two may blend together in your mind, creating the impression that the claim has actually been demonstrated.

A classic in this genre is the commercial for Bounty towels (the "quicker picker-upper") that features the following demonstration:

Two glasses containing equal amounts of liquid are shown. A sheet of Bounty is immersed in one glass, a sheet of "another leading paper towel" is immersed in the other. Then the two glasses are turned upside down. It appears that the Bounty towel has absorbed all of the liquid because nothing drips out; but some liquid comes out of the other glass, meaning that the other hasn't absorbed everything. What has been demonstrated? Here's Wrighter's commentary:

If you believe the pictures, then they have just proved that Bounty towels absorb more liquid than the other paper towel. But what did they actually say? "Bounty. The quicker picker-upper." They say that Bounty picks up faster than the other. They have shown you one thing, but they have said something else. Don't misinterpret what I'm saying. Bounty knows exactly what it's doing. They are presenting you with a new idea in paper towels: speed in absorption. But it's very hard to prove that two inanimate objects move at different speeds, so the demo they use is the closest they could come to it. They use the words to get you to see what they want you to see.

In Wrighter's analysis, the Bounty ad is designed so that the "show" and the "tell" will coalesce. The fact that the Bounty towel absorbs liquid more rapidly than "another leading paper towel" is not necessarily enough to make it better. Perhaps it absorbs less liquid but does so more quickly. Even if the details of Wrighter's analysis here are flawed, the point is a good one: Visuals—and the evidence they present—can be enhanced by the voice-over, thereby producing a different impression. So when viewing TV commercials in which a demonstration of a product in use is featured, be sure that you understand exactly what is being demonstrated. And don't allow the words (the "tell") to influence what you're seeing (the "show").

Dramatization

Dramatizations are just that: little pieces of drama with a cast of characters, actors and actresses to play the roles, a script, a director, a budget, a shooting schedule. Of course, they're made to look as spontaneous and lifelike as possible. Advertisers use them when they have a product that cannot easily be shown in action. For example, advertisers for detergents and bleaches find this approach a natural because it's hard to get a close-up of enzymes and additives "eating stains" from your clothes while they're tumbling around inside a washer. So they set up a situation that establishes a need for their product, cut to a close-up of the box or package in which it comes, then cut back to the situation to show the resolution. It's the before-and-after routine.

Typical of such TV commercials is one aired several years ago for Alberto VO5 shampoo. In outline, it begins by showing a woman (she's an actress, remember) before she washed her hair. Then we see her sudsing away, with lots of lather. Then, presto! her hair looks fantastic after that one shampoo with Alberto VO5. The impression created by this sequence is that the shampoo was responsible for her beautiful-looking hair. No doubt she did shampoo with the product. But that doesn't mean that washing with VO5 is the only thing that happened between the "before" and the "after." Never mind that the actress or model chosen had lovely hair to begin with; you may be sure that she also had her hair professionally set, dried, and combed after the shampoo. But none of this is alluded to. The visual impression that the shampoo alone was responsible is reinforced by the claim, "She's got hair she can wash and wear." This claim is meant to call to mind the wash-and-wear revolution in fabrics. Most consumers consider these fabrics a real godsend because they eliminate the need for ironing. The implication of "wash-and-wear hair," then, is that you'll be able to bypass some steps. This cannot be stated, of course. If you wash your hair, with Alberto VO5 or with any other shampoo, it still has to dry, you still have to comb it and style it and you may have to set it. But we never see this process. For in commercials, just as in plays, more of the action takes place offstage. The problem is that we have no way of knowing what has happened offstage. Even if we did, the immediacy of TV tends to lure us into forgetting the offstage activity.

Dramatizations are particularly effective at hammering away at our emotional foibles. The advertiser can zero in on some weakness in our self-image, such as our fear of being offensive (ads for dandruff removers, mouthwashes, and deodorants do this) or of being behind the times ("You mean, you haven't heard about new, softer, more absorbent Toilet Tish?"). How ecstatic the advertiser who stumbled across the word "halitosis" in the dictionary must have been! And think of the slogan invented for Wisk: "ring around the collar." We see the embarrassed wife, suffering what seems to be the ultimate ignominy: the public revelation of her inadequacy at the washing machine! "What will people think? They'll think I don't take good care of my husband, that I don't really love him." Now comes the answer to this severe trauma: "Wisk!" Such commercials seek to persuade not by offering reasons leading to a conclusion but by using stereotypes with all of their emotional attachments. The stereotype may be direct, as in the case of "ring around the collar," or indirect, as in the Virginia Slims cigarette ad: "You've come a long way, baby." The manufacturer attacks your fears, appeals to your desires, and hopes you'll look to its product for help.

As you watch these dramas unfold, remember what we said at the beginning: The people are actors working from a script, and the entire production is under the advertiser's control. While it is carefully designed to look spontaneous and lifelike, you won't see anything they don't want you to see. You won't see the people they interview with hidden cameras who do *not* praise the product to the hilt. That footage winds up on the cutting-room floor.

Conclusion

It seems appropriate to conclude with a comment about advertising. Charles Revson, founder of Revlon, is reported to have once said, "I don't sell cosmetics; I sell dreams." It's easy to get down on advertisers because of the tricks they play, the gimmicks they use, and the charades they sometimes engage in, pretending to be giving us arguments when they are doing something quite different. However, what makes all this possible, Mr. Revson was reminding us, are the dreams they tap into. They don't create those dreams. On that point, consider these lines from Graham Nash's song, "Teach Your Children":

> Feed them on your dreams
> the one they pick's
> the one you'll know by.

SECTION IV

Advanced Argumentation

♦

CHAPTER TWELVE

Constructing Arguments

Introduction

In Sections I and II, our subject was the identification, interpretation, and critique of short arguments or of segments from longer ones. Letters to the editor are necessarily brief (200 or 400 is the word limit for many newspapers, and magazines tend to print shorter letters). The more serious and important arguments that play a role in everyday discourse tend to be longer and more complex in structure than those we have looked at so far. You won't be adequately prepared for in-depth logical appraisal until you have mastered the moves required to analyze and critique these more extended arguments. We shall offer our method for handling these extended arguments in Chapter 13.

Before we turn to that task, however, there is another aspect of argumentation we have not as yet dealt with, and it is one whose treatment provides essential background for analyzing extended arguments. We are referring to the ability to construct a case for a thesis. In Chapter 3, we introduced the rudiments of argument construction. We pointed out that you have no right to be confident of your critical evaluation of someone else's argument unless you can support your critique. In this chapter, we hope to extend your understanding of the basic structure of argumentation by explaining how to go about investigating an issue in some depth and making a well-argued case for or against a particular position on it. To that end, we introduce an explicit account of the underlying dialectical pattern of argumentation.

Argumentation as Dialectic

If you want to construct something—whether it be an automobile engine or a sailboat, an after-dinner speech or an advertising campaign—you must first know its purpose. The same goes for arguments. A survey of the uses to which arguments are put shows that they can have more than one function.

Preeminently, arguments are used to persuade, and this is the role in which we have considered arguments so far. But they can also function to reinforce beliefs whose truth their audience already accepts. Political speeches at party conventions and religious sermons are examples of this type of argument. In these contexts, speakers literally preach to the converted, yet they commonly use arguments. Another use of arguments is for the purpose of inquiry. Here the person conducting the inquiry tests various alternative theses by seeing whether good arguments can be found to support them and whether the arguments that have been urged against them stand up. These are three central functions of argument: persuasion, reinforcement, and inquiry.

Whether used to persuade, reinforce, or inquire, all arguments have two things in common. First, their motivation is doubt about the truth of the claim that occupies the position of conclusion. The reason there are arguments about abortion and euthanasia, for example, is that people disagree about the right policies on these issues. There is no point, as we have seen in our discussion of problematic premises, in arguing about the self-evident or the obvious. An exception would be a hunt for arguments for a belief already firmly held, such as God's existence, or the independent existence of a world outside our bodies or of other minds besides our own. In such cases, the point of the argument is to explore backward from a conclusion to the premises needed to support it. It's those premises about which there is doubt or question.

Second, all three types of argumentation tend to involve people occupying two distinct roles. One is the role of the doubter or interrogator; the other is the role of the prover or arguer. In the case of solitary inquiry, in which the individual reflects alone, one person must switch back and forth between the two roles of doubter and arguer. In the case of one person's addressing an audience, which is the situation of an author and her readers, a speaker and his listeners, or a TV preacher and the viewers, the single person tends to take the role of arguer, and the audience, treated as a source of questions and doubts, is put in the role of interrogator. The doubter is also sometimes called the *questioner*, the *opponent*, or the *antagonist*. The prover is also known as the *answerer, respondent, proponent*, or *protagonist*. Since an argument consists of reasons intended to show that a claim is worthy of acceptance, one person (or persona) must bring forward the reasons, and another person (or persona) must ask for them. There can be more than one person playing each role, and one person can switch back and forth between the two roles.

These two characteristics of arguments—their motivation by doubt or questions and their structure as an exchange or dialogue between two roles—are central to understanding how to go about constructing them.

The structure of an argument means that you have to have some audience in mind. It may be a particular person or a special group, but it might even be any reasonable person whatever. The motivation of an argument means that you have to respond to the doubts or questions your audience may have about the claim you are arguing for. Thus any claim that you think is worth arguing for will have, on the one hand, reasons that lead you to consider accepting it, and on the other hand, reasons that have led others either to reject it or to question it. It follows that if you remain convinced that the claim is worthy of acceptance, you must believe yourself able to produce both good reasons for supporting it and good reasons for rejecting the grounds for criticizing or doubting it.

We have seen that in general terms, what makes an argument for a claim a good one is that its premises are acceptable, relevant, and sufficient. But how is it to be decided whether they succeed in meeting these criteria? Who is to say? The test is whether the argument resists the scrutiny of its critics. This means that doubts or objections about arguments must be resolved or countered. In general, whether an argument is a good one depends on whether it stands up to criticism.

When you argue fully for a claim, you in effect make a case for it. We borrow the term from the realm of legal trials, where attorneys "make the case" for the prosecution or for the defense. A case consists, at its core, of arguments in support of the claim (the *main* or *overall conclusion*), and the refutation of arguments against it. Criticisms of, or objections to, the arguments for the claim and attempts to support the arguments against the claim may also have to be responded to.

A case can get much more complex than this, but the basic structure always relates back to arguments *for* the claim and arguments *against* the claim.

One way a case can get more complex is when there is more than one argument in favor of the claim. We call each distinct argument for a claim a *line of argument* in the case. There can also be more than one objection to the claim and, since each of these objections must be refuted, more than one argument in answer to the objections.

A second complicating factor can be that the arguments defending the claim or attempting to refute objections to it can themselves come under criticism. This happens when, for example, after you present someone with an argument for a position you are trying to defend, that person finds fault with your argument. If you are to maintain your position, you must try to answer that criticism. Or again, it can happen that after you have argued against an objection to your position, someone finds fault with your "refutation" of the objection. At this point, you must respond to that criticism of your refutation. Since at every point where you present an argument in the process of making your case, there is always at least the theoretical possibility of a criticism of that new argument, you can see that this process of criticism and reply, criticism and reply, could go on indefinitely (in theory, at least). In fact, it is rarely necessary to go beyond a couple of moves before you have considered all reasonable objections to your arguments, assuming that your arguments are sound ones.

Now, combine the two complicating factors just mentioned. Imagine that (1) there are several arguments for the claim and several objections requiring refutation and (2) there are criticisms of those arguments and the need to produce further arguments to refute those criticisms, plus objections to those further arguments and the need for replies to them. You can see that making a complete case for a claim can be a lengthy and complex enterprise.

However complicated a case becomes, it boils down to arguments *for* a claim and replies to arguments *against* it. This pattern involved in making a case is what we call the *dialectical character of argumentation*.

Argumentative Inquiry

A proponent of a point of view tends to make arguments in situations in which that opinion has been put in doubt, and the proponent is eager to win over those who question the opinion. In such situations, the arguer has already decided that the conclusion is true or worthy of acceptance. But how was that decision arrived at? And what gives the arguer confidence that this opinion or position really deserves his or her assent and is worth going to the trouble to argue for?

In our view, before advocating a position to others, its proponent should investigate to see whether the position merits his or her support. Arguments will play a pivotal role in any such investigation. Below, we sketch one model or plan that you can follow if you want to investigate whether an opinion you happen to hold is worth your assent.

We suggest that you begin your investigation by treating your opinion not as a fact but as a hypothesis, a *possible* truth. Treat it as a focus for the question, Should I believe this claim? And try to leave your mind open to a "yes" *or* a "no" answer to this question, allowing the weight of the evidence or other grounds to determine your verdict. You can carry out an investigation to discover:

1. What support does the claim have (the pro considerations) and what grounds tell against it (the con considerations)? This investigation might entail some research. What arguments in favor of and against the claim have already been voiced by others? Once having researched the pros and cons, you'd do well to see if you can come up with any additions to each side yourself. You will find it useful, even necessary, to organize these arguments into distinct lines of argument. And while you are obviously trying to come up with the best arguments you can find or think of, at this point don't judge the merits of the arguments too closely; that belongs to the next step.

2. What are the relative merits or force of the pros and cons? Formulating the pros and cons isn't enough to tell you how good the arguments for and against the claim are. The arguments are likely to vary in their merits. If there are five arguments on each side, but those on the pro side are all bad while all those on the con side are forceful, clearly the verdict would not be a draw but a decisive confirmation of the contrary point of view. So the second stage of the investigation consists of assessing the merits of the pros and cons.

You are already well prepared for this evaluative investigation because you know how to bring the criteria of relevance, sufficiency, and acceptability to bear on arguments; to recognize fallacies; and to spot where arguments need improvement. This first evaluative move is, then, to render judgments of the arguments as they stand. If you researched the original pros and cons, you discovered that other people have anticipated you in this evaluative process. You certainly should make use of any critiques you find in the literature if you think they are sound.

Critiquing the main arguments for and against the thesis in question cannot be the final step. The goal, remember, is to investigate how good a case can be made for the thesis in order to see whether it is worthy of your endorsement. It's entirely possible that the arguments can be improved in response to the critiques just carried out. So the next step is to try to patch up, modify, qualify, extend, and, in general, make what improvements you can to those main pros and cons in the light of the critical points raised against them.

What will happen following the last stage of the inquiry is that in most cases a profile of the relative merits of pros and cons of the claim in question will begin to emerge. You are now in a position to make a judgment. Is the hypothesis confirmed or refuted? Does the claim after all deserve your endorsement and, if so, with any qualifications? Or should you reject it or regard it as unlikely or implausible?

Once you have carried out such an argumentative investigation, you are on solid ground if you want to convince others of a position's truth or falsity. Not only will you have a basis for your own point of view, you will also have most of the material you will need to make your case to your audience, because the considerations that led you to adopt your position may well convince others, too.

Having made such an investigation and decided that the position in question is worthy of support, you should next consider how to construct arguments that advocate it in order to persuade others of its tenability.

Constructing the Case

We have discussed what is involved dialectically in making a case for a claim. That is the ideal, or the model, that lies behind both inquiry-oriented and advocacy-oriented argumentation. And we have set out a method for investigating the merits of a claim. This method provides a basis for developing one's own opinions and also generates raw material that can be used in arguments to persuade others of the truth of a claim.

With these background points in place, we now offer some more specific advice about how to construct an argumentative essay, with particular attention to situations of controversy. As you will see, there is some overlap with the material we presented on constructing arguments in Chapter 3. An outline of the steps involved is presented in the box on page 250.

Identify the Problem, Question, or Issue

The first step is to make clear to yourself what the point at issue is and be prepared to say why it is controversial enough to generate argumentation. Here are some examples:

1. The issue is whether capital punishment is justified. There are many who want capital punishment reinstated, while others are convinced it should be abolished forever.
2. The question is whether the former Soviet republics can coexist peacefully. The former Soviet republics harbor many antagonisms toward each other.
3. The problem is to determine whether the deficit should be reduced drastically at all costs. Laissez-faire economists tend to think the deficit must be decimated; others think a fairly large deficit is not harmful to the long-term health of the economy.

Identifying the question and why there is a problem or controversy will put you on the track of the points that need to be covered in your argument.

ONE WAY TO COMPOSE A CASE

1. Identify the problem, question, or issue.
2. Make your position clear.
3. Present arguments for your position.
4. Defend your arguments.
5. Consider objections to your position.
6. Decide on your order of presentation.

Make Your Position Clear

Everything we said in Chapters 3 and 7 about being clear applies to this second step, with a few supplementary points.

You should be able to state your position (thesis, opinion, point of view, claim) in a single sentence or in a clause beginning with the word "that." For the above examples, you might say:

1. "My position is that capital punishment should be reinstated."
2. "I believe that there will be an uneasy coexistence for some years, with a few minor clashes but no major outbreak of hostilities."
3. "My opinion is that we should not be preoccupied with the deficit at the expense of new government social programs."

The most common mistake is combining an argument, or a fragment of an argument, with the statement of one's position. For instance, someone who wants to argue for the reinstatement of capital punishment might express his position like this: "Capital punishment should be reinstated because it is a deterrent to murder." But here the person's *position* is just that capital punishment should be reinstated. Part of his *argumentation* for his position is the premise that capital punishment is a deterrent to murder; that's not part of his conclusion. Don't combine the two in stating your position because when it comes time to consider objections, the confusion of position and argument will result in confusion between objections to the position and objections to the argument, which are entirely different.

Another mistake is to state two or more positions together when each requires a separate defense. Thus you will encounter this sort of statement of a position: "In my opinion, capital punishment should not be reinstated, and those who are lobbying for its return cannot be the devout Christians they claim to be." These are two distinct propositions. Even if one of them is true, it doesn't follow that the other is, too. Moreover, quite different kinds of evidence would be required to support each claim. Combining them at the outset invites nothing but confusion in the argument to follow. There is nothing wrong with holding and defending two or more distinct positions related to a single issue, but it is crucial to separate them and to defend them separately. (An exception to this rule is when what you are arguing for is precisely the conjunction of those two positions: "I will spend the year in Greece and complete my novel" or "She won over his confidence and then stole his money.")

Present Arguments for Your Position

Only with the third step does the actual "argument" start. Presumably you have reasons for holding your position instead of the alternatives to it that you referred to in explaining why there is a problem or question. If you conducted an investigation into your position first, it will have yielded arguments you can put to use here. This is where you state those arguments, starting with the strongest ones you have. You might want to *deliver* your strongest argument last, but how you write up or deliver the presentation of your case most effectively is a different matter from the task of building the logically strongest case, which is what we are concerned with here.

You might have one, or more than one, line of argument for your position. If more than one, keep the different lines of argument separate. For instance, if you are arguing for the reinstatement of capital punishment, you might think it is justified on the ground that it is a deterrent to murder, and you may also think it is justified because you believe it is the punishment that a murderer deserves. These are different kinds of reasons for favoring capital punishment, and their respective merits or flaws will be independent. When you turn to the consideration of possible objections to your arguments, you will want to avoid the confusion that could be caused by mixing up an objection to one line of argument with an objection to another. Keep each line of argument clearly distinguished from the others.

Write out each argument, and line of argument, as completely as you can. Spell out all the steps. If you recall the difficulty you had supplying missing premises for arguments you were trying to understand and evaluate in Chapters 4 through 9, you recognize the importance of making your arguments as fully explicit as possible. You might, for example, spell out your deterrence argument for capital punishment as follows:

1   The threat of being executed for murder is likely to deter a person who might want to commit a murder, and the state should do whatever it can to reduce the incidence of murder; so the state should reinstate capital punishment as the penalty for murder.

Since only the state can legally institute capital punishment, you need to include the second premise to connect your deterrence premise with the conclusion. Spell out such connections.

Defend Your Arguments

Your own arguments are no more privileged than those of other people. They, like others, must meet the standards of relevance, sufficiency, acceptability. If your arguments are to be logically sound, they must be fallacy-free. So the fourth step in developing your case is to consider any objections a reasonable critic of your arguments might raise. (This step corresponds to the evaluation of the pros and cons in an argumentative inquiry.) These are objections to *your arguments* for your claim, not objections to that claim itself (your main conclusion). What you should be doing at this point is trying to strengthen the arguments for your claim by testing those arguments against criticisms that a reasonable but skeptical observer might make.

There are at least a couple of ways you can put yourself into the position of critic of your own arguments. One is to identify the *kind* of argument you are offering in each case, in order to see if your particular argument meets the standards for arguments of that sort. Suppose it's a causal argument, for example. If so, and you are arguing to a general causal claim as your conclusion, have you established a systematic correlation between what you allege to be the cause and the effect? Have you considered and rejected alternative hypotheses? Suppose you've made an argument from analogy. In that case, are the two things you are comparing truly similar in the salient respect in which they must be in order to justify your conclusion? Suppose you have appealed to an authority. In that case, does your appeal satisfy the conditions for legitimate appeals to authority? If you are arguing in an adversarial context, have you fairly represented the views of the person whose interests conflict with yours and with whom you disagree? You get the idea.

The other way you can put yourself into the position of critic of your own argument is to pay attention to the points that have already been discussed and argued about in the controversy on which you are taking a position. These may pertain to premises in your arguments. You might have to do some research to discover such criticisms. In the capital-punishment argument, for example, you ought to be aware of (or to find out) the fact that people have presented evidence that they contend shows that capital punishment is not, in fact, a deterrent. The data purport to show, for example, that in those states where capital punishment has been abolished, the murder rate has not gone up. Since this contention appears to contradict the claim that capital punishment is a deterrent to murder, you will need to respond to it, if you want to use the deterrence argument.

What you need to do here, in general, is detach yourself from your own favorite arguments and look at them as a sympathetic critic might. Look for flaws to be removed and omissions to be filled in. The egocentric and ethnocentric attitudes discussed in Chapter 9 will do their best to obstruct you, but it is really in the interests of your own position that you learn to be a perceptive, constructive critic of your own arguments. Such criticism will expose to you their flaws, which you may then be able to correct. Your case will actually be made stronger, not weaker, by your insightful criticisms of it.

While the first move of defense is criticism, the second is further argumentation. At points where your critique exposes an undefended premise that is open to attack (for example, your "deterrence" premise), you can move to provide the needed argument or rejoinder. If you find that your conclusion was hastily drawn on the basis of a limited sample of the relevant kinds of evidence, you can seek out and present the additional evidence needed to nail down your case. If a premise is found to be irrelevant, you can move to supply the unexpressed assumption that was at work when you formulated the argument, the addition of which will make the irrelevance evident.

Where you find the criticism solid, however, you might want to make a strategic qualification. (Perhaps, for example, you decide that you want to defend capital punishment *only for those found guilty of first-degree murder*.) In other cases, the strength of the criticism will require you to abandon your argument altogether. Perhaps you got carried away initially and argued from a faulty analogy that you cannot repair or qualify. In that case, you need to look for another argument to replace the one you dropped, or you might be able to get along with the remaining ones if you had several in your basket to start with. Your case is strengthened, not weakened, by the addition of needed qualifications and by the excision of bad arguments.

Consider Objections to Your Position

Recall the pattern of dialectical argumentation: (1) arguments *for* a claim and (2) replies to arguments *against* it. So far we have dealt only with arguments for the claim. The fifth step in constructing a case for a claim is to state the strongest arguments *against your position* that you can think of. These are arguments that will have as their conclusion either (1) the proposition that your conclusion is false (or otherwise unacceptable), or (2) a proposition which, if true, would be incompatible with your conclusion. For example, if your conclusion is that capital punishment should be reinstated, there might be an argument with the conclusion that capital punishment should *not* be reinstated. Alternatively, or in addition, there might be an argument for the conclusion that murderers should receive life imprisonment without parole. If the conclusion of this argument were true, then your position, that capital punishment should be reinstated, is not; hence it is incompatible with your conclusion.

Keep in mind that the point of the exercise is to make the best case you can for your position. It is counterproductive, therefore, to look only at minor, easily answered objections to it. Look for the most convincing objections you can find or imagine because you have a good case for your position only if you can answer the best arguments that can be made *against* it.

These arguments against your position should be stated as fairly and fully as you can manage because you want to avoid misrepresenting the position you disagree with and thus risking setting up straw-person objections. But once you have presented these arguments, your next move is to try to show that they are *not* sound. Thus you will have to generate arguments that show that the objections to your position violate one or more of the standards of good argument and consequently do not establish their conclusions.

Once again, you may find that some of the objections make good points that require you to further qualify your position. However, if any of these arguments turns out to be completely cogent, you must abandon your position, at least in its present form, because these are objections not just against your present arguments for your position but against your position itself.

Assuming that you have presented and defended weighty arguments in support of your position and that you have refuted the best objections against it, the result is a strong case that your position is worthy of acceptance. And that is just what you set out to produce.

Decide on Your Order of Presentation

We have reviewed the steps to follow when constructing an argument for a position you wish to defend, and we distinguished between these steps in the dialectical process and the order of presentation you should follow when writing up your argument for presentation. It is advisable to practice by following a set order until the moves become automatic (which they do, in time). However, there is no heaven-sent edict that requires the arguments for a position to be set forth and defended first and the arguments against it to be considered and refuted second. Sometimes it is more effective, rhetorically, to reverse that order. For example, when your audience is under the impression that there are clear arguments proving your position false, it might be wise (other things being equal) to start by presenting your refutations of those arguments. You would thereby weaken the audience's predisposition to dismiss your position out of hand and make them more receptive to your later presentation of your arguments on its behalf. Or again, there is no reason in principle against a presentation that alternates arguments for and refutations of criticisms against, in sets of two. This approach does risk confusing your reader, though; and your presentation will not be persuasive if it is not clear.

There is another way you might want to rearrange the steps you followed in putting your argument together when you get to the stage of organizing it for presentation. You initially worked through an argument for your position, objections against it, then your responses to those objections. The last move sometimes consisted of providing additional argumentation to make good the defects in the original argument. Having spotted those defects, you might conclude that there's no point in repeating this whole process when you present your finished argument. Instead, it might be more effective if you produced the strengthened argument at the outset. However, this won't be a good policy when the (defective) objection is one your audience is familiar with and finds compelling. In that case you will need to address it at the outset in order to disabuse them of it and remove that presumption against your position.

An Example

It is time to illustrate the procedure for constructing an argumentative essay by working through an example. We won't take up a major controversy because to develop a case for a position on a major issue, such as the morality of abortion or the merits of a free-market economy, would take more space than we have available.

Our example comes from a minor dispute that ruffled feathers on our campus. A bit of background is in order. Our university runs an internal mail service delivering mail twice a day from a central post office to departmental offices, where departmental secretaries sort it and file it in faculty mail slots. You also need to know that in our city, one of the candidates for mayor in the recent civic elections (we'll call her Dr. Gibson), is also a professor on campus.

The student newspaper ran the headline, "University Unwittingly Sends Campaign Mail. Who's to Blame?" According to the story, one of the people working for Dr. Gibson's campaign, a colleague in her department (whom we'll call Schneider), had sent a flyer and a letter asking for contributions to Dr. Gibson's campaign to every faculty member through the university mail system. All the costs of sending this material except those connected with the mail distribution were borne by the Gibson campaign. But the newspaper was taking the position that Professor Schneider shouldn't have sent the letters through the university mail without paying costs. Was the paper right?

That is the question we shall examine. Professor Schneider didn't think he had done anything wrong, at least not morally wrong. He was quoted as saying that he couldn't find any written policy against sending campaign material through the university mail service. So we have a disagreement between Professor Schneider and the student newspaper; we have a controversy.

We are not sure what to think about this issue, so we will treat our argument construction from the point of view of argumentative inquiry. It does strike us as plausible to think the newspaper is right, so we will begin by taking the position, at least for the purpose of starting the inquiry, that Professor Schneider should not have sent the campaign literature through the university mail without paying for the delivery.

So far, we have identified the issue and made our position clear. The next step is to present arguments in support of our position.

Here are a couple of arguments that occur to us as we think about what might be said on behalf of the newspaper's position:

2   Argument *A*

1. The university should not take a partisan position on city politics.
2. By using his university connections and not paying for the mailing of the Gibson campaign literature, Professor Schneider compromised the university's nonpartisan position on local politics.
3. Professor Schneider should not have sent the Gibson campaign literature through the university mail without paying for it.

3   Argument *B*

1. By sending nonuniversity material through the university mail system without paying for it, Professor Schneider set a precedent that will allow other university and nonuniversity people to send nonuniversity material through the university system without paying.
2. It is undesirable to have people, whether connected with the university or not, send nonuniversity material through the university mail at no charge.
3. Professor Schneider should not have sent the Gibson campaign literature through the university mail without paying for it.

Notice that in both cases, the conclusion of the argument is the position we are inquiring into.

The next step is to go through each argument separately to see if it stands up to critical scrutiny. We'll leave Argument *A* to you and work through Argument *B*.

First we check the connection between the premises and the conclusion. The argument seems to go like this: "If an action of yours sets a precedent and it is a bad precedent, then you shouldn't have done it." To test this inference, we try to think of a counterexample. Could there be a situation in which the premises were acceptable but the conclusion was not? Could an action that sets a bad precedent ever be justified?

Some might say that if a great deal of good would result on a particular occasion from an action, then the action should be taken even if it sets a bad precedent. For instance, if someone not connected with the university saved a life by using university property (say, a fire extinguisher), then whatever the precedent set thereby, the action would be justified because the gain was so great. (This is the first objection to Argument *B*.)

Does this counterexample show that the inference from the premises to the conclusion in *B* is not sound? Here we move to the next step in our procedure and try to reply to the objection. We think that in fact, the example is not a counterexample. Using university equipment to save a life does not set a harmful precedent but a most desirable one. So the example does not give us a case where the premises are both true; that is, where the action sets a precedent, and it's a bad precedent. We cannot think of any further objections to the move from the premises to the conclusion in *B*, so we declare it acceptable (pending notification of some as-yet-unconsidered objection).

Now what about the premises themselves? Take the first premise. Does Professor Schneider's action really set a precedent? If his action is not judged wrong in this case, does that mean other faculty and nonuniversity people would have to be permitted to send nonuniversity mail through the campus system without paying?

One might object, first, that Professor Schneider is connected with the university, so his action does not set a precedent for nonuniversity people. However, in reply to this objection to the first premise, we would make the point that Professor Schneider was acting in his capacity as campaign worker for Dr. Gibson's campaign, not in his capacity as a university faculty member. Sure, his faculty status was what led the university post office to accept and deliver the campaign literature without question, but as sender of this literature he acted in the role of a campaign worker, not a professor. The objection does not, then, show that no precedent has been set for nonuniversity use of a university service.

Another possible objection to the first premise is that Professor Schneider was sending material relating to Dr. Gibson, another faculty member, so the material is not unrelated to the university.

But a similar reply to our previous one works here, too. Dr. Gibson is running for mayor in her capacity as a private citizen, not in connection with her faculty post or as a representative of the university. Since her connection with the university is not related to her mayoralty campaign, the campaign literature mailed by Professor Schneider on her behalf is nonuniversity material.

We will leave our testing of the first premise here. You may think of further objections that would have to be countered by anyone trying to defend this argument. We move on to the second premise of Argument *B*: It is undesirable to have people, whether connected with the university or not, send nonuniversity material through the university postal system without charge.

Is this really true? What would be the consequences if this were the policy? What problems would it create? It strikes us that the consequences would depend on the demand for this service. If outsiders wanted to use the university postal system for nonuniversity business once or twice a year, the burden on the mail delivery system would be insignificant. If such mail started to go through the system every day, however, the university might be forced to add staff or cut its own service. Thus, looking at the precedent from the point of view of its consequences, we would have to say that one must reserve judgment until there is some concrete evidence that it would be a burden on the mail system. This basis for assessing the second premise leaves us in the position of having to withhold judgment. Is there some other way to assess this premise, one that will give us a definite answer?

Here is one possibility: If there is a policy allowing free use of the university postal service by nonuniversity people or for nonuniversity purposes, then some people using the system will not be paying for it while others are. That makes it unfair. So even if the harm is minimal or negligible in terms of the cost to the university or the restriction of the service, there is an element of unfairness involved that makes the precedent undesirable.

As far as we can see, there is no disputing that the Schneider precedent allows for a certain amount of unfairness. Let us consider how strong a point this is. If only a very few people take advantage of the policy, and do so only rarely, then although the unfairness exists, it is a minor consideration. Thus, if this is all that can be said in support of the second premise, the result is that Argument *B* is not a terribly forceful objection to Professor Schneider's action.

Argument *B* gives us some grounds for accepting our position, though not overwhelming ones. Maybe Argument *A* will fare better under critical scrutiny. And there may be Arguments *C, D,* and *E* that we have not had the wit to assemble. Begging limitations of space, we cut off here any further consideration of the arguments for our starting position and turn now to arguments that might be framed against it.

Professor Schneider himself offered an argument that was quoted in the student newspaper. His argument ran as follows:

4   Schneider
1. There is currently no university policy explicitly prohibiting the sending of political campaign literature through the university mail free of charge.
a. When there is no policy against an action in a large institution, then that action is permissible.
2. It was not wrong for Professor Schneider to have sent the Gibson campaign literature through the university mail without paying for it.

You will notice that we have supplied a missing premise in order to make all the steps in the argument against our position explicit. We have tried to make the missing premise plausible by adding the qualifier "in a large institution." It seems particularly true in large institutions that one must be free to act when there is no policy explicitly prohibiting the action. The alternative of being free to do only what a specific policy *permits* would be too stifling. If Schneider's argument is sound, then our initial position is false. We must now examine this argument.

The inference from premises to conclusion stands up; indeed, we have supplied the missing premise to make sure it does. And we see no reason not to take Professor Schneider's word for it that there was no policy forbidding his action when he mailed out the campaign literature. So the question comes down to premise *a*. But it strikes us as a very weak link in the argument.

Our argument against premise *a* is that some actions can be dangerous or wasteful and, for that reason alone, should not be performed whether there is any policy expressly forbidding them or not. Thus premise *a*, taken as it stands, is false. To avoid this objection, we restate premise *a* as follows:

5   *a'*. When there is no policy against an action in a large institution, then, other things being equal, that action is permissible.

This rewording makes premise *a'* acceptable, but we now have to add a further missing premise in order to get to the conclusion, namely:

6   *b*. In Professor Schneider's case, other things *were* equal. So in the absence of a specific policy prohibiting it, there was no special reason for not mailing the literature.

The trouble with this second missing premise is that it is pretty controversial. Our initial arguments, *A* and *B*, both offered reasons why Professor Schneider should not have mailed the campaign literature the way he did. We cannot then grant premise *b* in Professor Schneider's defense without giving up the initial position we are investigating, so going along with *b* requires us to beg the question. Since *b* cannot be granted, then this argument fails to establish its conclusion that Professor Schneider did nothing wrong.

We have, so far, considered and rejected one objection to our position. Perhaps there are others that will fare better. If we want our inquiry to be complete, we must search for these additional arguments, but we will break off the inquiry at this point because we have already illustrated the dialectical procedure to be followed in trying to work out a position on an issue. Since this is the same procedure to follow in making a case for a position, you can look back over our discussion of this example as if we had initially committed ourselves to the position that Professor Schneider was wrong to have sent out the campaign literature for Dr. Gibson through the university mail without paying for it.

Conclusion

A good deal more could be said about the construction of arguments from the logical point of view, and volumes more from the rhetorical point of view, but in this chapter we have addressed what we believe to be the most important logical starting point: the dialectical structure of argumentation. Any complete case in support of a claim must have the structure we have described. Not all arguments will go to this length, nor do they need to, but any shorter argument can be identified as to where it fits in this dialectical pattern. It will be an argument for a position, a reply to an anticipated objection to an argument, or the refutation of an anticipated objection to a position.

You will learn through practice to provide just the right amount of argument called for and to direct it at the important points at issue. Keep in mind what we said at the outset, that each argument has its audience. Identify your audience, and direct your arguments to the dialectical challenges that come from that audience.

What is missing from this chapter is a taxonomy of the different types of argument, with recipes or hints for producing arguments of each type. Such a list might include arguments in support of recommendations of policies or actions, arguments in support of value judgments, and arguments in support of causal claims. Under these three general headings, we could list the variety of argument subject matters within each type. Arguments about values can be subdivided into arguments about moral, aesthetic, prudential, religious, and other values. There are arguments for theories in the social sciences and arguments for theories in the physical sciences; and within each grouping, the differences between particular scientific fields are relevant. Learning all of this requires, first, an understanding of and practice with the types of considerations common to arguments of each general type. For example, arguments recommending policies usually invoke a distinction between ends (or goals), and means of achieving those goals, together with an apparatus for ranking alternative means to a given goal. Second, one needs to learn something about each specific field about which one wants to argue. This calls for a well-rounded education.

Both these objectives are highly desirable. We believe that the first could be achieved in a course devoted entirely to the construction of arguments. The second requires a sound liberal education.[1] This text can do little more than try to set you on the road to an ability to formulate arguments, and so we hope that you expand and deepen this ability as your education proceeds. If you keep in mind the dialectical pattern of argumentation and try to employ it whenever you construct arguments, you will be starting out on the right foot.

EXERCISES

1. *Directions:*   Decide how many positions are expressed in each of the following sentences. If there is just one, restate it to make this clear. If there are more than one, state each one separately.
   a. Puerto Rico, which is now a commonwealth, should be made a state.
   b. Scotland should be allowed to secede from England on a twenty-five-year trial basis, with an option to revoke its secession and rejoin England after that period is up.
   c. Wealthy industrialized nations should share their wealth with third-world countries, but third-world countries should not have to share any increases in their wealth.
   d. If God exists, then evil is an illusion.
   e. While marriage is a desirable institution, it should not require sexual exclusivity.
   f. Mussolini was merely a banal thug, whereas Hitler was evil incarnate.
   g. The end of American imperial hegemony is at hand, but there is no new world power to replace it unless we count Japan.
   h. The twenty-first century belongs to China, not Japan.

2. *Directions:*   Decide which of the following sentences expresses just a position (or more than one position) and which expresses part of an argument combined with the statement of a position. Write out each position expressed separately, and mark it as such. Write out separately each premise offered as a partial argument for a position expressed, and mark it as such, identifying the position it is supposed to support.
   a. The breakup of the Balkan states signaled the fact that nationalist loyalties are alive and well even at the end of the twentieth century.

[1] Thanks to John McPeck and Mark Weinstein for reminding us of the need to emphasize this point.

b. No war between nuclear powers can be justified given that any such war entails the destruction of the international economy.

c. Springsteen has the best lyrics and the best sound around; he's simply the best rock 'n' roll musician of the last two decades.

d. Although the women's movement has made impressive gains in the past quarter of a century, its goals are very far from being realized.

e. One would have expected that after *Sex*, Madonna could not outgross herself further, yet she has continued to surprise and shock her fans.

f. Simply because of their immense populations, third-world countries will be setting the international political agenda for the next century.

g. If you can afford a wide-screen television set, you can afford to donate to local and international charities.

3. *Directions:* Identify at least three positions that could be taken on each of the following issues:

a. Noise in the library

b. Landlord-student relations

c. Gay and lesbian rights

d. Athletic scholarships

e. Equal pay for equal work

f. Affirmative action

g. Abortion rights

h. House husbands

i. The job training role of colleges and universities

4. *Directions:* Select issues from the list above, and formulate two arguments in support of and two arguments against each position that you identified for each issue. (Your instructor will tell you how many issues to select.)

5. *Directions:* Select an issue about which you have strong opinions. Identify a position on that issue with which you strongly disagree. Formulate three strong arguments in support of that position. (Avoid making up straw-person objections or trivial objections that are easily refuted or accommodated.)

6. *Directions:* Identify an issue that interests you but on which you have not yet taken a position. Set out the reasonable positions that could be taken on this issue that you know of or that you can discover through research, including the positions some people have actually taken. Make sure these positions are actually incompatible. Formulate as many reasonable arguments against each of these positions as you can. State as many objections to each of these arguments as you can.

7. *Directions:* Write an essay that follows the dialectical argumentative pattern on some issue that you consider important and that perplexes you.

CHAPTER THIRTEEN

◆

Analyzing Extended Arguments

The Method Explained

In previous chapters, we focused on what might be called *snippets*; that is, short arguments or excerpts from longer ones. Our reasoning was that it would be easier to learn to detect fallacies in a relatively uncluttered setting. The time has come to switch our focus and come to grips with more fully developed arguments. It is one thing to be able to identify fallacious reasoning in snippets and quite another to practice the art of logical criticism on "the real thing"—the longer pieces of reasoning that confront you in your everyday reading. The purpose of this chapter is to present a method for evaluating extended arguments, the toughest challenge that a student of argumentation can undertake.

By an "extended argument," we mean the entire passage as it occurs in its natural setting, whether in an editorial, an opinion piece, a letter to the editor, or a speech before the Senate. Such passages often contain several different but related arguments that have been rolled into one as the writer or speaker attempted to "make the case" for his or her position. Evaluating extended arguments presents special problems for two reasons: (1) such passages are too long for it to be practical to go over them with a fine-toothed comb and (2) such passages often contain more than one vulnerable zone. Hence a useful method of analysis must guide you in the task of extracting the essence of the argument, and must also guide you in ranking criticisms in their order of importance. Our method does that. And last, but most important, our method requires you to look at the weaknesses that you have uncovered and to consider as well the strengths of the argument and then produce an overall evaluation, locating the argument at some point in the spectrum:

strong argument ←———————————————————————→ weak argument

For ease of reference, we refer to the entire passage in which the extended argument occurs as the *text*. The process we describe will show you how to go about extracting the extended argument from the text, thereby compiling a subtext which then becomes the focal point of evaluation. In the remainder of this section, we introduce a five-step process for the analysis of extended arguments. In the following section, we illustrate how it works by applying it to a couple of examples. The five steps are listed in the box.

STEPS IN ANALYZING EXTENDED ARGUMENTS

1. Write a synopsis of the argument.
2. Identify the main premises and the conclusion.
3. Put the main premises into hierarchical order.
4. Evaluate the argument.
5. Write up your critique.

Write a Synopsis of the Argument

A preliminary step, it goes without saying, is a careful reading of the original text. Failure to grasp the entire sense of the text will skew your subsequent analysis and will make you vulnerable to a charge of setting up a straw person. Having read and digested the text, begin your analysis by constructing what we call a synopsis. By *synopsis*, we do not mean a mere summary or restatement of the text; we mean a logical description of the argument in the text, beginning with an identification of the main conclusion (whether implicit or explicit) and including a description of the various strategies used by the arguer to generate that conclusion.

To write a good synopsis, one must be able to use the paragraph structure of the original text intelligently and to describe how that unit contributes to the overall end of arguing for the conclusion. Most writers use the paragraph structure as their unit of development and attempt to present their case point by point. But some writers violate this practice, either by extending some point over several paragraphs or by introducing multiple points in one paragraph. Thus in blocking out the argument, learn to rely judiciously on the author's paragraph structure.

We recommend assigning a number to each individual paragraph of the text to facilitate reference to it. Read each individual paragraph with the conclusion in mind. Ask yourself, What role does this paragraph play in the argument as a whole? How does it advance the case for the conclusion?

The typical functions you will encounter are:

1 Providing background information

Explaining a crucial term in the argument

Making a comment or observation

Stating the conclusion

Stating (and defending) a premise

Defending a premise against general skepticism

Defending a premise against actual or anticipated objections

Defending the conclusion against actual or anticipated counterarguments

Summarizing an alternative position (prior to arguing against it)

Tracing the logical consequences of a premise

While writing the synopsis, weed out material that is extraneous to the argument. Such material includes:

2   Background information that provides the context of the argument

Explanations that play a nonevidentiary role in the argument

Digressions and asides

Repetition of points already made

Literary devices and flourishes

Below, we print the entire text of an argument, excerpts from which you have already seen. Read the entire text carefully. Write a synopsis; then compare your synopsis with ours, which follows the text. The paragraphs are numbered to facilitate reference.

3   1. Latest crime statistics from Denmark provide a striking illustration of the beneficial effects of that nation's experiment in pornography and will provide a powerful argument for those favoring the legalization and open availability of pornography in Canada.

2. According to the figures, sexual offenses against females in Copenhagen, the heart of the "dirty-picture" business, dropped 59 percent from 1965 to 1970. During the same five years, cases of exhibitionism or indecent exposure dropped 58 percent; peeping, 85 percent; child molestation, 56 percent; and verbal-indecency incidents, 83 percent. There was no noticeable effect on cases of rape and intercourse with minors.

3. According to one expert, pornographic material provides the psychosexual stimulation needed by those people who otherwise take illegal means to obtain such stimulation.

4. Whatever weight attaches to the moral or good-taste arguments against pornography, it seems doubtful that they will prevail, in the long run, over the increasingly liberal attitudes in modern society, particularly when the liberal position is buttressed by proof that legalizing pornography results in decline in sexual crime.

5. In Canada, pornography and the issue of legalizing it are probably still too laden with emotion to be the subject of dispassionate debate. As a result, unfortunately, the confusing situation with respect to pornography will probably continue.

6. It is unfortunate because the necessarily haphazard way in which we enforce pornography legislation cannot help but make the law and the process of its enforcement look ridiculous, thus undermining the respect for law on which every civilized nation depends.

Our synopsis of the argument follows:

The issue dealt with in this editorial is whether pornography should be made legal. The editorialist's position is nowhere explicitly asserted but is evident in the first and the fifth paragraph. We take the conclusion to be: "Pornography should be legalized and made openly available in Canada now." The argument has three phases. In paragraphs 1-3, the editorialist provides warrants for the conclusion by claiming (implicitly) that legalizing pornography reduces sex crimes. The first paragraph is introductory in function, anticipating the causal claim implicit in the second paragraph and supported by the statistics cited there. The third paragraph provides a hypothesis to support the correlation in the second paragraph. The second phase of the argument begins with the fourth paragraph, where the editorialist anticipates counterarguments to his conclusion; namely, the argument that opposes legalization on moral grounds and the argument that opposes it on grounds of "good taste." The arguer tries to undercut these arguments by claiming that they cannot withstand the force of growing liberal attitudes. The last phase of the argument takes place in the fifth and sixth paragraphs, where an attempt is made to show what the consequences of not legalizing pornography will be (undermining respect for the law).

The value of a good synopsis is that it highlights the main features of the argument, thus preparing you for the next step. Remember that a synopsis is not a mere summary or restatement of the argument but, rather, an overview of the original text, highlighting the functions played by its various parts.

Identify the Main Premises and the Conclusion

In order to identify the main premises and the conclusion (especially of longer arguments), you may need to sketch a tree diagram of the *macrostructure* of the argument. By "macrostructure," we mean the main branches of the argument, together with the conclusion. We distinguish this from the *microstructure*, the logical structure of internal arguments for individual premises.

We suggest that you start by drawing a diagram of the macrostructure, using the numbers to refer to the paragraphs and using your synopsis to indicate what role the paragraphs play, either singly or in blocks. Figure 13-1 is our diagram of the macrostructure of the argument just considered. Note that we have given a code name to each of the parts of the argument. That code name will vary from one argument to the next. And we have put the numbers of the paragraphs from the synopsis in the circle to indicate that "branch" of the argument. Beginning at the left of the diagram, we have placed what we have coded as the moral and "good-taste" objections (comprising the fourth para-

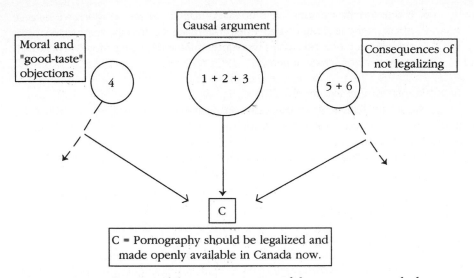

Figure 13-1 *A diagram of the macrostructure of the argument on whether pornography should be made legal.*

graph). Note that we have shown these objections with a broken arrow leading *away* from the conclusion (because that is the logical direction of an objection of this sort) and then we show a straight arrow taking that objection back to the conclusion, indicating that the arguer has attempted to counter that objection (whether successfully or not is another matter). In the middle, we have what we called the *causal argument*, comprising paragraphs 1-3 and leading directly to the conclusion. Then, at the right, we have a branch of the argument called "consequences of not legalizing." Again we show this as an objection.

Once you have a diagram of the macrostructure, you are in a position to "read off" the main premises. Our diagram shows that the argument has three main branches, all of which converge upon the conclusion. Thus, from paragraphs 1-3, we take the claim to be that "legalizing pornography would decrease sex crimes in Canada." Notice that this claim does not appear anywhere in paragraphs 1-3. We take it to be the claim that, in effect, summarizes the thinking in paragraphs 1-3. So it becomes our P1. Next, we look at the fourth paragraph and, again, summarizing what is stated there, come up with P2. Finally, we look at the right side, for the third branch, again looking to see what is implied in these paragraphs. Hence, the structure of the main argument is now clear.

4   P1: Legalizing pornography would decrease sex crimes. (paragraphs 1-3)
P2: The objections to legalizing pornography cannot withstand the force of growing liberal opinion. (paragraph 4)
P3: Failure to legalize pornography has the undesirable consequence of undermining respect for law. (paragraphs 5 and 6)
C: Pornography should be legalized and made openly available in Canada now.

Now that the structure of the main argument is before us, we are ready to begin the process of evaluation. Our procedure will be to look first at the main argument to see whether it is fallacious or not. After that, we must inspect the internal arguments provided in support of the main argument, if any. But here a question arises: Are all of the main premises of equal importance in the argument? For many arguments, the answer is "no." This realization points to the need for one more step prior to actual evaluation.

Put the Main Premises into Hierarchical Order

Once you've identified the main premises, you need to put those premises into hierarchical order. By "hierarchical order," we mean a list of the main premises in their order of importance. How do you determine this? In evaluating premises for importance, there are two factors to take into consideration: emphasis and weight.

Emphasis.   How much emphasis has the author placed on this particular branch of argument? The best way to answer this question is to see how much attention the arguer has given to the presentation of the premise. If, for example, in an argument running over some six paragraphs, the arguer spends three paragraphs developing one branch of the argument while spending only one paragraph on, say, the other two, it seems clear that the author places greater emphasis on the first branch. This consideration would place it above the others in the hierarchy. Major flaws in this branch will likely have greater impact on the argument than weaknesses in the others—a point that needs to be remembered when you turn to the evaluation.

Weight.   In making a case, an arguer will often summon all the arguments she can muster for the position even though some one or two of the arguments have a perceptibly greater capacity to support or generate the conclusion than do others. Thus, for example, an argument that a certain action is immoral would tend to have greater weight in showing it to be inadvisable than an argument that it is inconvenient.

In constructing the hierarchy, place the branches with greater weight at the top. For example, one might seek to develop the case for capital punishment by arguing both that it is a deterrent to murder (first branch) and that it is more economical than life inprisonment (second branch). Clearly the first branch should be put first in the hierarchy because by itself, it has (if well argued) considerable weight and also because the economic argument is given subsidiary emphasis by its positioning.

By judicious reflection on the branches of the argument and the factors of emphasis and weight, you should be able to rank the main premises in hierarchical order, with the most important ones at the top and the less important at the bottom, realizing that, of course, branches may be of equal, or coordinate, importance. The purpose of this ordering is clear: When you evaluate the internal arguments, your first move should be to inspect the arguments for the branches at the top of the hierarchy, and you should work your way down from there.

To put the main premises of the pornography argument into hierarchical order, list the branch or premise that is most important at the top, and give it a label or abbreviation.

5   P1: Causal argument
    P3: Argument from consequences
    P2: Argument against possible objections

A hierarchy is not complete without the reasoning in support of the ranking, so we provide the following justification:

6   P1 (causal argument) is the most important branch because it receives the greatest emphasis (the editorialist spends three out of the six paragraphs developing it) and because it has the greatest weight (for if legalizing pornography would decrease sex crimes, then that is a good reason for taking that action; sex crimes are highly repugnant and any way of reducing them deserves serious consideration). The second place in the hierarchy belongs to P3 (argument from consequences). Both factors, emphasis and weight, suggest this placement. The writer spends approximately two paragraphs in support of this point, and it has thrust: The well-being of society requires respect for the law, and the author claims that this respect is being threatened by present laws against pornography. The least important of the three premises is P2 (argument against possible objections). The editorialist mentions the objections but does not spell them out in detail, nor does he give them any systematic attention.

With this hierarchy to guide us, we now approach the task of evaluating the argument in an orderly (rather than a haphazard or hit-and-miss) fashion.

Evaluate the Argument

When you evaluate an argument, you will be looking for instances of fallacious reasoning. The first nine chapters of this text were aimed at preparing you to detect fallacious reasoning and—just as important—equipping you to defend your judgments. Those judgments, along with their defense, form the basis of your criticism of arguments. We recommend that you begin with the main argument and then deal with the internal arguments roughly in their order of occurrence in the hierarchy you've just constructed.

Main Argument.   First, look at the main premises: P1, P2, P3 . . . C. Ask yourself, Are these premises acceptable? Do they pass the acceptability requirement? Remember that this requirement applies mainly to premises that stand alone, without any support. If a premise has been argued for, then the issue of whether to accept it or not is the issue of whether the argument for it is a good one or not. Next, check the premises individually for relevance. Ask, Does *P*1 satisfy the relevance requirement? Then repeat the process for *P*2, *P*3, and so on. Finally, check for sufficiency: Do the premises, taken together, satisfy the sufficiency requirement? Do they provide enough support for the conclusion? Can you think of a way in which all the premises could prove to be relevant and acceptable and yet the conclusion not acceptable? Is there evidence that you need to have but do not have?

Whatever fallacies you find in the main argument, you need to take note of them and develop the necessary reasoning to support your charge. Any fallacy discovered in the main argument has a strong potential for becoming the basis for a major criticism of the argument.

Internal Arguments. After you have evaluated the main argument, the next step is to evaluate the internal arguments. Here is where the hierarchy constructed at the third step comes to the fore. Look first at the internal argument that supports the premise highest in the hierarchy. Any fallacy that occurs in that argument has the potential for becoming a major criticism of the whole argument. Once you have inspected the arguments for the first premise in the hierarchy, then repeat the process for the next premise in the hierarchy, and continue this process until you believe you have covered all of the internal arguments.

At the end of the process of evaluation, you will have a list of fallacy charges (and their justifications) against various premises—both main premises and internal ones. The final step is to introduce an order of priority among those charges. That is what is involved in going from evaluation to critique.

Write Up Your Critique

You are now prepared for the final and most important step in the process of analyzing extended arguments: critique. If the point of the exercise had been just to evaluate the argument as good or bad, you might well have stopped when you encountered what you thought was a serious fallacy. But the purpose is not just to evaluate but, rather, to offer the arguer criticism—enlightened feedback.

By a "critique," we mean an ordered and reasoned set of criticisms. It is not a critique to simply throw out as many fallacy charges as you've come up with, without thinking about their significance as criticisms.

After you have checked the main argument and the internal arguments and located any instances of fallacious reasoning, the task that remains is to write up your critique, showing proper discrimination. Begin by presenting the strongest criticisms and proceed by giving the criticisms next in order of importance. Do not stop until you've made all your important points. At some point in your critique, give credit for the good points the arguer made. Your critique should conclude with an overall judgment of the argument that adequately reflects both its strengths and its weaknesses.

In constructing your critique of an extended argument, by following two principles, you can keep your criticisms effectively focused and logical. These are (1) the principle of discrimination and (2) the principle of logical neutrality.

The Principle of Discrimination   The basic idea of discrimination can be put roughly as follows: In criticizing an argument, strive to get to the heart of the matter. A critic who gets sidetracked and expends all his or her energy criticizing peripheral flaws in an argument while major ones go unnoticed does not display the quality of discrimination. It would be comparable to a movie critic who spent most of her or his review berating the performance of a minor actor while failing to note weak performances by the principal performers. In requiring you to get to the heart of the matter, the principle of discrimination simultaneously proscribes the two most common faults in criticism of arguments: (1) nit-picking and (2) latching onto the first complaint that comes into your mind. Neither of these all-too-common tendencies makes for effective logical criticism.

If there is a fallacy in the main argument, then this criticism will normally take precedence over others. It should come first in your write-up. Often the problems will occur in the interior parts of the argument, and here the hierarchy constructed in the third step comes to the fore. Look first at the internal argument that supports the premise highest in the hierarchy. Any fallacy that occurs in that argument has the potential for ranking as a major criticism. A major criticism of an argument is one that has the following properties: (1) the criticism focuses on a premise (or argument for the premise) that is high up in the hierarchy and, therefore, crucial for the success of the argument and (2) the fallacy that occurs in that premise is a serious logical error.

In fact, fallacy charges are not all equally serious. A fallacy of relevance is, all else being equal, more serious than a fallacy of sufficiency. And a fallacy of sufficiency is, all else being equal, more serious than a fallacy that violates the acceptability criterion. Thus, a charge of *ad hominem* is probably a more serious charge than one of *problematic premise*. But we are speaking in general here, and you will need to consider the facts of the case in deciding how serious a fallacy charge is.

Discrimination in the sense just sketched is fundamental for the practice of cogent logical criticism. Unfortunately, the practice of discrimination, like that of sound judgment, cannot be codified in any set of rules, and nothing can substitute for sound judgment developed out of much practice.

The Principle of Logical Neutrality   The basic idea behind this principle is: Don't confuse substantive criticism with logical criticism. We don't mean to imply that there is a precise boundary between substantive criticisms and logical ones. Alas, the boundary is not easily drawn, but there are cases where the difference is clear. For instance, to reject an argument because one of its premises is problematic is to make a logical criticism of that argument; to reject it because one of its premises is false is to make a substantive criticism. Both are perfectly proper criticisms to make. The point we wish to make is that they are different types of criticism.

Let's work with the example alluded to above. The claim that a given premise is problematic is a claim about the logical status of that statement in a specified context; namely, within the argument into which it has been incorporated. To call that premise *problematic* is to point out that in this context, it fails to function adequately as a premise because it ought to have been defended but wasn't. However, that very same statement could occur in some other argument without being problematic. In saying, on the other hand, that a premise is false, we are making a statement about its relationship to the world that is independent of its occurrence in any particular argument. If the premise is false, it will presumably be false in any argument.

Consider an example from the current debate about abortion. One might challenge the position of those who favor abortion on demand by claiming that "those who support abortion on demand are guilty of bad argumentation because they assume that the fetus is not a person, but that is false." The critical point here is a substantive criticism. The critic's point is that the fetus is, in fact, a person. On the other hand, to claim that "those who support abortion on demand are guilty of bad argumentation because they assume that the fetus is not a person, but that is a *dubious assumption*," is to state a logical criticism. The critic's point is that the arguer has assumed a problematic proposition without supplying the defense that any such proposition requires. Of course, while it is possible in principle to distinguish between logical and substantive criticisms, in practice it can be difficult to do so. There are going to be gray areas, criticisms whose nature is not clearly one or the other. Our point here is that differences in philosophy or difference in values are real and important and should be labeled as such. Logic does not favor either side in this or any other debate.

The principle of logical neutrality requires that one be clear about the nature of the criticism one offers and that one not pass off substantive criticism under the guise of logical criticism.

Figure 13-2 on page 272 is a flowchart that represents our method of analysis as we have discussed it in this part of the chapter.

The Method Applied

In this section, we shall apply the five-step method to two extended arguments, one of them opposed to and the other in favor of capital punishment in Canada.

Against Capital Punishment

You have already seen an excerpt from the first argument below in the first section of Chapter 5. The entire argument is a long one but typical of the sort of passage one regularly sees and with which one needs to be able to reckon. Here is the original text, an opinion piece by University of Windsor psychology professor Lawrence LaFave that originally appeared in the *Windsor Star*. The paragraphs have been numbered to facilitate later reference.

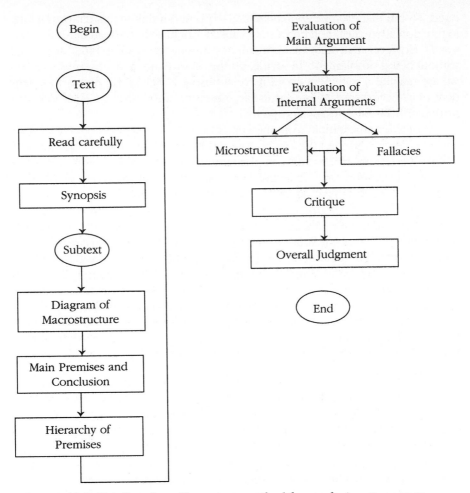

Figure 13-2 *This flowchart illustrates a method for analyzing arguments.*

7   1. Sir: The federal report by University of Montreal criminologist Dr. Ezzat Abdel Fat-
        tah (*Star*, December 16) appears to represent an excellent public service. The sta-
        tistics gathered seem to suggest that the death penalty fails to deter murder.

     2. Such findings are consistent with those in other countries, such as the United
        States. Statistics compiled in that country have provided less than no support for
        capital-punishment advocates. If anything, data there suggest that capital punish-
        ment increases the murder rate (even discounting those murders the state
        committed allegedly to deter murder). For instance, the more southern states of
        the United States, where capital punishment is still enforced, were found cursed
        with the highest murder rates.

3. Such statistics do not conclusively prove anything, based as they are on mere correlational (rather than experimentally controlled) data.

4. Since experimentally controlled data in this area are nonexistent, we are stuck with these mere correlations, but such facts do definitely seem to throw cold water on any argument that legal murder (i.e., capital punishment) acts as a deterrent to illegal murder.

5. The above is not the only kind of evidence that capital punishment fails to prevent illegal murder. For instance, some countries have publicly executed pickpockets. And while some pickpockets were being [hanged], others circulated among the observers, picking pockets.

6. Criminologists inform us that most murders are hot-blooded, and between relatives, acquaintances, or close friends. It is psychologically obvious that hot-blooded murder is impulsive, performed rashly by a person so overwhelmed by emotion that he or she has lost control (rather than by a cold-blooded calculator of the advantages and penalties involved).

7. Famous attorney Marvin Belli observed in one of his newspaper columns that of all the killers he has spoken with, none ever told him that just prior to committing the homicide he had stopped at the library to check on the penalty.

8. Imagine yourself a prisoner in the federal penitentiary in Arkansas of which criminologist Murton was warden. If you were a random prisoner there, then since only about a dozen of the several thousand convicts were on death row, chances would be a small fraction of 1 percent that you would have been sentenced for execution.

9. In that circumstance, how would you feel toward the men who, unlike yourself, were on death row? Chances are you would feel a profound sympathy for your fellow convicts and a profound hatred for a society that could do such a thing. At least that is what Warden Murton found.

10. And the reason is an axiom among social scientists: "The greater the love of the 'in' group, the greater the hatred of the 'out' group."

11. When you herd men into prisons, you tend to solidify them against a common enemy—the guards and others not in prison. If, in addition, you place a portion of them on death row, you so embitter against society the vast majority that will eventually be released that you increase the probability that when they do get out, they will commit hostile acts (including murder).

12. Sometimes after an execution, the victim is found innocent after all. Until science has found a way of restoring the dead to life, it is difficult to see how

anyone with a concept of justice should wish the legal executions of such innocent men on his conscience.

13. Who gets executed for murder is, in fact, probably much more closely associated with racial, sexual, and economic prejudice than it is with who actually commits murder.

14. In the United States, the number of poor black men who have been executed for murder is legion; the number of rich white women who have been victims of capital punishment can be counted on the fingers of one hand (and it would be erroneous to conclude that the latter group did not commit a large share of the murders).

15. The vast majority of Canadian police officers appear to favor capital punishment, especially when one of their colleagues is murdered in the line of duty. These police officers are entitled to their opinion.

16. However, the public should not take their views on this subject seriously, and the mass-communications media (with special reference to the *Windsor Star*) should not continue to give so much space to their views.

17. The reason is that it is difficult to conceive of a group more incompetent on the subject of capital punishment than police organizations. Two basic reasons for their incompetence in this area are: (a) police officers are too emotionally involved in the issue to think about it with the detachment needed for sound judgment and (b) the interpretation of the statistical and other evidence as to whether capital punishment acts as a deterrent is far beyond the modest intellectual achievements of typical police officers and their organizations.

18. Obviously, however, there are other reasons why many people favor capital punishment besides suffering under the apparent delusion that it acts as a deterrent.

19. Some people, perhaps convinced their own lives are failures, have become bloodthirsty and have a sadistic *need* for capital punishment. Having grown up in a so-called Christian culture, they may rationalize this need, convincing themselves that capital punishment acts as a deterrent.

20. Such individuals, regardless of how overwhelming the evidence becomes against capital punishment as a deterrent, will remain unconvinced.

That was Professor LaFave's argument. Here is our analysis of the entire argument:

The Synopsis.   We begin by identifying the conclusion, which is not difficult in this instance. Though much of the argument is given over to LaFave's attempt to argue that capital punishment is not a deterrent, the reasoning in paragraphs 18 and 19 makes sense only if we suppose LaFave to be against capital punishment, period. But LaFave's article was published in a Canadian paper for a Canadian audience. As the overall conclusion, therefore, we have, "Capital punishment should not be allowed in Canada." The bulk of this passage, paragraphs 1-11, deals with the question of deterrence. Here, LaFave develops two lines of argument. In paragraphs 1-4, he argues against the idea that capital punishment is a deterrent, using statistical grounds. In paragraphs 5-11, he offers us what is, in effect, a psychological argument for the same point. In paragraphs 12-14, the author attempts to show that a system of capital punishment will have undesirable consequences (in 12, he argues that innocent persons may be put to death; in 13 and 14, he argues that capital punishment is inequitably applied in practice). In 15-17 (the part we have seen before), LaFave attempts to defend his position by anticipating the objection that the police favor capital punishment. He tries to show that this is not a strong objection. In paragraphs 18-20, LaFave seems to be trying to take the ground out from beneath alternative arguments that would favor capital punishment.

Identification of the Main Premises.   The macrostructure of this argument may be seen in Figure 13-3. From this diagram, we can extract the main premises.

Figure 13-3 *A diagram of the macrostructure of the argument on capital punishment.*

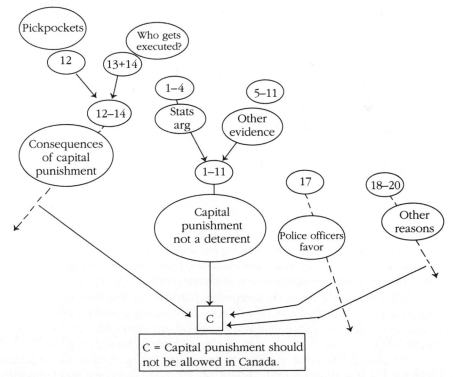

8   *P1*: Capital punishment is not a deterrent to murder. (paragraphs 1-11)

P2: A system of capital punishment has undesirable consequences. (paragraphs 12-14)

P3: The fact that police officers are in favor of capital punishment is not a good reason for having capital punishment. (paragraphs 15-17)

P4: Other reasons given for capital punishment are not good ones. (paragraphs 18-20)

Notice that we have indicated in parentheses beside each premise where in the original text of the argument we have drawn that premise from.

Hierarchy of Premises.   We place *P1* at the top of the hierarchy. LaFave devotes well over half of his argument to attempting to establish this premise, so it is given strong emphasis. Moreover, the issue of deterrence tends to dominate the debate so that if LaFave makes a strong case for his claim that capital punishment is not a deterrent, then his argument has force.

If we look to the criterion of weight rather than emphasis, we place *P4* next in the hierarchy. For in this part of the argument, LaFave proposes to show that other reasons given for capital punishment also fail. In combination with *P1*, *P4* makes a strong case. The next slot in the hierarchy belongs, we think, to *P2*. If there are good reasons for a particular policy, then its having undesirable consequences may just be an effect we have to live with. If, as LaFave alleges, there aren't good reasons, then the presence of undesirable consequences is a good, if subsidiary, reason for not adopting the particular policy. The last slot in the hierarchy goes here to *P3*. True, LaFave does give this branch of argument more than the cursory treatment given to *P4*. However, the weight of this premise is debatable. Even if it is true, as LaFave alleges, that we should not take the views of police officers with any great degree of seriousness, still, accepting this doesn't advance us markedly toward the conclusion. As we see it, then, the hierarchy of premises is:

9   *P1*: Deterrence argument

P4: Dismissal of other reasons

P2: Argument from consequences

P3: Opposition by police argument

We will evaluate the internal arguments in this order.

Evaluation of the Argument.   The main premises all pass the relevance test. Moreover, all of the main premises are argued for. Thus the only question that remains is whether *P1-P4* provide sufficient grounds for the conclusion. And we have already answered that question in constructing the hierarchy of the premises: if *P1*, *P4*, *P2*, and *P3* prove acceptable, then LaFave will have given a strong argument for his position. But he will need a strong argument for *P4* because in effect, he needs to convince us that there aren't any better reasons that he can't handle. However, we find the main argument here to be a strong one.

To evaluate internal arguments, we begin by inspecting the argument given for the first premise in the hierarchy, *P1*. Here there are two supporting arguments. The first one, paragraphs 1-4, is based on statistical grounds. We think that this argument is well turned out, properly qualified (LaFave grants that statistical arguments aren't conclusive in 3 but points out in 4 that we cannot have experimentally controlled data).

The second argument, paragraphs 5-11, is not as easy to characterize but is, broadly speaking, an empirical one, with three branches: In paragraph 5, LaFave claims that in cases where capital punishment was used against pick-pockets, it failed as a deterrent (implying that a fortiori, it will fail to deter murderers); in paragraphs 6 and 7, he argues that capital punishment doesn't deter the most common form of murder—hot-blooded murder; and in paragraphs 8-11, LaFave tries to turn the argument around, arguing that in fact, capital punishment acts as an *incentive* to murder.

The argument in paragraph 5 is undocumented and undeveloped, so we will be charitable and treat it as a colorful anecdote.

The argument in paragraphs 6 and 7 is another matter. Here, LaFave seems to be presenting a serious argument based on psychological reasoning. We want to examine the reasoning here more closely, and so we will take a look at microstructure. The basic assertions here are these:

10

1. Most murders are committed in hot blood (so we are informed by criminologists). (paragraph 6)

2. Murders committed in hot blood are rash, impulsive, uncontrolled. (paragraph 6)

3. Such murders are not committed by individuals who stop to weigh the advantages and penalties. (paragraphs 6 and 7)

The implicit conclusion to this line of reasoning must be that capital punishment would not be a deterrent in most cases. To reach this conclusion, LaFave must be making this assumption: Capital punishment can serve as a deterrent only if people consider the consequences of their actions prior to acting. Here we think LaFave has made a *dubious assumption*. One could argue that the threat of death serves to influence behavior by encouraging people to develop habits of action that comply with the law. The development of such habits would override momentary irrational impulses so that people would not have to stop and think. Since such a teleology strikes us as plausible and is not ruled out, and since the assumption mentioned above is necessary for LaFave's conclusion to follow, we charge LaFave with *dubious assumption* here. Because this is a serious charge against an argument which supports the premise highest in the hierarchy, we take charge of *dubious assumption* to constitute a *major* criticism of the argument.

Next, we review the argument in paragraphs 8-10. Here LaFave argues that if we have a system of capital punishment, then we may expect that prisoners who are released from prisons in which there are murderers on death row will be motivated to commit hostile acts (including murder) when they are released. The problem with this argument is that it turns on an empirical point: whether released prisoners (from certain institutions) do exhibit the tendency to commit hostile acts, including murder. The only compelling way to shore up this point is by providing the evidence, and since LaFave is clearly familiar with the body of evidence (paragraphs 1 and 2 make this clear), he should have called attention to it here. As it stands, this argument is based on inadequate evidence and hence is guilty of *problematic premise*. This is a relatively weak fallacy charge, but since it is directed at a fairly crucial part of his argument, it is a criticism of moderate strength.

The next branch of argument to be considered is *P4*. Here, LaFave purports to argue that other reasons (beside the deterrence argument) for favoring capital punishment are not good ones. The argument suffers from two flaws: *ambiguity* and *ad hominem*. We can draw a bead on the breakdown here if we note, first, that LaFave does not follow through on his promised line of reasoning. What we expect him to do is confront other arguments cited in support of capital punishment, especially the argument of retributive justice; that is, that to balance the scales of justice, a life must be taken in compensation. LaFave needs to address this argument because it functions prominently in the reasoning of those who advocate capital punishment. Instead, LaFave "psychoanalyzes" those who oppose his view. Instead, that is, of showing where their arguments break down, he diagnoses his opponents and calls them bloodthirsty and sadistic. Their arguments can be appraised without reference to the psychological states of those who advance them. LaFave commits *ad hominem* when he makes this irrelevant attack on the persons of those who defend capital punishment. Since *ad hominem* is a violation of relevance, this is a serious fallacy charge. And since this part of LaFave's argument is crucial to its success, this criticism is a strong one.

This leads to a second point. LaFave shifts the meaning of "reason" here. In paragraph 18, we suppose him to mean "reasons" in the sense of "logical reasons" for favoring capital punishment. Instead, in paragraphs 19 and 20, he speculates about psychological reasons why someone might favor capital punishment. The argument exploits this ambiguity, commits *ad hominem* in so doing, and thus fails to convince. We consider *ambiguity* a violation of the relevance criterion and so, once again, because this branch of the argument is crucial, we regard this, too, as a strong criticism.

The next premise to be considered is *P2*. Two criticisms emerge when we consider the argument given for that premise. First, we note that LaFave's premises refer us to raw numbers, whereas the implicit conclusion must be taken as referring to ratios or percentages. It may be true that the number of poor black men executed vastly exceeds the number of rich white women executed. But that may be explained simply by the fact that the number of poor black men who commit murder (and thereby become "eligible" for capital punishment) vastly exceeds the number of rich white women who commit murder. Absolute numbers are insufficient; we need percentages to support the claim of inequity. Hence LaFave's argument is guilty of *hasty conclusion. Hasty conclusion* is a fallacy charge of medium strength, and we are now at the third level of the hierarchy, which surely means that this is not a criticism one would want to feature too prominently in one's critique. (If, as seems likely, the additional evidence is readily provided, this charge of fallacy is not terribly damaging and would not have a prominent place in our write-up.)

Second, LaFave's data are taken from the United States, whereas his conclusion (if it is to yield evidence for the main conclusion) must be taken to apply to Canada. The assumption necessary here—that if capital punishment is unfairly applied in the United States, it must also be unfairly applied in Canada—strikes us as dubious. Though it would be naive to think that racism did not exist in Canada, it has never been shown to exist on the scale or in the intensity found in the United States. Hence LaFave's argument is guilty here of *dubious assumption*. This seems to be a moderate criticism.

Finally, we come to the argument for *P3*. On the surface, it looks as though LaFave commits *ad hominem* by attacking police officers rather than their position. However, in this dialectical context, the issue is credibility and that is what LaFave seems to question. He cites two reasons: (a) police officers are too emotionally involved in the issue and (b) they lack the competence to interpret the statistical evidence. As to the first reason, it remains to be shown that the police are so deeply involved in the issue that their capacity to think about it objectively has been impaired. As to the second reason, many police officers belong to unions or associations that have in their employ persons capable of handling statistical evidence. LaFave has given us two instances of *problematic premise* here.

We have completed our inspection of the entire argument and must now put our criticisms into an order reflecting our judgment of their relative importance, concluding with our overall judgment on the argument.

Critique.   Though LaFave's argument is not without its strong points, particularly in paragraphs 1-4, he has not presented a strong argument for his position. The main argument is solid, but there are logical defects in each of the four branches supporting the four main premises. In particular, the argument for *P1* (the claim that capital punishment is not a deterrent) suffers from both *dubious assumption* and *hasty conclusion*. These charges strike at the core of his argument and represent the strongest criticisms of his position. The next strongest criticisms are the charges of *ad hominem* and *ambiguity* in connection with *P4*, LaFave's attempt to dismantle other arguments for capital punishment. For his argument to be successful, he must address himself to substantive versions of these ancillary types of argument for capital punishment. The argument for *P2* has two flaws, one of which may be easily repaired; but the other (the assumption about the comparability of the United States and Canada) is not as easily remedied. The criticisms of his argument for *P3* (against police officers) are the least damaging, but this particular argument appears to be the least effective of the lot. All in all, then, LaFave's argument needs fairly extensive repair before it can be considered compelling.

For Capital Punishment

Having just subjected one possible case against capital punishment to criticism, and with the spirit of logical neutrality and balance to uphold, we examine an argument for the use of capital punishment in the United States.

11   1. The debate over capital punishment shares with discussions of other life-and-death decisions (those involved in abortion, for example, and those involved in euthanasia) the emotional tensions that surround extreme and irreversible acts. Carrying out a death penalty, undergoing an abortion, and unplugging a life-support system are all acts that do not permit any further relationships with the victim. Capital punishment differs from abortion and euthanasia, however, in that it is intended as a punishment. Neither the unborn fetus nor the terminally ill patient has committed a crime. Indeed, opponents of abortion and opponents of euthanasia commonly argue that these procedures are unjustifiable because the victims are innocent. They have not, in any sense, deserved punishment. People who argue in favor of abortion or euthanasia are sometimes invited to put themselves in the position of the victims of these procedures.

2. Opponents of capital punishment also invite those who argue in favor of it to put themselves in the position of the condemned man (it is usual to leave women out of consideration, and in fact far fewer women than men have been executed in the United States). This tactic, however, steers us past the point. For what is at issue is the guilt of the condemned man, and the emotional repugnance we may feel at being asked to sit on death row ignores the fact that *we* are not guilty.

3. Similarly off base is the widely used argument that capital punishment carries a terrible risk that innocent persons may be executed. It is argued that the possibility that one innocent person might be falsely condemned is enough, in itself, to make capital punishment illegitimate. For how can society compensate an innocent victim for its error?

4. But the issue is not whether capital punishment can or cannot be imposed without error. It is, rather, whether any person justly convicted of a capital crime should or should not be executed.

5. Since the death penalty cannot be regarded as a form of chastisement or rehabilitation, the heart of the debate may be located in the issue of its value as a deterrent. I set aside as irrelevant the question of retribution because torture is probably superior to execution as a means of paying back the offender. Torture, it might be noted, is the obvious target of the Constitution's objections to "cruel and unusual punishment."

6. As for the deterrent value of the death penalty, one must have recourse to statistical data. The issue is not whether some people may be deterred from committing capital crimes by the threat of execution, for everybody knows that some people are *not* deterred. The issue is whether you and I are deterred.

7. Here a comparison is needed. We need to consider the number of capital crimes, such as murder, committed annually, on a per capita basis, in a country

that is, in many respects, similar to the United States but has a different approach to the issue of capital punishment. Here, a good choice is England.

8. The population of England is about 42 million, or roughly one-fifth that of the United States. Between 1968 and 1977, England averaged about thirty-six murders per year, while the United States figure was about 5,000. In other words, the rate of murder in England during this decade was less than one twenty-fifth that of the United States.

9. Both countries had, during this period, a system of law that included capital punishment for murder. But in the United States, no condemned person was in fact executed between 1968 and 1977 except Gary Gilmore, who refused to appeal his conviction and, in fact, demanded that he be executed according to law. In England, by contrast, convicted murderers move speedily toward execution.

10. One might consider here the contrast between English and American laws on guns. The advocates of strict gun control in the United States are fond of connecting the relatively low rate of murder in England with England's very strict enforcement of laws respecting the registration and bearing of firearms. They argue that this enforcement protects the public.

11. But if this argument holds water, then surely it must follow that strict enforcement of laws respecting capital crimes should also yield results. One recalls how quickly hijackings ceased when sky marshals were shown ready to shoot skyjackers.

12. What we have now is a system that makes no sense. Knowing that they will, in practice, be condemned to life imprisonment, criminals convicted of capital crimes are ready to kill in order to stay out of prison. Those who are finally caught are forced to suffer the torture of lifelong incarceration. Meanwhile, the public receives no protection.

13. This is, indeed, "cruel and unusual punishment."

Here is our step-by-step analysis:

The Synopsis.   Although the author nowhere explicitly states the conclusion, we infer from paragraphs 5, 11, and 12 that she favors capital punishment. The first paragraph serves to provide lift-off for the argument, the writer comparing capital punishment with other life-and-death issues (euthanasia and abortion) and then distinguishing it from them. Its purpose seems to be to detach the opposition to abortion and euthanasia from the opposition to capital punishment. This paragraph is largely extraneous to the author's argument. In the second paragraph, the writer identifies a possible objection to her conclusion (put yourself in the position of the condemned) and then tries to defuse the objection (we are not guilty). In the third paragraph, the writer anticipates another common objection to her conclusion (there is a risk that an innocent person will be executed). This objection is countered in the fourth paragraph, where the author claims that this objection is beside the point. In the fifth paragraph, the writer sets forth the claim that is fundamental to her strategy: that the crucial issue in the debate is deterrence. In paragraphs 6-9, the writer presents facts which, she believes, show that capital punishment is a deterrent. In paragraphs 12 and 13, the writer tries to show that the absence of capital punishment has unacceptable consequences (the public is not protected, and criminals are subjected to cruel and unusual punishment), thereby arguing indirectly for a change in the present situation.

Identification of the Main Premises.   Our synopsis reveals four main branches of this argument as shown in Figure 13-4. From this diagram, we can read off the main premises.

12   P1: The argument against capital punishment based on sympathy for the criminal is ineffective. (paragraph 2)
P2: The argument against capital punishment that an innocent person might be executed is irrelevant. (paragraphs 3-4)
P3: The crucial issue is whether or not capital punishment is a deterrent. (paragraph 5)
P4: Capital punishment is a deterrent. (paragraphs 6-9 and 10-11)
P5: The lack of capital punishment creates risks for citizens and causes cruel and unusual punishment. (paragraphs 12-13)

Figure 13-4 *Four main branches of the argument for capital punishment.*

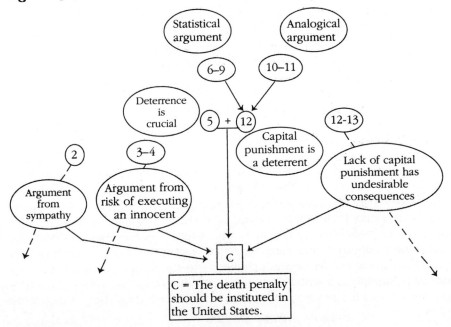

Hierarchy of Premises.   It is evident that for the author's purposes, *P*3 is the most important premise. Were it rejected, the argument would lose its main pillar of support. Second place in the hierarchy goes to *P*4, which itself is supported by two different arguments: the statistical argument and the analogical one. The author's emphasis on this line of argument is clear from the amount of space given to it. The next most important branch is that developed in *P*5 because the consequences named here are clearly unacceptable. Finally, and of coordinate (though little) importance are *P*1 and *P*2. The author's treatment of these arguments is sparse, and even if these arguments failed, there might be other (and stronger) arguments against capital punishment. Hence our hierarchy is:

5   *P*3: Deterrence argument is crucial.
      *P*4: Capital punishment does deter.
      *P*5: Lack of capital punishment has undesirable consequences.
      *P*1-*P*2: Sympathy and innocence.

Evaluation of the Argument.   The premises are all relevant to the conclusion and, taken together, would, if acceptable, provide enough evidence for the conclusion. Hence we turn our attention to the internal arguments for these premises, beginning at the top.

The argument for *P*3 is not developed in great detail, as the author has chosen to deal almost peremptorily with the other reason often brought forth to justify capital punishment: retributive justice (clearly the author is correct to set aside rehabilitation). The author's argument is an odd one, and we would ponder it at length if it were necessary. But since so much of recent debate has centered on the issue of deterrence, it seems a better use of time and energy to look carefully at the argument for *P*4.

The author presents two arguments for this premise. The first, drawn from statistical data, compares murder rates during the period 1968-1977 in the United States (where only one person was executed) and in England (where, she alleges, "convicted murderers move speedily toward execution"). Alas, our author has the facts quite wrong, for no one has been executed in England since 1965, when capital punishment was made illegal by an Act of Parliament. We recognize that this is a substantive rather than a logical criticism of the argument. However, it puts the argument in serious straits because it is not one that the author can readily repair. The comparison with England will have to be dropped. And if the writer wishes to offer a cogent statistical argument, she will have to offer a much more complete (and accurate) set of statistics compiled from both countries that do, and countries that do not, have capital punishment on the books. Since *P*4 is crucial, and since it turns out to be false, this constitutes a major criticism of the argument.

Ordinarily we would recommend that one continue the evaluation. But since the criticism appears disabling, it is questionable how much is to be gained by extending the critique beyond the discovery of what looks like a grievous criticism.

Critique. This argument has to be rejected. Its most important claim (that the deterrence argument is crucial) is not well argued, and the most crucial empirical claim is false. This is not a strong argument. Had the first criticism not been so telling, we would have gone on to inspect the rest of the argument because it is always possible that the criticisms can be rebutted and that our sense of discrimination has failed us, the result being that a more important criticism is placed further down the ladder than it should be. And we should mention that the purpose of criticism is not to shred an argument but to offer enlightened criticism and thereby enrich the dialectical process of the exchange. But in this case, we have encountered a substantive criticism of such magnitude that it damages the argument beyond repair. Though this will happen from time to time, our general advice is that one should carry out the process of evaluation to its conclusion.

Conclusion

The index of success we have in mind for this book is not whether it teaches you to spot fallacies, bad news reporting, or advertising gimmicks. Being able to do those things, while certainly not *un*important, is just a means to an end—the end being to become a better and more reflective consumer of attempts at persuasion. If this text makes you more vigilant and, at the same time, improves your ability to detect the various problems that occur in the myriad types of persuasive attempt we spoke of at the beginning of the text, then it will achieve everything we can reasonably expect it to.

EXERCISES

Directions: Use the five-step method to evaluate the following extended arguments. The first two are shorter and more straightforward than the last two. The third argument has already been seen in abbreviated form. And you have seen the argument to which the fourth exercise is responding: the LaFave letter on capital punishment found on pages 272 to 274.

1. *Background*: This letter deals with a proposal that a fine be imposed on the owners of dogs who relieve themselves on public property. The writer objects, saying:
   a. Why pick on dogs? What about other nuisances on city property? The suggestion made by the Parks Board that owners who allow their dogs to relieve themselves in the park pay a fine is ridiculous.
   b. Have they forgotten that the dog is an animal and, as such, cannot ask its master to "go to the washroom"? What is the owner to do? The owner pays a license fee for the privilege of keeping a dog. He also observes the law that forbids him to let his dog run loose.
   c. In taking his dog for a walk on a leash, he is within the law. The fact that the dog might have to perform a natural function is automatically included under the law because of the dog's status as an animal.

2. *Background*: The Okanagan Valley is a fruit-producing region located in the province of British Columbia in Canada. A letter about the health hazards associated with pesticides stated:

   a. It seems to me that people are going too far when they claim that it is not safe to eat apples and pears because pesticide sprays have been used on them.

   b. What they do not seem to realize is that sprays against fruit pests (the codling moth and the pear psylla, for instance) have been used in the Okanagan Valley for at least fifty years. If sprays were dangerous, it would surely have shown up by now in Okanagan medical records. I was born in the Okanagan Valley and lived there for thirty years, and I, my daughter, and my granddaughter seem quite healthy. I see no evidence of genetic damage.

   c. If sprays had not been used during all those years, the insects would have taken over, and there would now be no apples or pears, or else wormy ones. The entomologists are trying to find alternate ways of controlling insect pests, but entomologists are hard to come by.

   d. I suggest that an orchardist using spray is no more dangerous to the human race than is the automobile, which not only pollutes the air but uses a vital resource that is fast disappearing.

3. *Background*: In the late 1970s, the United States government passed a law making 55 miles per hour the maximum on all interstate highways. The stated purposes of the legislation were to conserve fuel and to save lives. The argument below is adapted from "Taking Stock of Speed," an opinion piece that appeared in *En Route* magazine, distributed by Air Canada. Len Coates argues against the speed-limit legislation.

   a. The time has come to repeal the 55-mile-per-hour speed limit. This backward step was originally justified in the name of saving lives and conserving energy. In fact, it accomplishes neither.

   b. True, the 55-mile-per-hour speed limit does conserve energy. But it does not conserve all that much energy. Indeed, properly inflated tires do more than the 55-mile-per-hour limit to conserve energy. That was the conclusion drawn by Charles Lave, a member of the Institute for Transportation Studies at the University of California, in a 1978 study using United States government figures.

   c. Furthermore, lowering the speed limit is an expensive way to save lives. It takes 102 man-years or $1.3 million to save one life by lowering the speed limit. There are cheaper ways to save lives. Smoke detectors, properly installed in houses, would save lives at the cost of $800,000 per life saved. Making dialysis machines more readily available would save lives at a cost of $600,000 a life.

   d. Not only does the lower speed limit not accomplish its objectives, but the cost of the lower speed limit in wasted time is enormous. Everyone knows that trucks run more efficiently at 70 miles per hour than at 50. And look at the time that your average business executive loses. Compare the time it takes to drive, say, 100 miles at 55 miles per hour rather than 70 miles per hour. It comes to almost thirty minutes of wasted time, a 27 percent differential. And I don't need to remind you that in business, time is money.

   e. The only significant opposition to raising the speed limit comes from bleeding hearts and professional do-gooders like Ralph Nader and company.

   f. The damage to the human spirit that the slowdown causes is even greater. Speed is what the automobile is all about. Speed is what this society is all about. Slowing down is what societies and nations do before they die. Surely the United States does not have this kind of death wish, does it?

   g. Finally, isn't it curious that the current economic malaise [the reference here is to the recession of 1982–1983] began just after the imposition of the 55 mile-per-hour limit?

   h. All in all, then, it is evident that the law making the speed limit 55 miles per hour should be repealed.

4. *Background*: This letter to the *Windsor Star* is a response to Professor LaFave's letter, analyzed earlier in this chapter:

   a. The logic of the professor's argument escapes me completely, and being a person of "modest intellectual achievements," a typical police officer, I defer to his superior intelligence.

   b. The first portion of Professor LaFave's letter indicates his knowledge of the United States and its customs; his lack of knowledge of Canadian police officers is apparent in the latter part of his letter and is exceeded only by his colossal vanity. After permitting police officers the luxury of having an opinion, he then instructs the public and the news media to ignore these opinions: "The Lord giveth, and the Lord taketh away."

   c. Admittedly risking the ire of Professor LaFave, I nevertheless would like to correct several of his mistaken assumptions regarding police officers (with whom it is glaringly evident he has had no social contact) and their views toward capital punishment. No rational person expects any punishment to halt murder, particularly the "hot-blooded" type "between relatives, acquaintances, or close friends." However, any experienced police officer knows that capital punishment is a definite deterrent to murder committed during the commission of another crime (robbery, rape, and so on).

   d. How do I know this? From more than twenty years of contact with criminals who have little, if any, knowledge of psychology but who realize that once capital punishment has been utilized, they have no hope of a life sentence, which today means a parole after seven to ten years and weekend passes in the interim.

   e. The murders that concern most police officers are murders committed for profit or to eliminate witnesses by cold-blooded professional criminals. And these are the murders that are increasing and will continue to increase until, heaven forbid, our country can be statistically compared to the United States.

   f. I can't offer a remedy for this situation, but possibly the professor, with his educational background, can. In fact, he may have offered a remedy in his letter, but if he did, it was hidden in his verbiage. Like most psychologists, he is familiar with the human mind as portrayed in his textbooks, but he fails to realize that there are, in every community, persons to whom the life of another means absolutely nothing, to whom several years in prison also means nothing, and whose only interest is in furthering their own ends.

   g. The value of capital punishment as a deterrent may be arguable, but there is no argument that today's "life sentences" are any deterrent. Our main concern is the safety of the public in our country, and we ask only that punishment of some deterrent value be incorporated into our laws.

   h. While Professor LaFave cannot "conceive of a group more incompetent on the subject of capital punishment than police organizations," I have no difficulty at all and suggest an organization composed of psychology professors of Lawrence LaFave's caliber.

Answers to Selected Exercises

Chapter 1

1. No argument. An opinion: a claim about the use of the word "basically" that is asserted without defense.

2. An argument. Conclusion: "If you are getting a refund, you should file your tax return early." The other claim, "If you file your return early and you're getting a refund, you'll have the money sooner to spend or invest," is clearly a reason supporting the conclusion.

6. An explanation. Weschler is explaining why he found the turbulent political events in Poland surprising. His explanation: Poland's material situation seemed to have improved dramatically since his last visit.

10. Proto-argument. The claim is unclear. It may mean that it is a sin to be homosexual (that is, to find only members of one's own sex sexually attractive), or it may mean that to have homosexual sex is a sin. It may mean both. The support is unclear. Is the note that "the vast majority of people once believed the same thing" a reason or just a historical observation? Where does the alleged unchangeableness of morality fit into the reasoning? Is homosexual activity wrong just because the lovers are not married? We don't think the author would think a homosexual marriage would justify sex between the partners.

    The elements of an argument are here, but until the writer has sorted out his or her thinking, it lacks the real structure of an argument. Hence it is a proto-argument.

Chapter 2

A. Passage from Chapter 1 Exercises

2. The statements:

    1. If you are getting a refund, you should file your tax return early.

    2. If you file your tax return early when you're getting a refund, you'll have the money sooner to spend or invest.

Tree diagram: 2
                        ↓
                        1

Missing premise:

a. It's good to spend or invest your tax refund sooner rather than later.

Revised tree diagram: $\overline{2 + a}$
                              ↓
                              1

B. Passage from Chapter 2 Exercises

  1. The statements:

    1. To fear death is to think ourselves wise without being wise.

    2. To fear death is to think that we know what we do not know.

    3. No one knows whether death may not be the greatest good that can happen to man.

Initial tree diagram: 3
                              ↓
                              2
                              ↓
                              1

Missing premise (goes with 3 to support 2):

a. To fear death is to think that death is a bad thing.

Revised tree diagram: $\overline{3 + a}$
                               ↓
                               2
                               ↓
                               1

Chapter 3

A. Exercises for evaluating arguments

  1. A good argument?

  2. Think about the sufficiency requirement.

  3. Think about the relevancy requirement here. How relevant is the comparison between offering a free trip to Disneyland and offering arms for hostages?

  4. Both of these assertions seem extremely controversial and bereft of support; think about the acceptability requirement.

Chapter 4

  4. Harris commits *problematic premise* at least twice in this argument. His claim that the first-degree murderer is least likely to repeat but more likely to repent is an important piece of evidence for the conclusion, but it lacks any defense and it is far from obviously true. He should have defended this claim. The next claim is also without support and ought to have been defended.

11. The arguer commits the fallacy of *irrelevant reason*. In order to defend the claim that the prosecutor is making a mistake in laying the charge, the arguer, in effect, puts forth the claim that the lady in question feels guilty and bad enough about what happened. (How this is known, we are not inclined to worry about.) This reason is irrelevant: The feelings and attitudes of those who have been involved in an incident like this have no bearing on whether a crime has been committed. The prosecutor must make the determination on the basis of the evidence. Hence the reason here is irrelevant to the conclusion.

Chapter 5

2. Talbert is guilty of an *ad hominem* here. The arguer has made an accusation against the columnist, in effect charging that Talbert had a false sense of self-importance. This is a criticism of him personally, but since his personality is part of the work he does in writing such a column, it is a legitimate target of criticism. Instead of responding to the arguer's criticism/argument, which he could have done by, for example, denying the charge, admitting the charge, or asking for examples so he could think about it, Talbert instead attacks the arguer personally. Talbert's comment implies that because the arguer chose to use a pseudonym, he (or she) has some psychiatric disorder. But this is an irrelevant attack upon the person of the arguer. His position can well be evaluated without any reference to his person. For the issue is whether or not Talbert is writing the kind of column he is supposed to be writing—and that has nothing to do with the psychiatric health of the author of this letter.

5. The newspaper's response is a classic case of *straw person*. The claim to which he or she is responding is that the media overload on bad news (which has certain consequences for the city) and that they often fail to report good news. The spokesperson extrapolates from this claim and imputes to the arguer the view that the media should "stop reporting crime" and that this alone will result in "a tremendous infusion of business" and the solution of the problems. But that was not the view taken by the critic, who was complaining about the ratio of negative to positive stories. The spokesperson then attacks this view as naive and as wishful thinking, which of course it is. But the original criticism was not at all naive. A great many critics have made this very claim. Unfortunately, when criticized in this way, the news media tend to become defensive, hiding behind distortions, as this newspaper did, or behind clichés like "Don't shoot the messenger" or "We don't make the news; we only report it." One would imagine that somewhere there is a more adequate defense of news-media practice, which must perforce include overlooking some, indeed many, good stories.

Chapter 6

5. This letter verges on a proto-argument because the author does not make explicit where she is going with the points she makes. Still, there is argumentative direction. A comparison is made between correcting the past injustices done to native peoples in North America by European invaders and correcting long-ago injustices to ancient Britons by various waves of invasions from northern Europe (by Angles and Saxons, then by Vikings and Jutes, later by Normans). The arguer seems to be claiming that if native North Americans should be compensated for the injustices of white European invasions, then original Britons should be compensated for the injustices of northern European invasions (that's the point of the rhetorical question). The latter seems silly

because there is no way to identify those dispossessed. So applying the principle of charity, we take that to be the arguer's point: Just as the latter compensation is absurd, so is the former. So we take the writer to be giving an argument from analogy to show that it makes no sense to compensate native peoples in North America for the past injustices of white European invaders.

The absurdity of compensating early Britons is due to the inability to identify those who suffered; their descendants have long ago been absorbed into the vast pool of later generations. But it is not so clear that we cannot identify a class of people in North America who continue to suffer from the injustices of the European invasion and land-grab. For example, native North Americans were dispossessed and required to live on reservations; their way of life was made impossible in most cases by the settlement of the wilderness and the extinction of the species of animals they relied on (for example, the buffalo). The list could go. In many cases, descendants of these early tribes *can* be identified, and in many cases these descendants continue to exist in deprived circumstances. So there is a group of people living today who continue to be disadvantaged as a result of the white European invasion and whose condition might be improved by compensation.

We conclude that the reasons why compensation makes no sense for early Britons does not clearly apply to native North Americans, and so the argument from analogy against compensating the latter does not succeed. We charge the fallacy of *faulty analogy*.

8. This news story, reporting statistics on the leading causes of death in the United States in 1990, contains no argument: No point is made; no conclusions are drawn. Obviously, then, there is no fallacious argument.

9. The minister was arguing that rock 'n' roll is a bad thing because it can be harmful—it can cause not only fornication but fornication that is careless about the consequences. He is giving an argument to a general causal claim. One piece of evidence is an alleged connection between listening to rock and having sex: Of 1,000 girls who became pregnant out of wedlock, 984 had sex while rock music was being played. Another is the hypothesis offered to explain this connection: There is a rhythm of sexual arousal to our bodies that responds to the rhythm of rock music.

How the minister could know that of a sample of 1,000 girls who became pregnant out of wedlock, 984 had sex while rock was playing is puzzling. This is not the type of data one hears about, and the sample is extraordinarily large; so we contend that the minister owes readers the basis for this claim: We thus charge *problematic premise*.

But even if we accept this data, there are problems with the evidence for the causal claim. First, the data does not support a correlation; we need to know that when rock music was *not* being played, the incidence of sex was significantly lower. The music might have accompanied all the activity of young people (we speculate that it did, as it does today), so the fact that it accompanied their sexual activity is, in and of itself, no evidence of its playing a causal role in their having sex or in their failing to make use of birth control devices. Second, even if there were a correlation between rock and sex, the hypothesis might explain the increased incidence of sex but not of *irresponsible* sex. If a potential partner said, "I think I'm HIV positive," we suspect that the rhythmic pressures of rock 'n' roll would not prevail over the inclination to avoid exposure to the AIDS virus, which would show that the music alone is not the determinant of irresponsible sex. We conclude that the minister also commits *questionable cause* in his argument.

Chapter 7

5. We're probably in the minority, but we have trouble understanding just what is meant these days by the term "parameters." It seems to have become a kind of all-purpose term referring to what? boundaries? conditions? limits? aspects? values? We're inclined to call this term *vague*, because we aren't sure what the "parameters of a literary genre" means. Further, the second reason given ("sets the tone for a new trend by drawing on . . .") also strikes us as *vague*. We don't know what the author is saying. It's not because we don't know the meaning of the individual's words but because when we put them together, we find ourselves perplexed.

11. We think this author is *equivocating* on the word "discrimination." Certainly in one sense of the word, the proposal would discriminate against smokers, but this kind of discrimination is very different from the kind referred to in the last paragraph. The discrimination shown by the Nazi government against Jews belongs to a completely different class; it was morally horrendous. It would be difficult to put the restrictions on smoking in public places in that category.

    There is something inappropriate about the writer's claim that smoking is "my own private business . . . even in a restaurant." On almost any reading of the term "private," this claim seems false. Certainly the arguer owes us justification for the application of "private" here. We would call it a *freeloading term*.

Chapter 8

1. We take it that this author is using a short form of the slippery-slope argument. The immediate conclusion is that there will have to be a reduction in the number of births, either voluntarily or enforced. The argument as follows runs: If such a reduction does not occur, the result will be (in a few steps: "before long") a situation in which people struggle with one another for bare survival ("the survival of the fittest"), which was the prehuman situation (and as such, presumably, is undesirable); therefore, such a reduction in the number of births should occur.

    None of the causal steps is spelled out, and we question whether the causal necessity envisaged is defensible. It strikes us that prosperous nations could organize food production and distribution much more effectively than they do now, and if that is so, we could feed a much larger world population. Also, since security and plenty seem to be accompanied by decreases, not increases, in the birthrate, increases in the standard of living in third-world countries can be expected to be accompanied by declining birthrates, without any special attention devoted to "limiting" the number of births. For these reasons, we think there is a case of the *causal slippery-slope* fallacy in this argument.

2. We don't think the editorial is arguing that taxing "free" car washes will lead us down a causal slippery slope to taxing our dreams. But we do think it is arguing from analogy that the car-wash tax sets a precedent that has such ridiculous implications that the tax is a mistake. The *Brandon Sun* argues that if the free car-wash tax is justified, then so is a tax on savings, on do-it-yourself projects, and on private car washes—all of which it claims would be ridiculous.

    We agree that the latter would be ridiculous taxes, but are they relevantly similar to the free car wash? We take it that the Manitoba government's view is that a "free" car wash with every fill-up of gas is like a coupon, something of value given to customer to elicit their business, and that such coupons are taxable. Our savings, or the car wash you do in your driveway, are not like coupons a merchant distributes to solicit business. Hence "free" car washes are not similar in relevant respects to savings or private car washes, and so the justification for taxing the former does not apply to the latter.

The *Brandon Sun* commits *faulty analogy* by claiming a precedent that does not exist.

9. We take the letter writer to be accusing doctors who sign their letters to the editor on nonmedical matters with a kind of *improper appeal* to their own *authority*. Why would they sign "M.D." to their letters unless it was to try to add a kind of credibility to what they said? The writer jokingly invents some silly alternative possibilities to make this point. We agree. In all such cases there is a violation of the "capability" condition because the doctors by hypothesis have no special competence in the matters they are writing about. There could, in some such cases, also be a violation of the "appropriateness" condition (perhaps no appeal to authority is fitting) or the "credibility" condition (perhaps the doctor has a conflict of interest on the issue). The "consensus" condition would not apply, because since we are not talking about authorities here, we are not talking about disagreements among authorities.

Chapter 9

1. The assumption here seems to be that it is permissible to cheat in a subject that is not your major and in which you have no interest. Needless to say, the authors of this text find this *assumption dubious*.

3. This passage is not an argument; it is an explanation we found in a Canadian history textbook. Yet the assumption buried in it clearly houses an ethnocentric attitude. When colonists married Indians, they "abandon[ed] all trace of civilization" because *it is assumed*, the Indians were uncivilized. This assumption overlooks the considerable richness of the culture of the indigenous peoples of this continent, a culture most Europeans neither understood nor cared to understand. This attitude is *ethnocentric*.

Chapter 10

Here are two brief newspaper stories and our analyses of them from the point of view of a consumer of news information.

British Voters Crush the Tories

1   The governing Conservatives have wiped out in local elections and suffered a stunning defeat in a special race for a parliamentary seat, a loss that Prime Minister John Major blamed on the economy.

The landslide in Thursday's vote cut the Conservatives' majority in the 650-member House of Commons to 19.

"People feel bruised, they feel hurt," Mr. Major said on Friday, "I think they were determined to give the Government a bloody nose."

Some Conservatives were calling for him to dismiss the Chancellor of the Exchequer, Norman Lamont, whose policies have been blamed for prolonging the recession.

The Conservatives suffered a surprising defeat in a special House of Commons election in Newbury, a prosperous southern England district that the party held for 69 years. The vote was called after the incumbent died in February.

"The people of this country will give them no more credit and today they have bounced the check," David Rendel of the centrist Liberal Democrats said. He won the seat with a huge 22,055-vote majority.

In the elections for the 47 county councils of England and Wales, the Conservatives lost all but one—Buckinghamshire—of the 16 authorities they had controlled. Conservatives lost to the Labor Party and the Liberal Democrats in their traditional heartland of southern England.

In April 1992, Mr. Major led the Conservatives to their fourth successive victory in national elections on promises of an imminent economic recovery and a strong currency and a pledge not to introduce new taxes.

But the pound was devalued last September and the Government now plans to raise taxes to control a growing budget deficit. But there have been signs of a modest economic growth.

"There is a strong feeling that this is something the country didn't have to go through," Anthony King, a professor government at Essex University, said of the recession of recent years.

"This does light a fuse under the Government which will require them to change course," said a leader of the Liberal Democrats, Paddy Ashdown.

Jack Straw, the Labor Party's environmental spokesman, said the result was "a really major slap in the face of the Government."[1]

The headline "British Voters Crush the Tories" sets the reader up to interpret the recent election results as a defeat of the British Conservative government whereas, in fact, a careful reader will notice that they were just defeated in county council elections and in a special parliamentary election for one seat in the 650-member House of Commons. Someone who read the headline only would get a very misleading impression of the significance of the vote in question.

Were the British voters in these election merely voting against the government's policies, or were they voting in favor of Labor or Liberal Democrat policies? The headline and lead paragraphs suggest the former interpretation. The Tory leader, Prime Minister Major, says the voters were giving the government "a bloody nose"—that is, a minor blow, but far from fatal. The other party leaders, in the last two paragraphs, say the voters were sending a more major signal to the government. There is no indication that British voters prefer Labor or Liberal Democrat policies. Will these results cause the British government to alter its policies? Without much more information, there are insufficient grounds for speculation about Mr. Major's government's prospects in a future general election or about the direction of British economic policies.

The larger question for the American reader is whether these election are portents of a change in the governing party in Britain and, if so, what that implies for American interests. Will the Clinton administration be influenced by possible voter opposition to tax increases in Britain? Will the British experience apply in current American politics?

South Africa Is Charging Rightist in Killing

2.   A leader of the pro-apartheid Conservative Party will be charged with murder in the killing of Chris Hani, a popular black leader, the police said today.

Brig. Frans Malherbe of the police told the South African Press Association that Clive Derby-Lewis would face charges along with his wife, Gaye, and Janusz Walus, a white extremist arrested after the assassination on April 10.

---

[1] "British Voters Crush the Tories," *The New York Times*, May 9, 1993.

Mr. Derby-Lewis's wife was charged by the police last week. The couple and Mr. Walus, who was charged previously, are scheduled to appear in court Wednesday.

Mr. Hani, the head of the Communist Party and a top official of the African National Congress, was shot to death in his driveway. The police arrested Mr. Walus shortly after and said the murder weapon was found in the car he was driving.

Mr. Derby-Lewis and his wife are high-profile opponents of government reforms to end white minority rule. Mr. Derby-Lewis is a former member of Parliament for the Conservative Party.[2]

This is a follow-up story to the major event of the assassination of senior African National Congress (ANC) party official Chris Hani—a murder that jeopardized negotiations between the ANC and the white South African government.

However, this brief report tells the reader very little. The arrested man is identified as a "white extremist," as the leader of a pro-apartheid party, and as, along with his wife, "high-profile" opponents of government reforms to end white minority rule. But many key questions are not answered here. How big and influential is the party that Derby-Lewis leads? What effect will his arrest have on the opposition to reforms? What effect will it have on daily violence among blacks and between blacks and whites in South Africa? More narrowly, since Derby-Lewis is not the man previously charged and arrested with the murder weapon in his car, what is Derby-Lewis's connection with the murder? Why is he being arrested?

In sum, this brief report is a snippet of information that raises more questions than it answers and hence is not particularly useful. The student of current events would have to file this information and add it to later information in order to answer the questions it raises.

Chapter 11

We think there are sufficient analyses in the body of the text to illustrate our approach.

Chapter 12

1. *a.* Two. (1) Puerto Rico is now a commonwealth. (2) Puerto Rico should be made a state.

   b. One. There is one proposal with a two-part rider that is part of it.

   c. Two. (1) Wealthy industrialized nations should share their wealth with third-world countries. (2) Third-world countries should not have to share any increases in their wealth.

   d. One conditional proposition—as it is.

2. *a.* Premise: The Balkan states have broken up in the early 1990s. Conclusion: Nationalist loyalties are alive and well at the end of the twentieth century.

   b. Premise: Any war between nuclear powers entails the destruction of the international economy. Conclusion: No war between nuclear powers can be justified.

---

[2] "South Africa Is Charging Rightist in Killing," *The New York Times*, May 9, 1993.

     c. Premise 1: Springsteen has the best lyrics of any rock 'n' roll musician around. Premise 2: Springsteen has the best sound of any rock 'n' roll musician around. Conclusion: Springsteen is simply the best rock 'n' roll musician of the last two decades.

     d. Two positions: (1) the women's movement has made impressive gains in the past quarter century. (2) The goals of the women's movement are far from being realized.

3. *a.* Issue: noise in the library.

     Position 1: There is too much noise from students talking in the library. Position 2: There should be background music played in the library to mask the background hum of conversation. Position 3: Anyone bothered by the noise in the library should either wear earplugs or not try to work there.

Chapter 13

We think there are sufficient analyses in the body of the text to illustrate our approach.

Glossary

A priori analogy, argument from. A particular type of argument from analogy that uses or relies on the following pattern: (1) a predicate is attributed to a first thing (a person, act, event, situation, and so on) in a premise, allegedly because of a set of properties it has (the "relevant properties"); (2) in a tacit or stated premise, the first thing is alleged to be similar to a second in the respect that both have the relevant properties; and (3) the conclusion is that the same predicate is, or should be, attributed to the second thing.

Acceptability. The quality of being acceptable; a premise is acceptable when it is reasonable to expect a member of the audience to take the premise without further support; one of the three criteria that govern logically good argumentation; each premise must satisfy this requirement.

Ad hominem. The fallacy that occurs when a critic irrelevantly attacks the person of the arguer as a means of discrediting the person's argument; a relevance fallacy; closely related to *tu quoque*, *poisoning the well*, and *guilt by association*.

Adversarial context. A context in which an arguer either attacks an opposing position or defends his or her own position against an attack; often found in speeches in Congress; the natural habitat of *straw person*, *ad hominem*, and *red herring*.

Ambiguity. The situation that occurs when one word has two or more different meanings and the context does not allow you to decide which one applies. When ambiguity in an argument prevents understanding which claims are made, there exists the fallacy we term *ambiguity*.

Analogy. A comparison between two or more things that notes a likeness or similarity between or among them—some property that they share. An argument from analogy is one that relies on the similarity between two or more things to conclude that a property known or alleged to belong to one also belongs to the other. See *A priori analogy, argument from,* and *Faulty analogy*.

Anecdotal evidence. Evidence consisting of one or a small number of personal experiences. Used in an argument, it leads to a species of *hasty conclusion*.

Argument. (1) An interaction, usually verbal, usually between two or more people (though we do "argue" with ourselves), which normally is occasioned by a disagreement of opinion. In this sense, we speak of "having an argument." (2) What it is that someone makes, assembles, or formulates—the person's reasons or evidence—as grounds or support for an opinion. A collection of claims (or statements) whose purpose is to lay out a route that leads from the acceptance of a set of the claims (these are called the *premises*) to the acceptance of the remaining, target claim (which is termed the *conclusion*). In this sense, we speak of "giving an argument" or of "making" or "constructing" arguments.

Assert. *Verb*: To assert a proposition is to state it as true—to go on record as believing that it is so.

Assumption. An unexpressed element of reasoning on which the expressed elements depend for their intelligibility or truth or cogency; in argumentation, assumptions required for the conclusion to follow plausibly from the premises are known as *missing premises* (also called *unexpressed premises, unstated premises, tacit premises, or hidden premises*).

Authority. In matters of belief or opinion, a person or source whose assertion that a proposition is true is (or is taken to be) a good reason for accepting the proposition, other things being equal. In matters of conduct, a person or body with the right to command obedience. See *Improper appeal to authority*.

Background. In connection with news reports, the context of events that precede and surround a particular event reported in the news in terms of which its full meaning and significance can be understood. *Background assumptions or knowledge* are the propositions knowledge of which must be shared by an arguer and audience for an argument to make sense and for its premises to be plausible to that audience.

Balance. In news reports, the property of fairly reporting the views of all parties with an interest in a matter of dispute or controversy.

Begging the question. The fallacy that occurs when the premise of an argument is either identical to or presupposes the conclusion whose truth/acceptability it is supposed to provide evidence for; a violation of the acceptability requirement; sometimes known as *arguing in a circle* or by its Latin name, *petitio principii*. Sometimes arguments appealing to common practice or to past practice beg the question because common or past practice is used to defend conduct the continuance of which has come into question.

Case. The total of arguments directly supporting a position and arguments attempting to refute criticisms, of both the position itself and the supporting arguments.

Causal claim. A claim that one thing is a cause or the cause of another. A *general causal claim* is a claim about a (the) cause(es) of all the members of a given class or type of things, events, or states of affairs. A *particular causal claim* is a claim about a (or the) cause(es) of a particular thing, event, or state of affairs.

Causal relationship. A relationship between two sets of factors such that one is a cause of the other.

Cause. A set of factors responsible for bringing something into existence or for changing it or for preventing it.

Cause, argument from a. An argument with a causal claim as one of its premises.

Cause, argument to a. An argument with a causal claim as its conclusion.

Claim. *Noun*: A statement that someone has asserted, or put forward, as being true. Premises and conclusions of arguments are all claims. *Verb*: To put forward a statement as being true.

Common practice, argument from. An argument in which allegedly wrong or otherwise inappropriate conduct is defended on the grounds that such conduct is customary or commonly practiced. See *Improper appeal to practice*.

Completeness. The quality of a news report of providing a full-enough account to permit the reader or viewer to have a more or less accurate and rounded understanding of the event(s) reported, leaving few questions unanswered and with no puzzling assertions or unexplained technical terms.

Conclusion. In the context of arguments, a claim, or opinion, that is backed up or supported by reasons or evidence. The *main conclusion* of an argument is the final, ultimate, or overall claim that the whole body of support offered is intended to back up.

Conclusion indicators. Words or phrases that precede clauses containing conclusions. Conclusion indicators, by the same token, indicate the presence of argument in the passage, and sentences preceding the sentences in which they occur normally contain at least some of the premises of the argument in question.

Connections. What to look for when reading or viewing news reports—the ways in which the events reported relate to you and to other issues, interests, and events (past, present, and future).

Correlation. A systematic covariance between two variables (properties or events) such that the occurrence of or a change in instances of one tend to be accompanied by the occurrence of or changes in instances of the other; usually an indication of some causal relationship involving the variables, but by itself insufficient evidence for any specific causal claim.

Criterial principle. A principle that states an essential condition for something. Popular sovereignty is a criterial principle because (according to it) a law must express the will of the people in order to have legitimacy.

Demonstration. In advertising, this term refers to a test or a test situation designed to show that one product is in some way better than another. *Example*: Squeezing the water from two brands of paper towel and showing a larger pool of water under one than under the other, implying thereby that the one with the larger pool of water under it absorbs more liquid.

Dialectical aspect (or pattern) of argumentation. The feature of arguments of being akin to conversations or dialogues, with an assertor or defender of a position in one role and questioners, doubters, or challengers in another.

Dramatization. In advertising, this term refers to a situation used to show or indicate some benefit to be derived from a product. *Example*: Showing a woman with dull and messy hair, showing her using a particular hair product, and finally showing the same woman with lustrous hair, implying that the final result was due solely to use of the product being advertised.

Dubious assumption. Our name for the fallacy that occurs when an arguer uses an assumption in an argument and that assumption is debatable and undefended.

Effect. That which is caused; the consequence of a cause; in a causal relationship, the factor that results from or is brought about by the causal factors.

Egocentric thinking. The tendency to view the world through the eyes of one's own ego and its interests.

Emphasis. The term used to describe how much importance the arguer attaches to a premise in his or her argument, usually determined by the amount of space devoted to developing and supporting the premise.

Equivocation. The fallacy that occurs when the arguer shifts the meaning of a term in the course of an argument and the argument requires that the term have the same meaning throughout.

Ethnocentric thinking. The tendency to view the world through the eyes of any of various ethnological factors: sex, gender, race, religion, nationality, and so on.

Euphemism. The substitution of a mild expression for a harsher one; for example, "passed away" for "died" or "bathroom" for "toilet." See *Obfuscation*.

Extended argument. An argument that has a longer and more complicated structure than the "snippets" used in this text to illustrate fallacies.

Fallacy. As used in this text, an argument that violates one of the criteria of good argument (relevance, acceptability, and sufficiency) and is committed frequently in argumentative discourse. Be advised that there is controversy in the literature about the best way to conceptualize fallacies.

False implication. The advertising strategy of making a claim that is true but wording it so as to imply something that is false. Thus "Introducing MicroTech" implies that the product is new. By the fundamental axiom of decoding advertising prose, if the ad implies rather than states, the best inference is that what is implied is false.

Faulty analogy. Our name for an argument from a priori analogy that fails to support the conclusion either because it is false or problematic that the predicate does, in fact, apply to the first analogue because of the relevant property set or because it is false or problematic that the second analogue does, indeed, share the relevant property set.

Formal logic. The discipline that studies valid implication relationships between sets of statements or propositions or inferences from one set of statements or propositions to another where the validity of the implication or inference is determined by its logical form.

Freeloading term. The term we give to the fallacy of using in an argument a term with a definite positive or negative evaluative component without providing sufficient justification of that embedded evaluation.

Genetic fallacy. A variation of *ad hominem* in which the arguer attempts to discredit the argument by discrediting its source or origin.

Gimmick. Any advertising strategy that attempts to make one of two things that are essentially equal appear to be better, to stand out; as in "you gotta have a gimmick if you want to get applause" (*Gypsy*).

Global relevance or sufficiency. The relevance or sufficiency of the premises in relation to the context of discussion and debate about the merits of the conclusion, going beyond the particular stated argument under investigation. See *Local relevance or sufficiency*.

Guilt by association. A variant of the *ad hominem* fallacy; attacking someone's position by attacking the person on the basis of some alleged association in the past or present when no such association exists or when, even if it did, it is irrelevant or does not constitute sufficient grounds for discrediting the person's position.

Hasty conclusion. Our label for the fundamental fallacy in which the sufficiency requirement is violated; arguing for a conclusion without providing sufficient evidence for it; sometimes called *hasty generalization* (though the conclusion of the argument need not be a generalization). See also *Anecdotal evidence* and *Unrepresentative sample*.

Headline. The name in print journalism for the title of a report printed in large type at the top of a story.

Ideology. An interest-bound point of view that bestows a sense of the legitimacy of their interests on those who share it and blocks them from appreciating that it is limited. The ideological role of the media. The ways in which the media share and propagate a broad world view.

Implication. (1) A relationship holding between statements or claims in which if one (or more) is true, then the other can normally be expected to be, too: "Ella is a brand new mother" implies "Ella has just given birth." (2) An act whereby one person means another to draw a conclusion from something the first person does or says. For example, if you say, "That door is freshly painted," your implication is usually that your listener should be careful about touching the door. A strict implication is a statement that strictly implies another in a case where, if the first is, in fact, true, the latter necessarily is true; the truth of the first statement and the falsity of the second statement would be inconsistent.

Importance. The "news checklist" item that calls for a judgment of whether an event deserves its prominence or even to be reported at all.

Improper appeal to authority. Our name for the fallacy of appealing to an authority for support in an argument when (1) it is inappropriate to appeal to any authority in such matters, (2) the particular source appealed to lacks either the competence or the opportunity to know anything about the matter in question, (3) there is disagreement about this matter among competent authorities, or (4) there is some question about the authority's credibility.

Improper appeal to practice. Our name for an argument from common practice or past practice that is fallacious either because there is, in fact, no such practice or because, in the circumstances, the existence of the practice is not relevant, or not sufficient, to justify or excuse the conduct being criticized.

Inconsistency. What occurs when two or more statements are made in a context where if one or more is true, then one or more of the others must be false. In other words, the truth of one or more is incompatible with the truth of one or more of the others. The fallacy of *inconsistency* occurs when an arguer puts forth two claims that cannot be taken as true/acceptable together, whether both claims are premises or one is a premise and one the conclusion; a variant of *problematic premise* because the acceptability requirement is violated.

Infer. *Verb*: To form or change a belief or other attitude, or to consider a possibility, on the basis of other information observed or believed, or of other possibilities.

Inference. (1) The act of inferring; thus, when you see me lifting the hood of my car, you might infer that I cannot get my car started. (2) The product of such an act—the claim that is inferred.

Informal logic. The discipline that studies the logic of argumentation from a normative point of view; that is, decides what is good and bad logic in argumentation where these properties are not dependent upon the logical form of the argument.

Inquiry, argumentative. An investigation into the belief-worthiness of a point of view; consists of finding and assessing the strongest arguments pro and con with a view to seeing how well supported the point of view is.

Internal argument. An argument the conclusion of which is also a premise being used to support a further conclusion.

Irrelevant reason. Our term for the fundamental fallacy in which the relevance requirement is violated; arguing for a conclusion on the basis of a claim that is not relevant to that conclusion; sometimes called *non sequitur,* from the Latin for "it does not follow."

Issue. What an argument is about, typically a topic or theme embedded in the conclusion of the argument in the sense that the conclusion is one position to take on the issue. For example, in the conclusion "Capital punishment should be reinstated," the issue is capital punishment.

Lex talionis. The ancient law limiting retaliation: "An eye for an eye; a tooth for a tooth." The point of the law (which defined a sort of combination of retribution and compensation) was that the penalty should be no worse than the crime: no more than an eye for an eye.

Local relevance or sufficiency. The relevance or sufficiency of the premises offered in the stated argument taken in isolation. See *Global relevance or sufficiency.*

Logic. The discipline that studies various types of reasoning with a view to developing criteria, procedures, and rules that will distinguish good arguments or inferences from bad and strong arguments or inferences from weak. See *Formal logic* and *Informal logic*.

Logical form. The pattern that emerges when the particulars of a statement or proposition are replaced by variables. *Example*: One logical form of "All moose can swim" might be "All X are Y" ("All creatures that are moose are creatures that can swim"); or, equivalently, "For anything A and any predicates x and y, if A is x, then A is y" ("For any particular thing, if the predicate 'is a moose' applies, then the predicate 'can swim' also applies").

Logical structure. The logical structure of an argument is the organization or alignment of the premises as they are set up to support the conclusion.

Major criticism. A criticism that has major impact on the argument, one that would cause the arguer to revise the argument drastically; determined by the strength of the fallacy charge and the position of the criticized premise in the hierarchy; the stronger the charge and the higher the premise is in the hierarchy, the more major the criticism.

Majority rule. The procedural decision-making principle that the support of a majority of the members of a body shall suffice to authorize any action or policy of that body.

Minor criticism. A criticism that has minor impact, one that the arguer can meet by making simple rather than significant revisions to the argument.

Missing conclusion. A claim or opinion that, judging by what is stated in the discourse and by the context, the author means to support or defend. (Also called *unstated conclusion, tacit conclusion, hidden conclusion, or unexpressed conclusion*.)

Missing premise. A claim that is (*1*) not expressed in the written or spoken argument but (*2*) must be added to an explicit statement in the discourse to make the set of stated premises relevant as support for the conclusion. When interpreting the argument offered by a particular author and addressed to a particular audience, any missing premises you add in reconstructing the argument should also be (*3*) likely to be accepted by the arguer and (*4*) ones the arguer would likely use in addressing that particular audience. (Also called *unstated premise, unexpressed premise, hidden premise, and tacit premise.* Sometimes a missing premise is what is referred to as the *assumption* of an argument.)

Necessary causal condition. X is a necessary causal condition of Y if Y will not occur unless X occurs.

Non sequitur. Latin for "it does not follow"; an alleged premise-conclusion connection in which the premise is irrelevant to the conclusion. See *Irrelevant reason*.

Obfuscation. A kind of euphemism or vagueness, except that here the arguer's intent is to obscure or conceal meaning ("The patient did not fulfill his wellness potential" for "The patient died").

Objectivity. In news reports, the (alleged) absence of advocacy for any point of view.

Opinion. A belief about or an attitude toward something.

Past practice, argument from. An argument in which allegedly wrong or otherwise inappropriate conduct is defended on the ground that such practice is traditional, that it has been standard conduct in the past. See *Improper appeal to practice*.

Poisoning the well. A variant on the *ad hominem* fallacy, one in which the arguer attempts to cast doubt on the arguer's position by making derogatory comments about the arguer. The arguer is the well; the attempt is to "poison" the source so that we will not take in (we will reject) any water (argumentation) drawn from it.

Popular sovereignty. The democratic political principle holding that laws should be based on the will of the populace.

Popularity. Our name for the fallacy of alleging that a claim is true or credible because it is widely accepted in circumstances in which popular acceptance is not relevant to, or else not sufficient for, accepting the claim. Another version of an appeal to popularity is the argument that a claim is false because it is *un*popular when such unpopularity is not an adequate reason for rejecting the claim.

Post hoc. Short for *post hoc, ergo propter hoc*, literally "after this, therefore because of this." A *post hoc* argument is an argument to a particular causal claim based exclusively on the premise that the effect in question followed (or immediately followed) the alleged cause.

Precedent, argument from. The argument that an action or policy should not be permitted because if it were, it would set a precedent that would justify similar, and undesirable, actions or policies.

Preemptive strategy. In advertising, this term refers to taking a standard feature or aspect of a product and building a claim around it, thereby "preempting" the truth for the product. *Example*: Claude Hopkins's claim that Schlitz bottles were "washed in live steam"—which was true of bottles for other brewers (though they didn't bother to say so).

Premise. In the context of arguments, a reason or item of evidence used in an argument to support a claim or opinion. (Alternative spelling: "premiss.")

Premise indicators. Words or phrases that precede clauses containing premises. Premise indicators, by the same token, indicate the presence of argument in writing or speech. The clause preceding a premise indicator, or following the clause it introduces, will often contain a conclusion of the argument.

Principle of charity. Originally a principle of interpretation, the principle of charity as applied to argumentation holds that the person whose writing we are dealing with should be given a fair, or *charitable*, reading. If we are in doubt about whether the text contains an argument, we should interpret it in the way that does the most credit to its author by maximizing its plausibility and cogency consistent with its context, its language, and what we know about the author's beliefs and intentions. When providing missing premises, we should do so in such a way as to neither overcommit nor undercommit the arguer.

Principle of discrimination. A principle of criticism of argumentation that requires the critic to begin his or her critique with the most important criticisms of the argument; in other words, the critic should focus most attention on the key issues and not spend much time on tangential points.

Principle of logical neutrality. A principle of criticism that states that the arguer should not seek to pass off substantive criticism as if it were logical criticism.

Problematic premise. Our name for the fundamental fallacy in which the acceptability requirement is violated; consists of putting forth, without any support, a premise that requires support or evidence.

Procedural principle. A rule about how the members of a body should proceed in carrying out their business.

Proto-argument. An attempt to persuade rationally by giving reasons for some claim which lacks a clear structure or in which some or all of the claim, the reasons, or the evidence are not clear.

Psychological appeal. In advertising, the use of words, graphics, or music to appeal to an emotion or to some other aspect of the human psyche. *Example*: The ring-around-the-collar commercials for Wisk detergent are aimed at a wife's desire for the world to think that she takes the best possible care of her husband.

Questionable cause. In general, our label for the fallacy of arguing *to* a causal claim as the conclusion without providing adequate support for it (see below); or the fallacy of arguing *from* a causal claim as one of the premises without supporting it when there are grounds for questioning the acceptability of the causal claim. Questionable cause is found in arguments both from particular and from general causal claims. In arguments from particular causal claims, it is (1) a recommendation based on a pure *post hoc, ergo propter hoc* inference without even connecting hypothesis proposed; (2) a recommendation based on a hypothesis offered to explain a correlation when alternative, equally plausible hypotheses exist and have not been ruled out; (3) a recommendation based on a claim supported only by a spotty correlation, one that hasn't been systematically established; or (4) a recommendation based on a claim supported by a correlation only, without other correlations checked out and found not to account for the cause. In arguments from general causal claims, it is a recommendation based on mistakenly taking what is merely one cause among others to be the only cause or the main cause; confusing a necessary causal condition with a sufficient causal condition.

Reciprocity. In argument interpretation and evaluation, being able to understand the point of view of another arguer, especially when one disagrees with it. Also, an exercise in which one arguer is required to repeat, accurately and to the satisfaction of another arguer, the position of that arguer and the arguments given for it.

Reconstructing an argument. Setting out explicitly the premises and conclusions, and their structure, of an argument stated or implied in a passage.

Red herring. The fallacy that occurs when an arguer introduces into the argument an irrelevant issue that has the potential of distracting attention from the issue.

Relevance. One of the three criteria that govern logically good argumentation; each premise of the argument must be relevant to (germane to, have a bearing on) the conclusion. The determination of relevance must be made taking into consideration every other premise of the argument. Relevance claims are always open to reconsideration. See *Global relevance* and *Local relevance or sufficiency*.

Relevant property(ies). In an argument from a priori analogy, the features the first analogue has (or must have) in virtue of which the predicate being transferred by the argument may be truly assigned to it. The second analogue must also have these features if the argument is not to be fallacious. See *A priori analogy, argument from*.

Rhetoric. The discipline that studies effective communication; often used to mean the way in which our thoughts are put into language. Sometimes used to mean flowery or overblown discourse, whether spoken or written, and sometimes used to mean insincere claims, promises that will not be backed by action.

Rhetorical question. A sentence that is interrogative in its grammatical form—its terminal punctuation is a question mark and its subject and predicate may be inverted —but that the author is, in fact, using to make a claim, not to ask a question.

Semantic claim. In advertising, the attempt to convince the consumer that one product is better based only on the names or words used to refer to it. *Example*: RCA's use of XL-100 as the name of one of their television sets.

Slippery assimilation. An argument of this pattern: *A* cannot clearly be distinguished from *Z* because *A* cannot clearly be distinguished from *B*, *B* cannot clearly be distinguished from *C*, and so on, until *Y* cannot clearly be distinguished from *Z*. Also called *sorites*.

Slippery-slope argument, causal. An argument with the following pattern: An action or policy should not be taken because if it is, it will cause a chain reaction that will result, ultimately, in an undesirable consequence. *Causal slippery slope* is our label for the fallacy consisting of a causal slippery-slope argument in which at least one of the alleged links in the causal chain is questionable or false.

Snippet. A short, focused argument, often a segment of a longer argument and usually dealing with just one issue.

Sources. In arguments, people or other authorities appealed to as the basis for premises.

In the news media, a source is the person or agency that gave the reporter the information or the occasion for the dissemination of the information (e.g., a press conference, a background interview).

Straw person. The fallacy that occurs when the arguer distorts and then attacks his or her opponent's position; so named because the distorted version is typically a "straw effigy," something that is more easily taken apart than the real thing.

Sufficiency. One of the three criteria that govern logically good argumentation; taken all together, the premises must provide enough evidence or adequate reason to warrant accepting the conclusion. See *Global relevance or sufficiency* and *Local relevance or sufficiency*.

Sufficient causal condition. X is a sufficient causal condition of Y provided that any time X occurs, Y will occur.

Support. A set of one or more statements supports another statement just when, if one accepts the former, one has some reason for accepting the latter.

Suppressed evidence. In advertising, information that is withheld in order to avoid showing a product in an unfavorable light. *Example*: Manufacturers of drugs may suppress information about their products' side effects or prices.

Tu quoque. A variation of *ad hominem* in which the arguer attempts to discredit an adversary's argument by charging that the opponent is guilty of the very thing which he or she condemns in others.

Two wrongs. Short for "two wrongs make a right." A two-wrongs argument is an argument in which someone tries to defend a person who has been criticized by citing an allegedly similar set of one or more actions (the wrongness of which is granted or at least not challenged) that was performed without blame, criticism, or sanction by someone else. A *two-wrongs* fallacy is a two-wrongs argument in which the lack of blame, criticism, or sanction for the second set of actions is either irrelevant or insufficient to establish the impropriety of blaming, criticizing, or otherwise sanctioning the action in question.

Unrepresentative sample. A *sample* is a subset of a collection of things that is used as the basis for a generalization made about the whole collection. When the sample does not contain the same distribution of the properties being generalized about as exists in the whole collection, it is said to be an *unrepresentative sample*.

Vagueness. The condition that occurs when the meaning of someone's speech or writing is unclear and that unclarity arises from the person's not having clearly communicated the meaning; when this occurs in an argument (that is, when either a premise or a conclusion is vague), we have the fallacy that we term *vagueness*.

Weasel. A term for a word used in advertisements to qualify or dilute the strength of a claim. Advertisers know that people notice not these words but what comes after them. *Example*: In the slogan, "Shield helps fight cavities," people hear only "Shield fights cavities."

Weight. The term used to describe how much support a premise (and its supporting argumentation) provides for the conclusion; some premises provide more weight than others.

Wire services. Private companies or cooperative agencies that distribute news reports to newspapers and to TV and radio stations. Wire services have their own reporters, who gather information and write news reports. Some wire services also distribute news gathered by their subscribers. The Associated Press (AP), United Press International (UPI), Agence France Presses (AFP), New York Times-Los Angeles Times, and Scripps Howard are wire services.

Index